What's Wrong with the Rorschach?

James M. Wood

M. Teresa Nezworski

Scott O. Lilienfeld

Howard N. Garb

What's Wrong with the Rorschach®?

Science Confronts the
Controversial Inkblot Test

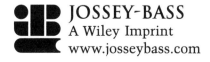

JOSSEY-BASS
A Wiley Imprint
www.josseybass.com

Published by Jossey-Bass
A Wiley Imprint
989 Market Street, San Francisco, CA 94103-1741   www.josseybass.com

Rorschach is a registered trademark of Verlag Hans Huber AG, Bern, Switzerland. This book has not been prepared, approved, licensed, or endorsed by any party associated with Verlag Hans Huber AG, Bern, Switzerland, the owner of the registered trademark "Rorschach."

Jossey-Bass books and products are available through most bookstores. To contact Jossey-Bass directly, call our Customer Care Department within the U.S. at (800) 956-7739, outside the U.S. at (317) 572-3986, or fax (317) 572-4002.

Jossey-Bass also publishes its books in a variety of electronic formats. Some content that appears in print may not be available in electronic books.

Designations used by companies to distinguish their products are often claimed as trademarks. In all instances where Wiley is aware of a claim, the product names appear in initial capital or all capital letters. Readers, however, should contact the appropriate companies for more complete information regarding trademarks and registration.

Library of Congress Cataloging-in-Publication Data

Wood, Jim, date.
    What's wrong with the Rorschach?: science confronts the controversial inkblot test/ James M. Wood, M. Teresa Nezworski, Scott O. Lilienfeld.—1st ed.
      p. cm.
Includes bibliographical references and index.
    ISBN 0-7879-6056-X (alk. paper)
1. Rorschach Test.   I. Nezworski, M. Teresa.   II. Lilienfeld, Scott O., date.   III. Title.
BF698.8.R5W66 2003
155.2'842—dc21   2002155627

Printed in the United States of America
FIRST EDITION
HB Printing   10 9 8 7 6 5 4 3 2 1

Contents

—✎— Acknowledgments

In writing this book and our previous publications on the Rorschach, we were sustained by the emotional support and substantive contributions of our colleagues and friends. We would like to thank the following supporters and contributors to our work.

To Lee Sechrest and Richard Bootzin of the University of Arizona, Russ Clark of the University of North Texas, and Pam McCauley of the Arizona Department of Corrections, who thoughtfully listened to our doubts about the Comprehensive System in the early 1990s and encouraged us to pursue the matter further.

To Elaine Walker, William Stejskal, Roy Malpass, and John Wiebe, colleagues and friends who listened to our ideas and offered agreement, disagreement, and thoughtful observations.

To Sena Garven, Deb Corey, James Billings, and Bianca Moehlmann, graduate students (some now colleagues) who have offered valuable insights and reflections.

To John Hunsley, Michael Bailey, Will Grove, Chris Barden, and Robyn Dawes, critics of the Rorschach whose insights we have freely borrowed.

To Ed Wagner, Carol Wagner, Ed Aronow, and Glenn Young, experts in the Rorschach who have provided us with valuable insights into the test.

To Helge Malmgren, whose Web site on the Classic Rorschach was indispensable for our understanding of European approaches to the test.

To Robert Archer and Radhika Krishnamurthy, who have gracefully maintained their neutrality in the current Rorschach debate, accepting legitimate arguments and data from both sides.

To Wayne Holtzman, whose insights regarding the history of the Rorschach were immensely helpful.

To Marvin Acklin, Thomas Shaffer, Philip Erdberg, and Mel Hamel, firm supporters of the Comprehensive System, who have been willing to publish empirical findings that do not always support its claims.

To Kasper Jorgensen and his Danish colleagues for their careful work on the test. And to Phil Carcena for his development of Rorscan, an excellent scoring and interpretive computer program for the Comprehensive System.

To Jack Gerber, John Wallace, Kim McKinzey, and Vicky Campagna, whose insights regarding the Comprehensive System have been incorporated into this book.

For their support and assistance in numerous ways, Howard Garb wishes to thank the following: from VA Pittsburgh Healthcare System—Georgette Bellucci, Stephen Perconte, and Jeffrey Peters; my wife, Flora, and my children, Merrick and Leanna; and my colleagues, Colleen Florio and William Grove.

To Dorothy Striegel, whose influence as a teacher inspired the literary aspects of this book.

To family and friends who read drafts of this book and offered valuable suggestions and criticisms, including James Coyne, Dan Deurloo, Richard McNally, Stevan Nielsen, Patrick Whalen, Randolph Whitworth, and Thomas Wood.

Special thanks to the woman identified as "Rose Martelli" and her children.

To historians of psychology whose publications and informal reflections have informed this book, including David Baker, Ludy Benjamin, John Exner, Ernest Hilgard, John Kilhlstrom, John Reisman, Donald Routh, and Leila Zenderland.

We also wish to thank individuals who have provided us with illustrations for this book including Richard Van Vleck and the American Artifacts Web site (http://www.americanartifacts.com) for his assistance in obtaining a drawing of Dr. Albert Abrams and the Dynamizer, Philip Schatz for his assistance in obtaining a copy of the Blacky Study, Sol Rosenzweig for his permission to publish a drawing from the Rosenzweig Frustration Study, and Gerald Blum for his permission to publish a drawing from the Blacky Study.

August 2002   JAMES M. WOOD
El Paso, Texas
M. TERESA NEZWORSKI
Dallas, Texas
SCOTT O. LILIENFELD
Atlanta, Georgia
HOWARD N. GARB
Pittsburgh, Pennsylvania

To Edward Aronow, Marvin Reznikoff,
and Edwin Wagner
Admired colleagues,
whose dedication to science matches
their devotion to the Rorschach.

The most costly of all follies is to believe passionately
in the palpably not true.

—*H. L. Mencken,* A Mencken Chrestomathy, *1949*

What's Wrong with the Rorschach?

CHAPTER ONE

A Psychological X-Ray

The Power of the Rorschach

The Rorschach has the dubious distinction of being, simultaneously, the most cherished and the most reviled of all psychological assessment tools.

—*John Hunsley and J. Michael Bailey,
"The Clinical Utility of the Rorschach," 1999*

Psychologists have been quarreling over the Rorschach Inkblot Test for almost half a century. From 1950 to the present, most psychologists in clinical practice have treasured the test as one of their most precious tools. And for nearly that long, many of their respected scientific colleagues have been trying to persuade them that the test is well-nigh worthless, a pseudoscientific modern variant on tea leaf reading and Tarot cards.

Introduced in 1921 by the Swiss psychiatrist Hermann Rorschach, the test bears a charming resemblance to a party game. A person is shown ten inkblots and asked, "What might this be?" Like swirling images in a crystal ball, the ambiguous blots tell a different story to every person who looks upon them. There are butterflies and bats, diaphanous dresses and bow ties, monkeys, monsters, and mountain-climbing bears. When scored and interpreted by an expert, people's responses to the blots are said to provide a full and penetrating portrait of their personalities.

Called a "psychological x-ray"[1] and "perhaps the most powerful psychometric instrument ever envisioned,"[2] the Rorschach is administered to more than a million people throughout the world each year. In the United States, where the test is used routinely in schools, mental health clinics, and legal cases, it's probably administered hundreds of thousands of times annually. And that's a conservative figure; in the early 1990s, it was estimated that the Rorschach is given over 6 million times each year worldwide.[3] Only one other personality test, the Minnesota Multiphasic Personality Inventory, is more popular.[4]

Psychologists often use the Rorschach to help courts determine which parent should be granted custody of a child. The test is used in schools to identify children's emotional and learning problems, and in prisons to evaluate felons for parole. Convicted murderers facing the death penalty, suspected victims of sexual abuse, young men seeking to enter the priesthood, airline pilots suspended from their jobs for alcohol abuse—all may be given the Rorschach by a psychologist who uses the test scores to make critical decisions about their lives.

As a way of introducing you to the mysteries of the blots, we'll begin by discussing the Rorschach responses of a fifty-year-old man who was recently given the test. We'll first describe the findings, then examine how they reflect this man's inner and outer realities. In this way you can develop a deeper understanding of the Rorschach and its purported powers.

A BLIND ANALYSIS OF RORSCHACH SCORES

Rorschach experts sometimes engage in *blind analysis*—interpreting test results without any information about a patient save age and gender. A blind analysis is an acid test of an expert's skill because all the interpretations are based on the inkblot results alone. Our blind analysis of this man's test results are based strictly on his Rorschach scores.

The interpretations are taken from recent books by John Exner and Irving Weiner, the two most influential contemporary authorities on the Rorschach. Psychologists who use the Rorschach often rely heavily on the guidelines supplied by these two experts. Especially important are Exner's manuals, which provide detailed, step-by-step rules for the interpretation of each Rorschach score. Weiner's interpretive guide is consulted for more in-depth understanding. In keeping with current practice, we've adhered closely to Exner's and Weiner's recommendations.

Impaired Thought Processes

A patient's statements while taking the Rorschach are written down verbatim in a transcript called a *protocol*. At the beginning of the interpretive process, the psychologist determines whether the images recorded in the protocol actually fit the shape of the blots. For example, one Rorschach blot is obviously shaped like a cat. If a patient looks at it and says that it looks like a cat, the response is considered to be of "good form quality." In contrast, if the patient says that it looks like a giraffe, the response is considered to be of "poor form quality," because a giraffe doesn't fit the blot's shape.

The Rorschach protocol of this man shows that he gave many responses with poor form quality. For example, in one blot he reported seeing an owl, even though the blot really doesn't look much like an owl at all. In another blot he reported seeing "two blue crabs doing a tango," a strange image bearing only the remotest resemblance to the blot itself.

Exner and Weiner's books indicate that the poor form quality of this man's responses is highly unusual and that he probably suffers from moderately impaired thinking and a significantly distorted view of reality.[5] It's likely that he tends to misinterpret events and the actions of people.

The man also gave several responses involving people in movement ("two women preparing dinner," "two dancing dervishes") and adopted a complex approach to the blots, weaving their diverse parts into unified images. According to Exner, these features of the Rorschach protocol indicate that the man is probably cautious and thoughtful, preferring to gather information and reflect on it before he acts.[6] He habitually approaches problem solving in an analytic way.

Severe Depression

Following the Exner and Weiner guidelines, the Rorschach clearly reveals the presence of severe depression. In the blots the man reported seeing "a Georgia O'Keefe painting of a cow skull" and "a blue rug with coarse fiber that's being pulled apart." Such images of death or damage can suggest that the man takes a depressive, pessimistic view of himself.[7] Furthermore, a disproportionate number of his responses focused on the black or gray features of the blots. In one blot he saw "a bat" and remarked on its black color. In another, he saw "the Eiffel Tower" and commented that it was gray. According to Exner's manual, the large number of such responses indicate that he's holding back his emotions.[8]

Exner's manual describes how a patient's Rorschach responses can be combined into a single "Depression Index." This man's score on the Depression Index is very high.[9] Using Exner's guidelines, one would infer that he has probably been suffering from extreme sadness and feelings of hopelessness for several weeks. The physical signs of depression, such as disrupted sleep, loss of appetite, and fatigue, are also likely.

Interpersonal Problems

The Rorschach results also indicate that this man has persistent problems relating to other people. One distinctive feature of the protocol is his tendency to see people in pairs, including "two Greek women dancing," "two medieval guys with hats on," and "two dwarves." According to Exner and Weiner, a profusion of such responses indicates that a person is preoccupied with himself, focusing egocentrically on himself and his problems.[10]

Another unusual feature is his tendency to see things in the white spaces within the blots. For example, one blot contains a large white space in the middle without any ink. He identified this white space, but not the blot itself, as "a jet." According to the manual, the many Space responses in his protocol indicate that he feels a great deal of anger, which probably hinders him from sustaining deep or meaningful relationships with other people.[11]

Also telling are the many fantasy figures that he saw in the blots. For example, he described one inkblot as "Tiger Lily from Peter Pan," and another as "Two laughing gargoyles." These responses, according to Exner's manual, reveal a tendency toward fantasy and suggest that the man's relationships with other people are based largely on his own imagination rather than reality.[12]

Mixed in with this man's self-preoccupation, anger, and guardedness is a paradoxical tendency toward dependency and clinginess in close relationships. This excessive dependency is revealed in his description of one blot as "a bullet popsicle." Exner's manual tells us that even a single "Food response" identifies a person as unusually dependent in his personal relationships.[13]

Nevertheless, some positive tendencies can also be discerned. In several blots he saw human figures engaged in enjoyable or cooperative activities, such as the "two Greek women dancing" or the "two women preparing dinner." According to the manual, these positive human images indicate that he's highly concerned about other people, relates to them effectively, and is probably regarded as likable and outgoing.[14]

THE ACCURACY OF
THIS RORSCHACH TEST

This blind analysis was based on definitive books by the leading current authorities. We also double-checked the results by running the scores through a popular computer interpretation program for the Rorschach. But is this interpretation accurate? Does it genuinely provide deep insight about *this* fifty-year-old man?

We can say with considerable confidence that it does not, as Jim Wood, the first author of this book, was the subject of the test. The results were based on a Rorschach recently administered to Jim by a well-qualified clinical psychologist who's trained and experienced in the standard methods for administering and scoring the test. Here are Jim's own observations on his test results:

Impaired Thought Processes

If the Rorschach is correct, then I deserve a great deal of credit for having overcome my mental disabilities. My undergraduate degree was from Harvard. I received a master's degree from Yale Divinity School and a Ph.D. in clinical psychology from the University of Arizona. I've published over thirty articles and book chapters, including several during the past year. It's unlikely that I'll ever win the Nobel Prize, but aside from my Rorschach results, there's little to suggest that my thinking is unusually impaired or that my view of reality is more distorted than average.

Severe Depression

Next is my so-called depression, which was purportedly revealed by a high score on the Rorschach Depression Index, some unpleasant images involving death or destruction, and several responses based on the black and gray aspects of the inkblots.

Depressed individuals are persistently sad, have little interest in normal activities, and feel fatigued. They often experience hopelessness and may have thoughts of death or suicide. They often have difficulty concentrating on matters as simple as reading a book or watching a television program. Sleep and appetite are usually disrupted.

I have none of these problems. My mood is normal, even a little cheerful. I'm interested in many activities, such as writing this book, taking care of small home improvement projects, and spending time with my family. My energy level is about average. My concentration is fine and so is my appetite. I sleep soundly, though my wife complains about my snoring.

How can it be that the Depression Index (usually called the *DEPI*) shows that I'm depressed even though I'm not? In fact, nearly all studies over the past decade have found that the *DEPI* bears little or no relationship to depression.[15] Despite the studies, the books of Exner, Weiner, and other Rorschach experts continue to claim that a high score on the *DEPI* is a strong indicator of depression. For this reason, many clinical psychologists still use it for this purpose.

What about the images of death and destruction that I saw in some blots, such as the cow skull from a Georgia O'Keefe painting? As it happens, there may be a slight relationship between such responses and depression, although the research evidence is conflicting.[16] However, the tendency of depressed individuals to see unpleasant images in the blots (if it exists at all) is probably too weak to be clinically useful, and many nondepressed individuals give such responses for other reasons. For example, I lived in Arizona and New Mexico for many years, and I own a book of Georgia O'Keefe's paintings. When I see one of her cow skulls in an inkblot, it probably has more to do with my Southwestern heritage and interest in art than with my mental outlook.

Similarly, the fact that I saw several gray and black objects in the blots probably has nothing to do with depression. In the 1920s and 1930s, some Rorschach experts advanced the notion that people who comment on the black or gray tones of the inkblots are "holding back" negative feelings such as anxiety and depression. There was no good scientific evidence to substantiate the idea then, nor has any compelling evidence been unearthed in the intervening seventy years. Nevertheless, Rorschach experts routinely interpret such responses as evidence of suppressed negative emotion.

Interpersonal Problems

Finally, according to the Rorschach results, I'm an interpersonal disaster—self-centered, dependent, guarded, and angry. When I took the test I fully expected this finding because practically everyone looks sick on the Rorschach. For instance, in one study conducted in the early 1980s, psychologists were asked to evaluate the Rorschach scores of a group of mental patients. Unbeknownst to the psychologists, the Rorschach results of some normal individuals were included with the patients' scores. The findings of the study were stunning: The psychologists classified nearly 80 percent of the *normal* individuals as having depression or serious character problems.[17]

Because about four out of five normal people look disturbed on the Rorschach, I consider myself to be in good company. Besides, most Rorschach interpretations regarding character problems lack solid scientific support and are probably no more valid than the predictions of a palm reader. For example, consider the "bullet popsicle" that I saw. According to the most respected books, even a single "Food response" indicates a high degree of dependency.[18] However, this interpretation is little more than opinion, unsupported by good evidence—even Exner has stated that "the findings concerning food answers are, at best, limited."[19]

Inconsistencies and Direct Hits

Although my test results provide an instructive example of how the Rorschach works, they're unsatisfactory from a scientific viewpoint. Perhaps you wondered if my prior knowledge of the test could have unconsciously influenced my responses to the blots. If this thought crossed your mind, let me encourage your healthy doubts. As this book will show, the Rorschach has thrived for eight decades precisely because many people have squelched their doubts and politely accepted the pronouncements of Learned Experts, without asking questions or requiring solid evidence. I hope that as you form your own opinions, you'll rely not on our personal say-so, but on the extensive body of research and historical information that's documented in the footnotes and references of this book.

In fact, there's really no way to know with certainty if I was unconsciously influenced when I took the Rorschach. After all, how could I be conscious of my own unconscious influences? I can only report that

I took the test straight, without trying to shape my responses or make them turn out a certain way.

Before setting aside my Rorschach, I'd like to mention a few other points that are especially interesting. First, as you may have noticed, several of my Rorschach results seem inconsistent or even contradictory. For instance, even though my thinking is supposedly distorted, my Rorschach scores also indicate that I'm reflective and analytic in my approach to problem solving. As another example, even though the Rorschach indicates that I'm self-centered, guarded, and angry in my interpersonal relationships, it also says that I relate well to other people and am well-liked.

A recent textbook on the Rorschach concedes that its results are "sometimes contradictory."[20] There are several strategies for dealing with these anomalies. Often the inconsistencies can be smoothed over or ignored when the final test report is written. Some psychologists even argue that the contradictions are a proof of the Rorschach's value: Human personality is complex and self-contradictory, they say, and the Rorschach results accurately reflect this fact.

One psychologist who uses the test in legal cases told me that an attorney once subpoenaed a computerized Rorschach interpretation from her files, and then pointed out its inconsistencies in court. To avoid further embarrassments of this kind, the psychologist stopped using computerized interpretations in her court cases. In this way, the contradictions could be kept safely out of sight of overly inquisitive lawyers.

Although most of the interpretations based on my Rorschach are incorrect, a few are direct hits that describe me quite well. For instance, consider the finding that I'm unusually thoughtful and reflective, and that I prefer to gather information and analyze situations before acting. I can vouch that the Rorschach is right on this point: As might be expected for a professor, I am more reflective and analytic than most people.

When I viewed the inkblots, I repeatedly saw people engaged in movement ("two dancing dervishes," "two women preparing dinner"). According to the Rorschach books, responses that involve human movement often indicate a thoughtful, reflective personality. In this case, the books may be at least partly correct. Several studies have shown that such responses tend to be slightly related to reflectiveness and self-restraint.

The Rorschach Test could easily be dismissed if it were all wrong. But the situation is complicated. Although the large majority of

Rorschach scores are either useless or scientifically unsupported, a few can provide genuine information about patients. If during the past fifty years clinical psychologists had tossed away the chaff of the test while retaining the few kernels of wheat it provides, the Rorschach might now be a limited but modestly successful psychological tool.

Unfortunately, the history of the Rorschach has proceeded in a different direction. In its current form, the few worthwhile scores of the Rorschach are buried among the many scores and interpretations that are pure moonshine. The situation would be humorous if it didn't regularly result in harm to innocent people. Psychologists using this test can and do cause serious damage to people's lives, as the following true story illustrates.

THE RORSCHACH AND CHILD SEXUAL ABUSE ALLEGATIONS

Rose Martelli was an Italian American from New England with a deep if unconventional religious faith. Although she belonged to the Catholic Church, she also attended services at fundamentalist Christian churches and sent money to television evangelists.

Rose never completely fit in at St Leo's, her Catholic parish. With her habit of reading the Bible each night for guidance and her enthusiastic references to "The Lord" as if he were a personal friend, she seemed more like a born-again Christian than a Catholic. Furthermore, as a low-income divorced mother, Rose was out of place in St. Leo's middle-class congregation. Living in subsidized housing with her teenage daughter and young son, Rose attended a junior college and worked only part-time at a low-paying job.

Allegations of Abuse

Rose's ex-husband was a salesman in a city in upstate New York. She was pregnant when she left him after only six months of marriage. When the baby, a boy named Noah, was born, a fierce court battle ensued over custody and visitation. Rose alleged that Donald Bell, her ex-husband, had been violent during their marriage. Then a week before the case was scheduled for trial, Amity Martelli (Rose's eight-year-old daughter by a previous marriage) suddenly reported that she remembered that Donald had sexually abused her when she was five.

The domestic court judge, clearly skeptical about the timing of the daughter's allegations, ruled that Donald should enjoy full rights as a father and regular unsupervised contact with his son. For a year or two Donald's visitations with Noah proceeded without serious incident. Then Rose began to revive the accusations she'd made during the custody dispute. She claimed that when Noah returned from visits with his father he sometimes bore unexplained bruises on his body and face.

Shortly after Noah's fourth birthday Rose began to call Child Protective Services (CPS), voicing suspicion that Donald was physically and sexually abusing him. When the CPS investigators asked for details, however, Rose was unable to do much more than repeat a few ambiguous remarks that Noah had let fall. CPS interviewed the little boy himself, but he didn't tell the investigators anything that suggested abuse.

Still, Rose's phone calls to CPS continued. It was the kind of case that investigators regard with weary skepticism. Unable to disregard Rose's charges but seeking a resolution, the CPS worker in charge of the case requested that she and her ex-husband submit to evaluation by a psychologist. Both parents agreed.

The Psychological Evaluations of Donald and Rose

Donald Bell's psychological report came back looking normal. Because he lived in a different state, Donald arranged an evaluation by a psychologist in the place where he was living. The report indicated that although Donald was psychologically distressed and absorbed with his own problems, he didn't exhibit the personality characteristics of a child molester.

In contrast, Rose's psychological evaluation revealed a person with extensive emotional and mental dysfunction. The psychologist appointed by CPS had administered several tests. Although most of them revealed no serious problems, the psychologist found many signs of psychological disturbance in Rose's Rorschach.

The psychologist reported that Rose was seriously disturbed and probably lacked genuine concern for her two children. In addition, the test revealed that Rose's thinking was so impaired that she distorted reality and the actions of other people. The psychologist speculated that Noah had made some ambiguous remarks about his father, which Rose had distorted in her mind until they seemed to constitute proof of abuse. Rose was willing to produce such allegations, the psychologist added, because she was extremely self-centered and probably unconcerned about the harm that could be done to her ex-husband and son.

As might be expected, the attitude of CPS changed substantially after receiving the psychologist's report. In a phone call, the case-worker told Rose about the test results and urged her to seek help from a therapist. Rose blew up and accused CPS of abandoning her and her children.

Aftermath of the Psychological Evaluation

In the months following the psychological evaluation, Rose continued to pester CPS with phone calls. Once she called from a hospital emergency room. She claimed that Noah had told a doctor, "My Dad peed in my mouth," and that bruising had been found in the boy's throat. CPS duly recorded this strange report but declined to investigate further.

Then, eight months after the psychological evaluations had been filed, an unexpected event dramatically altered the situation. Returning from a weekend visit with his father, five-year-old Noah told Rose that during their time together his father had slapped and yelled at him, then taken off his clothes and "poked him in the butt." Noah asked to see a doctor. Rose immediately drove him to a hospital, where Noah again described what his father had done to him. Bruises on his body were noted by medical personnel and a swab was taken of his rectum using a rape kit. The laboratory test revealed the presence of sperm.

A Fuller Picture of the Case

Because Jim Wood, the first author of this book, has professional expertise in the field of sexual abuse, Rose Martelli's lawyer contacted him to conduct a detailed review of this case. He read the legal documents and psychologists' reports, reviewed the medical records and CPS files, and most important, interviewed several people who had known Donald Bell and Rose Martelli for years. Here is Jim's account of what he gleaned by reading the record and making some phone calls.

DONALD BELL   Although Donald Bell currently worked as a car sales-man, his history revealed chronic employment problems. He was in his early forties, but had never held the same job for longer than a year. He'd been married four times, including his marriage to Rose. The positive evaluation sent to CPS from New York was grossly misleading, written by a psychologist who'd conducted a brief interview and then written his report without bothering to obtain independent information about Donald or the allegations against him.

Donald's real name was Joseph Rossi. He'd begun using the name of "Donald Bell" in his thirties for reasons that were unclear. Although Rose had said that he was physically abusive during their brief marriage, the CPS psychologist had treated this allegation as a manipulative distortion. However, documents showed that Donald had broken two of Rose's teeth within a few months of their wedding. He had also physically abused one of his prior wives.

Interestingly, the CPS psychologist had been given much of the information that I've described here. However, based on the Rorschach, the psychologist decided that Rose's bizarre reports were unreliable and could be discounted.

THE DAUGHTER'S ABUSE ALLEGATIONS   The allegations of sexual abuse against Donald by Rose's eight-year-old daughter Amity had been disregarded by the family court judge several years earlier. The CPS psychologist, without interviewing Amity, suggested that the girl might have been manipulated into making false statements. However, mental health records indicated that the psychologist should have looked into the matter more closely.

Amity had entered psychotherapy within a few months after Rose fled from her marriage to Donald. Treatment focused on the trauma that Amity had experienced from repeatedly seeing Donald batter her mother. It was only after several months of therapy that Amity began to tell her therapist about sexual abuse by Donald. The incidents she recounted were detailed and highly compelling.

ROSE MARTELLI   Finally, there was Rose herself, whom the CPS psychologist had characterized as emotionally disturbed, disordered in her thinking, and unempathic. The hard facts of Rose Martelli's biography and her psychological test findings (aside from the Rorschach) revealed a picture that was at striking variance with the psychologist's conclusions.

First, Rose didn't at all fit the label of "low-income mother" that was sometimes used to describe her. Although her income was temporarily low (as is often true of recently divorced mothers), she held steady employment throughout her twenties and thirties and was currently enrolled in training as a paralegal assistant. (She subsequently obtained her degree and, at the time of this writing, has completed many years of successful employment in her field.)

Second, the psychologist's conclusion that Rose lacked concern for her two children was manifestly wrong, according to people who knew the family well. They agreed that Rose was a devoted and intelligent mother. Her success at combining the roles of mother, student, and employee was inconsistent with claims that she was suffering from distorted thinking, mental impairments, and severe emotional disturbance.

Third and finally, Rose Martelli's religiosity was long-standing and well-known. She had a reputation for honesty. In the course of conducting my review of the case, I had the opportunity to check out many of Rose's so-called bizarre stories. In every instance that I investigated, I found that she'd been meticulously accurate. For instance, Noah's bruises following visitations with his father had been seen by reliable witnesses, including a Catholic priest.

Any opinion that Rose Martelli was habitually inclined to falsehood or distortion was contrary to everything that I could learn about her. Yet CPS had blindly accepted and acted on just such an opinion, based on a psychologist's interpretation of the Rorschach.

Rose Martelli's Rorschach After reviewing the documentary materials and conducting interviews of several key individuals, I was deeply puzzled by the psychological evaluation of Rose Martelli. This report, which had persuaded CPS to ignore her phone calls and the danger to her son, contradicted everything else that I'd learned.

At first I suspected that the psychologist who wrote it must have been incompetent. Only gradually did I realize that she'd done an adequate job according to the training she received. In fact, virtually all her errors could be traced to a single source: her reliance on the Rorschach Inkblot Test. The damaging conclusions about Rose—that she was emotionally disturbed, lacking in empathy, and distorted in her thinking—stemmed from this single test.

Why had the Rorschach so badly mischaracterized Rose? As a graduate student in clinical psychology, I'd been trained to use the Rorschach and become acquainted with its history. I knew that in the 1950s and 1960s the test had come under intense criticism for its lack of scientific support. It might well have been abandoned except for the Herculean efforts of one resolute psychologist, John Exner.

Beginning in 1974, when the test was at its lowest ebb, Exner began to publish a series of books describing his own approach to the Rorschach, which he called the "Comprehensive System." These thick volumes, which still appear every four or five years in new editions, have become the bible of the Rorschach over the past twenty-five years. They not only provide meticulously detailed instructions for administering, scoring, and interpreting the test, they describe extensive scientific research that seemingly supports it. Many clinical psychology graduate programs today train their students in the Comprehensive System, and hundreds of psychologists pay to attend Exner's "Rorschach Workshops" each year.

Searching for the Truth   Curious about the research described in Exner's books, I began to probe the scientific literature on my own. Collecting journal articles and dissertations, I was surprised to discover that, contrary to Exner's claims, most Rorschach scores lacked adequate scientific support. Far from being complete and balanced presentations of the scientific literature, Exner's writings were often one-sided, presenting research findings that supported the test while ignoring those that did not. The scientific basis for the Comprehensive System was weak at best and nonexistent at worst.

The psychological report on Rose Martelli, I eventually realized, was little more than a fantasy, a fictitious personality description based on Rorschach scores with little if any validity. If the results were carefully scrutinized one by one, they disintegrated.

As you may have guessed, several of Rose's Rorschach scores were similar to my own. Like me, she had a high score on the Depression Index, a scale invented by Exner. As noted earlier, studies by many independent researchers have found that scores on the Depression Index bear little if any relation to depression,[21] a fact that Exner never mentions in his books.

Rose's Rorschach, like mine, revealed the presence of "distorted thinking." In fact, research indicates that about 50 percent of normal people will be labeled in this way by the test,[22] although again Exner makes no mention of this problem. Rose's Rorschach, which contained numerous responses involving human movement, also indicated that she is a reflective person. This apparently contradictory Rorschach finding was smoothed over in the CPS psychologist's report.

Rose's Rorschach also contained a small element of inadvertent humor. Viewing one of the blots, she reported "A Thanksgiving turkey already eaten." Following the recommendations in Exner's books, the psychologist had interpreted this "Food response" as an indicator of extreme dependency: Rose was described as a clingy person who needed someone to lean on. However, the psychologist had missed two relevant details. First, Rose had come to the testing session during her lunch hour without eating anything since breakfast. It's possible that hunger may have turned her thoughts to food. Second, the date was December 5. About a week earlier, the top shelf in Rose's refrigerator had been dominated by the carcass of her family's Thanksgiving turkey. Already eaten.

Particularly damaging to Rose was the psychologist's characterization of her as self-centered and without empathy for her children. This conclusion was based on a "Reflection response" that Rose had supposedly given to one of the blots. A Rorschach response is scored as a Reflection if it refers to a mirror image or reflection, such as "An elf looking at himself in a mirror" or "A pine tree reflected in a lake." According to Exner's books, such responses are rare and virtually always indicate that a person is "narcissistic" and self-centered, with little regard for the feelings of others.

The claim that a Reflection response signals the presence of narcissism has never been substantiated by good research. In fact, researchers other than Exner have found that Reflections are quite common, occurring in the Rorschachs of nearly 30 percent of normal individuals. Because the blots are symmetrical, people often turn them sideways and comment that the image resembles a scene reflected in water. It's a normal and predictable response.

However, any discussion of these issues is irrelevant to Rose Martelli's Rorschach, for the reason that she never gave a Reflection response at all. The CPS psychologist simply made a scoring error. Rose had said that one of the blots resembled "a paper snowflake, like you make by folding a piece of paper and cutting it out." The psychologist mistakenly scored this as a Reflection response, even though it didn't involve a mirror or reflection. Scoring errors and disagreements are fairly common among psychologists who use the Rorschach, although the promoters of the test generally ignore this problem. This scoring error had caused Rose to be labeled as narcissistic and deficient in empathy for her children, leading CPS to ignore her pleas to protect her son.

Unfortunately, these insights about Rose's Rorschach came after the legal system had already taken action. A domestic court judge, overwhelmed by what he thought was contradictory and confusing evidence, awarded custody of Noah to his father. The boy went to live with his father in New York.

THE RORSCHACH MYSTIQUE

It would be comforting to believe that the story of Rose Martelli and her children is merely an isolated incident, and that a test as scientifically problematic as the Rorschach could never achieve widespread acceptance among educated professionals at the beginning of the twenty-first century. But just the opposite is true. Thanks largely to the enormous commercial success of the Comprehensive System over the past quarter century, the Rorschach is highly popular. Consider the following estimates from surveys in the past ten years:

- In surveys, the Rorschach typically ranks as the second most widely used personality test among clinical psychologists. (Number 1 is the Minnesota Multiphasic Personality Inventory, usually called the MMPI, a yes-no questionnaire that is used to identify psychological symptoms and disorders.)[23]
- 80 percent of Ph.D. clinical psychology programs emphasize the Rorschach in required testing courses.[24]
- 68 percent of specialist programs in school psychology include the Rorschach in standard training.[25]
- 33 percent of clinical psychologists in practice consider the Rorschach to be one of the most important tests they use.[26]
- 31 percent of psychologists who evaluate parents in custody evaluations use the Rorschach.[27]
- 35 percent of psychologists who evaluate children for abuse or neglect use the Rorschach.[28]
- 32 percent of psychologists who evaluate criminals for the courts use the Rorschach.[29]

Particularly striking are the numbers for forensic assessment: Between 30 percent and 35 percent of psychologists routinely use the Rorschach when they conduct custody evaluations, child abuse assessments, and criminal evaluations. As such statistics show, there was nothing unusual in the fact that the psychologist in the Martelli case used the Rorschach.

Nor was it unusual that the psychologist based her most important conclusions on the Rorschach, even though it was contradicted by other weighty evidence. Because the test is often considered unique in its power to reveal deep truths about a person, apparently inconsistent information is commonly reinterpreted to conform with the Rorschach results.

For example, the psychological report on Rose Martelli didn't mention that the seemingly bizarre stories she told about her ex-husband had been corroborated by other people. And the report minimized her exemplary performance as a mother: "Although Ms. Martelli strives to give the impression that she is a dutiful mother to her children, it is unlikely that she cares deeply about their needs when they conflict with her own." Thus Rose's positive qualities as a mother were explained away as mere illusion, and the negative Rorschach results accepted as the real story.

In the 1940s and 1950s the Rorschach was unblushingly promoted as a "psychological x-ray" that could penetrate surface qualities and reveal the inner secrets of an individual's personality.[30] Although they might claim otherwise, some clinical psychologists today still view the test as an x-ray or, to update the image, as a psychological brain scan. Rorschach experts tend to subtly disparage ordinary questionnaires like the MMPI, because they believe that such tests reveal only what patients are willing to report about themselves. By contrast, the Rorschach is said to uncover a deeper, "implicit" truth, even when the patient tries to conceal it.[31]

Despite its failure to live up to such promises, the Rorschach still possesses a palpable and powerful mystique. When introduced into the United States in the 1930s, it attracted a tiny group of enthusiasts who published their own newsletter and held meetings to discuss the test's subtleties. Because they made overstated claims that went far beyond the available scientific evidence, these early "Rorschachers" were widely regarded as cultish by other psychologists.[32]

Although the Rorschach eventually outgrew this stage and achieved broader acceptance, the somewhat clannish atmosphere surrounding its beginnings has never entirely dissipated. When serious devotees talk about the extraordinary richness and subtlety of the Rorschach, their voices are still likely to take on a distinctive, reverent tone that is almost never heard in discussions of other psychological tests. Mention of the Rorschach's well-known shortcomings is avoided as if in bad taste, and serious criticisms are often met with anger or outrage.

Perhaps nothing is more telling than the awe and deference shown toward the leading Rorschach experts, who are often treated with a reverence usually reserved for religious figures. A humorous real-life example involved a psychologist testifying in a criminal case. While preparing her evaluation, she had taken the unusual step of phoning John Exner and asking his opinion about the interpretation of a particular Rorschach score.

"Oh, that's right," the judge interrupted. "Exner is the Godfather of the Rorschach, isn't he, Doctor?"

"Oh no, your Honor," the psychologist smilingly replied, "He's the *God* of the Rorschach."[33]

PURPOSE AND ORGANIZATION OF THIS BOOK

The Rorschach is not merely a psychological test. It's also a social and scientific phenomenon. In this book, we tell the extraordinary story of how this creaky, flawed assessment technique, invented over eighty years ago, has become one of clinical psychology's most widely used tools, paradoxically still popular in an era when space stations are orbiting the earth and biologists are unlocking the secrets of the human genome.

In numerous articles published in professional journals over the past six years, we've alerted our fellow psychologists to the problems of the Comprehensive System for the Rorschach. In the present book, we hope to address not only our psychologist colleagues, but also professionals whose work can benefit from knowledge of the Rorschach's flaws (lawyers, judges, psychiatrists, social workers, counselors, disability evaluators, medical administrators, and health planners). We particularly hope that graduate students will read this book, as well as members of the general public with an interest in psychology, science, and pseudoscience.

The history of the Rorschach is fascinating because it reveals how the field of mental health practice has groped its way forward during the past century, influenced by science, salesmanship, wishful thinking, and a well-intentioned but often misdirected desire to understand the complexities of the human psyche. By examining the forces that have made the Rorschach successful, we can better understand the countless other fads and fallacies that have swept through clinical psychology, psychiatry, and social work.

As our story shows, there are powerful social and professional reasons why psychologists adopted the Rorschach seventy years ago and have clung to it ever since. And there are equally powerful scientific and ethical reasons why the test has been intensely criticized for the past half century, though usually to little effect.

A PREVIEW OF THE CHAPTERS

Most of the book follows a historical sequence. In Chapters Two and Three we tell how the inkblot test was invented by Swiss psychiatrist Hermann Rorschach shortly after World War I and spread to the United States during the Great Depression. Chapters Four and Five describe the heyday of the test in the 1940s and 1950s, when the Rorschach inkblots were often seen as a clinical psychologist's emblem, much like a mechanic's wrench or a doctor's stethoscope.[34] Chapters Six and Seven relate how research undermined confidence in the Rorschach, uncovering its flaws and failings, so that the test came under fiery attack from some of the country's leading psychologists in the 1950s and 1960s.

In Chapter Eight we'll tell the dramatic story of how John Exner saved the Rorschach in the 1970s with his Comprehensive System, and in Chapter Nine we'll describe the disconcerting revelations and new wave of scientific criticism that have recently cast doubt on that work. Chapter Ten discusses the possible fate of the Rorschach in years to come. Chapter Eleven addresses the fascinating question of why psychologists still cling to the Rorschach despite overwhelmingly negative research evidence and bad publicity for their profession. Finally, in Chapter Twelve, we'll explain why and how the Rorschach can be kept out of courtrooms and other legal settings. This last chapter on misuse of the Rorschach in forensic settings is dedicated to Rose Martelli and her children, as well as to all other individuals who have been inadvertently harmed by psychologists wielding inkblots.

WHAT YOU WON'T FIND:
PICTURES OF THE REAL BLOTS

In preparing this book, we had to carefully consider how many of the Rorschach's secrets should appropriately be revealed to nonpsychologists. On one hand, it's important that nonpsychologists be given enough information so that they can make an informed decision about the test and its scientific foundation. On the other hand, it's important not to compromise the integrity of the test.

We decided to take as our model a recent book written by four distinguished Rorschach scholars: Eric Zillmer of Drexel University, Molly Harrower of the University of Florida, Barry Ritzler of Long Island University, and Robert Archer of Eastern Virginia Medical School. Like us, these authors addressed their book to nonpsychologists as well as psychologists.[35] They provided numerous examples of Rorschach responses, and explained how these responses are scored and interpreted. Accordingly, we've written our book with about the same level of detail that these authors found appropriate.

An important concern is whether nonpsychologists reading this book might try to use the information it contains to fake the test. We want to state at the outset that this book is not intended for such a purpose. In our opinion, it's morally reprehensible to fake a psychological test. Furthermore, attempts to fake the Rorschach are ill-advised and likely to backfire. We discuss this issue at greater length in Chapter Twelve.

Sadly, there's something that we'd like to share with readers but can't—the actual Rorschach inkblots. Readers who have never seen the blots will naturally want to know what they look like, and because the copyright has apparently expired, there's probably no legal obstacle to printing them here. However, after giving the matter some thought, we've decided not to do so.

Psychologists have never quite made up their minds about whether the Rorschach inkblots can be safely revealed to nonpsychologists. On one hand, members of the profession are justifiably reluctant to reveal the materials of some psychological tests because their usefulness might be compromised. For example, if readers were to see the Rorschach inkblots in this book and later be given the test, they might give different responses than they would have otherwise, possibly invalidating the test results. For this reason, some psychologists become irate when copies of the Rorschach inkblots appear on the World Wide Web, as they do from time to time, or are otherwise revealed to the public.

On the other hand, there's educational value in showing the blots to nonpsychologists with a serious and legitimate interest in psychological assessment, and perhaps little danger of affecting their scores should they later take the test. For example, it's been reported that the Rorschach scores of psychiatric patients stay pretty much the same when they're given the test a second time, and even when they deliberately try to change their responses.[36] Research like this suggests that seeing the blots beforehand might not invalidate the test results.

Furthermore, the fact is that the cat—or the Rorschach—is already out of the bag. In the 1970s two psychologists published colored copies of the Rorschach blots in a hardback book for the general public called *The Nuremberg Mind*.[37] Moreover, John Exner's books, which contain pictures of the blots and extensive detail about their interpretation, are available for purchase by nonpsychologists from Barnes & Noble bookstores and Amazon.com. One of us even recently bought a set of used Rorschach cards for $20 on the Web, without being asked whether he was a psychologist. There's also an inexpensive paperback with the naughty title *Big Secrets: The Uncensored Truth About All Sorts of Stuff You Are Never Supposed to Know*.[38] It contains black-and-white outlines of the blots, as well the formula for Coca-Cola and the recipe for Kentucky Fried Chicken.

Because the Rorschach inkblots are already an open secret, there may not be much point in trying to protect their privacy. However, because the profession's ethics generally discourage the release of test materials to nonpsychologists, we've decided not to reproduce the blots here. Instead, we've chosen to provide readers with two imitation blots that resemble the originals. These black-and-white blots appear in Chapter Two. Readers can look at these blots or show them to their friends and ask "What might this be?" just as Hermann Rorschach did over eighty years ago when he created his test.

It's his story that we tell in the next chapter.

CHAPTER TWO

A Test Is Born
Origins of the Rorschach
Inkblot Technique

*HAMLET: Do you see yonder cloud that's almost
in shape of a camel?
POLONIUS: By the mass, and 'tis like a camel indeed.*

—*William Shakespeare,* Hamlet, *1600*

Everyone has seen a cloud shaped like an animal, or
a spooky face in the glowing embers of a fire. The human visual system
was naturally selected to detect meaningful shapes in an ever-changing,
ambiguous environment. Sometimes, when this part of our brain works
overtime, we're surprised to see a horse in the whorls of a wood table-
top, or a witch in the creases of a rumpled bedspread. The tendency to
see these serendipitous shapes is probably universal and long-standing.
There was almost surely a time when stone-age children stood together
on a hilltop, pointing at a cloud that looked just like a mastodon.

Phantom images of this kind have often been accorded deep meaning or magical significance, a phenomenon known as *pareidolia*. For
example, in an old form of fortune-telling called ovomancy, egg whites
were dropped into water and the future foretold from the swirling
shapes. A similar practice survives in the practice of telling fortunes
from tea leaves and coffee grounds.[1]

Occasionally the mysterious shapes produced by random processes
have crossed the line from magic to religion. Supposedly miraculous

images of Jesus, exciting much fervor, have been reported in such unlikely places as a burned tortilla and an Atlanta billboard advertising spaghetti.[2] As recently as 1993 pilgrims flocked to Watsonville, California, because an image of the Virgin Mary had been discerned in natural markings on the bark of an oak tree.[3] Following the destruction of the World Trade Center by terrorists on September 11, 2001, some individuals claimed that the face of Satan could be detected in television footage of the black smoke that billowed from the twin towers.[4]

There's something about the ambiguous, spontaneous shapes in egg whites, tea leaves, smoke, and inkblots that seems to excite the credulous, mystery-seeking side of human nature. Occasionally, the fascination with such images has inspired works of art. The great Renaissance artist Botticelli, who painted the familiar portrait of Venus standing on a scallop shell, is said to have sought inspiration by throwing a paint sponge against a wall, then finding pictures among the chaotic splotches of color.[5] In the mid-1800s the German physician Justinus Kerner published a book called *Die Klecksographie* (which can be translated as "Blot-o-graphy"), a somewhat melancholy volume that contained fifty inkblots arranged into odd pictures and accompanied by little poems.[6] His popular book set off a European fad called Blotto in which inkblots were used for fortune-telling and as a party game. Kerner believed that his inkblot images came from "Hades" and "the other world," so although Blotto was regarded as a pastime it also had a slightly occult flavor, much as Ouija boards do today. (Although highly popular in the late 1800s, inkblot games eventually disappeared from sight. However, a new inkblot game, Thinkblots, has recently appeared on the shelves of American toy stores.)

In the late 1800s and early 1900s, when psychology first appeared in universities as an independent scientific field, several European and American psychologists began to use inkblots in research.[7] Some investigators used inkblots to explore visual perception, hoping that the unfamiliar shapes would confuse and slow down the visual process and render it easier to study. Other early inkblot studies focused on memory processes. The most distinguished of these early researchers was Alfred Binet, the French psychologist who is best remembered for his pioneering work on intelligence. Binet experimented with inkblots as a measure of imagination and considered including them in his famous intelligence test.

By the time the Swiss psychiatrist Hermann Rorschach began his own studies between 1910 and 1920, a considerable body of scientific research that made use of inkblots had already accumulated. Inkblots were in the air. Rorschach's innovation lay not in his decision to use blots for research, but in his unique ideas about how they might be studied, and in his distinctive energy and creativity.

KLEX AND HIS INKBLOT TEST

When he was a young man, Hermann Rorschach's friends called him Klex, which in German means "Inkblot." Because his father was an art teacher and Hermann himself possessed a talent for drawing, the nickname was well-chosen. By a peculiar coincidence, it also foreshadowed the achievement that would make Hermann's name known throughout the world: the creation of the Rorschach Inkblot Test.

Born in Switzerland in 1884, Rorschach attended medical school in Zurich from 1904 to 1909. In that era, the Burghölzli Hospital at the University of Zurich was a leading European center of psychiatric research. Eugen Bleuler, who coined the term *schizophrenia* and published a seminal book on the disorder, was director of the Burghölzli. C. G. Jung, whose theories of archetypes and the collective unconscious later brought him international fame, was then a young, up-and-coming psychiatrist and Bleuler's assistant. During his medical studies, Rorschach was influenced by the scientific spirit and innovative ideas of both men.[8]

Young Rorschach was an intelligent and dedicated student with distinctively nonmedical interests. He felt a deep attraction to the visual arts, especially painting and drawing. Furthermore, he developed a passion for the people and literature of Russia and eventually married a young Russian doctor, Olga Stempelin. After Hermann received his medical degree in 1913, he and Olga lived briefly in Russia. However, they soon returned to Switzerland, where he found employment in a small insane asylum.

Photographs of Hermann Rorschach show an alert, handsome young man, tall and slender, with a short moustache. According to later accounts, he was even-tempered and generous, had a good sense of humor, and was deeply devoted to his wife and two children. Popular with his patients at the asylum, he kept a pet monkey that he sometimes brought to the wards. He enjoyed working in the hospital's wood shop, where he crafted small toys for his children.

As an obscure psychiatrist working in a small mental hospital, Hermann Rorschach would probably be forgotten today had it not

Figure 2.1.   Hermann Rorschach.
A Swiss psychiatrist who displayed talents in both research and art,
Hermann Rorschach created his famous inkblot test to explore the
relationship between perceptions and personality.
Source: Granger Collection, New York. Used by permission.

been for his enduring commitment to research. Like many psychiatrists educated in Zurich, Rorschach was impressed by Freud's daring
new theory of psychoanalysis, and he published several case studies
from a psychoanalytic perspective. Following the example of Bleuler
and Jung, Rorschach carried out systematic research studies, often
during his own personal time.

At first Rorschach's energies as a researcher focused on Swiss religious sects that would now be termed cults. For instance, he investigated one group whose leader, Johannes Binggeli, taught that his penis was sacred. Binggeli's followers considered his urine to be holy and sometimes used it in lieu of wine for Holy Communion. Binggeli practiced sex with young girls to "exorcise demons" and was eventually arrested for incest with his daughter.[9]

By studying such sects, Rorschach made several discoveries that even today would be regarded as significant. For example, he established that the same or similar cults had existed for centuries in Switzerland, and that they especially flourished in those parts of the country where weaving was a common trade. Participation in cults seemed to run in families; at times cult activity continued from generation to generation for as long as several centuries. These discoveries, though not earth-shattering, fill out our picture of Rorschach, because they indicate that he had a scientific instinct, a genuine talent and energy for uncovering fresh information through investigation.

Creating the Blots

In 1918 Rorschach set aside his study of cults and devoted himself to a much different research project involving inkblots. In the space of only three years, he developed a series of blots that could be used for testing, administered them to hundreds of patients and normal people, and published the book that firmly established his place in the history of psychology.

It's unclear how Rorschach first developed the idea of using inkblots as a psychological test, especially because he seems never to have mentioned the earlier inkblot research by Binet and other psychologists.[10] Like most Europeans his age, Rorschach almost certainly played Blotto during his childhood when the game was a fad, and he probably read Kerner's odd little book *Klecksographie* as an adolescent. According to later reminiscences by his wife, Rorschach was impressed by a historical novel about Leonardo da Vinci in which the great Renaissance artist described how he saw devils, monsters, and beautiful landscapes in the damp spots on walls and on the scum of stagnant water.

Rorschach carried out brief inkblot experiments with children as early as 1911 but set the topic aside for more than five years. His interest was revived by the dissertation of Szymon Hens, a Polish medical student working in Zurich.[11] Hens had tried without much success to distinguish psychotic patients from normal persons by comparing the images that they saw in inkblots. When Hens's inkblots were published in 1917, Rorschach decided to pursue the topic again.

Drawing on his talents as an artist, Rorschach created a collection of forty inkblots.[12] Some were made by dripping black ink onto sheets of paper, which he folded to create symmetric patterns. Others were created with delicately tinted colors. He deleted portions of some blots and enhanced others with a pen. It seems that the final versions, although based on real blots, were conscious works of art composed of ink drawings and watercolors.[13] After constructing a variety of these "quasi-blots," Rorschach began to experiment by showing them to patients and acquaintances and asking them to describe what they saw.

Early Scoring Categories

Based on his preliminary observations, Rorschach concluded that people's perceptions of the blots fell into several broad categories. For instance, some people tended to see movement (waiters serving food, a man falling into a pond), whereas others saw images characterized by color (fallen rose leaves, a brightly colored dress). Furthermore, different people focused their attention on different areas of the blots. If two people looked at the same blot, the first might see images in the tiny splotchy details at the blot's edge, whereas the second might describe the blot as a single image. Rorschach concluded that these diverse responses reflected fundamental personality differences. Accordingly, he developed a variety of scoring categories such as Movement, Color and Whole Card responses.

From his initial collection of blots, Rorschach eventually selected those that tended to elicit the scoring categories that struck him as most important. For instance, he selected several blots because they tended to evoke descriptions of people in motion (such as the "two women preparing dinner" that the first author of this book saw when he took the test; see Chapter One) or responses based on color. Using this first set of "Rorschach cards," he proceeded to administer the new test to over four hundred individuals, both normals and psychiatric patients.

Publication of Psychodiagnostics

Rorschach's first study of four hundred subjects yielded results that appeared to be almost exactly what he expected. When psychiatric patients and normal people described what they saw in the inkblots, they seemed to reveal their innermost personalities, intellectual strengths and weaknesses, and psychological problems. Rorschach swiftly wrote a book summarizing his research. One publisher agreed to publish the book but was willing to print only two blots in full size. The rest of the blots were to be miniaturized, apparently to save printing costs. With the help of a friend, Rorschach located a second publisher who agreed to print ten of the blots in nearly full size.[14]

Rorschach's book, *Psychodiagnostics,* was published in June 1921.[15] It was to be his only book. In the ensuing months he continued to develop his ideas about the test and delivered a lecture to the Zurich Psychoanalytic Society on the usefulness of inkblots in clinical practice. Except for a small circle of Rorschach's closest associates, however, psychiatrists paid little attention to his new test. His book sold only a few copies. He was disappointed and became uncharacteristically depressed by its cool reception.[16] Then, nine months after the publication of *Psychodiagnostics,* Rorschach entered a hospital complaining of abdominal pains. On the next day, April 2, 1922, he died from a perforated appendix with peritonitis. He was thirty-seven years old.

Rorschach's writings on the inkblot test were extremely limited. He left only the blots themselves, his book *Psychodiagnostics,* and his lecture to the Psychoanalytic Society, which was published posthumously.[17] Although Eugen Bleuler eulogized Rorschach as "the hope of an entire generation of Swiss Psychiatry,"[18] with his untimely death it seemed unlikely that his work would have an impact. Few or none of his contemporaries in Zurich foresaw that he had left behind a legacy that would be cherished and reviled by psychologists for the next eighty years.

RORSCHACH'S CENTRAL IDEAS: MOVEMENT, COLOR, AND *EB*

According to a popular stereotype about the Rorschach Test, responses to the blots are interpreted as Freudian symbols that represent unconscious thoughts and motivations. A threatening lion seen in a blot means that a person harbors unconscious aggressive impulses. Eyes mean that the person is paranoid and feels watched. Long, cigar-shaped objects mean—ah, that goes without saying, doesn't it?

Although some psychologists use the test in this way, Hermann Rorschach had something quite different in mind. Rorschach was interested not so much in the sexual or aggressive images that people saw, but rather in the *movement* and *color* of those images. If a woman saw an inkblot as a monster that reminded her of her father, Rorschach would probably have been most interested in finding out whether the monster appeared to be *moving,* and whether the *color* of the blot had affected the woman's choice of an image. Rorschach's central idea, to which he devoted the most pages in *Psychodiagnostics,* was that the perception of movement and color reveals a person's fundamental orientation toward reality.

Movement Responses

Rorschach defined a Movement response (*M*) as one in which respondents see a human engaged in movement, such as "two Alpinists climbing a mountain" or "a ballerina doing a pirouette." Somewhat paradoxically, Rorschach also scored some images of motionless people as *M,* such as "a vampire sleeping in a coffin" or "a child sitting at a desk." Such responses were scored as *M* because they were thought to exhibit "passive movement" or a state of muscular tension. Animals seen in the blots could also be scored for *M* if they were engaged in "human-like activity," but not otherwise. Thus, "two dogs performing in the circus" or "a bear on a bicycle" would be scored as *M,* but not "a cat catching a mouse."

Rorschach believed that individuals who give a large number of *M* responses are "introversive" or "turned inward" toward the world of thought and fantasy. In Rorschach's formulation, introversive people are reflective, intelligent, and creative, but tend to be awkward and have difficulty adapting to everyday realities. An extremely introversive person could be brilliant but socially inept, like the "nutty genius" characters in some movies.

Because people with many *M* responses are ostensibly introversive, it would seem to follow that people with only a few *M* responses would be extraverted. However, Rorschach's views of introversion and extraversion didn't follow this intuitive, symmetric pattern. According to his theories, a person with only a few *M* responses lacks the positive qualities associated with introversion such as intelligence and imagination, but doesn't necessarily possess extraverted qualities. Extraversion (which Rorschach called "extratension") is a completely different quality from low introversion, and shows up in the inkblots as Color responses, a topic that we'll discuss in the next section.

The notion that introversion is related to the perception of movement in inkblots may seem a bit odd to us, but Rorschach didn't simply pluck it from thin air. His idea was based partially on the work of John Mourly Vold, a nineteenth-century Norwegian philosopher who conducted extensive research on the relationship between muscular movement and dreams.[19] Mourly Vold believed that when muscular activity was inhibited during sleep, imagery involving movement (that is, dreams) was stimulated. He reported several experiments in support of his theory. For example, Mourly Vold asked a group of his students to sleep with a cloth tape wrapped around their ankles, to inhibit their nighttime movements. Consistent with his theory, the students reported a large number of dreams that involved highly active movement.

Building on Mourly Vold's ideas, Rorschach conjectured that introversion involves inhibited movement, and therefore that introversives should see more imagery involving movement when they view inkblots. Thus, although Rorschach's ideas about introversion and *M* responses may strike us as strange today, they weren't especially exotic in his era. (Rorschach did not address possible alternative explanations of Mourly Vold's finding, such as that the cloth strips might have disturbed the students' sleep and so affected their dream imagery, or that the students might have known of the hypothesis and consciously or unconsciously shaped their reports accordingly.)

Color Responses

The second central category in Rorschach's system was Color (today abbreviated as *WSumC,* for "the Weighted Sum of Color responses"). He defined a Color response as one in which a person's perception of the blot is influenced by the ink's color. For example, if a person described a red blot as "blood," or a blue patch as "the sky," the image was considered to be a "Pure Color" response. Rorschach regarded Pure Color responses as particularly important because they were based solely on the color of the blot.[20] Also significant were responses based on both the blot's color and its shape or form. For example, if a person reported that a blot looked like a lion because it had a tawny yellow color and the shape of a lion, then the response was scored as "Form-Color." For Rorschach, the crucial issue was whether color influenced a person's response to a blot. Thus, if a person said that a red and yellow area of the blot looked like "fire," Rorschach considered this a Color response even if the person did not explicitly mention the words "red" and "yellow."

Rorschach believed that Color responses are intimately related to *affect* (the experience and expression of emotion), and that individuals who give a large number of such responses are "extratensive" or "turned outward" toward the world of external reality. In Rorschach's formulation, extratensive people are socially adroit, practical, and adaptable to the demands of the outer world, but with a tendency to be restless, emotional, and impulsive. Rhett Butler and Scarlet O'Hara in the classic movie *Gone with the Wind* could be thought of as male and female versions of extreme extratension.

Just as an absence of *M* responses doesn't necessarily mean that a person is extratensive, an absence of Color responses doesn't necessarily indicate that a person is introversive. A person without Color responses is simply "non-extratensive," lacking the emotionality, practicality, and social adroitness of an extratensive, but not necessarily possessing introversive qualities. In fact, according to Rorschach, some pitiable individuals lack both extratensive and introversive qualities, as we'll discuss in the next section.

Rorschach's interest in Color as a scoring category, and his decision to include it as a basic element in his test, developed later than his interest in *M*.[21] In *Psychodiagnostics* he provided little explanation for his idea that Color responses are related to affect and extraversion. Without citing any research on the topic, he simply asserted that "it has long been realized that there must exist a very close relationship between color and affectivity," and he noted that in everyday speech we say that "everything looks black" to a gloomy person, and that a cheerful person sees the world "through rose-colored glasses."[22] Of course, such arguments based on common figures of speech constitute a feeble kind of evidence. For example, in common speech we say that a person disappointed in love is "heartbroken" and that a distressing piece of news is "gut-wrenching." If we took Rorschach's arguments on this point seriously, we'd have to conclude that a close relationship exists between internal organs and affect, and perhaps start scoring "Human Organ Responses" on the inkblot test. In fact, despite Rorschach's attempt to find supporting evidence, his ideas concerning Color responses were grounded in weak or minimal scientific evidence.[23]

The Balance of Introversion and Extratension: The Experience Types

Rorschach's "introversion" and "extratension" bore a family resemblance to the concepts of "introversion" and "extraversion" proposed a few years earlier by C. G. Jung. The similarity is understandable, considering that Jung and Rorschach lived in Zurich, were personally acquainted, and read each other's work.[24] However, Jung and Rorschach disagreed concerning the relationship of introversion to extraversion (extratension). Jung considered introversion and extraversion to be *polar opposites,* so that the conscious personality of a person was *either* introverted *or* extraverted. In contrast, Rorschach considered introversion and extratension to be independent and potentially compatible personality features, so that a person could be *both* introversive *and* extratensive.

Rorschach's conviction that introversion and extratension could exist simultaneously in the same person was expressed in the most important score in his test, the *Erlebnistypus,* which is usually translated into English as "Experience Balance" or "*EB.*" *EB* is the ratio between the number of *M* responses in a Rorschach protocol and the number of Color responses.[25] For example, if a patient gives 7 *M* responses and 2 Color responses, then *EB* is 7:2. According to Rorschach, this ratio reflects the "balance" between introversion and extratension within the personality, and reveals an individual's basic experience and orientation toward reality. Rorschach contended that every person fell into one of four "Experience Types," as indicated by *EB*:

- *Introversive.* Introversives are focused on "inner experience" and provide substantially more *M* responses than Color responses. Though they possess strongly introversive qualities such as intelligence and creativity, they lack the easy social skills and adaptability associated with extratension. One could say that Introversives "live too much in their own heads" and are awkward when handling the everyday details of life.

- *Extratensive.* Extratensives are focused on "outer experience" and provide substantially more Color responses than *M* responses. Extratensives are the mirror image of Introversives: Although they're adaptable and can relate easily to other people in social situations, they're lacking in imagination and emotional stability. At their worst, Extratensives could be described as flighty, impulsive, or shallow.

- *Dilated.* Dilated individuals (also called "Ambiequal") provide a moderate-to-high number of both *M* and Color responses. Dilated individuals have the best of both worlds because they possess a full measure of both introversion and extratension. They are thoughtful *and* socially adept, creative *and* adaptable to external reality. According to Rorschach, artists tend to belong to the Dilated type.

- *Coarctative.* Coarctative individuals provide a low and approximately equal number of *M* and Color responses. Coarctated individuals lack the resources of both the Introversive and the Extratensive types. These unhappy individuals possess neither the creativity and emotional stability of the Introversive nor the social ease and adaptability of the Extratensive. According to Rorschach, unintelligent people and depressed patients tend to belong to the Coarctative type.

MOVEMENT, COLOR, AND *EB*. JUST ANOTHER KIND OF HOROSCOPE?

Everyone knows people who fit Rorschach's four *EB* types. But the mere fact that it's easy to call such examples to mind doesn't mean that Rorschach's ideas are correct. After all, it's no more trouble to think of people who exemplify astrological sun signs, such as domineering Leos and well-balanced Libras, even though sun signs bear no relationship to personality.[26] So it's a fair question whether Rorschach's theories about introversion, extratension, Movement, and Color amount to anything more than a twentieth-century version of sun signs and horoscopes.

Contemporary Views of Introversion and Extraversion

Scientific research conducted since Hermann Rorschach's death provides overwhelming support for the concepts of introversion and extraversion. Psychology books now routinely identify "introversion/extraversion" as one of the "Big Five" personality traits (the other four are agreeableness, conscientiousness, neuroticism, and openness to experience).[27]

According to modern personality theory, introverts tend to prefer solitary activities, whereas extraverts seek and enjoy social contact. Introversion and extraversion are related to the way people spend their free time (introverts prefer to curl up with a good book or engage in solitary hobbies, whereas extraverts would rather hang out with their friends or attend a social function) and the type of employment they find most congenial (introverts do better in jobs that involve a substantial amount of time working alone, such as accounting or research, whereas extraverts thrive in jobs with substantial interpersonal contact, such as social work or sales).

In contemporary theories of personality, introversion and extraversion are conceptualized as polar opposites (a view closer to Jung's thinking than to Rorschach's). Introversion and extraversion have been shown to lie on a single continuum, with strongly introverted people falling at one extreme of the continuum and strongly extraverted people at the other. Most people fall toward the middle, being neither extremely introverted nor extremely extraverted.

C. G. Jung and, to a lesser extent, Hermann Rorschach are usually credited with introducing the concepts of introversion and extraversion into the field of modern psychology, and the general scientific acceptance of these concepts would seem to vindicate Jung's and Rorschach's ideas. However, the true picture is more complicated. The modern view is a modification of the ideas originally proposed by Jung and Rorschach, who believed that introverts and extraverts differ not only in their style of social contact but in the way they experience reality. According to both Jung and Rorschach, introverts direct their attention and interests to the "inner world" of fantasy and thoughts (turning inward), whereas extraverts direct their attention to the "outer world" of physical and social events (turning outward).

Although modern psychology's social version of introversion and extraversion has extensive scientific support, there's little solid evidence for Jung and Rorschach's idea that introversion and extraversion represent radically different ways of experiencing reality. Furthermore, Rorschach's picture of the four *EB* types is certainly incorrect. Although he thought that Introversive individuals tend to have abstract intelligence and to be socially awkward, research has shown no clear connection between introversion and intelligence, or between intelligence and social awkwardness. Similarly, although Rorschach portrayed Extratensive individuals as emotionally unstable, research has not substantiated this idea. Emotional instability is about as common among introverts as extraverts.[28]

M and *EB* as Personality Measures

A separate issue is whether Rorschach was right or wrong about *M*, Color, and *EB*. Are Human Movement and Color responses and the *EB* ratio related to introversion and extratension? The answer turns out to be *probably not*, but with a few interesting twists.

The most important questions about *EB* and *M* were explored vigorously by researchers in the 1940s and 1950s. For example, studies from that era demonstrated that *EB* bears little if any relationship to social introversion and extraversion.[29] Typical was a study by Wayne Holtzman at Stanford University in the late 1940s. Forty-six students who lived together in a close group setting were administered the Rorschach and asked to rate themselves and each other for shyness and sociability. Their *EB* scores were unrelated to the ratings.[30]

Research produced at least one encouraging finding, however. Rorschach had claimed that introversives are especially intelligent. Several studies provided support for this idea, showing that individuals who gave a high number of *M* responses tended to score above average on intelligence tests.[31]

Another set of intriguing findings in the 1950s suggested that there might be a relationship between *M* responses and physical activity, just as the theories of Rorschach and Mourly Vold would predict. Much of the research on this topic was carried out by Jerome Singer of Yale University and his colleagues using patients with schizophrenia.[32] In one study, patients were asked to write the phrase "New Jersey Chamber of Commerce" as slowly as possible, without lifting their pencil or stopping its motion. Patients with a high number of *M* responses were found to write more slowly than patients with a low number of *M* responses. In another procedure patients were asked to wait for fifteen minutes in a room where an observer surreptitiously noted how physically active they were. Patients with high *M* were less active than the patients with low *M*.[33]

Although Singer's results were tantalizing, the relationship between *M* and physical activity remained ambiguous. When another researcher used the pencil-writing procedure with college students instead of schizophrenic patients, he found no significant relationship between writing speed and *M*.[34] More important, even if *M* was related to a person's physical activity level or performance on a pencil-writing task, what relevance, if any, would these findings hold for the individual's everyday behaviors?

Singer proposed that both M and performance on motor tasks might be generally related to inhibition of impulses, so that individuals who give many M responses to the Rorschach, or are slow on the pencil-writing task, might be more inclined to inhibit their emotions or delay their actions. However, these speculations were never systematically substantiated. Although more than forty years have passed since Singer and his colleagues published their findings, there is still no solid evidence that M and pencil-writing speed are related to people's ability to inhibit their emotions, relate to other people, or perform important tasks in everyday life.

Researchers have produced other intriguing findings regarding M. Several studies suggest that individuals with many M responses in their Rorschachs tend to have a richer fantasy life than other people, with more daydreams and greater recall of nighttime dreams.[35] Individuals with high M also appear to be unusually accurate when asked to estimate (without a watch) how much time has passed in a given time interval.[36] Tantalizing as these tidbits are, they don't provide much support for Rorschach's contention that M represents one of the most fundamental aspects of personality. As a 1993 review of the literature on the topic concluded, research "has not eventuated in strong support for the hypothesis that M is particularly or even uniquely related to 'inner life.' . . . We really cannot say that we know the psychological 'meaning' of movement responses."[37]

Color as a Personality Measure

Findings regarding Color responses have been even less encouraging than those regarding M. Although Rorschach believed that the number of Color responses is related to affect and impulsiveness, research hasn't generally supported this idea. For instance, based on Rorschach's theories, psychologists in the 1950s assumed that groups characterized by impulsivity, such as psychopaths and delinquents, would show a relatively high number of Color responses. Instead, research indicated that these groups give an average or even below-average number of Color responses. Other studies that examined the relationship between Color and emotionality yielded negative or conflicting results.[38]

Despite the generally dismal results regarding Color, a few positive findings have emerged, just as with *M*. First, research has shown that young children give a disproportionately high number of Pure Color responses to the blots, and that the number of such responses decreases as the children grow older.[39] Second, it's possible that Color responses may be related to responsiveness to the physical environment.[40] For example, in one study in the 1950s, individuals who gave a high number of Color responses were more likely to notice and mention the physical details in their immediate environment and the testing room.[41] Third, several studies from the 1950s confirmed Rorschach's idea that depressed patients give a below-average number of Color responses.[42] However, more recent findings have been negative.[43]

Overall, research on Color responses has yielded unimpressive results.[44] As we noted earlier in this chapter, Rorschach never offered a good scientific explanation for why Color responses should be related to affect and impulsivity, so perhaps it's not surprising that his hypotheses haven't fared well.

Even Good Scientists Can Go Wrong

From the perspective of psychological science at the beginning of the twenty-first century, Rorschach's ideas about *M*, *WSumC*, and *EB* appear to have been largely mistaken. Of course, even good scientists can be misled by bad ideas. Sir Isaac Newton not only discovered the laws of gravitation and invented calculus, he believed in astrology and spent his later years conducting research on the subject. More recently, the brilliant Nobel Laureate Linus Pauling dismayed many of his fellow chemists by making extreme and ultimately discredited claims for the therapeutic value of Vitamin C for cancer and other diseases.

An important point can be made in Rorschach's favor as a scientist: He was correct when he hypothesized that people's *personality traits, beliefs, or emotions* can be closely related to how they *perceive* situations. Daily life is full of examples. Women seem to notice dirt more than men do. Children are more likely to hear the tinkling music of an ice-cream truck than their mothers are. In a more serious vein, psychological research has established some interesting links between personality traits and perception. For example, hostile children are particularly likely to perceive other children's intentions as hostile.[45] Similarly, anxious individuals are more likely than other individuals to notice threatening stimuli in their environment.[46]

Such findings show that Rorschach was at least heading in the right direction when he proposed a connection between personality and perception. His general idea was sound even though his hypotheses about *M* and *WSumC* were not. Looking back eighty years later, we can see where he got off track. Personality is most likely to affect perceptions when important *motivations* are involved.[47] Thus individuals are more likely to perceive hostility in the environment if they're highly motivated to protect themselves. Similarly, they're more likely to perceive threatening stimuli when they're concerned about issues of safety. In the absence of such motivations, personality does not seem to be closely connected with the perception of such simple visual categories as movement or color.

Rorschach clearly showed the qualities of a talented psychological researcher, although he was probably not the genius he has sometimes been called.[48] He had several good ideas and attempted to relate them to the scientific theories current in his time. Later in this chapter, we'll evaluate the scientific quality of his masterwork, *Psychodiagnostics*. But first, we'll take a moment to describe some of the other important scores in his test.

RORSCHACH'S OTHER SCORES

Rorschach included in *Psychodiagnostics* a variety of scores that he considered important, based on intuition and his observations while administering the test to hundreds of patients. Research during the past eighty years has shown that a few of these scores possess potential usefulness in clinical work. Others probably possess little value but deserve attention because they're still taken seriously by many psychologists and have been used to assess so many patients. These scores will reappear repeatedly in this book as the story of the Rorschach Test unfolds.

Response Frequency (R). One of the simplest scores yielded by Rorschach's test is *R*, the total number of responses that a patient gives to the blots. Most people report one to three images for each of the ten cards, so that *R* typically falls between ten and thirty. Perhaps not surprisingly, research has shown that *R* tends to be correlated (though somewhat modestly) with an individual's verbal intelligence. That is, individuals with high verbal intelligence tend to describe somewhat more things in the blots than do individuals with low verbal intelligence.[49]

Form Quality (F+ or F–). Rorschach thought it was important whether the images reported by a patient actually fit the shape of the inkblots. For instance, one of his blots closely resembles a four-legged animal. If a patient reported that this blot looked like "a cat," Rorschach considered the response to have "good fit" or "good form quality" (*F+*). In contrast, if a patient reported that the blot looked like "a hat" (which it definitely does not), Rorschach considered the response to have "poor fit" or "poor form quality" (*F–*).

Rorschach combined *F+* and *F–* to create a score called *F+%*—which is simply the result of dividing the number of *F+* responses by the sum of *F+* and *F–* responses. High *F+%* indicates a tendency to give responses with good form quality, whereas low *F+%* indicates the opposite. Rorschach reported that patients with schizophrenia have low *F+%*, and later researchers confirmed his observations. Low *F+%* is a valid (though not infallible) indicator of schizophrenia and other psychotic disorders.[50]

Color Shock. Five of the cards that Rorschach created are gray and white, whereas the other five contain color. He noticed that some patients seemed to have special difficulty with the colored blots. For instance, when given a colored card they might pause without saying anything, report that they couldn't see any images, or give a response that didn't really fit the shape of the blot. Rorschach concluded that these patients' thought processes had been disrupted by the emotion aroused by the color. He termed this phenomenon "Color Shock" and speculated that it indicated a neurotic repression of emotion. In other words, patients who responded oddly to the colored blots were thought to be experiencing strong emotion, but keeping it tamped down and out of awareness. Color Shock was intensively studied by researchers in the 1950s, as we'll discuss in Chapter Six.

Wholes (W), Details (D), and Small Details (Dd). As mentioned earlier, Rorschach observed that some responses tend to incorporate the entire inkblot into a single image. Rorschach called these "Whole" or "*W*" responses. In contrast, some responses are based on prominent areas of the blot ("This big splotch over here looks like a chicken"), or on small, relatively inconspicuous features ("This little squiggle on the bottom looks kind of like a face"). He used the term "Normal Detail" or "*D*" for images based on prominent areas of the blot, and "Small Detail" or "*Dd*" for responses based on smaller features.

We had an artist create the two blots that appear in Figures 2.2 and 2.3. There are several possible *W, D,* and *Dd* responses for these blots.

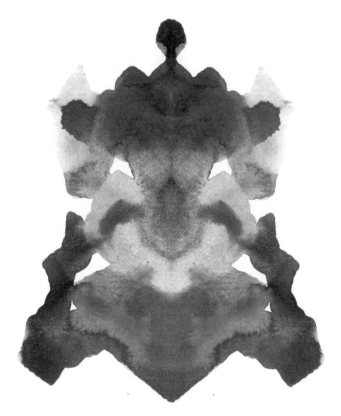

Figure 2.2.   Blot A.
What might this be?
Source: Copyright © 2002 Patrice N. Mozelewski. Used by permission.

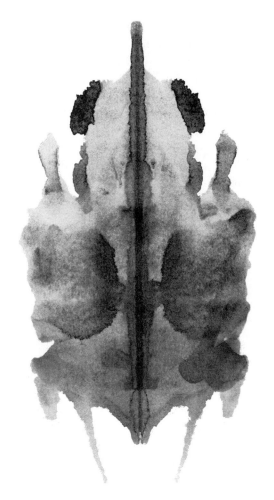

Figure 2.3.   Blot B.
What might this be?
Source: Copyright © 2002 Patrice N. Mozelewski. Used by permission.

For example, most people see Blot B in Figure 2.3 as a "bug" (a *W* response). A common response to the top two-thirds of Blot A in Figure 2.2 is "the head of a soldier with a big nose and moustache, wearing a helmet with a knob on top" (a *D* response). And the little knob at the top of Blot A has been identified as "a view from behind of a woman with her hair pulled back in a French braid" (a *Dd* response).

In Rorschach's opinion, *W*, *D* and *Dd* responses reveal both intellect and personality. Specifically, he believed that a high proportion of *W* responses indicates intelligence and the ability to integrate information imaginatively. In contrast, he thought that a high proportion of *D* or *Dd* responses are given by unintelligent individuals, "pedants," and "grumblers."[51] Although subsequent research hasn't borne out Rorschach's hypotheses about pedants and grumblers, it has provided support for his ideas about *W*. For example, one study found that the number of *W* responses with good form quality was correlated with problem-solving ability, although not with intelligence.[52]

Space Responses (S). The instructions for the inkblot test implicitly invite the patient to describe the blots: "What might this be?" However, Rorschach noticed that some patients report seeing images in the white spaces within the blots, outlined by the ink ("This white part here in the middle might be a face"). Because such Space responses (*S*) don't conform to the implicit test instructions, Rorschach believed that they indicate a "tendency to opposition."[53] Among extratensive people this opposition is ostensibly directed *outward* in the form of defiance, stubbornness, and argumentativeness, whereas among introversive people the opposition is supposedly directed *inward* as self-criticism and feelings of inadequacy.[54] Research on *S* and its relation to oppositionality hasn't provided clear support for Rorschach's ideas.[55] As one reviewer concluded, "we do not know what *S* responses mean."[56]

HERMANN RORSCHACH AS RESEARCHER

In *Psychodiagnostics,* Rorschach insisted that his ambitious new ideas were based on his own systematic observations, not armchair theorizing. He gathered data from over a hundred normal individuals and almost two hundred patients with schizophrenia, as well as smaller groups of epileptics, mentally retarded patients, and what he called "manic depressives" (patients with major depression or bipolar disorder). To conclude our discussion of Hermann Rorschach, we'll take a closer look at his study and examine its scientific strengths and weaknesses.

Group Study and Quantification

The research described in *Psychodiagnostics* has two features that elevate it above virtually all other psychiatric reports of its time. First, it was a group study involving two large samples of subjects (normal individuals and patients with schizophrenia). Today we take it for granted that most research involves substantial groups of subjects, but in Rorschach's era such studies were rare in psychiatry. Instead, case studies based on one or two subjects were the norm. For example, we can compare *Psychodiagnostics* with the books of Sigmund Freud, which often presented remarkably elaborate theories based on observations from a single case study. For many decades after the appearance of Rorschach's work, Freud's followers continued to rely heavily on the case study method, and Freud denigrated group studies as a method for testing his theories.[57]

The second striking feature of *Psychodiagnostics* is its emphasis on *quantification,* the use of numbers to represent findings.[58] By present-day standards, Rorschach's approach to numbers seems primitive. His book doesn't report even the simplest descriptive statistics, such as means (averages), standard deviations (a measure of the variability of scores across individuals), or percentages. Instead, the tables in *Psychodiagnostics* schematically display the range of scores that were obtained for different groups of people. For example, one table indicates that artists typically gave more than five *M* responses to the inkblots, people of normal intelligence gave two to four, and depressed patients gave zero.[59]

The tables in *Psychodiagnostics* are rough-hewn and approximate. After writing down scores for his subjects, Rorschach apparently eyeballed the numbers and then summarized his impressions. Although this approach now seems remarkably crude, it was a substantial improvement over most psychiatric research of the time. By 1921, the year *Psychodiagnostics* was published, numerical findings were routinely reported by psychologists who worked as researchers in universities. However, psychiatrists, who typically lacked research training, tended to lag behind.

Good science doesn't always require quantification. As an example, Eugen Bleuler (the Zurich psychiatrist whose work influenced

Rorschach) developed his brilliant insights about schizophrenia without resorting to numbers. Valuable scientific insights can sometimes be extracted from unaided clinical observation, particularly when a field of science is in its early stages. However, as a field advances, numbers become indispensable. For example, Bleuler never discovered one crucial fact about schizophrenia: its substantial genetic component. That insight was not established until the last third of the twentieth century, when statistical analyses of health records in Denmark revealed that the tendency of schizophrenia to run in families was at least partly heritable.[60]

Quantitative analyses can reveal patterns that are difficult to detect using ordinary observation. In addition, the *precision* of numerical analyses is of enormous value because it allows theories and data to be rigorously tested and scrutinized for errors. For example, Rorschach reported that the typical number of M responses given by depressed patients was zero. Subsequent research has shown that this number is much too low, and that the average number of M responses among depressed patients is probably between four and five.[61] The important point isn't that Rorschach was wrong about M in depressed patients, but that he reported his findings numerically, and with enough precision, so that later researchers could correct his mistakes.

Compared with other psychiatric studies of its time, the research reported by Rorschach in *Psychodiagnostics* is exemplary. One might expect his scientific findings to be exceptionally reliable as well. But herein lies an intriguing paradox. As our discussion of M, EB, and $WSumC$ has shown, Rorschach's central conclusions were often in error, in spite of his diligence as a scientist. How could Rorschach, one of the best psychiatric researchers of his time, be so wrong?

Source of Errors

A perusal of *Psychodiagnostics* reveals that Rorschach made several blunders that are all too familiar to scientists today. Research is full of hidden dangers. Scientists usually learn to avoid them through an unpleasant process, either by stumbling into these traps themselves or by reading about earlier researchers' mistakes. Only because researchers in psychology and psychiatry have been falling into jungle pits and mapping their locations for the past eighty years can we now see, with benefit of hindsight, where Rorschach went wrong and why.

First, Rorschach based many of his conclusions on samples that were too small. His group of patients with schizophrenia was fairly large (nearly two hundred subjects). Perhaps for this reason, his conclusion that patients with schizophrenia exhibit low scores on $F+\%$ has been confirmed by subsequent researchers.

However, Rorschach's other patient samples were tiny. For example, he reported results for only fourteen "manic-depressive" patients (in his time, mania and depression were often classified as a single disorder).[62] Some of these patients were probably manic rather than depressed, although his book doesn't provide details. Thus, his conclusions about the inkblot scores of depressed patients were based on no more than fourteen cases.

Second, aside from inkblot scores, Rorschach apparently lacked a sound method for measuring the personal characteristics of his subjects. For example, the tables in *Psychodiagnostics* show that he classified his normal subjects in a variety of ways, using such labels as *intelligent, imaginative, abstract, good–humored, indolent, negativistic, grumblers, stubborn,* and *apart from the world.* How did he measure such a wide variety of characteristics? Although his book doesn't provide an answer, it's clear that he didn't use formal tests such as Alfred Binet's intelligence scale.

Most likely, Rorschach relied on interviews and his own personal impressions, which nowadays would be considered inadequate for measuring such characteristics as intelligence, imagination, and negativism.[63] Unstructured interviews often have low validity.[64] It's sobering to realize that many of Rorschach's most influential conclusions—for instance that M is related to intelligence and imagination, and that S is related to negativism—were reached without good measures of intelligence, imagination, or negativism.

The third problem with Rorschach's study is subtler: He failed to keep inkblot scores completely separate from other information about his subjects. Rorschach both administered the inkblot test to subjects and evaluated their other characteristics (intelligence, impulsivity, and so on). The trouble with such an arrangement is that it opens the door to subjectivity, bias, and the common human tendency to find what one is expecting, referred to by psychologists as *confirmation bias.*[65]

For example, imagine that Rorschach the researcher is beginning to suspect that Color is related to impulsivity. He administers the inkblots to a man who gives a very high number of Color responses.

Afterward Rorschach estimates the man's impulsivity. Is Rorschach's estimate likely to be influenced by the Color responses? Will the responses cause Rorschach to give a higher estimate of impulsivity than he would have otherwise?

The answer, based on years of psychological research, is clear: Rorschach's estimate of the man's impulsivity is likely to be influenced by the Color responses, even if Rorschach tries very hard *not* to be influenced, and even if he *believes* he wasn't influenced.[66] At the conclusion of his study, Rorschach will find that, just as he expected, people who give a high number of Color responses are also impulsive. He typically won't realize that he helped to *create* this relationship by inadvertently giving higher estimates of impulsivity to subjects with a high number of Color responses.

The tendency of well-intentioned but incautious scientists to find what they expect is well-documented and accounts for some of the most fascinating stories in the history of science. We'll limit ourselves to mentioning only one, the case of the distinguished American astronomer Percival Lowell, who reported in the 1920s that while viewing the planet Mars he observed extensive canal systems constructed by intelligent beings, in accordance with earlier reports by the Italian astronomer Schiaperelli.[67] Lowell published detailed diagrams of the canals, which were apparently verified by some astronomers but fiercely disputed by others. When interplanetary probes eventually visited the planet and photographed it from a close distance, no canals were discovered, let alone intelligent beings. Lowell had found detailed evidence for what he expected, even though it wasn't there.

Expectations can shape and contaminate even careful scientific observations. For this reason, researchers over the past eighty years have learned to construct sturdy firewalls around their studies, so that one source of information is kept completely separate from another. If Rorschach were to repeat his study today, he'd be advised to arrange for one researcher to administer and score the inkblot tests, and for a separate researcher to evaluate the subjects' intelligence, imagination, impulsivity, and other characteristics. The two researchers would remain unaware of each other's findings until the end of the study, when the two sets of data could be compared. Only in this way could the integrity of the study be protected.

Rorschach's failure to take such precautions doesn't diminish his stature as a researcher who was far in advance of his time. However, the lack of appropriate safeguards probably explains, at least in part, why he reported many striking findings that later investigators have been unable to replicate. As we'll see, during the 1930s many psychologists in America accepted Rorschach's research results as a brilliant confirmation of his theories. In retrospect, it can be seen that his results fit his theories all too well. Eager to uncover the basic elements of human personality, Rorschach sometimes saw patterns in the data that weren't there, much as one of his patients might see a ballerina or a bear in the ambiguous contours of an inkblot.

Although most of Rorschach's insights about the inkblots were illusory, these illusions turned out to be infectious and enduring. Particularly in the United States, his obscure test was destined to become widely admired. In the next three chapters, we'll tell the rags-to-riches story of the Rorschach test in America, and describe how in a few decades the blots were transformed from the odd obsession of a small group of New York enthusiasts into clinical psychology's most prized diagnostic tool.

CHAPTER THREE

The Rorschach Comes to America

The Rorschach method does not reveal a behavior picture, but rather shows—like an X-ray picture—the underlying structure which makes behavior understandable.

—Bruno Klopfer, "Personality Aspects Revealed by the Rorschach Method," 1940

For several years after Rorschach's death, his test remained a purely Swiss phenomenon, kept alive by a few of his friends and colleagues. Only gradually did interest in the test spread to other countries. In the United States, however, the Rorschach ignited fads and controversies unknown elsewhere. The unusual and extreme reaction of American psychologists to the Rorschach was accounted for partly by the personalities of its promoters, and partly by the unique history of testing in the United States. In the present chapter, we'll explain how these factors contributed to the test's popularity and led to a heated fratricidal battle among the test's leading American proponents.

THE AMERICAN PIONEERS: BECK, HERTZ, AND KLOPFER

Because Hermann Rorschach's book *Psychodiagnostics* was unavailable in English during the 1920s and 1930s (a translation didn't appear until 1942), information about the inkblot test first spread among

American psychologists by word of mouth.[1] Emil Oberholzer, a Swiss psychiatrist and friend of Rorschach, taught the test to David Levy, an American psychologist. Levy introduced it to Samuel Beck, a graduate student in psychology at Columbia University in New York.[2] Beck in turn passed it on to his friend Marguerite Hertz, a graduate student at Western Reserve University (now Case Western Reserve University) whom he'd met while working as a reporter in Cleveland.[3]

Word Spreads: Samuel Beck and Marguerite Hertz

In 1932, ten years after Hermann Rorschach's death, Samuel Beck and Marguerite Hertz wrote the first two Ph.D. dissertations on the Rorschach Inkblot Test in the United States. These two young psychologists were destined to devote the next fifty years of their lives to the Rorschach, spreading the word and becoming legends in their profession. As Marguerite Hertz said toward the end of her life, "I have been happily wedded to the Rorschach."[4]

Beck was a gentle, earnest man who revered Sigmund Freud and Hermann Rorschach (whom he sometimes referred to as "the master").[5] Hertz was considerably more outspoken, an incisive writer and speaker who used her impressive adversarial skills to defend the Rorschach and prod her fellow "Rorschachers" into doing more research. Over the ensuing decades, Beck became widely respected for his sober, systematic approach to the Rorschach, whereas Hertz became equally respected for her blunt opinions and devotion to scientific rigor.

Beck and Hertz were both diligent researchers, well-trained in the psychological theories and techniques of their time. After receiving their doctorates, they immediately began collecting more data. By the end of 1935, Beck had published eleven articles on the Rorschach, including several in prominent journals.[6] At the same time, Hertz began to publish her findings on children and adolescents.

The Organizer: Bruno Klopfer

Thanks to the work of Beck and Hertz, interest in the Rorschach grew among U.S. psychologists during the early 1930s.[7] Unfortunately, no textbook on the subject was available (except in German) and only a handful of American psychologists knew the test well enough to serve as teachers. At Columbia University in 1934, a group of psychology graduate students began to search for a Rorschach instructor.

Although Samuel Beck had moved to Boston two years previously, the students discovered that Bruno Klopfer, a research assistant in the Anthropology Department, could administer and score the test. Klopfer agreed to meet with the students one night each week and teach them for a small fee.[8]

Klopfer was a Berlin psychologist who fled his country in 1933 to escape the Nazi menace.[9] Attracted by C. G. Jung, the famous Swiss psychiatrist whose work had influenced Hermann Rorschach, Klopfer moved to Zurich, where he entered analysis with Jung and worked in a position arranged for him. As a psychological technician, Klopfer learned to administer and score psychological tests. However, the position gave him little opportunity to pursue his chief interest, which was psychoanalytic psychotherapy. Although he learned to administer the Rorschach test, which had become fairly popular in Switzerland, he wasn't particularly interested in using it.[10]

Less than a year after moving to Zurich, Klopfer obtained a position as a research assistant at Columbia University under Franz Boas, one of the most influential figures in twentieth-century anthropology.[11] Again, the job wasn't a good fit for someone with Klopfer's interests and experience. However, the Great Depression was under way and he had a family to support.

When Klopfer began to meet with the graduate students from Columbia each week at his apartment, he intended to adopt a nuts-and-bolts approach, teaching them the basics of administering and scoring the Rorschach. However, the students soon complicated his task by pointing out ambiguities in the scoring rules that were difficult to resolve. Although we have no detailed records of these first meetings, it's not difficult to guess from articles published afterward the questions the graduate students must have raised.

For example, one early disagreement among the young Rorschach enthusiasts concerned the scoring of Card III, which contains one large black blot and three smaller red blots. Many patients report that the black blot looks like two people bowing to each other or holding a cauldron. Should responses that are limited to the black blot be scored as *W* (a "Whole" response, in which the whole blot is seen as a single image) or as *D* (a "Large Detail" response, in which a large blot on the card is seen as an image, but some blots on the card are disregarded)? The question is important because, according to Rorschach, *W* responses indicate intelligence and a capacity to organize perceptions, whereas *D* responses do not carry this interpretation.

Unfortunately, Rorschach had left contradictory scoring instructions. According to his guidelines, responses should be scored as *W* only if they included *all* of the blots on a card. Thus, if a patient described the black blot on Card III as two people but ignored the red blots, the response did *not* fit the definition of *W*. However, in apparent violation of his own rules, Rorschach elsewhere recommended that such responses to Card III should be scored as *W* because "the black figures are the essential parts of the plate."[12]

By opening this loophole, Rorschach created an ambiguity about the scoring of all the cards, not just Card III. If, as he said, *W* could be scored for the "essential parts" of Card III, shouldn't the same principle be extended to other cards? If so, what were the "essential parts" of each card? Klopfer himself proposed a special scoring category, "cut-off wholes," for responses like the one to Card III that included at least two-thirds of the blots on a card.[13]

Another early disagreement involved the scoring of movement. Why was *M* restricted to images of humans? Couldn't other types of movement responses indicate introversiveness, intelligence, and creativity?[14] Shouldn't responses like "a fish diving through the water" or "a rock smashing against a house" be scored as movement?

Such questions weren't resolved in Hermann Rorschach's book. After all, Rorschach had intended *Psychodiagnostics* to be a research report, not a detailed instruction manual. Furthermore, a lecture he'd given toward the end of his life, published posthumously in Switzerland in the early 1930s,[15] showed that he continued to tinker with the test after its publication, adding a new, rather vaguely described scoring category called "Chiaroscuro" (now called "Shading").[16]

The classes at Klopfer's apartment quickly evolved into lively meetings at which the scoring and interpretation of the Rorschach test were debated and minutely analyzed, sometimes into the wee hours of the morning. When additional graduate students from Columbia and New York University signed up, Klopfer added a second class, then a third. Based on his discussions with students, he began to develop a large number of new scoring categories.

By 1936 Klopfer had become the informal leader of a closely knit group of Rorschach enthusiasts. He began to publish a mimeographed newsletter called the *Rorschach Research Exchange*. In 1937 he established the Rorschach Institute, an organization of psychologists, social workers, and other professionals devoted to the test.[17] Both the newsletter and the Institute thrived, eventually evolving into the present-day *Journal of Personality Assessment* and Society for Personality Assessment.

Bruno Klopfer had a talent for forming close, empathic connections with people.[18] A magnetic speaker, he was characterized by one of his admirers as "the most enthusiastic, resourceful, and dedicated super-salesman of the Rorschach there has ever been."[19] Were it not for Klopfer's talents as an organizer and proselytizer, the Rorschach Inkblot Test probably never would have become as popular, or as controversial, as it is today.

THE APPEAL OF THE RORSCHACH

With impeccable timing, Klopfer launched his sales efforts in a market that was just beginning to expand. In the 1930s, clinical psychologists were seeking a test that promised to provide broad insight into their clients' emotions and motivations. The Rorschach fit the bill.

The Young Profession of Clinical Psychology

When the Rorschach test first appeared in America, clinical psychology was a tiny profession, viewed askance by physicians and many of the psychologists who worked in universities.[20] The first clinical psychology clinic in the United States, established at the University of Pennsylvania in 1896, treated children with learning problems.[21] For the next forty years clinical psychology was mainly a child-oriented profession, focusing on juvenile delinquents, children with mental retardation, and students with educational difficulties.

When the first effective intelligence tests were introduced into the United States around 1910 by psychologist Henry H. Goddard (a story we'll tell later in this chapter), the profession acquired an important new tool that enhanced its prestige. However, as clinical psychologists began using intelligence tests to identify children with mental retardation, they often encountered fierce resistance from physicians, who contended that only medical doctors should diagnose mental retardation.

Many psychologists who worked in universities also opposed the development of clinical psychology as a profession. They believed that the scientific base of psychology was still in its infancy, and that it was premature to set up clinics and establish a separate profession of clinical psychology. They tended to believe that psychologists should devote themselves exclusively to research, and that the application of psychological discoveries to clinical work should await further development of the science. So strong were the feelings on this issue that in the late 1920s the American Psychological Association did not grant membership to clinical psychologists unless they had published research in scientific journals.[22]

Dissatisfaction with Self-Report Personality Tests

During the 1920s and 1930s, most clinical psychologists worked with children and adolescents. Their most important duty was to administer intelligence tests. However, psychologists soon began using personality tests as well, hoping to shed light on children's emotional problems. There was a problem, though: The personality tests weren't particularly helpful. There was general agreement among psychologists about the definition of *intelligence* and how to measure it. In contrast, *personality* was a vaguer concept, and there was little consensus about what it was or how it should be measured. In fact, most psychology departments didn't even offer courses on personality in the 1920s and early 1930s.[23]

Most personality tests of the era were self-report inventories that asked a series of yes/no questions related to a single trait, such as sociability ("I like to relax by spending time with my friends") or anxiety ("I tend to be a worrier"). In clinical settings, such inventories were viewed as less than satisfactory for several reasons.[24] First, they relied on patients to provide accurate and honest reports regarding their own behaviors, attitudes, and thoughts. But what about patients who were unwilling or unable to provide such information? Many people (patients and nonpatients alike) are reluctant to discuss such sensitive topics as sexual activities, violence, or alcohol use. As one critic of self-report tests commented, the most important things about individuals are often what they cannot or will not say.[25]

A second problem with the self-report inventories of the 1920s and 1930s was their narrow focus. Typically they measured only one or two traits. Clinical psychologists yearned for a bigger picture, something more revealing than the bare information that a child was "introverted" or "anxious." A third problem was the inventories' lack of depth: At most they described *how* a patient behaved—not *why* a patient behaved a particular way.[26]

A fourth problem was that the most popular self-report inventory of the 1930s, the Bernreuter Personality Inventory, was ill-constructed and did a poor job of identifying psychological problems.[27] It's hardly surprising, then, that clinical psychologists of the era grew disaffected with the Bernreuter and similar tests, coming to believe that there was something inherently wrong with questionnaires.

In the 1930s many clinical psychologists and psychiatrists wanted a personality test that didn't depend on patients' potentially unreliable self-descriptions, and that provided a full picture of them as individuals.[28] The Rorschach, particularly as reshaped by Bruno Klopfer, seemed to fit this need. Klopfer claimed that the Rorschach could operate like an x-ray and penetrate deep into the individual without his or her awareness. As an article in Klopfer's *Rorschach Research Exchange* asserted, "It is just because the subject is not aware of what he is telling and has no cultural norms for hiding himself that the Rorschach and other projective methods are so revealing."[29] Such a claim was highly appealing to clinical psychologists.

In addition, whereas many self-report inventories yielded scores for only one or two traits (the Bernreuter yielded four), Klopfer's elaborate scoring system for the Rorschach yielded over fifty.[30] Poring over this wealth of data, psychologists could weave together various Rorschach scores in the intuitive manner suggested by Klopfer, and thereby produce a rich and nuanced portrait of a patient's personality.

Of course, "rich and nuanced" is not necessarily the same as "accurate," and therein lay the seeds of a bitter dispute that soon divided two of the Rorschach pioneers, Bruno Klopfer and Samuel Beck. Like Marguerite Hertz, Beck had been trained in the American approach known as *psychometrics,* which stresses the importance of evaluating a test in careful studies to ensure that it measures what it's supposed to. Beck and Hertz took it for granted that psychological tests, like medical tests, should be administered, scored, and interpreted systematically and objectively, and that their worth had to be demonstrated scientifically.

To Klopfer, who'd been trained in a much different European tradition whose roots were more philosophical than experimental, such psychometric ideas were new and alien. The coming clash between Klopfer and Beck had personal elements, but was mainly a conflict between two intellectual perspectives. In the next section, we'll describe how one of those perspectives—the American psychometric approach—developed during a national controversy over intelligence testing in the 1910s and 1920s and became established among

American psychologists by the time the Rorschach test appeared in the 1930s.

BEFORE THE RORSCHACH: THE RISE OF THE AMERICAN PSYCHOMETRIC APPROACH

The modern intelligence test originated in France nearly a hundred years ago. With the establishment of free public education in Europe and America during the 1800s, the number and diversity of children in schools increased drastically. In France and elsewhere, recognition grew that some "feebleminded" children (we would now say "children with mental retardation or developmental delays") could not learn as quickly as others and needed "special education" (a term that dates back at least to 1902).[31]

Alfred Binet and the First Modern Intelligence Test

Until the early 1900s there was no good procedure for identifying children with lower mental ability who required special education. Teachers were often asked to identify these children. However, as we noted in the last chapter, informal estimates of intelligence tend to be unsatisfactory. For example, a survey of Paris teachers revealed that they used widely different methods for estimating children's intellectual abilities. Many teachers mistakenly believed that a child's facial expression or head shape was useful for estimating intelligence.[32]

Several American and European psychologists in the late 1800s had attempted to develop what they called "mental tests" by measuring sensory and physical characteristics, such as muscular strength, reaction time, and sharpness of vision.[33] Sir Francis Galton, a cousin of Charles Darwin, was prominent among these early researchers. In the 1890s, however, the French psychologist Alfred Binet began to explore a much different approach, asking children to perform tasks that required judgment, comprehension, and reasoning.[34]

For instance, a child might be asked to put together a simple puzzle, or rearrange the words in a scrambled sentence. Over a period of fifteen years, Binet and his colleagues developed the first modern intelligence test, which was published in 1905 with revisions in 1908 and 1911. Like Rorschach, Binet died shortly after his test was developed and didn't live to see how popular it would become.[35]

Henry H. Goddard and the
Menace of Feeble-Mindedness

Binet's intelligence test was translated into English and published by Henry H. Goddard,[36] a psychologist at the then obscure Training School for Feeble-Minded Girls and Boys in Vineland, New Jersey.[37] Goddard, who had started his career as a teacher in Quaker schools, used Binet's test to identify children who needed special education. Children were classified according to their degree of intellectual deficiency. Those with the most severe retardation were classified as *idiots,* those with moderate retardation as *imbeciles,* and those with mild retardation as *morons* (a term of Goddard's own invention, based on the Greek word for *fool*).

Goddard's focus on retardation was natural, given that most clinical psychologists of his era worked with children with educational problems. He achieved national recognition and in 1914 published the standard book of his time on mental retardation, *Feeble-Mindedness.* The Training School at Vineland began to offer summer courses for teachers, who learned to administer intelligence tests and imitate the school's progressive educational practices. Goddard, charismatic and eloquent, inspired the psychologists and teachers who visited Vineland to become ardent advocates for his ideas.

Had Goddard limited his work to children with developmental delays, he would probably be regarded today as a benign figure and among the most eminent clinical psychologists of his time. Instead he's usually remembered as an overzealous idealist who embroiled the new field of intelligence testing in a disastrous public controversy.[38] This is because, in addition to his pioneering work on the educational use of intelligence tests with children, Goddard declared that feeble-mindedness was a hereditary condition caused by a single recessive gene, that it was responsible for myriad social ills, including crime, alcoholism, and prostitution, and that it posed an imminent threat to the moral fabric of America. In studies of prostitutes and juvenile delinquents, he claimed, IQ tests identified 40 percent to 90 percent as "mentally defective." "The feeble-minded person is a menace to society at the present moment," Goddard warned.[39]

In a highly influential and now notorious book, *The Kallikak Family,* Goddard traced the history of two branches of a single family, each descended from the same Revolutionary War soldier, Martin Kallikak.[40] In a youthful indiscretion, Martin had entered into an illicit liaison with a barmaid said to be feebleminded. The descendants of this union led lives marred by drunkenness, crime, poverty, and madness. In addition, Martin married a Quaker woman of good family, and the descendants of this marriage led lives of eminence and virtue, becoming government leaders, army officers, doctors, and ministers. Goddard concluded that the gene for feeblemindedness had been passed down through the barmaid side of the family and was responsible for its apparent degeneracy.

Goddard's study of the Kallikak family was seriously flawed from a scientific perspective. Because the character and intelligence of long-dead ancestors cannot be measured adequately with intelligence tests or estimated from interviews, information on 135 years of deceased Kallikaks was gathered mainly from the reminiscences of living Kallikaks—most of whom were judged to be feebleminded by Goddard's research team![41] Even though these oral histories were vague, incomplete, and lacking in solid corroboration, Goddard and his assistants used them to determine which Kallikak ancestors were feebleminded. Such retrospective determinations were subjective and appear to have been contaminated by the biases and preconceptions of Goddard's research team.[42] Like Hermann Rorschach, Goddard and his assistants employed a flawed research method that misled them into finding what they expected.

The scientific weaknesses of Goddard's book weren't recognized at first. Read widely by psychologists and nonpsychologists after its publication in 1913, *The Kallikak Family* influenced public policy for the next two decades. To keep supposed "degenerates" from transmitting hereditary defects to their offspring, many states passed laws requiring compulsory sterilization programs for the feebleminded. The case of Carrie Buck, an eighteen-year-old "defective" woman whose mother and seven-month-old daughter were labeled "feebleminded," was appealed to the U.S. Supreme Court. Goddard's book on the Kallikak family was cited in the appeal. Speaking for the court, Justice Oliver Wendell Holmes affirmed that the state of Virginia had the right to sterilize Buck: "It is better for all the world if instead of waiting to execute degenerate offspring for crime, or let them starve for their imbecility, society can prevent those who are manifestly unfit from continuing their kind. . . . Three generations of imbeciles are enough."[43]

The political implications of Goddard's ideas weren't limited to compulsory sterilization but extended to other areas. For example, when a high proportion of European immigrants tested by Goddard at Ellis Island were found to be "mentally defective," the results were used to promote immigration policies that restricted entry of supposedly inferior national groups such as Italians, Russians, and Poles.

Although Goddard's writings and findings were cited by supporters of sterilization and immigration restriction, he was ambivalent about such policies. Though not opposed to sterilizing feebleminded individuals, he preferred to isolate them in special institutions like the Vineland school. Furthermore, he believed that mentally defective immigrants from Eastern and Southern Europe could be successfully integrated into American society as menial workers: "People who are doing the drudgery are, as a rule, in their proper places. This fact should be recognized, and they should be helped to keep their proper places, encouraged and made happy, but not promoted to work for which they are incompetent."[44]

Criticisms of Intelligence Tests in the 1920s

Due largely to the energy and magnetism of Henry Goddard, during the 1910s intelligence tests spread rapidly across the United States. They were used to identify feebleminded schoolchildren, evaluate juvenile delinquents, and, during World War I, to identify military recruits unfit for service. The tests' practical value was difficult to deny. Even today intelligence tests serve a useful function in schools, courts, and the military. However, during the 1920s, at the same time that enthusiasm was at its highest, serious criticisms of the tests began to surface.[45]

First, Goddard's idea that feeblemindedness is transmitted by a single gene, and that low scores on intelligence tests unambiguously reveal the presence of this genetic flaw, came under heavy attack. Geneticists firmly rejected the single-gene idea.[46] In addition, overwhelming evidence accumulated that intelligence test scores can be influenced by such factors as a person's educational level or cultural background. Although heredity appeared to play a part in determining an individual's performance on the tests, environmental factors clearly did too. For example, a doctor who evaluated immigrants at Ellis Island pointed out that the word definitions required by intelligence tests were unsuitable for some cultural groups: "[It is] almost impossible for Americans to realize the narrowness of the lives of some of the poorer classes of the countries of Europe. . . . The farmer of southern Italy, tilling a few acres of land and living in a hut, the bare walls of which contain only one ornament, an unframed picture of the Madonna, and the only articles of furniture of which are a bed, a table, a chair or two, a few kitchen utensils and a little bedding, can hardly be expected to define the word 'charity.'"[47]

Another striking problem with the intelligence tests promoted by Goddard was their tendency to *overpathologize,* that is, to make normal individuals appear mentally defective. In an incident that was particularly embarrassing to American psychologists, the mayor of Chicago and several other politicians were administered the Binet intelligence test and received scores in the feebleminded range. "Who's Loony?" read the headline of a *Chicago Daily Tribune* story that ridiculed the legitimacy of IQ testing.[48] Serious questions were raised about Goddard's claim that most prostitutes and juvenile delinquents were mentally defective: Apparently IQ tests classified virtually *everyone* as feebleminded, even prominent citizens.[49]

Other troubling problems with IQ tests surfaced. Researchers noted that when different examiners gave the test, they sometimes used different procedures that affected the results. In addition, when children were given the IQ tests a second time, their scores sometimes varied widely between administrations. Thus, the same child might be classified as either "feebleminded" or "normal," depending on who administered the test and when it was given.[50]

Too large to be confined within the covers of scientific journals, criticisms of intelligence tests overflowed into the public forum. In 1922, Walter Lippmann, the most influential journalist of his day, published a devastating series of attacks on intelligence testing in the *New Republic.*[51] He wrote in response to recent books that claimed, on the basis of tests administered to soldiers during World War I, that the intelligence of the American public was substandard. As Lippmann mockingly reported: "A startling bit of news has recently been unearthed and is now being retailed by the credulous to the gullible. 'The *average* mental age of Americans,' says Mr. Lothrop Stoddard in *The Revolt Against Civilization,* 'is only about fourteen.'"[52]

Lippmann pointed out that such an idea was absurd: "It is quite impossible for honest statistics to show that the average adult intelligence of a representative sample of the nation is that of an immature child in that same nation. The average adult intelligence cannot be less than the average adult intelligence, and to anyone who knows what the words 'mental age' mean, Mr. Stoddard's remark is precisely as silly as if he had written that the average mile was three-quarters of a mile long."[53]

What made Lippmann's criticisms so deadly was his impressive grasp of the scientific issues involved. He fully acknowledged that intelligence tests were useful for identifying military recruits unfit for service, or for roughly sorting children into groups that were more or less likely to succeed in school. However, he perceptively identified several technical problems with the tests and argued persuasively that prominent psychologists of the day (including Lewis Terman of Stanford and William McDougall of Harvard) had used shaky research to promote the idea that distinctions among social classes were rooted in underlying hereditary differences in intelligence. Lippmann warned, "The real promise and value of the investigation which Binet started is in danger of gross perversion by muddle-headed and prejudiced men."[54] He also wrote, "They claim not only that they are really measuring intelligence, but that intelligence is innate, hereditary, and predetermined. . . . Intelligence testing in the hands of men who hold this dogma could not but lead to an intellectual caste system."[55]

Psychologists ineffectually attempted to defend themselves against Lippmann's criticisms. In an outraged and sarcastic response in the *New Republic,* Lewis Terman implied that Lippmann was a Communist and likened him to William Jennings Bryan, the populist leader who at the time was the country's staunchest defender of Biblical creationism.[56] However, Terman's attempts at smear accomplished little. The gist of Lippmann's argument—that many claims being made on the basis of intelligence tests were overblown, unsound, and without adequate scientific foundation—was correct. Lippmann's eloquent and well-reasoned articles, spiced with biting irony, tarnished the reputation of Terman and psychology and made an enduring impression on the profession and public.

Lessons from IQ Tests: Psychometrics

During the 1920s, intelligence testing, which had been clinical psychology's greatest public triumph, became its greatest embarrassment. The heated controversy had positive side effects, however, because it forced psychologists to think carefully about the scientific bases of psychological testing and to develop standards that could be used to evaluate the quality of tests.

By the 1930s an impressive body of knowledge and theory regarding psychological tests—now known as *psychometrics*—had taken shape. Experience with intelligence tests had led to the development and refinement of important concepts concerning psychological measurement, including norms, standardization, scoring reliability, correlation, test-retest reliability, alternate form reliability, and validity.

These seven fundamental concepts, well established by the 1930s, are still used routinely by psychologists to evaluate test performance. One could say that they provide a framework for "testing a test." A basic acquaintance with these ideas is essential to understanding the disagreements and controversies that have surrounded the Rorschach Inkblot Test from the 1930s until today.[57]

NORMS   Without a standard of comparison, test scores aren't informative. For example, suppose Amber received a score of 22 on the Binet intelligence test. Is Amber bright? Dull? Average? There's no way to know without more information. However, if we're told that the average score of children in Amber's age group is 17, then we can infer that she's probably bright. And if we're told that only 5 percent of children in her age group received scores higher than 21, we can infer that she's probably *very* bright.

As the example shows, test scores are informative only when they're compared with norms, which can be roughly defined as "the scores of an appropriate comparison group."[58] If we're testing the intelligence of an eight-year-old child, the appropriate norms should be based on the test scores from a "normative sample" of other children the same age. If we're testing an adult, the norms should be based on a normative sample of other adults, preferably adults in the same general age range as the person taking the test. Norms make it possible to determine where a person's test score falls relative to the scores of other people.

Although it seems obvious that the intelligence test scores of an adult should be compared with norms based on other adults, Goddard hadn't adopted this approach. The original Binet intelligence test, created for school settings, had fairly accurate norms for children, but not adolescents or adults. It's something of a puzzle why Goddard didn't construct normative samples himself, for example, by giving the test to a hundred normal adults and another hundred normal adolescents.

Instead, relying on children's norms and his own clinical judgment, Goddard decided which intelligence test scores were typical of normal adults and adolescents, and which indicated feeblemindedness. In other words, he made educated guesses. That he had guessed wrong became glaringly obvious when the Binet test misclassified the mayor of Chicago as a moron. In the absence of good norms, the test seriously overpathologized normal individuals, misidentifying them as abnormal. As we'll show later, similar problems of overpathologizing have plagued the Rorschach up until the present.

STANDARDIZATION   When psychology first appeared as a separate academic discipline in the late 1800s, it was a laboratory science. Early psychologists conducted painstaking studies to measure memory, reaction time, and visual perception. During that era the importance of standardization became clear. Each time a study was carried out, it had to follow precisely the same procedures. Otherwise, any effects observed by the researcher could be due to changes in procedure rather than to the phenomenon being studied. Furthermore, idiosyncratic variations in procedure could produce "random noise" and make measurements less precise.

Negative experiences with intelligence tests suggested that standardization was highly important for psychological testing. If two psychologists administered the same test, each should present the test items in the same way. Furthermore, it was crucial that psychologists follow the same administration procedures that had been used with the normative sample. Otherwise, an individual's test scores could differ from the norms simply because the test had been administered differently.

SCORING RELIABILITY   An obvious extension of the principle of standardization was that a test should always be scored the same way and according to the same set of objective rules. Otherwise, two psychologists scoring the same test responses from the same patient could arrive at strikingly different results, as had happened sometimes with Goddard's version of the Binet intelligence test. By the 1930s, the importance of scoring reliability (also called "interrater reliability") had become clear, and graduate students in psychology were admonished to carry out scoring in a consistent manner. However, it was not until several decades later that researchers began to examine the scoring reliability of psychological tests on a routine basis. They did so by assigning two psychologists to score the same group of tests. Reliability could then be evaluated by comparing the two sets of scores.

THE CORRELATION COEFFICIENT (r)   Before we discuss the remaining three psychometric concepts, it's necessary to understand the correlation coefficient (usually referred to as "r"). This coefficient is an extremely useful and versatile statistic that indicates how strongly two variables are related to each other.

To understand r, imagine that we're conducting a study to learn how strongly the variable "intelligence test scores" is related to a second variable "school grades." We administer an intelligence test to fifty normal schoolchildren, and then compare their test scores with their grades. In this example, school grades are measured on a scale from 65 to 100, where a score of 65 represents failure and 100 represents perfect grades. We then construct a graph that compares the test scores (along the bottom of the graph, called the "x axis") with the school grades (along the side, called the "y axis").

Figure A.1 in the Appendix shows four different graphs of what we might find. In graph A, the children's intelligence test scores and grades are *perfectly* related. In fact, the relationship is so perfect that if we know a child's test score we can predict that child's grades with absolute precision. For instance, a child in graph A with an "average" intelligence test score of 100 has school grades of 80. A child with a "very high" test score of 130 has grades of 95. When the relationship between two variables is perfect, as in graph A, r is 1.00.

Now consider graph B, which shows a less than perfect relationship between intelligence test scores and grades. The correlation coefficient is 0.90. In this case, we're still able to predict children's grades from their test scores, but with slightly less precision. For example, three different children in graph B have the same intelligence test score of 130, but somewhat different grades (92, 94, and 98). At best we can predict that children with test scores of 130 have grades "around" 95. Similarly, we can predict that children with average test scores "around" 100 will probably have grades "somewhere" between 75 and 90. Although imprecise, an r of .90 allows us to make predictions about individual children that are in the ballpark.

As the other graphs in Figure A.1 show, when the relationship between test scores and grades becomes weaker, r slips closer and closer to zero. When r goes down to .50, as in graph C, there's still a visible relationship between test scores and grades, but any predictions are very rough. For example, we can predict that children with high intelligence test scores (above 120) will generally have grades that are average (80) or better, and that children with low test scores (below 80) will generally have grades that are average or worse. Although such predictions are rather hazy, they may be helpful under some circumstances (for example, if we want to select a subgroup of the children for an enrichment class).

When the r dips as low as .30, as in graph D, the relationship between test scores and grades is barely visible to the naked eye and our predictions are very rough indeed. For instance, we can predict that on average children with intelligence test scores above 100 (the dots on the right side of the graph) have somewhat higher grades than children with test scores below 100 (the dots on the left side). But although we can make such general statements about different groups, it would be futile to make predictions about individual children based on their test scores.

For example, children with the lowest test scores (at the far left of the graph) have grades that are generally in the average range (around 80). And two children with test scores above 100 have the lowest grades in the entire group. Generally speaking, a correlation of .30 is almost useless if we're trying to make predictions about individuals, but it can sometimes be helpful if we want to make broad predictions about one group compared with another. The same is true for correlations below .30, except that our ability to make predictions—even about groups—becomes very limited when r is as low as .20 or .10.

The idea of the correlation coefficient was introduced in the late 1800s by Sir Francis Galton and refined by the great statistician Karl Pearson.[59] By the 1930s, psychologists realized that it was an extremely useful tool for evaluating the psychometric properties of tests. For example, correlations frequently are used to describe results on test-retest reliability, alternate-form reliability, and validity.

TEST-RETEST RELIABILITY   During the controversy over intelligence testing, it was noted that if a child was tested on two different occasions, the scores from the two administrations sometimes varied widely.[60] Such findings were disturbing because intelligence was supposed to be a stable, even hereditary, characteristic, and shouldn't fluctuate markedly from one test administration to the next.

By the 1930s, psychologists had come to recognize that test-retest reliability (sometimes called *temporal stability*) was an essential characteristic of tests designed to measure stable characteristics. If the same patients were tested on one occasion and retested within a relatively short time period (for example, within a few weeks or months), the scores should be approximately the same on both occasions.

Of course, the phrase "approximately the same" is rather loose, but a consensus has arisen among psychologists that test-retest reliability should be at least .80 or .85 for brief time periods.[61] Modern intelligence tests have test-retest reliabilities of .90 or higher for brief time periods.[62]

Graph A in Figure A.2 (in the Appendix) presents the hypothetical scores of fifty schoolchildren who were given the same intelligence test at Time 1 and Time 2. Each dot represents one child, with the test scores for Time 1 plotted along the x-axis (at the bottom) and the scores for Time 2 plotted along the y-axis (at the side). Test-retest reliability between the two occasions is .90. Most children obtained scores at Time 2 that were approximately the same as their scores at Time 1. However, as the graph shows, even with a reliability of .90, a few children obtained markedly discrepant scores on the two occasions.

Whereas modern intelligence tests have test-retest reliabilities of at least .90, the average test-retest reliability of present-day Rorschach scores is about .80 over brief time periods.[63] As an example, Graph B in Figure A.2 presents the hypothetical test-retest scores of fifty schoolchildren who have taken the Rorschach on two occasions (the scores have been kept between 60 and 140 to make comparison with graph A easier). The test-retest reliability between the two occasions is .80. Comparing graph B with graph A, we can see that there are more discrepancies in children's scores between Time 1 and Time 2 when reliability is .80 than when reliability is .90.

ALTERNATE-FORM RELIABILITY   The real point of studying the test-retest reliability of a test is to determine whether it yields *consistent* results. However, there are problems with administering exactly the same test twice and comparing the scores.[64] First, *memory* effects may artificially inflate the similarity of scores between the test and retest. For example, in one study the Rorschach was given to the same psychiatric patients twice, about three days apart. Approximately two-thirds of the images reported by the patients were the same both times.[65] In all likelihood, the patients simply remembered what they said three days previously.

A second problem is that test-retest reliability can be misleading if we're measuring *characteristics that are changeable and unstable.* For example, anxiety can be a very unstable characteristic. A person may be very anxious when tested today (say, because there's a layoff pending at work), but not anxious at all when retested a year from now. The test scores at the first and second testing may be inconsistent, not because there are problems with the test but because anxiety itself is inconsistent.

By the 1930s, psychologists had devised a simple strategy for getting around these problems called *alternate-form reliability.* The idea is to create two versions of the same test, and use these alternate forms in a test-retest study. For example, a child could be given Version A of an intelligence test one day, and Version B six months later. Because the versions are different, practice and memory effects are largely or completely eliminated.

The alternate-form approach also works with tests that measure unstable characteristics. For example, a person could be given Version A of an anxiety test now and Version B fifteen minutes later. Because the time interval is short, the two versions of the test should yield similar scores. If they don't, the results suggest that the test doesn't yield consistent results.

VALIDITY   The bottom line for any psychological test is its validity: How well does it measure or predict what it's supposed to? Since the 1930s, psychologists have required that the validity of a new test be demonstrated in well-controlled studies.[66] It isn't enough for presumed experts to assert on the basis of their personal experience that a test is valid.

When a test is used in schools, hospitals, courts, and other real-world settings, there's a need to demonstrate its *criterion validity.* Criterion validity refers to "the effectiveness of a test in predicting an individual's performance in specified activities."[67] For example, studies of criterion validity have examined the effectiveness of intelligence tests in predicting school performance. The results indicate that the correlation between intelligence test scores and school grades tends to be about .50.[68]

This .50 validity coefficient is important because it provides evidence that intelligence tests measure an important aspect of mental ability. If the correlation between intelligence test scores and school grades were only .10 instead of .50, we might wonder whether the tests measure what they're supposed to. The .50 validity coefficient also tells us how much precision we can expect if we try to predict a student's school grades from his intelligence test scores. Looking back at graph

C in Figure A.1, we can see that when $r = .50$ our predictions are necessarily rough. Intelligence tests don't provide us with a high degree of precision in predicting school grades.

The criterion validity of a test can also be demonstrated by showing that it correlates with other tests. For example, children are often given standardized achievement tests that measure their performance in reading, arithmetic, and other school subjects. Among children, the correlation of intelligence test scores with arithmetic achievement scores is about .70, and the correlation with reading scores is about .60.[69] Thus, intelligence test scores predict performance on achievement tests with more precision than they predict school grades.

As these examples show, whenever we ask, "Is this test valid?" we must also ask, "How valid and for what purpose?" For example, intelligence tests have approximately .70 validity for predicting math scores, but close to .00 validity for predicting skill in most sports. Statements about test validity should specify the size of the validity coefficient and the criterion being predicted.

A Psychometric Exemplar

By the 1930s, American psychologists had not only accepted the basic psychometric ideas discussed here, but had seen what these principles could accomplish. The highly respected Stanford-Binet Intelligence Test, introduced by Lewis Terman in 1916, provided an exemplar. Terman (the same psychologist who locked horns with Walter Lippmann in the *New Republic* in the 1920s) revised and extended Binet's test to improve its psychometric properties. He provided detailed instructions for the standardized administration and scoring of the test, and norms based on a thousand children and four hundred adults.[70] The test-retest reliability and validity of the Stanford-Binet were widely studied, and a new edition was published in 1937, including a parallel version so that alternate-form reliability could be examined.

Terman's test provided a benchmark against which other tests could be measured.[71] When the Rorschach test was introduced into the United States, its promoters sometimes enthusiastically compared it with the Stanford-Binet.[72] Both tests were said to be highly innovative and clinically useful, rivaling each other in importance. However, such comparisons became harder to maintain as the psychometric weaknesses of the Rorschach became evident. If any comparison was to be made, it was between the Rorschach and the crude version of the Binet intelligence test used by Goddard in the 1910s. However, this didn't become clear to American psychologists until the 1950s and 1960s.

THE SCHISM BETWEEN BECK AND KLOPFER

Now we return to the 1930s and the impending schism between Samuel Beck and Bruno Klopfer. Their conflict had its roots in their differing approaches to psychological testing and the Rorschach.

Bruno Klopfer's Resistance to Psychometrics

Compared with Samuel Beck and Marguerite Hertz, Bruno Klopfer in the 1930s was a scientific lightweight.[73] A clinical practitioner rather than a researcher, he had worked in educational settings before coming to the United States and had served as director of a school for "problem children."[74] He had twelve years of Freudian training and experience and (as we mentioned earlier) spent a year studying with C. G. Jung.[75] He was also influenced by the ideas of phenomenological psychology, which were more closely linked with philosophy than with research-based psychology.[76]

Although Klopfer was an intelligent man, his background in the theories of Freud, Jung, and phenomenology had not prepared him for American psychologists' hard-nosed approach to testing. As a result of his European background, he "was somewhat surprised and taken aback by the American emphasis on norms and standardization."[77] In the eyes of his admirers, he "chafed at the meaningless psychometrics of that era"[78] and "steadfastly refused to bow to sterile quantification."[79]

The extent of Klopfer's resistance to psychometrics can be seen in the fact that his subsequent textbooks on the Rorschach, published in the 1940s through the 1960s, included no norms.[80] Instead, in the 1946 edition, he took a potshot at the idea: "In an effort to compensate for the seeming 'subjectivity' of the Rorschach method . . . some Rorschach practitioners have over-emphasized the necessity for the accumulation of great numbers of records, as if the accumulation and summarization of these records would lend at least the appearance of objectivity to the method. It scarcely seems necessary at this time to suggest the futility of such a procedure."[81]

In the late 1930s Klopfer published an article in the *Rorschach Research Exchange* that asked, "Shall the Rorschach method be standardized?"[82] His answer was negative, although he conceded that "refinement" or "rationalization" of administration and scoring instructions could be desirable for beginners.[83] Particularly telling was his condemnation of those he had labeled as "extremists": "Orthodox 'experimentalists' demand that the Rorschach method be free from all 'subjective' elements. To reduce that point of view ad absurdum, we could say that they want to establish standardized tables where the scoring and interpretive value of every single Rorschach response could be looked up. They want to reduce the scoring and interpretation to a seemingly foolproof, mechanical, and, therefore, 'objective' procedure."

Although Klopfer thought such views ridiculous and extreme, they represented mainstream psychometric trends in American psychology that ultimately prevailed. As we'll see, his "ad absurdum" example eventually came true: In the 1990s, John Exner published detailed tables and decision rules so that, just as Klopfer had feared, the scoring and interpretation of virtually every Rorschach response could be looked up.[84]

The Debate in the Rorschach Research Exchange

Given their dramatically different perspectives, it was unavoidable that Samuel Beck and Bruno Klopfer would disagree about the Rorschach. Beck thought the test should be developed and used in accordance with psychometric principles; Klopfer did not. Because both men intended to put their own stamp on the test, the disagreement was bound to lead to competition and conflict.

At stake was the future direction of the Rorschach in America. Given his own prolific publication and research record, Beck probably expected that he, and perhaps Marguerite Hertz, would play a dominant role in shaping and disseminating the test, as Lewis Terman had done with the Stanford-Binet. In contrast, Klopfer had never published a single article on the Rorschach, much less a research article, except in his own *Rorschach Research Exchange*. That a nonresearcher—someone apparently oblivious to the basic scientific principles governing test usage—should set the future course for the Rorschach was unthinkable to Beck.[85]

For his own part, Klopfer regarded the Rorschach as a complex clinical tool that could best be developed by clinicians like himself who possessed rich and extensive experience in its use. He saw no reason why the future of the test should be dominated by psychometrically oriented psychologists who, in Klopfer's vivid metaphor, sought "the sacrifice of the intrinsic potentialities of the Rorschach method on the altar of a fetishistic goddess 'Statistic.'"[86]

An early warning of the impending struggle appeared in a 1936 article by Beck, which criticized some European approaches to the Rorschach as overly subjective. In line with the psychometric approach, Beck stressed that the scoring, administration, and interpretation of the test should be standardized on the basis of objective research evidence.[87] Although the article didn't specifically mention Klopfer (in fact, at the time he wrote the article Beck may have been unaware of Klopfer's activities in New York), it clearly opposed attempts to take the Rorschach in a "subjective," nonpsychometric direction.

In 1937 Beck published *Introduction to the Rorschach Method,* which became known as "Beck's *Manual.*"[88] It provided detailed instructions for administering and scoring the test. Klopfer responded by writing an unfavorable review in the *Rorschach Research Exchange.*[89] This was the first time that either Klopfer or Beck had criticized the other in print. Klopfer also published his own set of instructions for administering the Rorschach, thereby providing an alternative "manual" to Beck's.[90]

Beck responded to Klopfer's negative review with a reply, also published in the *Rorschach Research Exchange.*[91] A few months later, in a stunning escalation of the controversy, Klopfer devoted almost an entire issue of his journal to commentaries on Beck's work. Ten different psychologists and psychiatrists weighed in, all of them with something critical to say about Beck,[92] although (as we'll see a little later) one of them was also critical of Klopfer.

Most of the commentators, like Klopfer, were unenthusiastic about a psychometric approach to the Rorschach. For example, the English psychiatrist Arthur Guirdham protested that "this search for objective validation goes too far" and warned against the "deadly accuracy of psychometry."[93] The Swiss psychologist Marguerite Loosli-Usteri remarked that "any exclusively numeric approach to the test must needs be a failure" and "a mere analysis of statistics can never be satisfactory."[94] And the American psychiatrist John D. Benjamin said that he had no quarrel with professionals who used "objective quantitative" tests, but "I do, however, protest against the attempt to make over the Rorschach into one of them at a very real sacrifice of its enormous potentialities."[95]

Although journal editors are expected to maintain a judicial impartiality toward participants in a scholarly controversy, such was clearly not the case in the 1937 debate between Beck and Klopfer. By publishing ten articles critical of Beck, Klopfer had clearly stacked the deck against his opponent. Relations between the two men deteriorated even further and by 1940 all communication between them ceased.[96] As one author put it, "Subsequently the relation between Klopfer and Beck seems to have been one of mutual splendid isolation."[97]

Specific Issues That Divided Beck and Klopfer

A profound and fundamental difference in perspective led to the schism between Beck and Klopfer. It's worth looking at some of the specific issues that divided them, because the fine points of the disagreement are still relevant to how the Rorschach is used today. We'll describe the three most important issues that separated Beck and Klopfer: the scoring and interpretation of Shading, Movement, and *F+* and *F–*.

SHADING   As we mentioned earlier, after publishing *Psychodiagnostics,* Rorschach developed a new scoring category that today is called "Shading."[98] According to Rorschach, a Shading response is determined by "light and shadow" rather than "color."[99] For example, he scored Shading for the following responses: "a column of smoke," "dark mountains on a map," and "a parkway between dark trees that loses itself in the distance."[100]

Rorschach conceded that the psychological meaning of such responses wasn't entirely clear, but speculated that they indicated timidity, cautiousness, and a tendency toward depression.[101] He added that Shading responses emphasizing *depth, distance, or perspective* (such as the description of a parkway that "loses itself in the distance") were particularly important indicators of caution, depression, and feelings of alienation.[102]

Rorschach presented no research to support his ideas about Shading, and his treatment of the topic was rather perfunctory. Among the psychiatrists and psychologists who used his inkblot test in the following years, there was a feeling that he died before he could explore the full meaning of Shading responses.[103]

Other thinkers attempted to take up where Rorschach had left off. In 1932 the Swiss psychiatrist Hans Binder introduced several new categories of Shading that went considerably beyond what Rorschach described.[104] Binder's approach attracted considerable interest and is still used in Europe. A few years after the appearance of Binder's work, Klopfer introduced his own Shading categories, eventually evolving five separate shading scores that, he claimed, had important interpretive differences.

When Beck published his *Manual* in 1937, it didn't include either Binder's or Klopfer's new Shading scores. Instead, the *Manual* adhered closely to what Rorschach had originally described.[105] Beck made only a single minor change: He created a separate score for "Vista" responses, the subgroup of Shading responses with depth, distance, or perspective that Rorschach had considered indicative of depression.

Beck's conservative approach to Shading was one of the points that Klopfer criticized in his negative review of the *Manual*. Beck responded that although research might eventually shed more light on the meaning of Shading responses, in the meantime he preferred to stick closely to what Rorschach had said about them.

MOVEMENT   In the mid-1930s, the young Polish psychologist Zygmunt Piotrowski sometimes participated in the meetings of Klopfer's New York group. In 1937, Piotrowski published a brief article in the *Rorschach Research Exchange,* suggesting that the Rorschach should be scored not only for human or human-like movement (*M*), as Rorschach had proposed, but also for the movement of animals, such as "a lion pouncing," and for the movement of inanimate objects, such as "a rock rolling" or "a bomb exploding."[106]

Klopfer agreed with Piotrowski's suggestions about scoring and introduced his own ideas on how the new Rorschach variables should be interpreted. According to Klopfer, animal movement in the Rorschach (scored as "*FM*") represents "the influence of the more instinctive layers within the personality." Thus, a large number of *FM* responses in a patient's Rorschach protocol indicate that he is "living in a level of instinctive prompting below his chronological and mental age." Klopfer said that inanimate movement in test responses (scored as "*m*") represents the feeling that one's inner impulses are uncontrollable, so that a large number of *m* responses are a "danger signal" that inner conflicts are disrupting the patient's life.[107]

Beck forcefully opposed Piotrowski's and Klopfer's ideas about animal and inanimate movement responses. In the *Rorschach Research Exchange* he voiced two criticisms. First, these new ideas were inconsistent with what Rorschach and his closest associates had thought about the meaning of movement. Second, the ideas were purely speculative and lacked scientific support: "They [Klopfer and Piotrowski] are rather facile in adding scoring categories suggested without sufficient clinical evidence and without any produced experimental support. . . . *FM* and *m* are unnecessary elaboration of scoring, not yet proved to represent any psychological process not indicated in *M*. . . . One trouble with Rorschach interpretation is, unfortunately, too much reading of personality description into the record."[108]

F+ AND F–   As we described in Chapter Two, Rorschach introduced the score *F+* to indicate that a response to an inkblot possessed "good form" or "good fit." Responses that did *not* fit the blot were scored as *F–*. For an entire protocol, the number of *F+* responses was divided by the total number of *F+* and *F–* responses, yielding a score called *F+%*. The *F+%* came to be regarded by early Rorschachers as an indicator of patients' intellectual capacity or their tendency to "see their world accurately."[109]

Although the basic idea of *F+* and *F–* seems straightforward, these scores have led to endless disagreement among Rorschach enthusiasts. The difficulty arises when a psychologist sits down to score actual Rorschach protocols and must decide whether responses display "good form" or "poor form." The line between the two isn't always clear-cut.

In the early days of the test, scoring decisions about "form quality" were made using a three-part rule that Rorschach suggested:[110]

- If the response is "frequently recurring," that is, given by many normal individuals (for instance, seeing two people bowing in Card III), then it's scored *F+*.
- If the response is uncommon but fits the blot at least as well as the "frequently recurring" responses, then it's scored *F+*.
- Otherwise it's scored *F–*.

However, this approach had two problems. First, which responses were "frequently recurring"? Rorschach hadn't left a list or even indicated specifically what he meant by *frequently.* Was a response frequent if it was given by 25 percent of normal individuals? By 10 percent? By 5 percent? Because Rorschach didn't clarify these issues, each psychologist who used the test had to decide where to draw the line. Thus an important element of subjectivity was introduced, leading to scoring inconsistency.

The second problem lay in determining whether an uncommon response fit the blot at least as well as "frequently recurring" responses. Such a determination necessarily involved substantial subjectivity, first in deciding which responses were "frequently recurring," and second in deciding whether the uncommon response was a better, worse, or equal fit compared with the "frequently recurring" ones.

To reduce the subjectivity of scoring for F+ and F−, and to increase the likelihood that two psychologists scoring the same Rorschach protocol would arrive at similar scores, Beck's *Manual* provided what is now called a "form quality table," a list that indicated which responses on each card should be scored as F+ or F−. In creating this table, Beck generally followed Rorschach's ideas: Responses that were given frequently by a group of healthy subjects, or that fit the blots at least as well as the frequently occurring responses, were generally listed as F+, with the remaining responses listed as F−.

However, there were some weak points to Beck's procedure. For example, like Rorschach himself, he didn't specify exactly what he meant by *frequently*. Furthermore, diverging from Rorschach's procedure, Beck classified some responses as F− if they were given frequently by "feeble minded" individuals.[111]

In his review of Beck's *Manual* in the *Rorschach Research Exchange*, Klopfer rejected "a purely quantitative determination of F+ and F−."[112] Arguing that a "qualitative" approach was usually more appropriate, Klopfer proposed a set of principles that a psychologist could use in deciding whether a response had "keener form" or "negative qualities."

In fact, Klopfer had no great affection for Rorschach's approach to scoring F+ and F−.[113] Within a decade of his debate with Beck, Klopfer abandoned Rorschach's F+% and replaced it with his own "Form Level Rating," which depended on a complex set of "qualitative" rules for scoring the fit of Rorschach responses.[114]

Marguerite Hertz and the Schism

Before leaving the breach between Beck and Klopfer, it's interesting to note the role played by Marguerite Hertz, the third American pioneer. Hertz was among the ten psychologists and psychiatrists who had commented on Beck's article in the *Rorschach Research Exchange*. Her comment was by far the longest, and was notable for its clear thinking. It was entirely even-handed in its treatment of Beck and Klopfer, taking well-aimed shots at both.

Marguerite Hertz criticized Beck, not because he had attempted to standardize the scoring of *F+* and *F−*, but because he had done a sloppy job of it. She took him to task for not clearly explaining how he had constructed his form quality tables, and for classifying some responses as *F−* because they had been given by feebleminded individuals. Hertz pointed out that a response should be classified as *F+* or *F−* on the basis of its fit to the inkblot, and not because a particular type of person had given it.

Hertz appeared more tolerant than Beck toward attempts to develop new scoring categories for shading and movement: "In the process of working with the test, many supplementary factors invariably suggest themselves. . . . It has frequently seemed necessary to add new categories or to refine certain ones already in existence. Therefore the writer [Hertz] cannot censure Klopfer's group as severely as Beck does because they in their experience find additional categories significant."[115]

However, Hertz's choice of words was careful. She didn't go so far as to say that she actually *approved* of Klopfer's new categories, only that she didn't "censure" them "as severely." Although willing to consider Klopfer's new scores, she regarded them with skepticism: "The writer [Hertz] has on many occasions felt that Klopfer's group was refining the scoring to the extent of becoming involved in a maze of symbols."[116]

On a crucial issue Hertz separated herself from both parties in the debate, aligning herself more strongly with the psychometric approach than even Beck had. In his reply to Klopfer's review, Beck had made a bow to the "artistic" use of the Rorschach test by gifted clinicians: "The Rorschach test, as a subjectively used instrument in the hands of individuals having experience with many clinical groups and themselves having good clinical insight, can be accurately used for a penetrating understanding of the whole personality."[117] Hertz rejected this idea. Before the test could be used in the "subjective" or "artistic" way described by Beck, she wrote, "there must be assurance that the test has been subjected to definite universal principles so that all who use it will have approximately the same results. It must satisfy fundamental criteria of validity, accuracy, reliability, and objectivity. Whether it is successful and serviceable as a scientific instrument depends upon the extent of which these are met."[118]

Thus Hertz "out-Becked" Beck himself, uncompromisingly declaring the primacy of objective evidence and such mainstream psychometric concepts as standardization, reliability, and validity. Her stance was inimical to Klopfer as well, but he printed her comment along with the others in the *Rorschach Research Exchange*. In the ensuing years, Hertz maintained a civil relationship with both Beck and Klopfer but went her own way. Working independently, she evolved her own approach to the Rorschach, based on systematic collection of data. Reflecting on the alienation among the three Rorschach pioneers, John Exner wrote: "It would appear that while Klopfer had reached out for a role of Rorschach leadership in America for himself and the *Rorschach Research Exchange*, his reach had been too forceful, or rigid, or both, thereby causing some of the significant Rorschach experts of the time to withdraw from him either partially or completely."[119]

A NEW WAY OF THINKING ABOUT TESTS

By rejecting the application of psychometric ideas to the Rorschach, Bruno Klopfer had placed himself in an intellectual no-man's-land. Without the psychometric approach, he could not call on well-accepted psychological principles to justify his approach to the test. Moving swiftly, however, he began promoting a new way of thinking about tests that was much different from the psychometric approach. Within a few years of his breach with Beck, Klopfer set forth four interlocking principles that eventually exerted enormous influence in the field of clinical psychology, especially in the 1940s and 1950s, and even up until the present time: clinical validation, interpretation of "configurations," the artist versus the novice, and the projective hypothesis.

Clinical Validation

In the late 1930s, Klopfer began to argue that the value of Rorschach scores should be evaluated by what he called "clinical validation."[120] At first he seemed to mean that clinicians should interpret the Rorschach without knowing anything else about the patient, and then compare the Rorschach findings with case notes, other test results, or observations. If the Rorschach interpretation was consistent with these sources, then it could be considered valid.

Of course, this was the approach that Rorschach had followed when developing the test—but such a procedure is likely to be highly subjective. If the clinician who administers the test is also the person who gathers and evaluates the outside information, there's a substantial risk that conscious or unconscious biases will produce an overestimate of the match between the Rorschach results and the outside information. As we discussed in Chapter Two, the term for this problem is *confirmation bias.* We'll return to both these sources of error at greater depth in Chapter Seven, but for now it's enough to point out that Klopfer failed to recognize this flaw in his approach, just as Rorschach had.

Klopfer's idea of "clinical validation" was soon expanded to mean that testimonials and case studies could establish the validity of the Rorschach test. The value of objective studies was often minimized. For example, Morris Krugman, the first president of Klopfer's Rorschach Institute, conceded in his presidential address of 1939 that the validity of the Rorschach had not been "mathematically demonstrated."[121] However, in lieu of objective studies, Krugman cited "testimony from reputable workers in the various schools of psychology and in widely different situations as to the validity of the Rorschach." Although such testimony was not "ideal" from a scientific point of view, he admitted, it was nevertheless "impressive." And, he continued, "Even more impressive is the Rorschach worker's daily experience of constructing a personality and behavior picture of an individual without knowing anything about him except the responses to the ten cards, comparing that picture with what is learned from an intensive study of case material, from a psychiatric examination, from numerous interviews, and from various psychological tests, and not only finding close correspondence, but frequently throwing new light on the personality, that is substantiated on further investigation by other means."

The field of medicine had been dealing with similar issues for many years. Experience had taught that testimonials from patients or physicians about the effectiveness of medical procedures could be unreliable and highly misleading. Medical treatments and tests based on such shaky evidence could lead to widespread quackery, as had been illustrated in the infamous case of Dr. Albert Abrams and his Dynamizer.[122]

A highly respected San Francisco physician and former president of the California State Medical Society, Abrams began marketing the

Dynamizer in the 1920s. This device, he claimed, detected certain electronic vibrations of the human body called the "Electronic Reactions of Abrams" or "ERA." Although undetectable by ordinary scientific instruments, ERA could supposedly be felt by a doctor who was attached to the machine. When wired to the Dynamizer, a physician could purportedly sense a patient's ERA and diagnose disease—using only one drop of blood or a single hair.

Although derided by the *Journal of the American Medical Association,* the device became a medical fad. Thousands of doctors bought a Dynamizer and used it for diagnosis, apparently convincing themselves that they were detecting ERA through their hands while hooked up to the machine. Enthusiasm for the device waned only when the device was exposed as a fraud in a series of articles in *Scientific American.*

In promoting the idea of "clinical validation," Klopfer, Krugman, and other advocates of the Rorschach were ignoring valuable lessons from the history of medicine and, in effect, lowering the standards that psychologists used to evaluate tests. Recognizing this problem, some psychologists of the era warned against accepting Rorschach scores as valid on the basis of clinical experience. For example, Donald Super of Columbia University reminded his colleagues: "Unorganized experience, unanalyzed data, and tradition are often misleading. Validation should be accomplished by evidence gathered in controlled investigations and analyzed objectively, not by the opinions of authorities and the impressions of observers."[123]

Marguerite Hertz was also outspoken on this issue: "The chief objection to clinical validation is its lack of scientific procedure. Most clinical studies are characterized by few cases, inadequate controls, failures to control the techniques employed, and failure to standardize the research procedure. Case studies all too frequently include highly subjective diagnoses and dogmatic assertions. . . . Their findings are inconclusive . . . and await further research."[124]

Unfortunately, such warnings were generally disregarded. For the next three decades clinical psychologists continued to use the Rorschach test for many purposes that had little support except clinical validation.[125]

Configural Interpretation

In the early 1940s, drawing on the theories of psychologist Lawrence Frank,[126] Marguerite Hertz contrasted the supposed shortcomings of self-report personality tests with the virtues of the Rorschach.[127] In the highly respected journal *Psychological Bulletin*, Hertz criticized self-report questionnaires because they were supposedly based on an "atomistic conception of personality" in which the individual was conceptualized as "a bundle of characteristics, each subject to identification, segregation, and measurement." In contrast, she claimed, the Rorschach approached the individual "as a living, functioning whole, a dynamic synthesis" and allowed the clinician to view "the organization, interplay, and uniqueness" within the personality.[128]

Hertz's view was shared by Klopfer. He used this idea to explain why the test must always be interpreted in light of its "configuration." Because the Rorschach was based on a "total-action picture of the personality,"[129] Klopfer argued, the process of interpreting Rorschach results was necessarily more complex than with self-report questionnaires. Other tests could "achieve their results by adding up the scores," wrote Klopfer, but "such a summative procedure is impossible in the Rorschach method. . . . The Rorschach practitioner is concerned not with the sum of components but with a configuration or 'Gestalt.'"[130]

What Klopfer seemed to mean was that there was no straightforward relationship between any particular Rorschach score (such as *M* or *FM*) and its interpretation. Rather, the scores had to be interpreted together as a "configuration."[131]

An important result of Klopfer's theory about configural interpretation was that it allowed his followers to dismiss negative findings concerning the test's validity as irrelevant. Morris Krugman (the president of the Rorschach Institute who had spoken so glowingly about clinical testimonials) explained: "Psychologists have come to recognize that a complex instrument like the Rorschach cannot yield a simple score that may be validated by the application of a Pearson or other correlation, but that the entire configuration must be compared with the clinical picture obtained with such procedures as the full case study or the psychiatric examination. In other words, validation must be by clinical rather than by mathematical processes."[132]

Thus linking together the principles of configural interpretation and clinical validation, Krugman rejected any possibility that the validity of the Rorschach could be evaluated with standard psychometric methods.

Of course, the assertion that only "configurations" and not "simple scores" had interpretive meaning contradicted statements by Rorschach and Klopfer himself, who both claimed that many scores on the test correspond to such qualities as intellectual capacity (*W* and *F+%*), stubbornness (Space responses), impulsivity (*WSumC*), and depression (Vista responses).[133] Such assertions could be tested by ordinary validity studies and analyzed with correlation coefficients.

But scientific studies on these relationships were often dismissed because, as Krugman contended, such research didn't take into account the test's complexity. Objective research, so the argument went, was simply not sophisticated enough to capture the complexity of the Rorschach. As an observer of the era reported, "many Rorschach authorities have discouraged submitting the test to critical investigation."[134]

Rorschach Artists

In his debate with Klopfer in the *Rorschach Research Exchange*, Beck conceded that certain "artists" could "subjectively" extract from the test a "penetrating understanding of the whole personality" based on their great experience and clinical insight.[135] The existence of such virtuosos was well-accepted among Rorschach enthusiasts.

Klopfer presented the typical view: A psychologist could learn to administer the test in a few months. To reach the "next stage of proficiency"—being able to interpret the test without supervision—the psychologist must study under an expert for about three years.[136] Beyond this "stage of proficiency," however, there lay yet another level of expertise that, according to Klopfer, few could attain: "The interpretation of a Rorschach record, especially the construction of a complete individual personality picture, presupposes such a wealth of general psychological experience that only a limited number can ever learn to realize the full potentialities of the method."[137]

Thus, Klopfer delineated the hierarchy of Rorschach users. At the bottom were the "administrators," next were the merely "proficient," and at the top were the "limited number" who could use the test to its full potential. The Rorschach artists at the top were so skillful, Klopfer claimed, that they could provide "a complete picture of the individual personality" from "blind interpretation" of the Rorschach material alone, without any other clinical information or test scores. Less proficient Rorschachers might have to draw on other sources of information, but the true Rorschach virtuoso needed only the blots.[138]

Klopfer's views came to be shared by virtually everyone who used the Rorschach in the following decades. Rorschach proponents took it for granted that a great chasm divided "novices" from true artists.[139] Mere neophytes—usually graduate students—often stood in awe of the "wizards" who had mastered the test.[140]

These elitist assumptions proved highly influential, particularly because they meshed well with the psychoanalytic movement. Psychoanalysts became increasingly prominent during the 1940s and similarly tended to be elitist and authoritarian.[141] However, such a stark hierarchical structure represented an important shift within the field of clinical psychology, which had heretofore taken an egalitarian approach to testing.[142] For example, as we mentioned earlier, in the 1910s Henry Goddard assumed that the Binet intelligence test could be used by ordinary schoolteachers who attended his summer program at Vineland.

By the 1930s there was recognition that the proper use of intelligence tests required more educational background and experience than a summer program could provide. However, proficiency in intelligence testing was considered well within the grasp of ordinary graduate students. There was no elite group of "intelligence test artists." Lewis Terman was widely admired because of his scientific contributions to the Stanford-Binet, not because he displayed a seer's skill in interpreting its results.

The ideas propounded by Klopfer departed from the American psychological tradition in another important way: The highest point in the Rorschach hierarchy was attained through clinical *experience,* rather than through scientific *knowledge.* American clinical psychologists had always recognized that clinical experience was an important part of training. For example, graduate programs in clinical psychology typically required students to complete supervised internships in clinical settings with real patients, in addition to standard coursework and participation in research. However, Klopfer's ideas elevated clinical experience to a much higher level of importance while minimizing the importance of scientific training.

This change in emphasis would exert a profound influence on the field of clinical psychology for decades to come. Henceforth, many Rorschach artists would make confident pronouncements about patients based on "clinical experience," even though scientific evidence might be lacking for these formulations or even contradict them. If research failed to confirm clinical insight, so much the worse for research. Clinical experience trumped science.

The Projective Hypothesis

In 1906, Eugen Bleuler, the renowned Swiss psychiatrist who influenced young Hermann Rorschach, wrote: "Every psychic process, each action, exactly in the form that it is carried out, is possible for a given individual only in the manner determined by his past experience. Every particular act represents the whole man. The intent to infer the entire personality from the individual's handwriting, the physiognomy, the shape of the hand, or even the style and the use of the shoes are not aspirations without a basis."[143]

In the late 1930s, Bleuler's idea was refined by the American psychologist Lawrence Frank. Frank shared Bleuler's idea that every act of a person was revealing: "The personality process might be regarded as a sort of rubber stamp which the individual imposes upon every situation by which he gives it the configuration that he, as an individual, requires."[144]

A central weakness of self-report questionnaires, Frank said, was that they prevented a person from fully expressing himself as an individual, and instead forced him to fit into socially defined categories.[145] The solution was to present the person with an unstructured stimulus or "field," such as inkblots, and ask him to respond. "We may . . . induce the individual to reveal his way of organizing experience, by giving him a field (objects, materials, experiences) with relatively little structure and cultural patterning so that the personality can project upon that plastic field his way of seeing life, his meanings, significances, patterns, and especially his feelings. Thus we elicit a projection of the individual personality's *private world* because he has to organize the field, interpret the material and react affectively to it."[146]

Thus Frank introduced "the projective hypothesis," a remarkably durable notion that's still sometimes used to explain how the Rorschach and similar tests are supposed to work. Frank, who had a tendency to introduce metaphors from physics into his articles, likened the Rorschach and other "projective" tests to x-rays, a metaphor that Bruno Klopfer soon adopted.[147]

Frank's first paper on the projective hypothesis was well-timed. In 1935 Christiana D. Morgan and Henry Murray of Harvard had introduced the "Thematic Apperception Test" or TAT.[148] Radically different from most other psychological tests of the era, it consisted of a series of drawings depicting ambiguous scenes. The person taking the TAT was asked to tell a story about each picture. For example, one of the drawings depicted a distressed man standing beside an unclothed woman (apparently unconscious) who was lying on a bed. A story about this tantalizing scene might include themes of love, violence, fear, or guilt, which, it was believed, would reveal the teller's personality.

The projective hypothesis offered a plausible psychological rationale that Henry Murray used to justify the TAT. More important to our story, the projective hypothesis provided justification for the Rorschach, as Frank soon explained in an article in the *Rorschach Research Exchange.*[149] His explanation of *how* the Rorschach worked (leaving aside the unsettled question of *whether* it worked) leant an aura of intellectual respectability to the test by linking it to the psychological concepts of the time and a broader group of "projective" tests such as the TAT.

Eventually Bruno Klopfer renamed the Rorschach Institute and the *Rorschach Research Exchange.* They became the Society for Projective Techniques and the *Journal of Projective Techniques,* respectively. These changes revealed his success in establishing a broad intellectual and organizational counterforce to the American psychometric approach.

Henceforth, the Rorschach, the TAT, and other projective tests would be seen as new and exciting alternatives to traditional psychological tests. Such concepts as clinical validation and the projective hypothesis, promoted and developed by the Society for Projective Techniques and its journal, would exert an enormous impact on clinical psychology during the 1940s and 1950s. The Rorschach would soon be psychology's most cherished test. In the next chapter we'll describe these glory days of the Rorschach.

CHAPTER FOUR

Rorschach Rules!

*Few, if any, psychodiagnostic methods have leaped
into prominence with the velocity exhibited by the
Rorschach test.*

—*Florence Goodenough,* Mental Testing:
Its History, Principles, and Applications, *1949*

In 1940 the Rorschach Inkblot Test was the passion of
only a few psychologists, most of them living in New York City. Among
their colleagues these enthusiasts had a reputation for being cultish and
obsessed with the minutiae of scoring.[1] As the psychoanalyst Robert
Lindner wearily observed, for the average clinical psychologist "the
cultism of Rorschachers, their allegiances, their bickerings and jeal-
ousies, bore and distract him; so also do their endless disputes over—
let us say—the criteria of distinction between one F and another."[2]

Over the next ten years, the Rorschach would be transformed from
"a cult in which only the initiated may serve"[3] into clinical psychology's most widely used personality test. By 1950 the test was taught in
graduate programs throughout the United States and studied by
researchers at Harvard, Yale, Stanford, and the University of Chicago.[4]
It had become the subject of more journal articles and dissertations
than any other test.[5] In the present chapter, we'll discuss the reasons
for this astounding turn of events.

WHY THE RORSCHACH BOOMED IN THE 1940S

Writing in 1949, J. R. Wittenborn of Yale called his colleagues' attention to a striking paradox. Despite a lack of scientific support, the Rorschach test had left behind its cultish origins and become respectable: "Today, graduate instruction in the Rorschach method is offered in departments of psychology where less than a decade ago more conservative phases of clinical psychology were shunned. At present, reservations concerning the inkblot test are rapidly becoming unfashionable. Since from the standpoint of relative progress little more is known about the inkblots than was known by Rorschach, this rapid acceptance requires comment."[6]

Wittenborn shrewdly identified four reasons why the Rorschach had flourished: the publication of numerous books and articles on the test, the enthusiasm of its promoters, the rising influence of psychoanalysis, and broad social changes in Americans' attitudes toward mental disorders and a growing demand for psychological services.

Books and Articles on the Rorschach

The year 1942 was an important one for the Rorschach. Previously no books on the Rorschach had been available in English, but in that year two textbooks appeared. The first, *Clinical Application of the Rorschach Test* by Ruth Bochner and Florence Halpern, was criticized as simplistic by reviewers.[7] Nonetheless, its brief, straightforward approach made it appealing, and it was purchased eagerly by psychologists in the military during World War II.[8] Although Bochner and Halpern's attention to scholarly fine points was minimal (in fact, neither had a Ph.D. at the time),[9] their book became so popular that a new edition was published in 1945.

The second Rorschach textbook to appear in 1942 was a volume by Bruno Klopfer and psychiatrist Douglas Kelley. Describing the administration, scoring, and interpretation of the test in painstaking detail, *The Rorschach Technique* became a standard text in graduate programs and was destined to exert enormous influence on the practice of clinical psychology in the 1940s and 1950s.[10] A second, somewhat expanded version was printed in 1946.[11] Klopfer also began to disseminate his ideas about the Rorschach by offering summer workshops, first in Crafts, New York, then in other cities throughout the United States.[12]

Also appearing in 1942 was the first published English translation of Rorschach's *Psychodiagnostics*. However, because the book provided only limited detail about scoring and administration, it was unsuitable as a nuts-and-bolts introductory text and was mainly of interest because of its importance to theory.

Samuel Beck published a two-volume introduction to the test in 1944 and 1945 (a third volume appeared in 1952). The title of his book, *Rorschach's Test*, underscored the point that Beck, unlike Klopfer, was adhering closely to Rorschach's own ideas. Beck's conservative approach appealed to many psychologists, and his book was exceeded in popularity only by that of Klopfer and Kelly.[13]

The year 1946 saw the appearance of another massive text that would prove highly influential, the two-volume *Diagnostic Psychological Testing* by David Rapaport, Merton Gill, and Roy Schafer of the famed Menninger Clinic in Topeka, Kansas. This book introduced the idea that psychologists should conduct assessments using a "battery" of several tests, such as an intelligence test, the Rorschach, the Thematic Apperception Test (TAT), and a Word Association Test. The results could then be combined to provide a full picture of the individual's psychological functioning. "Test batteries" became popular among clinical psychologists and continue to be widely used. Rapaport and his colleagues also introduced a new scoring category for the Rorschach, "Deviant Verbalizations," which we'll discuss in detail in the next chapter.

With the publication of these new books, the Rorschach spread beyond the limits of New York City and throughout America. For several years they were virtually the *only* available textbooks that dealt with the clinical assessment of adults.[14] In the absence of alternatives, they were widely adopted by instructors in clinical psychology programs.

As we noted earlier, scholarly journals were also disseminating information about the test. More articles were being published about the Rorschach than about any other psychological measure.[15] The scientific quality of these articles left much to be desired. Paul Meehl of the University of Minnesota, probably the most prominent clinical psychologist of his generation, commented: "One of the sad facts about the Rorschach literature which is disturbing to those American psychologists who are interested but skeptical is the pitiably small number of studies which can really be called 'validation' studies in any respectable sense, buried among a great mass of investigations whose titles would suggest that they were systematic studies of validity, but which turn out not to be so at all upon reading."[16]

However, sober assessments like Meehl's were more than counter-balanced by the upbeat claims of Rorschach proponents.

Enthusiastic Promoters

As noted in Chapter Three, Bruno Klopfer had likened the Rorschach to an x-ray of the psyche, claiming that an expert could derive "a complete picture of the individual personality" from the inkblots alone. During the 1940s respected figures in clinical psychology came forward to offer further testimonials. For example, Saul Rosenzweig concluded in 1944: "Few trustworthy and penetrating psychological tools are available for the study of the total personality and among these the Rorschach procedure is probably the most distinguished."[17]

Furthermore, prominent journals published exaggerated claims regarding the scientific evidence for the test. For example, in the *Journal of General Psychology,* Philip Harriman advanced the dubious claim that the research base of the Rorschach was comparable with that of intelligence tests: "Now the corpus of literature on Rorschach methodology rivals in bulk, if not in quality as well, the published research on the Binet-type test."[18]

Similarly, in the *Journal of Consulting Psychology,* Bruno Klopfer asserted: "Twenty-one years of routine research have proven more than ninety per cent of his [Rorschach's] assumptions correct and even many of his hunches which seemed wrong at first glance proved to be pointing in the right direction on further scrutiny."[19] (In all fairness to Klopfer, he probably did not intend to mislead readers when he made these inflated claims. His idea of research was much looser and only remotely related to what American psychologists understood by the term.) Given such positive publicity in psychology's top journals, it's little wonder that the popularity of the Rorschach began to boom in the 1940s.

There were also attempts to disseminate the test to professions besides psychology. One book on the Rorschach for psychiatrists claimed to provide a quick road to insight. Psychiatrists were told that the book "permits almost immediate interpretation of personality trends and suggests clinical diagnoses."[20] The jacket of another text promised: "By simple procedure, taking a few minutes to administer and evaluate, psychiatrist, psychologist, psychiatric social worker, educator, or counselor may now avail himself of the fruits of research of many years in the Rorschach method."[21]

Such claims went too far even for such Rorschach boosters as Bruno Klopfer, who regarded the test as a delicate instrument that should be reserved for highly experienced clinicians.[22] The idea that a social worker or teacher might use it to reach instant insights seemed absurd and dangerous. Although the Rorschach never became widely used by nonpsychologists, such books helped to spread the test's reputation as an unsurpassed measure of personality.

The Rising Influence of Psychoanalysis

As luck would have it, the Rorschach rode into prominence on the coattails of an even more powerful trend of the 1940s, the rise of psychoanalysis. Sigmund Freud had traveled to America as early as 1909 and lectured to eminent psychologists on his new psychoanalytic theories.[23] However, for the next three decades his ideas exerted only minor influence on research and clinical practice in America.[24]

By the late 1930s, though, the influence of psychoanalytic concepts was on the rise. Americans' late-blooming interest in Freud was apparently due to several factors. Probably the most important was Adolph Hitler's accession to power in Germany in 1933. Hitler's Nazis were hostile toward psychoanalysis, which they called a "Jewish science."[25] Soon a wave of German psychoanalysts emigrated to the United States, Bruno Klopfer among them. Other distinguished émigrés included Erich Fromm, Karen Horney, and Otto Fenichel, three innovative psychoanalytic thinkers whose books were influential in the United States during the 1940s and 1950s.[26]

Although Freud's theories were complex and far-reaching, three of his ideas had an especially important impact on the Rorschach in the 1940s and 1950s. First was his view that human thought and action are powerfully affected by unconscious motivation. According to Freud, people don't really know why they think or do many things, because the reasons for their thoughts and actions are buried in the unconscious.

Second was Freud's emphasis on the importance of unconscious factors in psychological disorders. According to psychoanalytic theory, the problems of many psychiatric patients can be traced to their unconscious sexual and aggressive impulses, especially those they felt toward their parents in early childhood.

Freud's third influential idea was that dreams represent, in symbolic form, a person's underlying unconscious conflicts. By interpreting the meaning of dream symbols, Freud taught, a psychoanalyst can peer into the unconscious and gain insight into a patient's impulses and conflicts.

The emphasis of psychoanalytic theory on the unconscious presented a problem for self-report questionnaires. When answering items on a questionnaire, it was thought, patients could describe only what they knew about themselves and, by definition, couldn't accurately report what was in their unconscious. In contrast, the Rorschach had no such limitations and supposedly revealed things about patients of which they were unaware. Thus the rise of psychoanalysis contributed to discontent with "mere" self-report tests and deflected psychologists' interest toward the Rorschach and other projective techniques.

The close connection between psychoanalysis and the Rorschach was evident from the 1930s onward.[27] In 1939 Samuel Beck advised that a background in psychoanalysis conferred "a great advantage" on a Rorschach interpreter.[28] Bruno Klopfer took the position that the Rorschach was compatible with all accepted theories of personality, not just psychoanalysis.[29] Nevertheless, as the psychoanalytic theorist Ernest Schachtel pointed out, Klopfer "constantly uses such concepts as spontaneity, inhibition, control, pseudo-control, repression, sublimation, some of which seem to stem from the psychoanalytic theory of personality which has influenced Rorschach's personality concept."[30]

All the influential Rorschach textbooks in the 1940s were written within a psychoanalytic framework.[31] Marguerite Hertz observed: "Most of us have been influenced by psychoanalytic theory. . . . The psychoanalytic treatment of the determinants of mental life, the use of such concepts as mechanisms of defense, symbolism, conscious and unconscious motivation, and more, have been incorporated into Rorschach interpretation."[32]

Ironically, in *Psychodiagnostics*, Hermann Rorschach said that his inkblot test possessed only limited use as a psychoanalytic tool, and he explicitly discouraged its use as a means of exploring the unconscious.[33]

THE TRANSFORMATION OF CLINICAL PSYCHOLOGY IN THE 1940s

Although J. R. Wittenborn of Yale had identified four reasons for the Rorschach's rise to prominence in the 1940s, he singled out one as fundamental: America's response to mental disorders was changing, so there was a growing demand for psychological services.[34] The Rorschach, along with the field of clinical psychology, was propelled in the 1940s by broad currents of social and economic expansion.

World War II and Clinical Psychology

During World War I, psychologists had shown that they could contribute to the war effort by giving intelligence tests, eliminating recruits who were unfit for service and identifying bright soldiers who would make good officers. It had been a massive undertaking (intelligence tests were administered to over 1,750,000 American soldiers from 1917 to 1919)[35] and psychologists had learned to do the job efficiently.

When the United States entered World War II in 1941, military commanders already recognized the value of intelligence testing. There was an instantaneous demand for clinical psychologists to administer tests to the millions of new recruits who were flooding into the armed services. In addition, the role of psychological testing expanded during World War II to encompass not only the measurement of intelligence but the identification of psychopathology. There was recognition that some recruits might be ill-suited for military service, not because they were of low intelligence but because they suffered from emotional problems that could impair their ability to function as soldiers.

Mass psychological testing of soldiers during World War II provided a great boost to the Rorschach,[36] which was regarded as the best available instrument for identifying abnormality. Because the Rorschach was too time-consuming to be given individually, psychologists Molly Harrower and Marie Steiner devised a Group Rorschach that could be administered to large numbers of recruits at the same time.[37] The Rorschach blots were projected onto a screen at the front of a room and recruits wrote down their responses on a paper form. Harrower and Steiner eventually streamlined their procedure by developing the Multiple Choice Rorschach Test.[38] The test form listed several alternative responses. When a blot was flashed on the screen, soldiers were told to select the response that most closely matched their own impressions.[39]

World War II permanently transformed the profession of clinical psychology. Many psychologists who'd been trained in nonclinical areas such as learning, perception, or education were inducted into the army and suddenly expected to function as clinicians. Researchers who'd been running rats in mazes before the war were issued orders to learn the Rorschach.[40] Their introduction to the technique came from books by such true believers as Bochner and Halpern, rather than from university instructors more skeptical toward the test and its lack of scientific foundation.

The field of clinical psychology had traditionally dealt with children and educational problems, but the war shifted the profession's emphasis to adults and serious mental disorders. Although a few clinical psychologists had been employed in mental hospitals before the war, the 1940s marked the first time that large numbers of psychologists worked side by side with psychiatrists. Psychoanalytic ideas, which had been gaining ground among psychiatrists, rapidly began to spread among clinical psychologists.

Postwar Demand for Services and the New Face of Clinical Psychology

With the end of World War II in 1945, the Veterans Administration (VA) hospital system faced the daunting task of providing services to the war's 16 million veterans, as well as 4 million veterans of earlier wars.[41] The need for psychiatric services was critical. Mental disorders accounted for more than half of VA hospitalizations.[42]

The number of psychiatrists in the VA system fell far short of the demand for services. The shortage of mental health workers became even more serious when in 1946 the U.S. Congress created the agency now known as the National Institute of Mental Health (NIMH), which was granted "a broad mission to promote mental health as well as to deal with mental illness."[43]

In 1947, the VA and the U.S. Public Health Service (which contained NIMH) approached the American Psychological Association (APA) and worked out an arrangement to meet the burgeoning demand for mental health professionals.[44] The APA agreed to identify graduate programs that could provide acceptable training in clinical psychology. The VA and Public Health Service agreed, in turn, to provide funds to these programs to train more clinical psychologists.

APA committees worked on the project for two years under the leadership of psychologist David Shakow. Their efforts culminated in the summer of 1949 when seventy-three representatives from the VA, the Public Health Service, and psychology departments from throughout the United States met for two weeks at the University of Colorado in Boulder and approved principles for the training of Ph.D.-level clinical psychologists.

These principles, which came to be known as the Boulder Model for clinical training, included several important precepts:

- Ph.D. students in clinical psychology should receive scientific and statistical training comparable with that of other graduate students in psychology.
- Clinical students should be trained as researchers and required to complete dissertations based on their own scientific investigations.
- Clinical students should take courses dealing with specific clinical topics (such as psychopathology and psychotherapy).
- Training should include a year-long internship, during which students worked under supervision in a mental health setting.

The Boulder Model's concept of clinical psychologists as "scientist-practitioners" was rapidly adopted by graduate programs throughout the United States. In the late 1940s and early 1950s, thanks to the "superfluity of riches"[45] flowing from the federal government, the enrollment of students in clinical psychology programs mushroomed. The number of such programs multiplied from fewer than five in the early 1940s to twenty in the late 1940s, and to forty-five by 1956 (eventually climbing to near two hundred).[46]

Scientists and Practitioners, Empiricists and Romantics

By the end of the 1940s, the field of clinical psychology only remotely resembled what it had been a decade earlier. From a small collection of practitioners working mainly with children, clinical psychology had been transformed into a rapidly growing, well-funded profession that overlapped substantially with psychiatry. Henceforth its earlier role in educational settings would be relegated to a separate profession known as *school psychology.*[47]

From its inception, the new clinical psychology tried to weave together roles and ideas that were not entirely compatible, eventually leading to tensions with other areas of psychology and within clinical psychology itself. One potential source of conflict was the idea from the Boulder Model that clinical psychologists should be trained as both scientists and practitioners. In the ensuing years few clinical psychologists actually became researchers. Instead, the large majority found their place as practitioners, seeing patients and providing psychotherapy. Their professional and financial interests were sometimes much different from those of researchers.

The tensions between professional psychology and research psychology reached crisis levels in the 1980s, when the practitioners wrested control of the APA from the scientists.[48] In 1988, feeling that their values and financial interests were no longer represented, many research psychologists broke away from APA to found a separate organization, the American Psychological Society.[49]

Even more deep-seated than the division between scientists and practitioners in clinical psychology has been the split between *empiricists* and *romantics* (a terminology suggested by psychiatrist Paul McHugh of Johns Hopkins University).[50] According to scholars of intellectual history, two broad trends can be discerned in European and American thought over the past few centuries. One trend (which McHugh calls "empiricist" but historians might call "enlightenment")[51] holds that reason, objectivity, and empirically verifiable evidence provide the surest road to knowledge. The other trend (which both McHugh and the historians call "romantic") teaches that intuition, empathy, and subjective insights can provide a deeper and more authentic understanding than can mere reason.

Physics, chemistry, and biology had romantic influences in the 1800s, but by the beginning of the twentieth century they had become thoroughly empiricist. In the social sciences and the arts, however, and in psychiatry and psychology, romantic ideas have continued to exert a strong influence. For example, practitioners of psychodynamic psychology fall mainly in the romantic category. Psychodynamic psychology encompasses the schools of thought that have been built upon Freud's ideas.[52]

Within clinical psychology, the empiricist and romantic traditions have existed side by side from the time of the Boulder Conference onward. The empiricist tradition has emphasized systematic scientific research as a foundation for psychological knowledge, the use of psychometrically sound tests and procedures for assessment, and the interconnectedness of clinical psychology with such other scientific areas as learning theory, cognitive psychology, and neurosciences.

In contrast, the romantic tradition has emphasized clinical judgment and experience as a basis of psychological understanding, the use of intuitive assessment techniques such as dream interpretation and projective tests to gain insight into motivation and personality, and psychodynamic and other "depth" approaches to personality.

The adherents of these two traditions haven't always regarded each other kindly. In moments of irritation, empiricists may refer to romantics as "mystics," whereas the romantics may call empiricists "bean counters."[53] Over the years some universities have developed a reputation for tilting strongly in one direction or the other. For example, the University of Minnesota's highly regarded Ph.D. program in clinical psychology developed a reputation for "dustbowl empiricism" in the 1950s and still leans strongly in that direction. In contrast, the psychodynamically oriented Ph.D. program at Adelphi University in New York has strong romantic tendencies.

Despite such examples, the majority of graduate clinical programs lie somewhere between the extremes, so that most clinical psychologists receive some training in both empiricist and romantic traditions. For example, although all four authors of this book have strong empiricist backgrounds and are active researchers, we also have our softer, romantic sides. Two of us first entered the field of psychology because of our fascination with the (romantic) ideas of Sigmund Freud and C. G. Jung. Two of us are highly experienced in the (romantic) art of dream interpretation, and one has undergone two years of Jungian analysis. One of us continues to be deeply influenced by the tenets of Attachment Theory, which has its (romantic) roots in psychoanalytic thinking.

As readers may have already surmised, the great Rorschach schism of the 1930s was at bottom an empiricist-romantic dispute, with Bruno Klopfer representing the romantic position, and Samuel Beck (and especially Marguerite Hertz) representing the empiricist stance. The controversies that have engulfed the Rorschach from the mid-1950s to the present have also reflected this split.[54] In fact, the entire discipline of clinical psychology uneasily straddles the dividing line between romanticism and empiricism like a California mansion built directly astride the San Andreas fault.

The WAIS and the MMPI

Although our focus is on the Rorschach, its place in clinical psychology can't be fully understood without pausing to mention two other psychological tests: the Wechsler Adult Intelligence Scale (WAIS) and the Minnesota Multiphasic Personality Inventory (MMPI). Like the Rorschach, both rose to prominence after World War II.

THE WECHSLER ADULT INTELLIGENCE SCALE   The WAIS was introduced in 1939 by David Wechsler, a psychologist at Bellevue Psychiatric Hospital in New York.[55] In many ways the WAIS resembled Louis Terman's Stanford-Binet Intelligence Test. A patient was asked to perform a series of tasks, such as putting together colored blocks to form a pattern or giving the definitions of vocabulary words. However, the WAIS, unlike the Stanford-Binet, was designed specifically for use with adults and introduced technical improvements over previous intelligence tests. One important innovation was Wechsler's decision to base IQ scores on the means and standard deviations of normative groups, rather than on the older concept of "mental age." Another was his introduction of separate scores for "Performance IQ" and "Verbal IQ."[56]

The WAIS (known in its early days as the "Wechsler-Bellevue") was widely adopted by clinical psychologists in the late 1940s and early 1950s. In 1949 Wechsler introduced another version, the Wechsler Intelligence Scale for Children (WISC).[57] The WAIS and WISC have been revised several times over the years and continue to be the most popular intelligence tests among clinical psychologists.

THE MINNESOTA MULTIPHASIC PERSONALITY INVENTORY   The MMPI was clinical psychology's first highly successful personality questionnaire. Patients were asked to respond to 566 true/false questions, such as "I often feel sad" or "Sometimes I hear strange voices that other people can't hear." Their responses to these items were used to determine scores on several clinical scales, such as a Depression scale and a Schizophrenia scale.

Developed in the late 1930s and early 1940s by psychologist Starke Hathaway and psychiatrist J. C. McKinley of the University of Minnesota, the MMPI was created using a strategy that was innovative for its time. Earlier tests of psychopathology such as the Bernreuter Personality Inventory had been developed using what was called the "rational approach." In this approach, mental health experts write questions that, in their opinion, are related to particular mental disorders. These rationally chosen items are then used to construct the test.[58]

Although the rational approach can sometimes be an effective way to create a test, it didn't work well with the Bernreuter and other clinical tests of the 1920s and 1930s.[59] Hathaway and McKinley decided to take a different tack, which became known as the "empirical approach."[60] The basic idea was simple: They administered a large variety of questions to patients with a particular diagnosis, say "depression," and then compared the answers of the depressed patients with the answers given by nonpatients. The questions that depressed patients answered differently from normals were used to construct a "Depression" scale. The method was called "empirical" because it didn't depend on theories about how the patients with a diagnosis *should* answer but instead relied on how they *actually did* answer.

Besides the clinical scales of the MMPI, such as Depression and Schizophrenia, the test included several *validity* scales designed to identify patients who might be answering the questions deceptively. One of the validity scales was designed to identify patients who were "faking bad" by exaggerating or fabricating psychological symptoms. Two other validity scales were intended to identify patients who were "faking good" by underreporting symptoms or trying to paint an overly rosy picture of themselves.

Research has shown that the MMPI validity scales do a fairly good job of identifying patients who are trying to appear sicker or healthier than they really are. In the early days of the test there was also some hope that if a patient were found to be faking, the validity scales could be used to adjust the other scores to what they *would have been* if answered honestly. Thus, it was hoped, the MMPI might yield an accurate picture of a client's personality in spite of attempts at deception, and so might function (as the Rorschach was supposed to) as an "x-ray of the psyche." Unfortunately, attempts to adjust MMPI scores in this way have been generally unsuccessful.[61] If a patient answers deceptively on the MMPI, a psychologist using the validity scales can often detect faking, but usually can't do much beyond discarding the rest of the test scores as uninformative.

In the late 1940s and 1950s the MMPI's popularity among clinical psychologists lagged behind the Rorschach's, in part because of opposition from Bruno Klopfer and his associates. It was apparent to some psychologists that "the Rorschach Institute and its successor, the Society for Projective Techniques, viewed structured personality measures such as the MMPI with suspicion, if not downright hostility."[62] Not until the 1980s did the MMPI clearly pull ahead. It's now clinical psychology's most widely used personality test, with the Rorschach in second place. In 1988 the MMPI was revised, given a new set of norms, and renamed the MMPI-2, the version of the test still in use.

It's somewhat unsettling to realize that the three tests most commonly used by clinical psychologists today, the WAIS, MMPI-2, and Rorschach, are pretty much the same ones that psychologists were using half a century ago when the profession was taking shape. In some ways, there has been less change in personality assessment than in other fields. By now extensive research has been conducted on all three tests and we know quite a bit about what they can and cannot do. But in the 1950s, even though the scientific evidence was often sparse, clinical psychologists were confident in their tests and especially proud of the Rorschach, which was fast becoming an emblem of the profession.

A New Status Symbol

Researcher and historian of psychology Ernest Hilgard of Stanford University has pointed out that the Rorschach rose to prominence at just the right moment, when clinical psychologists were beginning to move en masse into psychiatric settings and work side by side with psychoanalytically oriented psychiatrists.

In earlier years the relationship between clinical psychology and psychiatry was often strained. For example, as we noted in Chapter Three, psychologists in the 1910s and 1920s ran into serious opposition to their efforts to diagnose mental retardation, which physicians (including psychiatrists) regarded as a medical condition. In the 1930s, when psychiatrists and psychologists worked together in child guidance clinics, the status of psychologists was distinctly inferior. In case conferences "the psychologist was usually called upon for IQ scores, and perhaps numerical scores on an inventory such as the Bernreuter test, and then was either dismissed or expected to keep quiet."[63]

During the postwar era, however, the status of clinical psychologists rose abruptly.[64] In this new situation, Hilgard notes, the Rorschach gave the clinical psychologist an important advantage:

If the psychologist was an expert on the Rorschach, which required subtle interpretation, the psychologist had secrets to share and was listened to with some deference because the psychologist now made clinical diagnoses that had previously been disallowed. To be able to talk of free-floating anxiety and color shock based on the patient's responses commonly caused many heads about the table to nod in assent as others on the staff recognized something that had been seen in the patient. This was worth a great deal to the self-image of the psychologist, even though doubts arose over the accuracy of the test by statistical standards.[65]

Whereas an intelligence test like the WAIS or a personality inventory like the MMPI might have stronger scientific support, such mundane tests lacked the mystique of the Rorschach, which was becoming clinical psychology's new status symbol.[66]

THE CARNIVAL OF PROJECTIVE TECHNIQUES

During the heady days of the 1950s, enthusiasm for the Rorschach and other projective techniques soared. In Klopfer's *Journal of Projective Techniques* (changed from the *Rorschach Research Exchange* in 1948) one could find discussions and research on such well-known tests as the Rorschach and TAT, as well as descriptions of tantalizing new projective techniques such as the Szondi test, Draw-a-Person Test, and Cypress Knees Test.

Soon projective techniques of all shapes and sizes were used with children and adults to identify maladjustment, uncover unconscious conflicts, and assign diagnoses. As one commentator observed, a "boom town excitement" had taken over clinical psychology: "News of a 'good' test, like news of striking oil, has brought a rush of diagnostic drillers from the old wells to the new and has quickly led to the formation of a new elite."[67]

The Incredible Infallible Rorschach

In the 1950s there was no longer a single Rorschach test. The term was used for several different techniques that varied widely, although all used Rorschach's ten inkblots. Samuel Beck, Bruno Klopfer, and Marguerite Hertz had all developed different methods for administering, scoring, and interpreting the test. In addition, as we'll discuss in the next chapter, two other psychologists, Zygmunt Piotrowski and David Rapaport, introduced their own distinctive Rorschach systems.

By 1957 there were five major American systems for using the Rorschach,[68] not to mention a 1958 textbook by the Danish-Swiss psychologist Ewald Bohm, which described yet a sixth, distinctively European approach to the test.[69] The existence of so many systems seriously retarded scientific progress.[70] If a study reported findings for one Rorschach system, there was no way to be sure whether similar results could be obtained with the other systems, because they differed considerably in their approach to test administration and scoring.

The situation was even more disorderly, verging on chaotic, among practicing psychologists, who routinely combined features of the different systems in idiosyncratic ways. For instance, Marguerite Hertz reported that many clinicians scored a Rorschach protocol using one system, but then compared the results with the norms (results for normal clients) of another system.[71] Given the differences in scoring and administration among the various systems, such a practice was absurd, analogous to administering one intelligence test and interpreting the results with norms from another.

Besides stitching the various Rorschach systems together into a bizarre quilt, many psychologists were interpreting patients' responses to the inkblots as if they were dream images whose symbolic meaning could be psychoanalyzed. This *content approach* to the Rorschach encouraged a kind of comic-book Freudianism. Patients who described one of the blots as an "alligator eating a chicken" were said to be sadistic and probably psychopathic.[72] Those who reported water imagery, such as a river or a lake, were described as dependent, ineffectual, and sexually inadequate.[73]

Although such practices lacked a scientific basis, they were often applied with great self-confidence. The Rorschach came to be regarded as "clinical psychology's most mysterious and powerful magic,"[74] revealing hidden secrets and unveiling deep truths. Many psychologists came to believe that it was virtually never wrong. So widespread was this attitude that even Samuel Beck, whose esteem for the Rorschach was enormous, felt compelled to speak out against "the aura of infallibility which some examiners generate around the test, together with the complementary readiness of their working colleagues to accept the findings."[75]

Marguerite Hertz noted the same trends. Although recognizing that many Rorschach devotees were going too far, she seemed to think that the excesses were due to individual aberrations and lapses, probably by psychologists who didn't really understand the test. The true experts weren't going overboard, she insisted a little defensively. It was simply untrue, she wrote, that "we claim that we can understand the past history and the dynamic personality characteristics of the individual and can predict reactivity to life situations from the responses to inkblots." Quite the contrary, Hertz flatly declared, "No such claim has ever been made."[76]

Apparently Hertz had never read *The Rorschach Technique* by her colleagues Bruno Klopfer and Douglas Kelley. In the opening pages of their popular textbook, Klopfer and Kelley made precisely the claim that Hertz wanted to disavow. Without blinking or blushing, they asserted that a skilled interpreter—using the Rorschach and nothing else—could obtain "a complete picture of the individual personality" through "blind interpretation."[77] If many a psychologist in the 1950s was succumbing to the temptation to act like "a fortune teller with his Rorschach crystal ball,"[78] the reason was not ignorance or hubris, as Hertz seemed to think. Such practices had been specifically encouraged by that "super-salesman of the Rorschach," Bruno Klopfer himself.[79]

Blind Interpretations and Rorschach Wizards

The first recorded "blind interpretation" of a Rorschach inkblot test was performed by Rorschach himself (it's included as an addendum in most English translations of *Psychodiagnostics*).[80] His colleague Emil Oberholzer had given him a patient's inkblot responses, which Rorschach interpreted at great length (twelve printed pages). Oberholzer, who psychoanalyzed the patient, read Rorschach's interpretation and testified, "I have nothing to add to the 'blind' diagnosis made by Rorschach. . . . I could not have given a better characterization of the patient . . . though I had him under analysis for months."[81] Oberholzer noted, "[Rorschach's] experience with the test . . . combined with the acute psychological insight and scientific talent with which Rorschach was endowed, made it possible for him to bring the interpretation of the results to a remarkably, almost dizzily, high state of refinement."[82]

Because Rorschach himself had set the pattern, it's unsurprising that Bruno Klopfer claimed that blind diagnosis, based on the inkblots alone, could supply all the information necessary to understand a patient's personality. Psychologists who had seen Klopfer interpret the Rorschach used such phrases as "crystal-ball gazer" or "sheer telepathy" to describe his uncanny skills.[83] Samuel Beck, though generally more conservative than Klopfer, established a similar reputation by publishing a book that presented his own lengthy blind diagnoses for eight patients.[84]

During the 1950s, the ability to make blind diagnoses came to be regarded among American psychologists as the mark of a true Rorschach virtuoso. Stunning performances by these Rorschach wizards converted many graduate students of the era into true believers.[85]

For example, one highly respected researcher reported how, during his clinical internship at a VA hospital, he attended case conferences at which the famed Marguerite Hertz interpreted Rorschachs.[86] Her astute observations based on the test were "so detailed and exact" that he at first regarded them with great skepticism. However, his doubts dissolved the day that he and a fellow student presented Hertz with the Rorschach protocol of a patient they'd seen in therapy for several months and knew very well: "We fully expected Hertz to make errors in her interpretation. We were determined to point these out to the group. . . . We were shocked, however, when Hertz was able to describe this patient after reading only the first four or five responses and examining the quantitative summary of the various scoring categories and ratios. Within 25 minutes Hertz not only told us what we already knew but began to tell us things we hadn't seen but which were obviously true once pointed out."[87]

This experience had a lasting effect on many budding psychologists. Although recognizing that the scientific evidence for the Rorschach was inadequate, they often became convinced that certain seasoned clinicians, with extensive experience and deep intuition, could extract impressive insights from the test.

A few clinical psychologists of the 1950s were skeptical about blind diagnosis, which they regarded as "a parlor trick" or "at best a stunt."[88] Indeed, the performances of Rorschach wizards bore more than a superficial resemblance to palm reading and crystal ball gazing. However, few graduate students of the era were prepared to recognize this connection. In general, blind analysis tended to make a profound impression on the budding psychologists who witnessed it. Indeed, it's hard to see how anyone unfamiliar with the tricks of palm readers could fail to be bowled over by the amazing insights that virtuosos seemed to extract from the Rorschach.

The High Birth Rate of Projective Techniques

When Lawrence Frank proposed the "projective hypothesis" in 1939, he suggested that many ambiguous situations and stimuli could be used to reveal a patient's true personality. For example, he mentioned that important information could be garnered from handwriting, finger paintings, or clay creations.

Psychologists wasted no time following up on these hints. During the 1940s and 1950s, an exotic carnival of projective techniques paraded through the pages of the *Journal of Projective Techniques* and other psychological journals.[89] Most of these tests lacked a scientific foundation and had little to recommend them beyond the enthusiastic claims of their promoters.

Perhaps inevitably, one enterprising psychologist invented a test that amounted to a "Rorschach for the blind."[90] The testing materials consisted of several cypress knees—gnarled woody outgrowths that form on the roots of cypress trees. A blind person taking the "Kerman Cypress Knee Projective Technic" was asked to feel the twisted shape of each cypress knee, describe the images it brought to mind, and tell a story about it.

Some projective techniques for children used dolls, balloons, or cold cream. A child who burst a balloon was regarded as showing a sign of aggression, while one who rubbed in the cold cream was said to have a preoccupation with anal eroticism and the smearing of feces.[91]

The profusion of new techniques was so rich and strange (one reviewer referred to "the amoeba-like birth rate of projectives")[92] that even Albert Rabin, one of the most prominent scholars in the field, penned a review entitled "Do we need another projective technique?"[93] He concluded that although many ill-conceived and poorly designed projective tests were flooding the market, there was plenty of room for well-constructed and properly validated techniques. Here we'll mention a few of the new tests, either because they drew considerable attention when they appeared or because they became a lasting part of psychology's landscape.

One interesting early projective test was the Tautophone, developed by two eminent clinical psychologists, David Shakow and Saul Rosenzweig, based on an idea of the famous behaviorist B. F. Skinner.[94] The stimulus was a phonograph record on which voices that were not quite intelligible could be heard conversing. Patients were asked to guess what was being said.[95]

Another intriguing novelty was the Szondi test, developed in Europe and introduced into America in the 1940s. A patient was shown forty-eight photographs of faces and asked to select those he most liked and disliked.[96] Unbeknownst to the patient, the photographs depicted individuals in various psychiatric categories, including sadistic murderers, homosexuals (then regarded as mentally disordered), and individuals with paranoid schizophrenia.

The Szondi pictures chosen by the patient supposedly reflected his own underlying needs. For example, if the patient said that he liked the photographs of sadistic murderers, this indicated that he accepted his own needs for "aggressive love." If he said that he disliked photographs of homosexuals, this indicated that he was unable to accept his own needs for "tender love." The Szondi excited interest in the early 1950s and a *Szondi Newsletter* was established for its admirers. American researchers eventually concluded it was worthless, although the test is still used in many parts of Europe.[97]

A myriad of projective techniques that involved telling stories based on pictures also surfaced around this time. The TAT was developed in 1935 (see Chapter Three).[98] Even today, it remains the second most frequently used projective technique after the Rorschach. The TAT consists of cards depicting ambiguous situations, mostly involving people. One of the TAT stimuli, Card 16, represents the epitome of ambiguity in projective techniques: it's entirely blank. Examiners ask respondents to tell a detailed story in response to each card. The stories ostensibly reveal respondents' underlying needs and perceptions of others.

The psychoanalytically oriented Blacky Pictures consisted of eleven cartoons portraying the adventures of two puppies, Blacky and Tippy. One cartoon showed Blacky chewing on his mother's dog collar. Patients were asked to tell a story about this picture and answer various questions. Their responses were thought to reveal unconscious feelings of "oral sadism" and other psychoanalytic concepts. Another cartoon showed Blacky watching as Tippy's tail was cropped (see Figure 4.1). This cartoon supposedly elicited "castration anxiety" (if the patient was male) or "penis envy" (if the patient was female).[99]

A wide variety of projective drawing techniques rose to popularity in the late 1940s and early 1950s. Most involved drawings of human figures.[100] For example, in the Draw-a-Person (DAP) test (there were also a Draw-a-Dog test, a Draw-a-Family test, and a Draw-a-Person-in-the-Rain test), the patient was asked simply to "draw a person."

Figure 4.1.   Cartoon from the Blacky Pictures.
Blacky watches as a knife descends on Tippy's tail. The image supposedly
elicits castration anxiety in males and penis envy in females.
Source: Copyright by Gerald Blum. Reproduced by permission.

After completing this task, the patient was asked to draw another person, but of the opposite sex from the first drawing.

The interpretation of human figure drawings seemed limited only by the psychologist's imagination. For instance, Karen Machover, the author of a highly influential book on the topic, advised that if the drawn figures included toes, this represented "an accent on aggressiveness that is almost pathological in nature." She noted that "structurally, the neck is the link between the body (impulse life) and head (intellectual, rational control)." Therefore, she advised, "the neck is often singled out for graphic emphasis by individuals who are disturbed about the incoordination of their impulses and their mental control functions." Emphasis on buttons, Machover said, appeared in the drawings of "dependent, infantile, and inadequate persons," whereas emphasis on pockets was "associated more specifically with affectional or material deprivation as background for psychopathic adjustment."[101]

Although few projective techniques lived up to the expansive claims of their creators, a handful proved valid and clinically useful. Three notable successes were the Goodenough Draw-a-Man test, the Rosenzweig Picture-Frustration Study, and Loevinger's Washington University Sentence Completion Test.

The Goodenough Draw-a-Man test bears at least a superficial resemblance to the Draw-a-Person test. Introduced in the 1920s by

Florence Goodenough of the University of Minnesota, author of a classic textbook on *Mental Testing,* the Draw-a-Man test has an appealingly simple format: The patient (usually a child) is merely instructed to "make a picture of a man; make the very best picture that you can."[102] The drawing is scored for accuracy and complexity, with points assigned for body parts, articles of clothing, proportion, and perspective.[103]

The Draw-a-Man test can be administered and scored quickly and its scores exhibit a reasonably strong correlation (.50 or higher) with such intelligence tests as the Stanford-Binet.[104] It has proven useful as a rough measure of intelligence, especially with children who won't cooperate with lengthier intelligence tests.

A second fairly successful projective technique is the Rosenzweig Picture-Frustration Study (see Figure 4.2), which has the distinction of being featured in Stanley Kubrick's film *A Clockwork Orange.* The patient is shown a series of cartoons, each depicting a person in a frustrating situation. For example, in one of the cartoons a schoolboy is being told by a girl that she isn't going to invite him to her birthday party.[105] The patient is asked to describe what the frustrated person (in this case the schoolboy) would say in response to the unpleasant situation. Research has shown that this test has some validity as a measure of aggressiveness.[106]

From a scientific point of view, the Washington University Sentence Completion Test (WUSCT)[107] is probably the most successful projective technique.[108] Jane Loevinger, a researcher in St. Louis, designed the test to measure "ego development," the degree to which a person is autonomous, aware of her own faults, and accepting of herself as she really is.[109] The test consists of thirty-six sentence stems, such as "When people disagree . . . " or "I most regret that . . . " (these aren't the actual stems, but are similar to them). Patients are asked to complete the sentences. Their responses are scored for the degree to which they reflect a complex appreciation of individuals and interpersonal relationships.

Research has shown that the WUSCT is a valid measure, probably reflecting qualities that in ordinary language we call *maturity, understanding,* and perhaps even *wisdom.*[110] For example, it correlates positively with measures of empathy and moral development, and negatively with delinquency.[111] However, the WUSCT is virtually never used by clinical psychologists in their daily work, and has been limited almost exclusively to research applications.

Figure 4.2.   Cartoons from the Rosenzweig Picture-Frustration Study.
Most research has shown that responses to the Rosenzweig Picture-
Frustration Study bear a relationship to aggressiveness.
Source: Copyright © 1976 by Saul Rosenzweig. Reproduced by permission.

The neglect of the WUCST by clinicians can be contrasted with the widespread popularity of such projective drawing techniques as the DAP. Karen Machover, with her strange ideas regarding toes, buttons, and pockets, has exerted a far greater impact on the ordinary testing practices of psychologists than have such sophisticated workers as Jane Loevinger and Saul Rosenzweig.[112] Even today, a psychologist who tests a child is far more likely to use the Draw-a-Person test than one of the better-validated projective techniques.[113]

Despite decades of negative research findings, projective drawings are still used by American psychologists to resolve delicate issues of overwhelming importance, such as whether a child has been sexually abused.[114] Anne Anastasi, author of a classic textbook on psychological testing, summarized the situation: "Projective techniques present a curious discrepancy between research and practice. When evaluated as psychometric instruments, the large majority make a poor showing. Yet their popularity continues unabated."[115]

But we're getting ahead of ourselves. Let's return to the 1940s and 1950s and look at important new developments with the Rorschach Inkblot Test during those decades.

CHAPTER FIVE

The Many-Portaled Quandary

Balkanization of the Rorschach

To Rorschach? or not to Rorschach? The newcomer to this much debated instrument finds himself before a many-portaled quandary. Not one but several tests confront him and all bear the name Rorschach.

—Samuel Beck, *"Review of the Rorschach Inkblot Test,"* 1959

The 1940s and 1950s were the Golden Age of the Rorschach. As projective tests soared in popularity, new ideas about the inkblots appeared and innovation became widespread. In the 1930s the Rorschach community split into three camps: Klopfer, Beck, and Hertz. During the ensuing decades, the number of variations would multiply until there seemed to be almost as many approaches to the Rorschach as there were psychologists using it. In this chapter, we'll describe new approaches to the Rorschach that evolved during the 1940s and 1950s.

THE SIGN APPROACH TO THE RORSCHACH

In 1937, the young Polish psychologist Zygmunt Piotrowski published an article in the *Rorschach Research Exchange* that articulated what he called the "principle of interdependence of Rorschach components."

Individual scores on the Rorschach test could not be interpreted in isolation, Piotrowski said. Rather, they had to be interpreted as a whole, so that the meaning of one score modified the meaning of others. As we discussed in Chapter Three, Bruno Klopfer adopted this idea, teaching that Rorschach interpretations are based on the overall "configuration" or "Gestalt" of the scores.

In the 1940s and early 1950s, several researchers attempted to apply the configural approach to Rorschach scores in a systematic, quantifiable way. One of the most ambitious examples was the "Inspection Technique" developed by Ruth Munroe of Sarah Lawrence College. She developed a list of twenty-seven Rorschach "signs" of "maladjustment," such as these:[1]

- More than one white Space response appeared in the protocol.

- The number of Color responses was more than twice the sum of Movement responses, or the number of Movement responses was more than twice the sum of Color responses.

The signs in a protocol were added up and combined according to an "extremely complex" system of rules to yield an overall score of maladjustment.[2]

Munroe's Inspection Technique was vulnerable to the criticism that, despite its complexity, it still oversimplified the configural approach used by virtuoso clinicians. However, as we noted in Chapter Three, Klopfer's description of the configural approach probably exaggerated the complexity of the interpretive process. In daily clinical practice, and indeed in Klopfer's books, many interpretations were based on single Rorschach scores or on straightforward combinations of two or three scores. Furthermore, Munroe stated explicitly that her approach mirrored how the Rorschach was commonly interpreted by clinicians: "I have relied upon generally accepted judgments as to what constitutes clinically significant deviation in Rorschach performance."[3]

No one contradicted Munroe on this point, and her work was published in 1942 in Klopfer's *Rorschach Research Exchange*. Thus, it's probably fair to conclude that her system for measuring "maladjustment" did not greatly oversimplify the configural approach, and that it may even have adopted a more sophisticated approach to interpretation than did most clinicians in their daily work.

In several articles and a monograph, Munroe reported research findings that showed that the Inspection Technique was successful at predicting the academic success of students at Sarah Lawrence College.[4] Her work was warmly praised by prominent researchers, including Donald Super of Columbia University and Paul Meehl of the University of Minnesota.[5] However, in a pattern that was to become depressingly common for Rorschach studies, most other researchers were unable to replicate Munroe's impressive results.[6] Eventually the Inspection Technique was abandoned.

At about the same time that the Inspection Technique was garnering attention from psychologists, several other Rorschach researchers developed similar lists of "neurotic signs" of maladjustment. All these innovative scales suffered a fate similar to that of the Inspection Technique: After a brief period of enthusiasm and positive findings, their promise failed to materialize and they were abandoned. Looking back at this body of research in 1971, Marvin Goldfried, George Stricker, and Irving Weiner concluded that "the search for neurotic signs represents a brief and inglorious chapter in Rorschach research."[7]

However, such a conclusion is probably too harsh and overlooks two important points. First, the signs developed by Ruth Munroe and other researchers in the 1940s represented a reasonable attempt to quantify how psychologists of the era were using the Rorschach to identify "maladjustment" and "neurosis." The failure of the signs suggested that perhaps the Rorschach wasn't as infallible as it was supposed to be, even when a configural approach was used.

Second, the early work on neurotic signs opened a pathway that Rorschach researchers were to follow for decades to come. For example, from the late 1940s through the 1960s, researchers developed new lists of Rorschach signs for other psychiatric conditions, such as Wheeler's signs for homosexuality, Irving Weiner's "color stress" sign for schizophrenia, and Hughes's signs for organic brain damage. Even Bruno Klopfer proposed a list of signs, the Rorschach Prognostic Rating Scale, that could be used to predict patients' outcomes in psychotherapy.[8]

Perhaps most important, the lists of neurotic signs in the early 1940s foreshadowed the work of John Exner, who in the 1970s and 1980s introduced a large number of similar Rorschach "indexes," such as the Egocentricity Index, the Depression Index, and the Obsessive Style Index, which were designed to measure a variety of personality characteristics. Exner's indexes were similarly calculated by scoring individual signs and combining them into a composite score. In conception and form, Exner's indexes were direct descendants of the sign approach that flourished in the 1940s and 1950s.

THE CONTENT APPROACH TO THE RORSCHACH

Whereas the lists of signs developed by Munroe and others emphasized systematic scoring and quantification, there appeared in the 1940s a new approach to the Rorschach that was unsystematic, resistant to numerical analysis, and immensely appealing to adherents of psychoanalytic theory. The "content approach" to the Rorschach was based on the loosely psychoanalytic premise that the images seen by patients in the blots are like dream figures, with symbolic meanings that can be revealed through interpretation.

Content versus Structural Approaches to the Rorschach

In the 1940s, under the influence of psychoanalytic theory, the distinction between *content* and *structure* took on special importance for Rorschach interpretation. *Content* consists of what a patient reports seeing in the blots—animals, human figures, x-rays of internal organs, articles of clothing, and so on. *Structure* consists of the formal aspects of the inkblot images and mainly concerns three issues:

- *Location.* Is the image based on the Whole blot (*W*), or on Details (*D* and *Dd*)?
- *Form Quality.* How well does the image fit the shape of the blot (*F+* or *F–*)?
- *Determinants.* What perceptual features of the blots (Movement, Color, Form, Shading) have "determined" what's seen?

As we discussed in Chapter Two, Hermann Rorschach was far more concerned with structure (location, form quality, and determinants) than with content. As a psychoanalyst, he recognized that the images seen in the blots could be interpreted symbolically, but he believed that they were only occasionally informative: "The test cannot be considered as a means of delving into the unconscious. At best, it is far inferior to the other profound psychological methods such as dream interpretation and association experiments. This is not difficult to understand. The test does not induce a 'free flow from the unconscious' but requires adaptation to external stimuli."[9]

The Father and Mother cards . . . and More

According to some accounts, Hermann Rorschach began to show interest in inkblot content in the months before his death.[10] However, the topic was generally ignored for the next two decades, until the publication of the little textbook by Bochner and Halpern that became popular during World War II (see Chapter Four).

In the 1942 edition of their book, Bochner and Halpern offered a handful of content interpretations in a straightforward, gently dogmatic way. For example, they said that Rorschach responses that include human images reveal "an interest in the self and in others," whereas responses that include body parts (arms, legs, heads) are "characteristic of people who show concern with body parts, that is, the hypochondriacs, the unintelligent, the nervous, the pedants, the depressed and the stereotyped, and some psychotics."[11] Bochner and Halpern's text, which adopted a nuts-and-bolts approach to the Rorschach, offered no explanation of how the authors arrived at their notions concerning Rorschach content.

In the book's second edition, which appeared in 1945, Bochner and Halpern substantially expanded their discussion of Rorschach content. For instance, they suggested that personality factors could be inferred from the types of animals that patients saw in the blots: "Interpretations consistently dealing with aggressive fighting animals reflect strong feelings of hostility and aggression. . . . Where the mild, timid animals are the rule, the prevailing attitude will be found to be a somewhat insecure, essentially passive one." Responses that involved supernatural or imaginary beings were regarded as a bad sign: "Such figures as ghosts, dwarfs, giants, angels, witches, etc., have a connotation somewhat different from that of the ordinary human answers. They represent an immature, childlike, or wishful way of thinking."[12]

Bochner and Halpern also introduced the idea, destined to become widespread, that certain Rorschach cards tap patients' unconscious feelings toward their parents. Specifically, they suggested that Card IV, which is often seen as a large man or monster, "may suggest the father or authority in general. . . . Its dark quality and overwhelming character are particularly disturbing to those for whom parental authority is still an unresolved problem." Similarly, the blots on Card VII, which are often seen as two female faces, "give this card a feminine quality, frequently with maternal implications."[13]

Thereafter Cards IV and VII became known as the "Father" and "Mother" cards. Patients' responses to these cards were interpreted as revealing attitudes toward parental figures and toward males and females in general. For example, if a woman remarked that the "arms" of the "man" on Card IV looked skinny and weak (as in fact they do), her response was considered ominous. An article in the *Journal of Projective Techniques* by psychologist Fred Brown advised that such an uncomplimentary description of the Father card indicated "penis envy" and "a degradation of the male arising out of a sour-grapes rationalization for the lack of male prerogatives."[14]

Similarly, Brown explained, if a patient perceived Card VII, the Mother card, as "stuffed animals," two interpretations were possible. Perhaps the patient regarded women as playthings, "created for the purpose of providing amusement." Alternatively, especially among female patients, the response indicated "a refusal to grow up and assume heterosexual responsibilities."[15]

By the early 1950s, the idea that began with the Father and Mother cards had been expanded by Brown and other writers to include all the Rorschach cards.[16] Because Card I is the first card shown to a patient, responses to it were said by Brown to indicate "the manner in which the patient responds to a new and challenging situation."[17] Card II, which is often seen as "clowns" or "puppy dogs," was said to evoke "childhood experiences and feelings."[18] Card III contains two human figures that seemingly possess breasts and penises. Therefore responses to this card were said to bring out "attitudes toward one's own conception of sexual identification and role."[19]

So it went with all the cards. Card V revealed childhood memories of having seen one's parents engaged in intercourse. Card VI reflected unconscious attitudes toward sex and "phallic worship." Card IX revealed "anal" concerns and paranoia.[20] Card X revealed "oral" fantasies.[21] Thus, in the new "content" approach, the Rorschach came to be viewed as a set of ten psychoanalytic x-ray plates, each exposing a different assortment of Freudian fixations and unconscious complexes.

Robert Lindner's Forty-Three Content Responses

During the 1940s and early 1950s a series of Rorschach theorists embellished and expanded the content approach even further. Particularly prominent was the psychoanalyst Robert Lindner, whose non-fiction book *Rebel Without a Cause* provided the name and (very loosely) the story of the classic movie starring James Dean. Whereas Bochner and Halpern introduced the idea that particular Rorschach cards evoked unconscious themes, Lindner tended to adopt a more fine-grained approach.[22] He identified forty-three specific responses to the blots that, in his experience, carried a very definite meaning. For example, he warned that certain negative responses to Card IV were associated with suicide: "The 'suicide card' is an apt name for Card IV. Responses containing such projections as 'a decaying tooth,' 'a rotted tree trunk,' 'a pall of black smoke,' 'something rotten,' 'a burned and charred piece of wood,' appear in severe depressive states with suicidal overtones and self-annihilative thought content. Where the response to this area frankly mentions death, however, there is a fair prospect that the patient will benefit from convulsive therapy."[23]

Similarly, Lindner identified a small blue blotch on Card X as interpretively important: "The response 'an extracted tooth' to this small area is to be expected from chronic masturbators and patients with serious conflicts over masturbation."[24]

In like manner, he cautioned about patients who responded to a certain area above the white space on Card II: "Where the responses 'a pair of pliers' or 'some sort of tool' are given, they usually mask the obvious phallic symbolism of the shape and denote hesitancy in coming to grips with an underlying sexual problem."[25]

Although Lindner's ideas were viewed with caution by some Rorschach experts, they were published in the *Journal of Projective Techniques* and widely discussed.[26]

Phillips and Smith

The new approach to Rorschach content pioneered by Bochner, Halpern, Brown, and Lindner culminated in 1953 with a well-known book by Leslie Phillips of Clark University and his collaborator Joseph Smith. The text began with what (for the Rorschach) was an admirably modest statement: "This book . . . is composed largely of statements about relationships between Rorschach performance and other behavior. Unfortunately, few of the relationships which are asserted have been corroborated; most represent guessed-at laws. They are perhaps best employed with equal parts of faith and skepticism."[27]

Of course, *all* popular Rorschach texts were little more than almanacs of "guessed-at laws." What was "refreshing" about Phillips and Smith was their willingness to say so honestly.[28]

With admirable clarity and considerable erudition, Phillips and Smith discussed all the usual Rorschach topics, such as Color responses, Movement, and Shading. They cited relevant work by other psychologists and presented data from their own patients to substantiate important points. With respect to scholarship, their discussions were clearly superior to the popular text by Klopfer and Kelley, and more wide-ranging and inclusive than the books of Samuel Beck.

If Phillips and Smith had stuck with the usual Rorschach topics, their book would probably have excited little controversy. But rather than simply following the well-worn path trodden by their inkblot forebears, they took the mildly innovative step of including a detailed chapter on content analysis. It's been a sore spot for some Rorschach experts ever since.[29]

With the same meticulous care that characterized the rest of their book, Phillips and Smith listed each type of Rorschach content in alphabetical order, from "animal" to "war," and illustrated the symbolic meaning of each with numerous examples. Their interpretations were not particularly wild or extravagant, at least compared with the articles being published in the *Journal of Projective Techniques*.

Furthermore, when Phillips and Smith proposed new interpretations for particular kinds of content, their suggestions often had a surface plausibility, or at least a clear connection with the psychoanalytic theories of their day. Here are some of their content interpretations, many of which have had a lasting influence on Rorschach interpretation:

- *Clothing* content, such as "tuxedo" or "hat," generally suggests "sensitivity to external social forms." However, certain types of clothing responses such as "man in disguise" or "person in masquerade costume" can also indicate suspiciousness and a tendency to believe that "things are not what they seem."[30]

- *Food* content, such as "ice cream cone" or "carrots," symbolizes "dependency needs and is associated with insistent demands for nurture."[31]

- *Imaginary and mythological figures,* such as "Merlin," "Bugs Bunny," or "angel," indicate an interest in other people, just as

Human content does, but suggest an "anxiety about interpersonal relations and a tendency toward social isolation."[32]

- *Islands* seen in the blots reflect "the feeling of being alone and rejected."[33]

- *Art* content, such as "design," "drawing," or "decoration," is associated with "fastidious attitudes and esthetic interests" and is found in people who tend to "lack vigor and intensity, act properly, often prudishly and, in general, avoid any turbulence or emotional expression."[34]

Phillips and Smith also presented an interesting discussion of *sexual* content. The Rorschach inkblots contain at least ten details that clearly resemble penises or vaginas, although few people actually say so when they take the test.[35] The intriguing mystery is whether these blatant genital images were created deliberately by Hermann Rorschach. Although *Psychodiagnostics* says nothing on the topic, it's difficult to believe that Rorschach, versed as he was in the sex-drenched theories of psychoanalysis, somehow overlooked all the naughty pictures in his blots.

Phillips and Smith opened their discussion of sexual content in the Rorschach test with some commonsense observations. They pointed out that normal individuals are more likely to report sexual imagery in the blots if they're friends of the examiner and therefore willing to speak candidly. They also noted that some "liberated" individuals, or patients in psychoanalysis, are more likely to report sexual imagery, presumably because they've grown accustomed to talking freely about such matters.[36]

Having issued these caveats, however, Phillips and Smith flatly warned that an "emphasis" on sexual content is most "blatant" among schizophrenics. The reason, they explained, is that sexual content often represents an attempt to compensate for repressed homosexuality: "In all groups, those males who emphasize sex content display both an inadequate heterosexual adjustment . . . and a tendency toward homosexual attachments. In schizophrenic men this desire for homosexual companionship is almost always inverted into a fear of men. This is the classic paranoid defense first delineated by Freud. Thus an emphasis on sex content by schizophrenic men may be used to infer paranoid ideation and delusions even when other paranoid signs are absent."[37]

Reactions to Phillips and Smith

Not surprisingly, the speculations in Phillips and Smith's book drew criticism from such scientifically oriented psychologists as Lee J. Cronbach of Stanford. He pointed out that the book's interpretations were plausible, but that "the cables of evidence anchoring them to reality have all the tensile strength of moonbeams."[38]

Although this reaction from psychology's empiricist wing was foreseeable, Phillips and Smith's book received unexpected jabs from Douglas Kelley, a fellow Rorschacher and Bruno Klopfer's coauthor. Writing in the *American Journal of Psychiatry*, Kelley commended certain aspects of the book, but undercut his praise with sharp remarks: "Probably the best approach to this book . . . is simply to accept the fact that it represents a viewpoint and that the authors' statements, especially in terms of clinical meaning, may be true in some cases and not in others. . . . If the title were changed to read 'Rorschach Speculations—Our Method,' it could be highly recommended."[39]

Kelley singled out the chapter on content analysis for special criticism: "The hazard here in adapting from the text a meaning for an individual response is higher than in any other section, since what may be significant to one person may be coincidental to another. Generally such 'dream book' interpretations are risky and this section of the book should be approached with greatest caution."[40]

In retrospect, Kelley's negative comments seem ironic, considering that his and Klopfer's textbook was at least as speculative as Phillips and Smith's. At the time, Klopfer's *Journal of Projective Techniques* was publishing pieces on the Rorschach that were just as far-fetched, though not nearly so scholarly, as Phillips and Smith's chapter on content analysis.

Why did Kelley single out Phillips and Smith's book for criticism? Several explanations seem possible. Among them, there's a remote possibility that Kelley was trying to sabotage a potential competitor. Shortly after Phillips and Smith's book appeared, Bruno Klopfer published a book that covered many of the same topics.[41] Kelley's review might have steered readers away from Phillips and Smith's text and toward Klopfer's work.

Second, Phillips and Smith's straightforward list of Rorschach content interpretations apparently struck Kelley as oversimplified and naive, like the dime-store "dream books" that his review sarcastically mentioned. Phillips and Smith presented their ideas so unambiguously that they could be easily subjected to straightforward testing by researchers. By contrast, as we noted in Chapter Three, Klopfer and his followers had gone to great lengths to deny the legitimacy of scientific tests of the Rorschach.[42] The real problem with Phillips and Smith's book, then, may have been its clarity and forthrightness.

The third and most plausible explanation for Kelley's pique is that he realized, quite rightly, that content interpretation represented a potentially revolutionary approach to the Rorschach that threatened to overshadow or even overthrow the traditional structural approach of Klopfer and Beck. Content interpretation possessed a powerful subversive appeal because it dovetailed so neatly with the psychoanalytic assumptions of the 1950s. Most clinical psychologists and psychiatrists already accepted the Freudian view that dream images have symbolic and sexual meaning. It was only a short step to accept Rorschach content interpretation. In fact, the content approach bore a much more obvious connection to Freudian theory than did the structural approach.

In retrospect, Kelley's unfriendly review of Phillips and Smith's book can be identified as the first cannon shot in a limited-engagement conflict that's been fought among Rorschachers ever since. From the 1950s to the present, the Rorschach establishment has always emphasized the importance of structural interpretation, whereas a vocal minority of Rorschach scholars has persistently championed the virtues of the content approach.[43]

Defenders of the structural approach have typically used two standard strategies for dealing with their content-oriented opponents. First, members of the "structural establishment" (particularly the Klopfer and Exner systems) have primly criticized the content approach as simplistic ("dream-book") and speculative. As noted earlier, such criticisms seem somewhat ironic, because the structural approach can be equally simplistic and speculative. However, by assuming an air of righteous scientific indignation toward the content approach, defenders of the structural approach can appear, at least momentarily, as true skeptics and empiricists.

The establishment's second strategy for dealing with content interpretation has been limited accommodation. Like a government that's unable to defeat rebel forces and so cedes them limited control through what it calls "power sharing," the traditional Rorschach systems have gradually accepted some elements of content interpretation, though always maintaining them in a subordinate position.

The first Rorschach systematizer to embrace this strategy was Bruno Klopfer. In 1954, the year after the appearance of Phillips and Smith's book, Klopfer published a textbook that cautiously incorporated several of the new ideas about content interpretation, including the Father and Mother cards.[44] Although he didn't cite Phillips and Smith, Klopfer used language very much like theirs to express his reservations about the content approach: "The kinds of hypotheses to be presented in this chapter are based on the whole backlog of dynamic personality theory as well as the clinical experiences of many people with whom the present writer has been associated. They are presented not as facts, but as working hypotheses, hunches, or guesses."[45]

Although Klopfer didn't typically characterize his ideas about the Rorschach as mere "hunches or guesses," in the case of content interpretation he called attention to the shaky nature of the evidence. In this way, while making a conciliatory nod toward content analysis, he emphasized its second-class status. Apparently adopting a pragmatic "if you can't beat 'em, join 'em" attitude, Klopfer grudgingly made room for the content approach. In the 1930s, he fiercely battled against ideas about the Rorschach that differed from his own. By the early 1950s, he learned that limited accommodation could be a more effective strategy.

NEW RORSCHACH SYSTEMS: PIOTROWSKI, RAPAPORT, AND BOHM

Although the Klopfer and Beck systems were preeminent during the 1940s and 1950s, other interesting approaches to the Rorschach appeared during this period and were destined to exert an impact on how the test was used.

Zygmunt Piotrowski and Perceptanalysis

The Polish psychologist Zygmunt Piotrowski has already popped up several times in our story. It was Piotrowski who in 1937 proposed that human movement (M), animal movement (FM), and inanimate movement (m) responses all have important and distinct meanings. He also introduced the principle of "the interdependence of Rorschach components," which Klopfer adopted under the name of interpretation of "configurations."[46]

EARLY ACCOMPLISHMENTS   Piotrowski may well be the most erudite and original thinker who ever dedicated himself to the Rorschach test. Trained in experimental psychology, philosophy, and symbolic logic, he traveled from Poland to New York in 1929 to pursue postgraduate studies at Teachers College of Columbia University.[47] In the early 1930s he attended some of the graduate student seminars at Bruno Klopfer's apartment, where he developed an interest in the Rorschach.[48]

Piotrowski's early work on the test was strikingly original, especially considering that most Rorschachers of the 1930s were marching in lockstep behind either Klopfer or Beck. In addition to formulating his ideas about *M, FM,* and *m* and the "interdependence of Rorschach components," Piotrowski conducted research on patients with what were then called "organic" brain disorders, such as brain tumors and Korsakoff's syndrome. He identified a list of Rorschach signs that differentiated these patients from individuals with psychiatric disorders.[49] Later researchers confirmed his findings and the "Piotrowski signs" for organic brain disease became well known among clinical psychologists.[50] He seems to have been one of the first Rorschach researchers to compile a list of signs for diagnostic purposes, an innovative idea that was soon applied to the identification of maladjustment and neurosis.

Although at first influenced by Klopfer, Piotrowski soon developed his own distinctive ideas about the Rorschach, eventually publishing his system in a 1957 book, *Perceptanalysis: A Fundamentally Reworked, Expanded and Systematized Rorschach Method.*[51] "Perceptanalysis" was Piotrowski's own term for inkblot tests and other techniques that sought to understand personality through perception.

Impressive and quirky, *Perceptanalysis* reflected its author's unique mind and breadth of scholarship. Piotrowski was a fascinating conversationalist whose thoughts could leap rapidly from naval history to Freud, then to Michelangelo.[52] His book on the Rorschach displayed a similar breadth of learning. As one commentator admiringly remarked: "What other author of a scientific textbook on psychological concepts and procedures has a reference list that includes books and studies in multiple languages, where books and studies on hard science, art, and literature stand side by side? What other author uses Nietzsche to explain the universality of the human movement response, credits Leonardo Da Vinci with the first 'ink blot' procedure, uses Hamlet's soliloquy to illustrate shading responses . . . and describes the meaning of color responses through the Indian philosopher, Bhagavan Das?"[53]

PIOTROWSKI'S APPROACH TO MOVEMENT RESPONSES   As we discussed in Chapter Two, the most important variable in Hermann Rorschach's inkblot experiment was M (Human Movement), which he regarded as an indicator of introversiveness or "turning inward." Piotrowski shared Rorschach's views regarding M but went far beyond them, arguing that an individual's M responses provide an in-depth picture of "his unconsciously as well as consciously determined, preferred modes of handling interpersonal relationships."[54]

In *Perceptanalysis,* Piotrowski demonstrated his approach to M responses by reinterpreting a protocol that Rorschach had discussed more than thirty-five years earlier. (In fact, this was the same protocol that was used in Hermann Rorschach's "blind analysis," which we discussed in Chapter Four.) The patient had given four human movement responses: "two clowns," "two dandies who bow very formally and greet each other, in white tie and tails, and top hats in their hands," "two human bodies in a bent over position with legs hanging down," and "a little man, who grasps the red with one arm and takes a step."[55]

Piotrowski explained how these four responses revealed the patient's "prototypal roles in life."[56] Two of the M responses (the dandies bowing, and the bodies bent over) were "compliant" or "passive," and a third (the little man taking a step) was only "timidly active." From this Piotrowski inferred that the patient assumed a "prototypal role" of compliance and dependence in his relationships with other people.[57]

As a second example, Piotrowski presented a protocol that included four M responses: "two people trying to tear something apart," "a couple of Negroes with a fish," "a couple of women," and "a tree playing the violin or some musical instrument."[58] Piotrowski extracted four main insights from these responses.

First, he focused on the image of the tree playing a violin. He noted that playing the violin is "an exhibitionistic act; it attracts the attention of others." However, the patient attributed this action to a plant rather than to a human, indicating a "strong suppression" of his impulses. From these clues, Piotrowski inferred that the patient's prototypal life role involved a conflict between a strong desire to exhibit his talents in front of other people and a tendency to feel bashful about doing so.[59]

Second, Piotrowski pointed out that the patient had given two *M* responses that involved aggression: the two people tearing something apart, and the African American figures with a fish (Piotrowski considered this second image aggressive because "it ends in the death of the fish"). These two responses indicated a "readiness to compete openly with others when vital personal values are involved."[60] Although the patient suppressed his exhibitionistic impulses (the tree playing the violin), he was apparently more willing to express his aggressive and competitive impulses openly.

Third, Piotrowski noted that in three of the *M* responses (including the tree), "the legs are immobilized and the activity is limited to the arms and/or mouth." From these responses, he inferred that "the patient's main formal aggressiveness would be limited, being expressed either orally through biting remarks or through other not very conspicuous activities."[61]

Fourth and finally, Piotrowski thought it significant that the patient had been vague about the sex of the two people tearing something apart and the two African Americans with a fish. These responses, said Piotrowski, "suggest homosexual tendencies" and, with other information from the protocol, indicated that "the patient does not feel well in the biopsychological role of a man."[62]

As can be seen, Piotrowski's approach to *M* responses, which he developed in the 1930s, shared much with the symbolic content interpretations that had become widespread in the 1950s. In fact, it could be argued that Piotrowski, ever the innovator, had introduced the content approach even before it appeared in Bochner and Halpern's 1942 handbook.

Piotrowski's ideas about other kinds of movement responses were ingenious twists on his ideas about *M*. He said that animal movement responses (*FM*), like *M* responses, reveal "prototypal roles," but that *FM* reflects roles that appear during "diminished consciousness" (for instance, when a patient is intoxicated) or that the patient has assumed in childhood. Thus, if a patient reports gentle *FM*, such as a "butterfly alighting" or a "dog sleeping," the interpreter might infer that the patient will become quiet and unassertive after a few drinks, or that he was quiet and unassertive as a child.[63]

In contrast to *M* and *FM*, Piotrowski said, inanimate movement responses (*m*) reflect prototypal roles in life that the patient would like to assume but can't: "The *m* can be compared to an attic where are stored away those personality trends which would lead to an inner conflict if they were expressed outwardly although they are desirable and accepted by the individual himself."[64]

For example, if a patient's protocol includes *m* responses such as "flying planes" and "exploding bombs," these images may indicate the patient's unfulfilled desire to "handle personally vital human relationships in an easy, effective, spontaneous, and effortless manner."[65]

REACTIONS TO PIOTROWSKI'S IDEAS   Piotrowski's ideas have generally been neglected by American Rorschachers. There seem to be three reasons why his system never caught on. First, his timing was poor. Had Piotrowski published *Perceptanalysis* in the late 1930s or early 1940s, his Rorschach system might have attracted a substantial number of followers. Instead, by the time his book appeared in 1957, the Rorschach community, like the U.S. political world, had pretty much settled down to a two-party system, with the Klopfer and Beck methods commanding the allegiance of most clinical psychologists. Piotrowski's position was much like that of an independent party candidate, who might be able to exert some pressure on the major parties, but couldn't hope to win a large proportion of votes.[66]

A second negative factor was Piotrowski's failure to develop good norms or support his ideas with solid scientific evidence. As Marguerite Hertz tartly observed, Piotrowski's *Perceptanalysis* "is par excellence an exposition of his personal views, beliefs, and procedures. Despite the fact he states as one of his goals, 'to contribute to the process of tidying up and tightening perceptanalysis as a scientific procedure,' there is little evidence to indicate why he considers his procedure 'scientific.'"[67]

In the decades since Piotrowski's book appeared, research has provided some support for a few of his hypotheses. Most significantly, Edwin Wagner and his colleagues have found that the number of "exhibitionistic" *M* responses tends to be higher in some groups, such as drama majors and strippers, in a way that Piotrowski would have predicted.[68] However, Piotrowski's ideas are numerous and complex, and little research has been conducted on them. Today, as in the 1950s, his Rorschach system hangs in midair like an enchanted castle without a sturdy scientific foundation.

Finally, there may have been a third, less tangible, factor that interfered with the acceptance of Piotrowski's ideas: He sometimes said or did things that seemed a bit eccentric. For example, in *Perceptanalysis* he claimed that "Rorschach produced more than an experiment or a test. He created a new, systematic, independent, and comprehensive science."[69]

Although most clinical psychologists in the 1950s held the Rorschach test in high esteem, few would have endorsed Piotrowski's idea that it formed the basis for an "independent and comprehensive science." In a review of *Perceptanalysis*, Herman Molish, a colleague of Samuel Beck, took Piotrowski to task for making such a grandiose claim: "Rorschach did not in essence create a 'new science.' What he devised was an experimental procedure that can be applied within the framework of a science of personality."[70]

Nor was this the only instance in which Piotrowski seemed to go overboard in his claims. For example, he continued to refer to the test as a "psychological x-ray" until at least 1982,[71] although even the most ardent Rorschachers had abandoned this metaphor many years earlier. Piotrowski also developed a system of dream interpretation,[72] based on the same principles espoused in *Perceptanalysis*, and offered "instant analyses" to people who called in their dreams to a radio talk show.[73]

Although Piotrowski may have been discounted by some psychologists because of his unconventionality, others who knew him vouched for his integrity, humor, kindness, and sheer intelligence.[74] Several of these positive qualities are evident in *Perceptanalysis*, which exudes an unmistakable mental energy that sets it apart from virtually all other books on the Rorschach.[75]

Any fair evaluation of Piotrowski must take into account the fact that he, like Bruno Klopfer, came from a European background that was substantially different from the American tradition of clinical psychology, with its emphasis on psychometrics and objective research.[76] Within the European tradition, it wasn't unusual for experts to spin interesting speculations based on intuition, clinical wisdom, the writings of previous experts, and theory. This point also applies to our discussion of Ewald Bohm later in this chapter.

Furthermore, when Piotrowski was right, he could be *really* right. In *Perceptanalysis*, he made the prediction (which was very strange in 1957) that Rorschach interpretations could one day be performed mechanically: "We shall be able to feed the Rorschach data, scored, classified, and counted according to objective rules, into a machine which will take the drudgery out of thinking consistently in terms of many variables and which will make the interpretation of the scored test data perfectly reliable."[77]

This notion didn't sit well with some orthodox users of the test, who believed that Rorschach interpretation depended on clinical wisdom and experience. For example, Herman Molish, who criticized Piotrowski for calling inkblot interpretation a "new science," considered the idea of mechanical interpretation to be far-fetched: "Certainly the goal is expansive and not wholly realistic. . . . One wonders how the psychologist would be 'fed' into such a machine to equate for . . . the psychologist's knowledge of human personality and of psychopathology."[78]

Despite such skepticism, Piotrowski made his "expansive" idea of machine interpretation come true, developing the first computer program to interpret the Rorschach.[79] Similar programs were eventually written for John Exner's popular Comprehensive System for the Rorschach. At the beginning of the twenty-first century, Piotrowski's idea of machine interpretation no longer seems strange. Psychologists commonly use some form of computer assistance when scoring and interpreting the Rorschach.

David Rapaport, Ego Psychology, and Deviant Verbalizations

Another innovator of the 1940s and 1950s was David Rapaport, whose idea of using the Rorschach to measure "Deviant Verbalizations" represented one of the most important extensions of the test since Rorschach's time. One writer observed, "Many would agree that Rapaport's contributions in this area are second only to those of Rorschach himself."[80]

Trained as a psychologist in Hungary, Rapaport emigrated to the United States in 1938 and worked at two of the country's leading psychoanalytic institutions, first the Menninger Clinic in Kansas and later the Austen Riggs Center in Stockbridge, Massachusetts.[81] Soon after arriving in America, Rapaport injected new ideas into the field of psychological testing. In 1942 he introduced American psychologists to the Szondi,[82] the projective test described in the previous chapter. In 1946, he and his coauthors published the two-volume *Diagnostic Psychological Testing*,[83] which popularized the idea of "test batteries" and became "virtually a bible among students and practitioners engaged in psychodynamically oriented psychological assessment."[84]

Diagnostic Psychological Testing not only explained how intelligence tests and projective techniques could be used in conjunction, but provided more than a hundred tables and fifty graphs that seemed to support the validity of the Rorschach and other projective tests.[85] These data soon proved to be an embarrassment, however. Several prominent critics, including Quinn McNemar of Stanford University, identified numerous problems with the book's statistics and methodology.[86] Eventually it was reprinted with the tables and graphs removed.[87]

Among its "countless pages of deceptively impressive statistical tables,"[88] *Diagnostic Psychological Testing* introduced the idea of Deviant Verbalizations.[89] Rapaport was particularly interested in how "thought disorder" (disruption of thought processes and speech) manifested itself in the Rorschach responses of patients with schizophrenia. In their book, he and his colleagues identified twenty-five types of Deviant Verbalizations on the Rorschach that indicate the presence of thought disorder.

One type of Deviant Verbalization, "Contaminations," involved "the unrealistic fusion of two separate ideas or images"[90] from the same or adjacent areas of a blot. For instance, Card III contains a small red area that people sometimes identify as either "a spot of blood" or "an island."[91] One of Rapaport's patients with schizophrenia described this red spot as "this bloody little splotch here . . . bloody little island where they had so many revolutions."[92] This response was a Contamination because the patient had combined two normal responses ("blood" and "island") into a single unrealistic response (a "bloody island" with "revolutions").

"Peculiar Verbalizations" and "Queer Verbalizations" were two other categories identified by Rapaport and his colleagues. Peculiar Verbalizations are responses that sound strange but might conceivably make sense in certain contexts: "a cranial skull," "two legs raising each other." Queer Verbalizations are responses that "would sound strange in any context," such as "the echo of a picture," "a split color," or "an artistic design of a fly's boot."[93]

As one might surmise from these examples, if a patient gives a substantial number of Deviant Verbalizations, there's reason to suspect abnormal thought and speech processes. Research has shown that even though normal individuals typically give a few Deviant Verbalizations, patients with schizophrenia tend to give substantially more.[94] Furthermore, certain Deviant Verbalizations (such as Contaminations) are a particularly bad sign, as they occur very rarely, except in the Rorschach protocols of patients with schizophrenia and similar psychotic conditions.[95]

Rapaport's approach to Deviant Verbalizations has formed the basis for all subsequent attempts to measure thought disorder using the Rorschach. The most successful application of his ideas is the Thought Disorder Index, a complicated scoring system developed by Philip Holzman of Harvard and his colleagues, which is still used by researchers who study the causes and nature of schizophrenia.[96] John Exner's Comprehensive System for the Rorschach also contains a highly simplified thought disorder index, "*WSum6*," based on Rapaport's ideas.[97] Another recently developed scale of this type is the "TETRAUT" of Edwin Wagner ("TETRAUT" is an abbreviation, based on Greek, for "four autisms").[98]

Although Rapaport's work on thought disorder constituted his major contribution to the Rorschach, he also exerted an *indirect* influence on the test through his students. It's sometimes said that the true importance of a scientist should be gauged not by his own work, but by the work of his graduate students. According to this criterion, Rapaport is by far the most influential psychologist in the Rorschach's history.

David Rapaport was an irritable, authoritarian teacher with a reputation for terrorizing students.[99] When asked why he liked to frighten his protégés, he said, "Learning occurs in a setting of anxiety. . . . If there is no anxiety, there is no learning."[100] Despite his unorthodox teaching philosophy, an exceptionally large number of Rapaport's graduate students went on to become prominent researchers and theoreticians, including Philip Holzman of Harvard, Sidney Blatt of Yale, Robert Holt of New York University, Lester Luborsky of the University of Pennsylvania, Martin Mayman of the University of Michigan, and Roy Schafer (author of an influential book on the psychoanalytic interpretation of the Rorschach).[101] Speaking on behalf of many members of this illustrious group, Robert Holt wrote in tribute: "To have been Rapaport's student was an experience on which most people look back with strong ambivalence, yet gratitude. He made endless demands on students, but never more than the demands on himself."[102]

Ewald Bohm and the European Rorschach Tradition

Any list of major Rorschach figures in the 1950s has to include the Danish-Swiss psychologist Ewald Bohm.[103] Bohm's writings became influential among European users of the test, although U.S. psychologists have disregarded him for some of the same reasons they neglected Piotrowski. Bohm's most important book wasn't published in the United States until 1958 (only a year after *Perceptanalysis*). By then American Rorschachers had already formed a two-party system based on Beck and Klopfer, so there was little chance that either Bohm's or Piotrowski's work would be widely accepted.

Bohm's book was close in spirit to Samuel Beck's work, and in fact was translated into English by Beck and his wife Anne.[104] Like Beck, Bohm had a deep respect for Rorschach and tried to remain faithful to his ideas, introducing relatively few changes and additions.

Rorschach's *Psychodiagnostics* was a compressed, disjointed book and its prose was sometimes difficult to understand. Bohm's special contribution was to take Rorschach's ideas and present them in a clearer, more systematic format. Perhaps because he shared a European intellectual background with Rorschach, Bohm was able to explain his ideas in a particularly illuminating way. Besides providing a lucid and faithful rendition of Rorschach's thought, Bohm helpfully explained the nitty-gritty details of test administration and scoring that had been skimmed over in Rorschach's book.

Although we don't have room for a detailed description of Bohm's work, we'll take a moment to discuss his ideas about "shock," which illustrate the strengths and weaknesses of the European Rorschach tradition that he exemplified. As we discussed in Chapter Two, Rorschach reported that some patients acted strangely when presented with the five colored inkblots, a phenomenon he called "Color Shock."

After Rorschach's death, his European followers elaborated the concept of shock. For example, Marguerite Loosli-Usteri of France used the term "Kinesthetic Shock"[105] to describe the behavior of patients who seemed to have special difficulty giving *M* responses. Kinesthetic Shock was thought to indicate a blockage in mental processes that involved movement and to be characteristic of patients who were "stiff" or overly tense. Similarly, Hans Binder of Switzerland introduced "Dark Shock," which was similar to Color Shock but manifested itself in response to the darker blots, particularly Card IV, and supposedly indicated "anxiety about anxiety" (worrying that one might become anxious).[106]

Bohm's book thoughtfully discussed the ideas of Loosli-Usteri and Binder, then elaborated on other kinds of shock, including "Red Shock," "Blue Shock," "Brown Shock," and "White Shock."[107] Although his lengthy reflections on the topic were scholarly and intelligent, they lacked a solid foundation in scientific research.

Bohm's book, and his treatment of shock in particular, exemplified a European scholarly approach to psychological testing that was quite different from the American psychometric tradition. As a scholar in this tradition, Bohm showed a penetrating understanding of Rorschach's ideas, a knowledge of basic psychological findings that bore on the inkblot test (for instance, in the field of perception), a detailed knowledge of what other scholars such as Loosli-Usteri and Binder had written, and an outstanding ability to synthesize these sources and formulate new hypotheses.

What Bohm lacked, however, was the tough-minded attitude of the psychometric tradition, which demanded objective evidence of a test's reliability and validity. Bohm believed in Color Shock because it had been reported by a respected authority (Rorschach). Similarly, he accepted Kinesthetic Shock and Dark Shock because they were elaborations of the already accepted idea of Color Shock, had been vouched for by the respected authorities Loosli-Usteri and Binder, and had been generally accepted by psychologists who used the inkblot test. In short, he was guided mainly by tradition and the consensus of learned experts.

In the American psychometric tradition, which had arisen during the disasters of intelligence testing in the 1910s and 1920s, consensus among experts wasn't sufficient to establish a test's value. However, European psychology had a different history, tradition, and set of standards. Bohm's scholarly book represented the best in that tradition.

It would be a mistake, though, to conclude that psychologists on the European and American sides of the Atlantic held diametrically opposed ideas about the Rorschach. Although American psychometric ideas didn't exert much influence on Bohm or other European users of the Rorschach, influence had spread in the opposite direction, so that leading American Rorschachers showed definite European leanings. In the concluding section of this chapter, we'll discuss the later years of Samuel Beck and Bruno Klopfer.

GRAYING PIONEERS: BECK AND KLOPFER

By the 1950s, Samuel Beck and Bruno Klopfer had become revered figures in clinical psychology. Their textbooks introduced a generation of graduate students to the Rorschach. Although not always in agreement, their ideas about the test were widely regarded as authoritative.

Samuel Beck After 1940

After a brief period at Harvard University, Samuel Beck settled in Chicago, where he headed the Psychology Laboratory at Michael Reese Hospital and served on the faculty of the University of Chicago. As we've already mentioned, he published the three-volume *Rorschach's Test* in the 1940s and early 1950s, which was reissued in a new edition in the 1960s. Dense and sometimes ponderous, *Rorschach's Test* wasn't particularly appealing as a textbook, at least for beginning graduate students, although it was prized as a resource for advanced users of the test.

A gentle, scholarly man, Beck liked to quote from Shakespeare and other classics. Only one topic could consistently shatter his equanimity: Bruno Klopfer. Although a leading figure in the field of projective testing, Beck declined to join the Society for Projective Techniques (the new name of Klopfer's Rorschach Institute) until the early 1950s. Thereafter, although he sometimes attended the Society's meetings, he seems never to have had a kind word for Klopfer. In 1959 Beck wrote: "Except for the use of Rorschach's inkblot figures and some of his letter symbols, the [Klopfer] technique has now so little in common with Rorschach's test . . . that it represents a quite different approach. . . . It would go far toward clearing up the present state of confusion if Klopfer and his associates ceased to identify their method by the term 'Rorschach.'"[108]

As this quote shows, Beck liked to emphasize that he, not Klopfer, remained true to "Rorschach's test" as it was originally conceived. Beck had a good point. For example, if one compares the books of Beck, Bohm, and Klopfer with Rorschach's *Psychodiagnostics,* it's clear that Beck and Bohm lie solidly within a European tradition that adhered closely to Rorschach's ideas (with some cautious elaborations such as Kinesthetic Shock), whereas Klopfer took off in several new directions.

Beck was justified in identifying himself as more orthodox than Klopfer. Nevertheless, it was probably a bad sign that he placed so much emphasis on fidelity to Rorschach's concepts. Although religious leaders and theologians routinely support their ideas by referring to the words of Jesus, Luther, or Mohammed, the "argument from authority" doesn't carry much weight among scientists. Scientific knowledge grows and changes with time, so that the ideas of even great scientists like Newton are often modified or replaced in light of new evidence.

In his clash with Klopfer in the 1930s, Beck supported his position by appealing to authority (Rorschach) and science (the psychometric tradition). In the 1940s and 1950s, however, Beck gradually drifted away from psychometrics. Although he continued to carry out research, Beck began, like his arch-rival Klopfer, to minimize negative findings if they contradicted the "clinical validity" of the Rorschach.[109] Furthermore, adopting Klopfer's position that the Rorschach was too complicated to be evaluated by standard research methods, Beck asserted: "Let it be said at once and unequivocally that validation such as is sought in a laboratory experiment is not at present to be expected for whole personality findings, whether by the Rorschach test or by any other. The measure of validity must be limited to indicating a *direction*. It cannot be a number such as a correlation or other coefficient."[110]

Some of Beck's contemporaries viewed this transformation with dismay. Donald Super disapprovingly noted Beck's tendency to appeal to authority rather than research: "There is no hesitancy, it seems, in accepting . . . [an] opinion of Rorschach's as evidence, despite a quarter-century of subsequent work with the inkblots, without citing evidence on the point."[111]

Similarly, Lee J. Cronbach commented unfavorably on Beck's failure to come to grips with negative research findings: "We find Beck turning his back on research evidence in the way that is too common in the literature and in the conversation of clinicians, by saying, in effect, 'Evidence or no evidence, these propositions have clinical validity.'"[112]

Beck's New Rorschach Scores

Throughout his career Samuel Beck strove to keep faith with the legacy of Rorschach. However, he cautiously introduced a few innovations, new test scores that he hoped were reasonable extensions of "the Master's" insights. Because these scores are still used today in the popular Comprehensive System for the Rorschach, we'll take a moment to describe a few of them.

ORGANIZATION ACTIVITY (Z)   Rorschach had noticed that some responses to the cards incorporate the entire inkblot into a single image. He called these "Whole" or "W" responses, and speculated that they are a sign of intelligence, because they indicate that the person can organize disparate pieces of information into one concept.

Taking Rorschach's insight about *W* as a starting point, Beck developed a numerical score "*Z*" (for "Organization") to indicate the level of organization in every inkblot response.[113] For example, Card V contains a simple black blot that many people describe as "a bat." Because "bat" responses to Card V don't require much organizational effort, they receive a low *Z* score.[114] In contrast, Card X consists of a large number of colored splotches arranged in a complicated pattern. Only a few people see these splotches as a single, unified scene. If they do, they receive a high *Z* score.

When a patient has finished taking the Rorschach, the *Z*s for all responses can be added together to yield "*Z sum.*"[115] Beck viewed this score as "an index of the intellectual energy as such . . . and the intelligence functioning per se."[116] Research findings have generally confirmed that *Z sum* is related to intelligence.[117]

TEXTURE RESPONSES   In the 1930s, Bruno Klopfer introduced several new Shading scores that went far beyond Rorschach's ideas. Beck's refusal to accept these innovations had contributed to his schism with Klopfer (see Chapter Three).

Rorschachers therefore raised their collective eyebrows when in 1949 Beck publicly made a partial about-face and adopted one of Klopfer's Shading categories, which was called "Texture." Texture is scored for Shading responses that depend on the sense of touch. For instance, one of the Rorschach blots resembles a bearskin rug. People sometimes stroke their fingers across it, remarking how it appears to be fur. Beck admitted that he hadn't conducted any research on Texture responses, but speculated that they reflect "erotic needs" that have been "unsatisfied" during childhood.[118]

EXPERIENCE ACTUAL (*EA*)   Finally we come to the Rorschach score that, in Beck's opinion, marked the culmination of the test's development and a major advance in Western culture. As we discussed in Chapter Two, the three central scores in Rorschach's test were *M* (Human Movement), *WSumC* (the sum of Color Responses), and *EB* (the ratio of *M* and *WSumC*). For decades, Beck had been content to follow in Rorschach's revered footsteps. However, in a 1960 chapter titled "Experience Actual," Beck unexpectedly claimed to have discovered a score even more important than *EB*.[119]

The chapter was unusual, if not unique, in the history of American testing. Taking excursions into phenomenological philosophy, Beck carefully prepared readers for a great revelation. Finally he unveiled his insight. Rorschach had computed *EB* by taking the ratio of *M* to *WSumC*. However, Beck had reached the profound realization that *M* and *WSumC* should be *added*. Their sum, which he termed the "Experience Actual" or "*EA*," supposedly revealed depths of the personality only hinted at by *EB*. "The essential fact is that the experience actual—and hence my new symbol, *EA*—reflects the inner state in the subject's present mental phase—the inner state as total psychological vitality, whether exerting pressure outwardly or converted into dream living."[120]

Beck left no doubt that *EA* represented a momentous step forward in human understanding and a resolution of the existential riddle presented by the *Ding an Sich* (the ultimate reality of things themselves) of philosopher Immanuel Kant: "By means of the total *Erlebnistypus*—the Experience Actual—the test sounds the depth experience, the inner, emotionally most intense mental life of the other. The test thus makes the bold effort of crossing the Kantian chasm to the *Ding an Sich*."[121]

As readers familiar with philosophy will recognize, Beck's claim to have traversed "the Kantian chasm to the *Ding an Sich*" was utterly preposterous, like a claim to have invented a perpetual motion machine. However, for psychologists there has always been a more mundane issue: What exactly did Beck mean? He seems to have been saying that *EA* was a pure measure of what some thinkers have called "psychic energy" or "vital force." *EA* was subsequently imported by John Exner into the Comprehensive System, where it still plays a central role in Rorschach interpretations. However, there has never been any compelling evidence for Beck's mystical claim that *EA* represents the "total psychological vitality" of the individual.[122] In fact, it's difficult to imagine how such a claim could even be tested.

Bruno Klopfer After 1940

The 1940s and 1950s were good years for Samuel Beck but perhaps even better for his old foe Bruno Klopfer, who rose rapidly to prominence in the new, expanding profession of clinical psychology. Klopfer's textbook *The Rorschach Technique*, coauthored with Douglas Kelley, was published in two editions and adopted by clinical psychology programs across the country. After teaching a few years at

Figure 5.1.   Bruno Klopfer, Circa 1959.
The great publicist and "super-salesman" of the Rorschach in the
United States, he founded the Society for Personality Assessment
and the *Journal of Personality Assessment.*
Source: Bruno Klopfer Biological File, UCLA University Archives,
Los Angeles, California. Used by permission.

Teachers College of Columbia University, Klopfer moved in 1947 to
the University of California at Los Angeles (UCLA), where he became
a clinical professor of psychology.[123]

As the title "clinical professor" indicated, Klopfer's main duties were
to train graduate students and supervise their clinical work, rather

than to conduct research and publish articles. His arrival at UCLA coincided with the postwar boom in clinical psychology, when federal dollars were pouring in and graduate programs expanding. There was a nationwide shortage of psychology professors with sufficient clinical background to staff the new programs. With his twenty-five years of clinical experience, Klopfer was a rarity.

Klopfer set out "to help his students develop clinical and intuitive ability."[124] In seminars at UCLA he demonstrated his legendary ability to extract amazing insights from the Rorschach.[125] Klopfer's vision had been impaired since childhood, so when interpreting the Rorschach he sometimes had to hold the cards close to his eyes to see them clearly. It was rumored that he was actually *smelling* the cards to extract insights.[126]

Klopfer remained editor of the *Journal of Projective Techniques* until 1971 (a total of thirty-six years), although he seems to have delegated the everyday business of running the journal to a series of executive editors. From the mid-1950s through the early 1970s he published an updated version of his popular Rorschach text from the 1940s and a three-volume set entitled *Developments in the Rorschach Technique*.[127] His interests led him into new areas. For example, he became intrigued with the idea that personality factors influence cancer, and reported that by using the Rorschach he could distinguish between patients with fast-growing and slow-growing tumors.[128]

A magical aura surrounded Klopfer, and his followers regarded him with a special awe that harkened back to the Rorschach cultism of the 1930s.[129] For example, in 1960, psychologist Pauline Vorhaus published a devotional history of Klopfer in the *Journal of Projective Techniques* that began: "This history of Bruno Klopfer is written more for those readers, present and future, who do not themselves know the man, than for those of us fortunate enough to call him friend or teacher. *We* do not need a history to 'know him.' But for those others, the question will arise, as it must always arise concerning great men of every period, what forces or influences in his life and in himself have shaped him into the particular kind of great man he turned out to be?"[130]

Thus, without the slightest trace of irony or humor, Vorhaus eulogized Klopfer as a "great man" whom future generations would be eager to understand. Her views were not unique. In 1966 the Society for Projective Techniques and Personality Assessment bestowed on Klopfer its highest honor, a prize named "The Great Man Award."[131]

Yet even as Klopfer received this crown, the gusts of a great storm could be heard howling outside the palace of projective tests. For nearly twenty years, psychological researchers—most of them devoted users of the test—had been finding that the Rorschach didn't live up to the expansive promises that had been made for it. By the mid-1950s, some of the Rorschach's most prominent friends had become its sharpest critics. And by 1966, when Klopfer received his award, the crisis had become so dire that even the test's defenders were coming close to conceding defeat. This is the story that we tell in the next two chapters.

CHAPTER SIX

Scientists Look at the Rorschach

Widespread use of the Rorschach has resulted in a clinical validity that is not always substantiated by statistical validity. The literature on validation highlights a few seemingly "positive" findings in a context of many apparently "negative" findings and contradictory results.

—Bruno Klopfer, 1960, quoted in Klopfer and Davidson, The Rorschach Technique: An Introductory Manual, *1962*

T he Rorschach achieved amazing success in the decades following World War II. As clinical psychology's most popular test, it grew and flourished, a new profession's icon and emblem. Yet even as the Rorschach's clinical reputation soared, its scientific stock began to plummet.

In the late 1940s and early 1950s, many tough-minded psychologists took a tolerant view of the Rorschach. Although recognizing that scientific support for the test was weak, they respected the Rorschach's excellent reputation among clinicians and looked forward to the appearance of solid studies that would demonstrate its strengths. Typical was the attitude expressed by Florence Goodenough in her classic 1949 textbook, *Mental Testing*. Drawing an analogy from child development, Goodenough said that the Rorschach was ending one stage in its maturation and entering another: "It was perhaps natural enough that a large number of the studies made up to the present time have been exploratory rather than thoroughgoing. . . . But the Rorschach method has now reached a point of development where a more critical attitude is desirable. That it is capable of yielding information of considerable value for the study of the individual seems reasonably certain, but much winnowing is still needed to separate the wheat from the chaff."[1]

This tolerant, cautious optimism was shared by other leaders in the field of psychological testing. There was a burst of eager research. Journal articles and dissertations on the Rorschach multiplied, many of high quality.[2]

The results were unsettling. In study after study, the Rorschach failed to perform as expected. Despite some positive findings, a dismal picture began to predominate, so that by the mid-1950s former friends of the Rorschach were beginning to call the test a failure. During the ensuing years the research evidence would become only bleaker, reaching crisis proportions by the mid-1960s.

FAILURES OF GLOBAL INTERPRETATION

In the early 1940s, Bruno Klopfer and Marguerite Hertz had denigrated self-report questionnaires as "atomistic," comparing them unfavorably with the Rorschach, which supposedly offered a fuller picture of the "whole personality." In an elaboration of this idea, Klopfer claimed that Rorschach scores had to be interpreted as a "configuration" or "Gestalt," so that the meaning of each score was modified by others (see Chapter Three).

The configural approach championed by Klopfer came to be known as *global interpretation*. In a series of studies in the 1940s and 1950s his ideas were put to the test: Highly trained interpreters were given patients' Rorschachs and asked to make decisions based on global evaluations of the test results. Because the interpreters were given complete test protocols, they could interpret the meaning of each score in the context of other scores. Rorschach enthusiasts were confident that the outcome of these studies would reveal the test's extraordinary power.

Predicting Success in Pilot Training and Clinical Psychology Training

Not long after World War II, the first important Rorschach failures were reported in two widely read articles in the *American Psychologist*.

The first came from J. P. Guilford of the University of Southern California, one of psychology's best-known researchers. He described an extensive study that had used tests to predict the success of candidates in a pilot training program in the Army Air Force. According to Guilford, "it was regarded as very important that the Rorschach test should be given full opportunity to show what it had to offer in a personnel-selection setting." However, "the results were almost entirely negative."[3] Neither individual Rorschach variables nor the global judgment of the Rorschach examiner bore a statistically significant relationship to candidates' success in training.

Guilford further reported that the Rorschach had been given to approximately 150 hospitalized psychiatric patients, but that their scores were not significantly different from those of aviation students. He commented: "The fact that it failed to discriminate anxiety cases and psychoneurotics as a group from presumably normal individuals of about the same age and the same sex is noteworthy, to say the least."[4]

Finally, Guilford reported a finding that called into question the notion of global interpretation. Some test scores (from tests other than the Rorschach) had been able to predict the performance of the pilot trainees. In virtually every case, these scores had outperformed the predictions made by experts using the Rorschach: "Quite generally, it was found that intuitive judgments and predictions based upon them were quite inferior to objective scores in terms of correlation with training criteria."[5]

In other words, when experts used a global approach to the Rorschach, they were *less* accurate than if they simply used a few scores from other tests in an atomistic manner. Thus, not only did the Rorschach perform poorly, so did the global approach to test interpretation.

The second *American Psychologist* article bearing bad news for the Rorschach was by E. Lowell Kelly and Donald Fiske.[6] These researchers had carried out an ambitious project to determine which assessment techniques could predict the success of graduate students in clinical psychology programs.

In Kelly and Fiske's study, students entering graduate school were evaluated with an impressive battery of tests and assessment procedures, including the Miller Analogies Test (a measure of intellectual ability), the Rorschach, the TAT, "objective" personality tests (questionnaires), intensive interviews, and credential files listing the students' prior histories and accomplishments. The students were followed for several years after entering clinical psychology programs and their performance was rated by both their professors and clinical supervisors.

The results were clear: "The most efficient clinical predictions, in terms of both validity and economy of data, are those based only on the materials contained in the credential file and in the objective test profile."[7] In other words, the best prediction of students' performance came from the relatively inexpensive job histories, school records, and questionnaires. The most consistent test predictors of success turned out to be the Miller Analogies Test and a straightforward vocational questionnaire. Although a Sentence Completion test showed some promise, in general the Rorschach and other projective tests proved to be of no value for predicting students' classroom performance or their success as researchers or therapists.

The Rorschach's utter failure as a predictor of vocational success in these two studies was disconcerting. After all, the test's promoters had confidently touted it as an all-purpose measure of personality and urged its use in personnel selection (some still do).[8] Particularly embarrassing was its poor showing compared with more economical paper and pencil questionnaires. According to Bruno Klopfer, Lawrence Frank, and Marguerite Hertz, the Rorschach was supposed to represent a great improvement over "atomistic" questionnaires.

Identifying Psychological Problems and Diagnoses

Although the Rorschach had crashed and burned as a personnel selection tool, there remained the possibility that it would fare better as a psychodiagnostic test. After all, Rorschach had developed the test in a psychiatric setting and many of its scores were thought to reflect psychological disturbances.

But here too the news turned out to be discouraging. A major study was conducted at the University of Texas at Austin by Wayne Holtzman and S. B. Sells. Holtzman was a young researcher who had developed an enthusiasm for the Rorschach while a graduate student at Stanford. Funded by the Air Force, he and Sells collected data on a hundred aviation cadets. Half of the cadets had been highly successful in flight training school, whereas the other half had been eliminated from the program because they developed "overt personality disturbances."[9] Thus the Holtzman and Sells study, like the two we've already described, was concerned with job success. The difference was that these two Texas researchers focused on failures due to psychological maladjustment.[10]

Holtzman and Sells enlisted prominent psychologists to participate, including such leading Rorschach experts as Bruno Klopfer, Zygmunt Piotrowski, and Molly Harrower. Each of these experts was given a packet of background information and test results (including the Rorschach and other projective tests) for a group of twenty cadets. They were instructed to sort protocols into two categories: successful completion of program or failure to complete program due to psychological problems.

The results were sobering. Because each psychologist evaluated twenty test packets, the number of correct guesses expected by chance alone was 10.0. In fact, the average number of correct guesses achieved by the psychologists was 10.2—almost exactly what would be expected if the experts had sorted protocols by flipping a coin.[11] When the performance of individual psychologists was examined, the results were no better: "None of the psychologists was able to predict adjustment to training significantly better than chance with the global approach to test evaluation."[12] Holtzman found the results of this study so disappointing that he began to look for alternatives to the Rorschach—a story we'll tell in the next chapter.

Studies by other researchers yielded similar results. Richard Newton at the University of Pittsburgh examined the Rorschach's ability to identify maladjustment. He assembled case histories and Rorschach protocols from individuals in five diverse groups, including normal individuals, patients with neuroses, and patients with schizophrenia. He found that ratings of "adjustment" based on the Rorschach were not significantly related to patients' diagnoses or to ratings based on case histories.[13] In other words, when psychologists used the Rorschach globally, they rated normal individuals, patients with neuroses, and patients with schizophrenia as equally maladjusted.[14]

At the University of California at Berkeley, Marguerite Grant and her colleagues examined the validity of the Rorschach as a measure of maladjustment among adolescents who were randomly selected from the community at birth and followed in a longitudinal study.[15] Psychologists rated the adolescents for adjustment based on the Rorschach, whereas case workers made adjustment ratings based on extensive interviews conducted over a period of years. Grant and her colleagues found no significant relationship between the Rorschach ratings and the ratings based on interviews.

Guinevere Chambers and Roy Hamlin at the Western Psychiatric Institute and Clinic in Pittsburgh reported both good and bad news for the Rorschach. Psychologists were given Rorschach protocols from patients and asked to sort them into five diagnostic categories. The psychologists were able to perform this sorting task "better than chance." However, their success was due mainly to their ability to identify patients with severe mental deficiency. Otherwise, their accuracy was mediocre. Chambers and Hamlin concluded: "This degree of success is certainly not impressive enough to justify expansive claims for the value of the Rorschach as a technique in identifying patient groups."[16]

In a similar study by Stewart Armitage and David Pearl at the Battle Creek VA Hospital, experienced psychologists used the Rorschach to identify diagnoses of patients with schizophrenia, neuroses, or character disorders. The overall number of correct diagnostic judgments was not significantly above chance, although the psychologists exhibited modest success at differentiating patients with schizophrenia from the other two groups.[17]

Lloyd Silverman at New York University reported slightly better results. Clinical psychologists were given results from the Rorschach and other projective tests for several young criminals, and were asked to provide ratings for character traits, psychological defenses, interpersonal behavior, and other criteria. The accuracy of the psychologists' ratings was better than chance but low.[18]

The most influential study on global interpretation in the 1950s was a horse race among the Rorschach, TAT, and MMPI carried out by Kenneth Little of Stanford and Edwin Shneidman of the Los Angeles VA Neuropsychiatric Hospital. The editors of the *Journal of Projective Techniques* selected twelve Rorschach experts to participate, including such prominent figures as Zygmunt Piotrowski, Walter Klopfer (Bruno's son), and Bertram Forer (the journal's executive editor).[19] Experts on the TAT and MMPI also participated.

Little and Shneidman's report filled an entire issue of *Psychological Monographs*.[20] They found that *none* of the prominent personality tests of the day—the Rorschach, the TAT, or the MMPI—performed well on the tasks for which clinical psychologists commonly used them, such as making diagnoses or assessing personality. The performance of the twelve Rorschach experts was generally slightly worse than that of the TAT and MMPI experts.

Notably, Little and Shneidman found that the Rorschach experts in their study tended to see mental illness almost everywhere, even when it wasn't present. When asked to evaluate Rorschach protocols of normal individuals, Rorschach experts assigned them such labels as "passive dependent," "hysterical personality," and "schizoid character." *Not a single Rorschach expert correctly identified normal individuals as normal.* One patient was identified as schizophrenic by three out of four Rorschach experts, even though he was a psychiatrically normal IBM repairman who was in the hospital for a hernia operation.[21]

Although the MMPI generally performed poorly, it tended to do somewhat better than the Rorschach. For instance, when given the MMPI results of the same normal individuals evaluated by Rorschach experts, three out of twelve MMPI experts correctly identified the patients as normal, compared with none of twelve Rorschach experts. None of the MMPI experts misidentified a normal individual as psychotic, whereas four of twelve Rorschach experts made this mistake. When given the test results of patients with such psychotic disorders as schizophrenia, nine of twelve MMPI experts correctly diagnosed psychosis, compared with seven of twelve Rorschach experts.[22]

For most research-oriented psychologists, findings like these permanently dislodged the Rorschach's halo. By the late 1950s, many thoughtful observers concluded that the Rorschach was largely useless for detecting and diagnosing psychological disorders. Since the early 1940s, enthusiasts had talked about the test as though it was as powerful as an x-ray, uncanny as a crystal ball. But a steady stream of negative results showed that the Rorschach wasn't so special after all. If anything, it wasn't even as good as the humdrum MMPI.

Using the Rorschach with Other Information: Does It Add Anything Worthwhile?

By the late 1950s, research had shown that judgments based on the Rorschach had poor validity. However, there remained the possibility that the test might be more useful if combined with other sources of information. In fact, this is how the Rorschach is generally used in clinical practice. A psychologist may use the Rorschach to generate hypotheses, and then confirm or support these hypotheses by consulting other sources of information, such as case files, interview data, or other test results. Little and Shneidman mentioned this issue in their classic article.[23] Although these researchers had found low validity for the Rorschach, MMPI, and TAT, they noted that the results might have been different had the tests been presented together as part of a test battery.

To examine this possibility, several researchers in the late 1950s and 1960s conducted studies in which the Rorschach and the MMPI were used in combination with each other and with other sources of information. In this way, investigators were able to evaluate whether validity increased when the Rorschach was added to other data.

For example, in a 1959 study at the University of Minnesota, Lloyd Sines gave various combinations of clinical and test data to a group of diagnosticians. He found that when he provided diagnosticians with basic biographical information, then added information from an interview, the interview information improved the diagnosticians' ability to describe patients accurately.

However, contrary to what Sines had expected, when the diagnosticians had already been given the biographical and interview information, the addition of either the MMPI or the Rorschach failed to improve accuracy. In fact, the effect of making Rorschach results available was frequently—and paradoxically—to *decrease* diagnosticians' accuracy. The most accurate group of diagnosticians used biographical information, interviews, and the MMPI, but *not* the Rorschach.

Three important findings emerged from the work of Sines and similar studies.[24] First, research showed unequivocally that the most valuable source of information about a client—far more valuable than psychological tests—is the client's history. Thus, when trying to understand or diagnose a patient, clinical psychologists should always conduct a thorough interview and read the case file. In general, the more biographical information that can be collected, the better. This may not seem like an earth-shaking discovery unless we remember that the popular textbook by Bruno Klopfer and Douglas Kelley had taught that a case history was unnecessary for a highly skilled psychologist using the Rorschach.[25]

Second, although detailed and reliable biographical information is usually more useful than the MMPI for making diagnoses and evaluating clients' personalities, research showed that biographical information and the MMPI *together* are slightly better than biographical information *alone*. In other words, the MMPI adds a small amount of "incremental validity" above and beyond what can be obtained from biographical information and an interview.

Third and most relevant, research showed that when psychologists already have biographical and interview information, the addition of the Rorschach is unlikely to improve their ability to make diagnoses or evaluate clients' personalities. To the contrary, some studies (like the one by Sines) have found that psychologists tend to become *less* accurate with the addition of the Rorschach.

Despite such findings, many psychologists from the 1950s to the present have continued to rely heavily on the Rorschach, even when it conflicts with biographical information and MMPI results (for example, consider the psychologist who evaluated Rose Martelli, described in Chapter One). Such an approach is doubly backward—backward because it reverses the correct order and puts the weakest source of information first (the Rorschach), and backward because it's forty years behind the times and out of step with scientific evidence.

Positive Findings:
Diagnosing Psychosis and Estimating IQ

The research findings on the Rorschach weren't entirely negative. Studies showed that the test achieved limited success in identifying patients with psychoses, and impressive success in estimating intelligence. However, this good news failed to arouse much enthusiasm, for reasons we'll discuss.

IDENTIFICATION OF PSYCHOSES   In Little and Shneidman's famous study, Rorschach experts showed some ability to identify such psychotic disorders as schizophrenia. They assigned a diagnosis of "psychosis" to 58 percent of psychotic patients but only 17 percent of nonpsychotic patients. The Rorschach experts had done better than flipping a coin, although not as well as the MMPI.[26]

Subsequent studies confirmed that clinical psychologists interpreting a Rorschach can perform somewhat better than chance when trying to evaluate whether a patient is psychotic.[27] However, the same is true for psychologists reading patients' answers on an intelligence test.[28] The irrational thinking and odd speech of psychotic patients can be detected in reasonably good excerpts of what they've said in response to any demanding verbal task, such as the Rorschach or an intelligence test.[29] For instance, when asked about the proverb, "The early bird gets the worm," a patient with schizophrenia might reply, "What you do depends on what time the worm wakes up. The worm has to wake up before you eat it."

Despite its above-chance performance, the Rorschach has never generated much excitement as a clinical test for schizophrenia, bipolar disorder, or other severe mental disturbances (useful as it can be as a research measure of psychosis or thought disorder, as we discuss elsewhere). Because psychotic disorders involve gross impairment of a patient's contact with reality, they usually aren't hard to identify. For example, patients with schizophrenia may hear voices that other people can't hear, or be convinced that the CIA is pursuing them. Thus in clinical practice a diagnosis of schizophrenia is usually established by an interview with the patient and conversations with the patient's family or friends. However, when it's not clear from an interview if a psychotic condition is present, psychological tests, including the Rorschach, can be helpful.

ESTIMATION OF INTELLIGENCE   The second Rorschach success story was more impressive and (for a while) more mysterious. During the 1950s several studies demonstrated that experts could estimate intelligence from the Rorschach with almost unbelievable accuracy. According to several dependable research reports, there was an astounding .70 correlation between experts' estimates of intelligence based on the Rorschach and patients' scores on such intelligence tests as the WAIS.[30]

The high accuracy of the experts was puzzling because several studies from the 1950s showed that individual Rorschach scores such as *M, R,* and *W* typically display only a low correlation ($r < .30$) with scores on intelligence tests.[31] How had the experts managed to make highly accurate predictions of intelligence based on such low correlations? Were the experts somehow combining the Rorschach variables in a way that boosted their predictive power?[32] This seemed unlikely. Several researchers tried this approach, by using a statistical rule to combine the most promising Rorschach variables into indexes of intelligence. However, such indexes weren't consistently accurate, and their performance was substantially inferior to what the experts were able to achieve.[33]

The clever solution to this scientific puzzle came from Hannah Davis at Columbia University and Thomas Trier at the University of

California at Berkeley.[34] These two young psychologists independently arrived at the same hypothesis: that the crucial factor was patients' *vocabulary*. Since the time of Binet, psychologists had known that vocabulary is an excellent predictor of intelligence test scores.

To test her hypothesis, Davis first asked psychologists to estimate the intelligence of teenagers and young adults from their Rorschachs. As in other studies, the experts' estimates correlated .70 with scores from an intelligence test.[35]

Davis then went a step further. She created a list of all the words that each subject had used while responding to the Rorschach cards. The word lists for each subject were given to a different group of psychologists, who were asked to estimate intelligence from the words alone. Their estimates correlated .71 with intelligence test scores!

Trier's study added two new twists. First, he gave the Rorschach protocols of patients to a group of clinicians and asked them to pick out the seven "most sophisticated" words. Then he gave these words to a second group of clinicians and asked them to estimate the patients' intelligence. The clinicians' estimates of intelligence, based on only seven words from each patient's Rorschach, correlated .74 with intelligence test scores.

Next Trier went to *The Teacher's Word Book of 30,000 Words,* which listed the frequency with which words are used in magazines, books, and other sources.[36] He calculated the average frequency of the "most sophisticated" words used by each patient. This rough measure of patients' vocabulary correlated .77 with intelligence test scores. The "word book" approach actually did slightly better than the expert clinicians!

Such findings were interesting but deflating. On the positive side, they confirmed, as Bruno Klopfer and others had contended for twenty years, that a skilled clinician could extract something important from the Rorschach, namely intelligence as indexed by vocabulary level. Less flattering was the discovery that the clinician didn't need to be a wizard to do so. One could do at least as well by circling the most sophisticated words in a Rorschach protocol and looking up their frequency in a book. Furthermore, it was disappointing that vocabulary level substantially outperformed such traditional Rorschach scores as *M, W,* and *F+%.*

The work of Davis and Trier has generally been ignored by Rorschach experts. Current books on the test don't even mention the strong correlation between Rorschach-based vocabulary and intelligence test scores.[37] Perhaps the findings have been ignored because they make the Rorschach seem less mysterious.

UNEXPECTED PROBLEMS COME TO LIGHT

In its early days, the Rorschach's outsider status worked to protect it. Because top-notch psychological researchers seldom paid it much attention in the early 1940s, the Rorschach hadn't been subjected to close scientific scrutiny. It had coasted to success in the postwar boom mainly on the basis of enthusiastic testimonials and a handful of (mainly second-rate) studies in the *Rorschach Research Exchange*.[38]

But the test's popularity in the late 1940s and early 1950s sowed the seeds of its undoing. Bruno Klopfer and his followers disparaged the psychometric approach and minimized the importance of research. However, when the Rorschach became psychology's most favored test, widespread research was inevitable. As energetic investigators from Yale to Stanford began churning out well-designed studies, unexpected problems came to light.

Overpathologizing: Making Nearly Everyone Look Sick

As early as 1950, a few shrewd observers such as Seymour Sarason and J. R. Wittenborn of Yale had warned that the supposedly infallible Rorschach could sometimes be wildly wrong, misidentifying healthy individuals as gravely disturbed or even psychotic.[39] At about the same time, Marguerite Hertz noted the tendency of many clinicians to see mental disturbance in normal Rorschachs: "Time and time again we see interpretations of adolescent records in which the interpreter stresses personality deviations and psychoneurotic disturbances, sometimes even more serious pathology. Yet these very matters may be seen as not abnormal when judged by the normative material available."[40]

Hertz, ever optimistic, seemed to believe that such lapses could be attributed to the carelessness of individual clinicians who failed to compare their results with tables of norms for relatively normal individuals. Only over the ensuing years did the full magnitude of the problem become evident. Research showed that the cases noted by Sarason, Wittenborn, and Hertz, far from being isolated, were examples of the Rorschach's general tendency to overpathologize normal people.

We've already mentioned the famous study by Little and Shneidman, in which Rorschach experts consistently misidentified normal individuals as seriously disturbed, with three of the four experts misdiagnosing a normal IBM repairman as schizophrenic. Other researchers also reported similar findings.

For example, Ann Lawler Brockway and her colleagues at Washington University in St. Louis studied a group of "adjusted" normal men and found that many of their Rorschach scores fell into the "maladjusted" range. Similarly, Marguerite Grant and her colleagues at the University of California at Berkeley found that Rorschach experts diagnosed "maladjustment" in two-thirds of adolescents randomly sampled from the community[41]—an implausible figure because, contrary to common stereotypes, adolescence is not a period of marked emotional disturbance for most individuals.[42]

At the University of Chicago, William F. Soskin demonstrated the biasing effects of the Rorschach.[43] Soskin gave psychologists true-life biographical information about a relatively normal man called "David."[44] The psychologists were told about twenty-five different psychologically revealing situations in David's life and asked to guess how he reacted to each one. After the psychologists indicated their answers, Soskin gave them David's Rorschach. Again they were asked to guess how David reacted to the twenty-five situations.

Soskin actually knew how David reacted to the various situations and so could rate the psychologists' predictions for accuracy. He found that the psychologists became slightly *less* accurate about David after they saw his Rorschach. More important, the Rorschach substantially biased their guesses in a negative direction, so that they began to "err quite consistently in the direction of overestimating the degree of maladjustment."[45] In other words, clinical psychologists who examined David's Rorschach tended to see him less accurately and as much sicker than he really was.[46]

Such findings had serious implications, because they strongly suggested that clinical psychologists who used the Rorschach were overperceiving psychopathology. However, such Rorschach leaders as Klopfer and Beck disregarded the problem, and most clinical psychologists followed suit. Although the meaning of these findings was clear by 1960, clinical practitioners generally ignored them. A witty

1973 article, *Alice in Rorschachland*, lampooned Rorschach practitioners "who search only for pathology, not for health."[47] Although the article occasioned some laughter, there's no evidence that it affected how psychologists used the test.

Ironically, the Rorschach's tendency to overpathologize may have helped to persuade clinicians of its great value. A test that labels most people as sick—even on an arbitrary basis—will often be correct *in clinical settings.*

For example, suppose that a test arbitrarily labels 75 percent of patients as either depressed, troubled in their interpersonal relationships, or both. Such results, though arbitrary, will usually be accurate, because most patients seen by clinicians are depressed or have troubled relationships. The test may seem uncannily sensitive. Of course, if clinicians were to administer the test to a large group of healthy adults, they would find (as Rorschach researchers did in the 1950s) that the test also arbitrarily identifies most *normal* individuals as maladjusted. But clinicians seldom assess healthy adults as part of their daily work.

Thus even an arbitrary test that makes nearly everyone appear disturbed can appear impressively sensitive, deceiving clinicians who base their opinions on firsthand observation. There seem to be two possible remedies for this "overpathologizing illusion." First, clinicians can rely on published research from well-controlled studies, rather than on personal experience, when evaluating the validity of test scores. But of course, that's precisely what Bruno Klopfer and other experts persuaded psychologists *not* to do with the Rorschach.

Another, more "clinical" remedy was first suggested by David Shakow and his colleagues, in a 1947 report on clinical training that laid the groundwork for the famous Boulder Conference (see Chapter Four). The famous "Shakow report" recommended that students in clinical psychology should work with both normal and abnormal individuals: "We have just made the point that the student should have contact with clinical material throughout the four years of training. *Equally important* is the need for contact with normal material. Opportunities should be provided to enable the student to become acquainted with the range of normal and borderline persons who never establish clinical contacts. *Such training is essential in order to keep the student balanced in his interpretation and understanding of the abnormal*" (emphases added).[48]

The Problem of *R*

Of all the scores introduced by Rorschach in *Psychodiagnostics,* none would appear to be less interesting than *R*—the total number of responses that a patient gives to the inkblots. Not surprisingly, *R* bears a modest correlation with intelligence test scores, is lower in people with developmental disabilities than in people with normal intelligence, and is not quite as high among grade school children as in older children. In short, people with higher mental abilities report more images in the inkblots than individuals with lower abilities. Other than that, *R* bears little if any relation to personality or psychological disorders.

Yet as researchers found in the 1950s, the drab and unassuming *R* is the power lurking behind the Rorschach throne, the unnoticed figure in the background that influences nearly everything else about the test. The reason is that as patients give more responses to the inkblots, *R* goes up *and so do most other scores on the test.*

The classic article on the problem, "Relationships Between Rorschach Scoring Categories and the Total Number of Responses," was published in 1953 by Donald Fiske of the University of Chicago and E. Earl Baughman, then at the University of Wisconsin.[49] Fiske and Baughman collected 633 Rorschach protocols and examined the relationship of *R* to the thirty most important Rorschach variables. The results, laid out in easy-to-read tables, were devastating: More than 60 percent of Rorschach variables had correlations over .30 with *R,* and several had correlations over .50.

R is the ocean, and other Rorschach variables the boats that rise and fall on its tides. The influence of *R* creates serious problems. For example, since the time of Rorschach, Space responses have been interpreted as an indication of oppositionality or stubbornness. However, Fiske and Baughman's tables showed that patients who give more responses to the test are substantially more likely to give Space responses. Patients with fewer than twenty responses to the test gave an average of one Space response, patients with twenty to thirty responses gave about two Space responses, and patients with thirty-five or more responses gave about three Space responses. Thus the very patients who are most cooperative with the test (by giving more responses) are, paradoxically, those most likely to be identified as oppositional and stubborn.

It may seem that "the problem of *R*" could easily be solved by dividing each Rorschach score by the total number of responses. However,

Fiske and Baughman showed that dividing by R doesn't work well and can create problems of its own.[50]

Fiske and Baughman instead proposed that researchers develop new inkblot tests based on the Rorschach. With these tests, the same number of responses would be collected from each patient to avoid the problem of R. In fact, this idea was eventually pursued by Wayne Holtzman at the University of Texas. However, most clinical psychologists continued to use the Rorschach just as they always had. They either ignored the problem of R or optimistically assumed that they could somehow adjust their interpretation of Rorschach scores in their heads to take R into account.

"The Rorschach Is an Interpersonal Situation"

In the late 1930s and early 1940s, Bruno Klopfer and his colleagues enthusiastically embraced the "projective hypothesis" of psychologist Lawrence Frank (see Chapter Three). Frank had criticized personality questionnaires because, he claimed, they simply measure conformity to society's expectations. An individual taking a questionnaire feels pressured to conform and answer in ways that seem socially appropriate, Frank said: "When we ask an individual to tell what he believes or feels or to indicate in which categories he belongs, this social pressure to conform to the group norms operates to bias what he will say and presses him to fit himself into the categories of the inventory or questionnaire."[51]

The great virtue of projective tests, Frank contended, is that they bypass the problem of conformity by eliminating social pressure from the testing situation. When shown an inkblot or ambiguous picture, respondents have no preconceptions about how they're supposed to perform. Free from social expectations, they will reveal their own "private world" of personal meanings and feelings.[52]

Frank's first contention—that people occasionally distort their answers on questionnaires to appear socially desirable—has been repeatedly confirmed by research since the 1940s. For example, some clients underreport their symptoms on the MMPI. However, Frank's second proposition—that projective tests can somehow bypass social pressures and magically reveal an individual's untainted private world—turned out to be a naive fantasy. As research in the 1950s showed, projective test scores are probably even more susceptible to social influence and distortion than are questionnaires.

In a classic 1960 article, Joseph Masling of Syracuse University reviewed an extensive scientific literature and concluded, "the studies cited here presented strong evidence of situational and interpersonal influences in projective testing."[53] Studies showed that individuals taking the Rorschach and other projective tests can "fake good" and "fake bad," just as with self-report questionnaires. Furthermore, Rorschach scores can change substantially depending on the purpose of the testing, the instructions given to the person taking the test, and the examiner's personality. Some of the most striking findings were as follows:

- People change their scores on the Rorschach, depending on the reason they're being tested. For example, people are likely to alter their responses to the test and be more careful in what they say if they believe they're being evaluated for a "serious emotional disturbance."[54]

- If an examiner provides subtle reinforcement by nodding after each Rorschach response or saying "good," the person will tend to produce more responses. For example, the examiner may unconsciously be encouraging a client to feel comfortable and give more responses. Because the number of responses (R) affects many other scores, the overall effect of such reinforcement can be substantial.[55]

- If an examiner provides reinforcement after a particular type of response (for example, a Human Movement response), the person will tend to produce more responses in that category.[56]

- Different examiners can consistently elicit different kinds of Rorschach responses. Thus, if two examiners both give the Rorschach to the same individual, the results may be different. Such differences can't necessarily be eliminated by instructing examiners to follow the same standardized testing procedures.[57]

- Friendly examiners often elicit more responses and more normal-looking Rorschach scores than do unfriendly or distant examiners. In other words, Rorschach scores can reflect the personality of both examiner and respondent.[58]

Frank had claimed that projective techniques are immune to the effects of social influence, but research showed just the opposite. Because the Rorschach and other projective tests are administered one-on-one, the opportunities for suggestiveness and social influence are, if anything, more substantial than with questionnaires. For clinicians who used the Rorschach in daily practice, these findings had disquieting implications. As Walter Klopfer warned his colleagues: "It seems that anyone experienced with the administration of the Rorschach test must surely concede . . . that the subject can be greatly influenced by the examiner. Manifesting great interest in responses . . . can certainly increase their number and their 'richness.' On the other hand, an examiner in a hurry certainly can reduce the length of the protocol and the number of details provided. The Rorschach is an interpersonal situation."[59]

Color Shock

The idea that Color responses reflect emotion and impulsivity originated with Hermann Rorschach (see Chapter Two). In the absence of good scientific evidence, he pointed to common figures of speech as support for this idea ("Everything looks black to me"). Not surprisingly, subsequent research failed to confirm his conjecture. For example, researchers found that delinquents and other impulsive individuals don't produce a high number of Color responses.[60]

Rorschach's closely related ideas about Color Shock proved popular among his followers. Color Shock is supposed to occur when a patient reacts strangely to a card that contains color. As Samuel Beck explained: "[Rorschach] observed that the color figures presented to the Subject at certain positions in the series produce a startle. It manifests itself by momentarily misshaping the subject's reaction pattern, most obviously in the intellectual sphere, but with effect also on the creativity activity and in the affective experience. . . . It is a phenomenon of neurosis and is therefore in reality neurotic shock."[61]

Although European theorists later identified a variety of other kinds of shock involving specific colors, as described in the discussion of Ewald Bohm's work in Chapter Five, Samuel Beck and Bruno Klopfer emphasized only two: Color Shock and Shading Shock.[62] Beck, in his characteristically systematic way, developed fourteen objective scoring rules for Color Shock. For example, in Beck's system patients' responses to the cards were timed with a watch to see if they took longer to react to the colored than black-and-white cards.

The idea of Color Shock began to crumble, however, following a classic study by Richard Lazarus, then a graduate student at Johns

Hopkins University. Lazarus gave the Rorschach to high school students on two different occasions. On one occasion the students were shown slides of the Rorschach cards in full color, on the other they were shown gray-and-white versions. Lazarus found that the students showed an equal amount of Color Shock for both sets of cards. In other words, Color Shock occurred even if the cards were gray and white! Lazarus concluded that "color played a minimal role, if any, in producing the 'color shock' indices."[63]

During the 1950s, the implications of Lazarus's discovery were verified by other researchers.[64] Particularly influential was a series of elegant studies by E. Earl Baughman, the same researcher who collaborated with Donald Fiske in the classic study of R we've already described. Baughman tested hundreds of subjects with Rorschach cards that had been modified in unusual ways.[65] For example, like Lazarus, he used one set of cards that was entirely gray, black, and white. Another set showed the outlines of the cards, but without any shading or color.

Baughman's findings overwhelmingly confirmed what Lazarus had found: "Color Shock" had nothing to do with color. Patients showed the classic signs of Color Shock regardless of whether the cards were colored or gray and white.[66] Rorschach's hypothesis about shock—that the color of the blots activates emotion and disrupts thought—was apparently in error.

In *Psychodiagnostics* Rorschach specifically cited Color Shock as evidence that his hypothesis about color was correct. Color Shock, he claimed, "reaffirms the internal relationship which must exist between color perception and the dynamics of affectivity."[67] However, when the notion of Color Shock was discredited in the 1950s, the leading Rorschach advocates showed little inclination to alter their allegiance to Rorschach's color hypotheses. In a new version of *Rorschach's Test* in the late 1960s, Samuel Beck staunchly reaffirmed his belief that Color Shock, when present, is a virtually infallible indicator of neurosis.[68]

Seemingly Positive Findings

From the late 1940s through the 1960s, hordes of eager researchers tramped back and forth over the Rorschach landscape like prospectors in newly discovered gold fields. Besides the highly visible studies already discussed, hundreds of smaller studies examined the validity of individual Rorschach variables.

By the 1960s, the picture emerging from this energetic activity had become clear, even to the test's strongest proponents. Bruno Klopfer acknowledged that researchers reported many negative and contradictory results, but only "a few seemingly positive findings."[69]

In his allusion to "a few seemingly positive findings," Klopfer was probably referring to three indisputable facts about the Rorschach that had been established by dozens of studies. First, as mentioned earlier, many Rorschach variables bear a consistent though modest relationship to intelligence. These include several traditional scores introduced by Rorschach (*M, R, P, W,* and *F+%*), as well as a few variables developed by later innovators (such as "developmental level" and "organizational activity").[70]

The second consistent finding was that a few Rorschach variables (especially *F+%* and Deviant Verbalizations) are related to schizophrenia and other psychotic disorders.[71] The third finding was that children's scores on the Rorschach differ from those of adults and change as children grow older.[72]

A few isolated Rorschach indexes also made a good showing in the 1950s and 1960s. Zygmunt Piotrowski's signs of organic brain damage received support in several studies.[73] Bruno Klopfer had developed a complex index, the Rorschach Prognostic Rating Scale, which was moderately successful at identifying patients who benefited from psychotherapy.[74]

Somewhat disconcertingly for Rorschach traditionalists, two indexes based on thematic "content" also performed well. In 1949, Abraham Elizur introduced a scale to measure hostile Rorschach responses ("animals fighting," "people arguing"), and a second scale to measure anxious responses ("a frightening giant," "a person hanging over a cliff").[75] Research showed that scores on the Elizur Hostility scale were modestly related to violent behavior, and that scores on the Anxiety scale were related to patients' anxiety as rated by themselves and others.[76]

A few other interesting findings about the Rorschach emerged, but almost nothing that was solidly established.[77] For example, as we discussed in Chapter Two, studies by Jerome Singer of Yale suggested that Human Movement responses (*M*) are related to physical activity, and he speculated that *M* is more generally related to inhibition.[78] However, this intriguing idea wasn't explored in depth by other researchers or shown to relate to important everyday behaviors and personality traits. As Leonard Eron, a well-informed if critical commentator on the test, dryly commented: "There is some slight evidence that human movement responses are an index to cognitive inhibition and the ability to inhibit motility, although even these minimal claims have not uniformly been replicated."[79]

So it was with most other Rorschach variables. Research results were often negative or (to echo Samuel Beck's words) "chaotic and confusing."[80] Writing in the respected *Mental Measurements Yearbook* in 1965, Eron tersely summed up twenty years of Rorschach research: "The monotonous overall conclusions have been that there is little evidence to support the claims made for the technique by its proponents. The results of research published subsequent to the last edition of the yearbook have not perceptibly altered this grim picture of the reliability and validity of the Rorschach procedure."[81]

Because of the negative findings reported by researchers, it was inevitable that psychologists who used the Rorschach would soon be faced with a crisis.

CHAPTER SEVEN

The Rorschach in Crisis

The rate of scientific progress in clinical psychology might well be measured by the speed and thoroughness with which it gets over the Rorschach.

—*Arthur Jensen, "Review of the Rorschach Inkblot Test," 1965*

B y the late 1950s, many thoughtful psychologists had come to realize that they'd been led on a twenty-year-long wild goose chase. Not only had the Rorschach failed to live up to its lofty reputation, there was disturbing evidence that it tended to misidentify normal individuals as maladjusted, even psychotic.

How could psychologists have been so wrong about the Rorschach for so long? Where had they been misled? These questions were puzzling. Only gradually did the answers become clear. In the heady years after World War II, when their profession mushroomed into prominence, clinical psychologists had naively accepted a whole set of plausible notions that on closer inspection turned out to be wrong.

In the early 1940s, Bruno Klopfer and his colleagues cobbled together a set of interlocking ideas that provided an intellectual framework for the Rorschach and other projective tests (see Chapter Three). Klopfer proposed that the Rorschach's value had been established by "clinical validation" instead of objective studies, that virtuosos could extract remarkable information from the test based on their extensive clinical insight, and that the test's seemingly marvelous properties could be explained by the "projective hypothesis." These ideas had become so widespread that many clinical psychologists in the 1950s had come to regard them as common sense.

Starting in the 1950s, however, a few doubters began to subject these preconceptions to closer scrutiny. We've already discussed how the projective hypothesis was undercut when research demonstrated the Rorschach's susceptibility to situational influences, including the style of the test administrator.

The idea of clinical validation and the seemingly amazing performances of Rorschach wizards were also subjected to the hard-headed scrutiny that has been the greatest strength of American psychologists. In the following sections we'll explain why and how the theoretical edifice erected by Bruno Klopfer and his colleagues in the 1940s eventually collapsed under the accumulating weight of scientific evidence. Then we'll describe the onslaught against the Rorschach by its critics and even some of its friends during the late 1950s and early 1960s.

THE ILLUSION OF CLINICAL VALIDATION

As we've already noted, Bruno Klopfer asserted that the Rorschach's value could be demonstrated by the procedure he called "clinical validation." According to Klopfer, a clinician could conduct a blind analysis of a patient's Rorschach and then validate his impressions by checking whether they matched information from other sources, such as interviews or case files. Klopfer and other Rorschach experts claimed that the test had been validated thousands of times in this way, and that psychologists' testimonials to its success unequivocally demonstrated its value.

As we explained in Chapter Three, the field of medicine had already learned that clinical validation is an unreliable method, vulnerable to self-deception. For example, when the quack Dr. Albert Abrams of San Francisco marketed his Dynamizer in the 1920s, it became a fad in the medical community. Thousands of apparently sincere physicians bought a Dynamizer and vouched for its effectiveness based on their personal clinical validation.

The Rorschach, it turned out, was more like the Dynamizer than any of its advocates cared to admit. Thousands of psychologists in the 1940s and 1950s had come to believe that the Rorschach was well-nigh infallible, revealing a broad array of personality characteristics and psychological disorders. But studies of global interpretation and individual Rorschach variables revealed that this belief was wrongheaded, if not absurd.

The idea of clinical validation is seductively appealing because it seems to make perfect sense. After all, if intelligent and highly educated doctors and psychologists have tried a new procedure and given testimonials to its success, surely they can't all be wrong.

Yet the historical record unequivocally shows that they *can* be wrong, and over the past fifty years psychologists have come to understand why.[1] In Chapter Six, we described one way—the "overpathologizing illusion"—that a worthless test can fool intelligent clinicians. If the test overpathologizes by making normal people appear maladjusted, this flaw will not be detected by mental health professionals in clinical settings who rarely test well-adjusted individuals. Even if the test makes clients appear to possess more psychopathology than they really do, clinicians may not notice the problem, particularly if they believe that the strength of the test lies in its ability to reveal psychopathology undetected by interviews and other tests.

In this section, we'll briefly describe two other mental illusions, "confirmation bias" and "illusory correlation," that can mislead professionals who place their trust in clinical validation.

Confirmation Bias

It's no big secret that people tend to notice and remember information that's consistent with their prejudices. Republicans have a long memory for the sneaky shenanigans of Democratic politicians but exhibit partial amnesia for the sins of their own party leaders. Democrats show the same pattern of selective recall, but in reverse. The same bias has been demonstrated repeatedly in psychological research. In a classic study, researchers asked Princeton and Dartmouth fans to watch a video replay of a much-disputed 1951 Princeton-Dartmouth football game. Princeton fans reported seeing far more infractions on the part of Dartmouth players than Princeton players, whereas Dartmouth fans reported precisely the opposite.[2]

As these examples illustrate, people tend to seek out and pay attention to information that confirms their cherished beliefs, while ignoring or criticizing information that contradicts them.[3] This general human failing, called *confirmation bias,* was described four hundred years ago by Francis Bacon, the English jurist and philosopher sometimes called the father of modern science: "The human understanding when it has once adopted an opinion draws all things else to support and agree with it. And though there be a greater number and weight of instances to be found on the other side, yet these it either neglects and despises, or else by some distinction sets aside and rejects, in order that . . . its former conclusion may remain inviolate."[4]

To see how confirmation bias can mislead even a highly educated physician or psychologist, consider the procedure for clinical validation that Bruno Klopfer promoted. Here's what Klopfer recommended: "We have to develop on the basis of a 'blind diagnosis' a personality picture of our subject as detailed as we can make it by using all the Rorschach categories available with their supposed significance. Then we compare the results of our blind diagnosis with the personality picture which we can gain from all other sources of information (observation, case history, test results, etc.)."[5]

Now picture Klopfer going through this procedure. First he makes his blind diagnosis based on the Rorschach. Then he checks to see if it fits the personality picture of the patient from other sources. What does he see? As we know by now, Klopfer was a man of strong opinions who was devoted to the Rorschach. Do we believe—in fact, can we easily imagine—that when he carried out the procedure of clinical validation, he was impeccably objective and impartial? Or instead, wouldn't we expect him to show some favoritism, focusing his attention on those instances in which the Rorschach scored a remarkable success, while excusing or explaining away those instances in which it seemed to have missed the mark?

We don't know exactly what Bruno Klopfer said and did when he conducted clinical validations for his thousands of cases. However, the point is that the procedure of clinical validation invites bias, so that in light of what we know about people in general and Bruno Klopfer in particular, there's ample reason to doubt that his validations of the Rorschach were impartial and even-handed. This observation is not a personal reflection on Bruno Klopfer, because such bias is deeply ingrained in most, if not all, people, scientists included.

Of course, Klopfer wasn't the only Rorschacher who carried out clinical validations. Thousands of other psychologists used the procedure and gave testimonials to its value. Could all those highly educated psychologists have been wrong?

This question has two answers. First, despite their Ph.D.'s, psychologists aren't immune to the biases we've discussed. Few clinicians who used the Rorschach were truly neutral or objective toward the test. After all, to become even minimally competent as an interpreter according to Klopfer or Beck's standards, a psychologist had to spend about three years in apprenticeship.[6] Thus, any Rorschacher who was competent enough to conduct a clinical validation was already committed to the test and probably biased in its favor.

Second, contrary to what we might assume from the testimonials of Klopfer and his followers, not all experts who carried out clinical validation of the Rorschach found the results satisfactory. Over the years several notable psychologists defected from the ranks of "true believers."[7] For example, in the mid-1950s, Joseph Zubin, a noted Rorschach researcher at Columbia University, began publicly expressing his misgivings about the test as it was commonly used. In a classic article titled "Failures of the Rorschach Technique," he searchingly described the test's problems. Among other things, he forcefully rejected the idea of clinical validation: "Subjective validation of the testimonial variety, in which he who comes to scoff remains to pray, will not be commented on further. This type of evidence is so clearly discountable as utterly unscientific, that it is not even to be counted among our failures."[8]

Eventually Zubin and his colleagues developed a new approach to the Rorschach that they hoped would prove more useful than traditional systems.[9] Nor were they the only prominent users of the test to express dissatisfaction. For example, Wayne Holtzman of the University of Texas and Lee J. Cronbach of Stanford gradually moved away from the Rorschach after a period of initial enthusiasm.

Illusory Correlation

In a classic series of studies in the 1960s, Loren and Jean Chapman of the University of Wisconsin discovered "illusory correlation," a fascinating phenomenon that helps to explain how clinical validation can go wrong.[10] The Chapmans noticed that clinical psychologists often expressed strong confidence in projective test scores that research had shown to be virtually worthless. Instead of scorning the psychologists as foolish or incompetent, the Chapmans wondered whether they might be the victims of a mirage, a subtle trick of the mind that was distorting their clinical judgment.

The Chapmans began by contacting clinical psychologists who used the Draw-a-Person test and asking them which aspects of patients' drawings they found to be associated with such personality traits as suspiciousness or intelligence.[11] Based on their experience with patients, the clinicians identified several associations or "correlations" between drawings and personality traits. Drawings that emphasized broad shoulders or a muscular build were said to be more common among men who had doubts about their masculinity. An emphasis on eyes was associated with suspiciousness, a large head with intelligence. Although these ideas had been discredited by research, the clinicians believed them to be correct based on their personal experience.

The Chapmans next carried out a study to determine whether college students could be induced to perceive the same correlations between drawings and personality traits that the psychologists reported.[12] Students were shown a series of drawings from psychiatric patients that included the various features identified by psychologists—broad shoulders, large eyes, oversized heads, and so on. Each drawing was accompanied by a pair of statements that supposedly described the patient, such as

The man who drew this
1. is suspicious of other people.
2. is worried about how manly he is.

Although the drawings came from real psychiatric patients, the statements accompanying the drawings were bogus. The Chapmans had deliberately paired the drawings with the statements so that there was *no relationship or correlation between them*. For example, the statement that the patient "is suspicious of other people" was equally likely to accompany a drawing with normal-sized eyes and a drawing with large eyes.

After viewing the drawings, students were asked to indicate which features of the drawings were associated with which personality traits. Of course, the Chapmans had ensured that no such associations existed. Nevertheless, the students, just like the clinicians, reported that broad shoulders had been more common in the drawings of patients who doubted their own manliness, that an emphasis on eyes was associated with suspiciousness, and that large heads were associated with intelligence.

In a later study using the Rorschach instead of the Draw-a-Person test, the Chapmans found essentially the same thing.[13] Students reported seeing a correlation between certain Rorschach responses and patients' personality characteristics, even though no such correlation existed in the test protocols. Again, the nonexistent correlations reported by the students were very similar to the correlations reported by psychologists based on their clinical experience.

Visual illusions can trick the eye (actually, the brain) into perceiving things that aren't really there. Apparently the mind can similarly be tricked into perceiving illusory correlations between test responses and personality traits.[14] In other studies, the Chapmans showed that illusory correlations are most likely to occur when there is a "verbal association" between a particular test response and a particular personality trait. For example, when people are asked which part of the body is most closely associated with intelligence, they tend to identify the head, and when asked which part is most closely associated with suspicion, they tend to identify the eyes.[15] Apparently when students and clinicians report that they observed an association between certain test responses and personality traits (big heads and intelligence, eyes and suspiciousness) they may actually be reporting what they *expected* based on verbal associations.

Loren and Jean Chapman's research helped to explain why clinicians' faith in the Rorschach and other projective techniques remained powerful despite overwhelming negative evidence from objective studies.[16] The findings regarding illusory correlation provided yet another reason—in addition to those already known for years—why clinical validation of the Rorschach was a bad idea. As Donald Super of Columbia had warned more than two decades earlier: "Unorganized experience, unanalyzed data, and tradition are often misleading. Validation should be accomplished by evidence gathered in controlled investigations and analyzed objectively, not by the opinions of authorities and the impressions of observers."[17]

RORSCHACH WIZARDS, ASTROLOGERS, AND MIND READERS

Clinical psychologists tend to have a pragmatic attitude toward their tests. Although respected as useful tools, the WAIS and MMPI aren't typically held in special awe. The Rorschach, in contrast, still possesses a subtle mystique that first became widespread in the 1940s and 1950s, when almost every clinical psychologist could relate stories about the fabulous feats of Rorschach wizards (see Chapter Four). Without meeting a patient, and relying solely on the blots, Rorschach virtuosos could arrive at insights that struck many hard-headed onlookers as almost magical. In terms of sheer emotional impact, one stunning blind analysis by a Rorschach wizard could outweigh a hundred negative research articles. As Joseph Zubin observed: "Blind analysis is one of the spectacular aspects of the Rorschach technique and has probably been the most important factor in the acceptance of the Rorschach."[18]

By the early 1960s, however, the astounding success of Rorschach wizards had become a puzzle in need of an explanation. Research had revealed that Rorschach virtuosos don't possess any miraculous powers. For example, in the study by Holtzman and Sells described in Chapter Six, Bruno Klopfer, Zygmunt Piotrowski, and Molly Harrower couldn't guess which aviation cadets would fail as a result of personality disturbances. And in the study by Little and Shneidman, Rorschach experts (including Piotrowski) consistently misdiagnosed a normal IBM repairman as schizophrenic.

Such findings presented a striking paradox. If Rorschach wizards stumbled so badly in controlled studies, how could they produce such amazing performances in blind analyses? In the following sections, we'll discuss the fascinating answers to this question.

A Few Simple Tricks

Thanks to two shrewd commentators of the late 1940s, it's apparent that some Rorschach wizards achieved their success by resorting to tricks, although they may not have done so intentionally. In an astute and sometimes humorous article published in 1949, J. R. Wittenborn and Seymour Sarason of Yale identified three simple stratagems of Rorschach interpreters that tended to create a false impression of infallibility.

The first was as old as the Delphic Oracle of ancient Greece, whose notoriously ambiguous prophecies were crafted to turn out correct, no matter which direction events took. The Oracle once told a king that if he went to war he'd destroy a great nation. Encouraged, he launched an attack and was disastrously defeated. The prophecy wasn't wrong, however. After all, the oracle hadn't said *which* nation the king would destroy.[19] Wittenborn and Sarason noted that Rorschach interpreters resorted to a similar tactic, delivering "ambiguous phrases or esoteric Rorschach clichés which can be given almost any specific interpretation which subsequent developments may require."[20]

Second, Wittenborn and Sarason observed, Rorschach adepts sometimes ensured their success by making inconsistent predictions that covered all bases: "A less artful, but nevertheless effective practice, involves including in the interpretations widely separated statements which can have an almost contradictory implication; one or the other of these statements may be employed according to the requirements of the circumstances. Such resourcefulness on the part of the examiner is often ascribed to the test itself."[21]

Third, Wittenborn and Sarason observed, Rorschach interpreters sometimes enhanced their reputations by giving impressive interpretations *after* they learned the facts of a case: "Some clinical psychologists, when told about some clinically important features of a patient, say, 'Ah, yes. We see indications of it here, and here, and here.'"[22]

Despite their skepticism about such practices, Wittenborn and Sarason still held a favorable opinion of the Rorschach and didn't regard all psychologists who used it as charlatans. In fact, it's difficult to believe that all Rorschach wizards of the 1940s and 1950s were conscious fakes. The explanation is almost certainly more complicated than that. But before proceeding further, we'll pause to discuss the psychology of astrology and fortune telling.

The Barnum Effect

In the late 1940s, Bertram Forer (the future executive editor of the *Journal of Projective Techniques*) published an eye-opening study that he called a "demonstration of gullibility." After administering a questionnaire to his introductory psychology class, he prepared personality sketches. For example:

> "Disciplined and self-controlled outside, you tend to be worrisome and insecure inside. At times you have serious doubts as to whether you have made the right decision or done the right thing. You prefer a certain amount of change and variety and become dissatisfied when hemmed in by restrictions and limitations. You pride yourself as being an independent thinker and do not accept others' statements without satisfactory proof. You have found it unwise to be too frank in revealing yourself to others."[23]

Forer asked the students to rate their own sketches for accuracy on a scale from 0 (poor) to 5 (perfect). The students gave the sketches an average rating of 4.2, which indicated very good accuracy. More than 40 percent of students said that their sketch provided a perfect fit to their personality.[24]

The results seemed to show that the personality questionnaire possessed a high degree of validity. However, there was a diabolical catch: Forer had given all the students the *same personality sketch,* which he manufactured using horoscopes from an astrology book. The students had gullibly accepted this boilerplate personality description as if it applied to them uniquely as individuals.

Although the statements borrowed from the astrology book were seemingly precise, they applied to almost all people. Psychologists now call such personality statements "Barnum statements,"[25] after the great showman P. T. Barnum, who said, "A circus should have a little something for everybody" (he's also credited with "There's a sucker born every minute").

As Forer had discovered, people tend to seriously overestimate the degree to which Barnum statements fit them *uniquely.*[26] For example, students in one study who were given Barnum statements disguised as personality test results responded with glowing praise: "On the nose! Very good. I wish you had said more"; "Applies to me individually, as there are too many facets which fit me too well to be a generalization"; "Surprisingly accurate and specific in description."[27]

The Barnum effect probably explains why many people believe in astrology, even though it has been shown to be worthless in scientific studies.[28] French psychologist Michel Gauquelin placed an ad in a Paris newspaper and offered to provide free horoscopes on request. To all readers who responded he sent the same horoscope, that of a notorious murderer. "Ninety-four percent of those receiving the horoscope praised the description as accurate."[29]

Recipients of a Barnum personality description are more likely to be impressed if they believe that it was personally tailored for them.[30] For example, participants in one study rated Barnum descriptions as much more accurate if they were told that it had been written for them "personally." In another study participants were given a bogus horoscope and asked to rate its accuracy. Those who were told that it had been prepared by an astrologer who knew the year, month, and day of their birth rated it as more accurate than those who believed that it was based merely on the year and month.[31]

Fortune Tellers and Psychics

Like practitioners of astrology, palm readers and other self-proclaimed psychics have long used Barnum statements (along with a few other stratagems) to create a false impression that they know the personality, the past, and even the future of people they've never met.[32] In fact, a pamphlet currently sold in many magic shops explains how novices can create a reputation for paranormal powers simply by using the personality description from Bertram Forer's classic Barnum study.[33] Budding palm readers are instructed to study a client's hand, then intone (in words directly from Forer) "Disciplined and self-controlled outside, you tend to be worrisome and insecure inside. At times you have serious doubts as to whether you have made the right decision or done the right thing."

The name for such bogus psychic practices is *cold reading*. Skillful cold readers apply the Barnum principle in many ways, for example by spicing their readings with statements like these: "You're working hard, but you have the feeling that your salary doesn't fully reflect your efforts," or "You think that somewhere in the world you have a twin, someone who looks just like you."[34] Such statements appear personal and individualized, but in fact are true of many or most American adults.

Experienced cold readers commonly tailor their Barnum statements to fit the age, gender, and social class of a client. For instance, with a well-dressed man in his late fifties or early sixties, it's usually safe to use age-specific Barnum statements like these: "You've been taking more time recently to pursue a special interest," "You have some pain and problems with your feet," or "You dislike driving at night." Although such group-specific Barnum statements don't apply to all people of all ages, they're usually true of individuals who belong to a particular age, gender, and socioeconomic group.

After being warmed up with Barnum statements, most clients relax and begin to respond with nonverbal feedback, such as nods, smiles, and eye movements. An astute cold reader follows up accordingly. For instance, if the client responds with puzzlement when told that he experiences inner doubts, the psychic can smoothly add, "but these moments of hesitation are usually transitory."

In most psychic readings, there arrives a moment when the client begins to work for the reader, actively supplying information and providing clarifications. It's at this critical juncture that a skillful cold reader puts new stratagems into action, such as the technique called the *Push*.[35] A psychic using the Push begins by making a specific prediction (even though it may miss the mark), then allows feedback from the client to transform the prediction into something that appears astoundingly accurate:

PSYCHIC: I see a grandchild, a very sick grandchild, perhaps a premature baby. Has one of your grandchildren recently been very sick?

CLIENT: No. I . . .

PSYCHIC: This may have happened in the past. Perhaps to someone very close to you.

CLIENT: My sister's daughter had a premature girl several years ago.

PSYCHIC: That's it. Many days in the hospital? Intensive Care? Oxygen?

CLIENT: Yes.

By using the Push, a cold reader can make a guess that's wildly off target appear uncannily accurate. The Push and other techniques are effective because, by the time the cold reader begins using them, the client has abandoned any lingering skepticism and is in a cooperative frame of mind, thereby helping the psychic to "make things fit."

Intriguingly, scholars who have studied the psychology of palm reading and astrology agree that although some psychics are conscious frauds, many sincerely believe in their paranormal powers.[36] For example, Denis Dutton of the University of Canterbury in New Zealand (and editor of the highly regarded Web publication *Arts and Letters Daily*) tells the true story of a young scientist who became intrigued by astrology. Preparing horoscopes for friends and clients, he was told that his readings were "amazingly accurate." His eyes were opened, however, when after receiving the usual enthusiastic reaction from a satisfied client, he found that he'd mistakenly given the customer the wrong horoscope. Deflated, the young scientist came to an embarrassing realization: "His great success as an astrologer had nothing whatsoever to do with the validity of astrology as a science. He had become, in fact, a proficient cold reader, one who sincerely believed in the power of astrology under the constant reinforcement of his clients. He was fooling them, of course, but only after falling for the illusion himself."[37]

A similar story has been told by psychologist Ray Hyman, professor emeritus at the University of Oregon and author of a classic article on cold reading.[38] As a young man, Hyman was originally doubtful about the validity of palm reading. But after trying it himself, he became persuaded that it could work magic, particularly when he received a great deal of positive feedback from clients. In fact, he became a fervent believer in palm reading and made a side living from it for some time.

Then one day a friend suggested that Hyman provide his interpretations backwards, giving clients interpretations that were exactly the *opposite* of what the palm reading textbooks suggested. To Hyman's amazement, the backwards interpretations were received equally well (if not better) by clients. This sobering experience persuaded him that the success of palm reading had nothing to do with the substantive content of the interpretations.

As such cautionary tales illustrate, Barnum statements can fool both the client who believes them and the naive psychic who believes the client.

Rorschach Wizards: Three Explanations

Having taken a detour into the realm of astrology and palm reading, we're ready to return to the land of Rorschach wizards. We'll begin by considering three plausible explanations for the spectacular performances of Bruno Klopfer, Marguerite Hertz, and other Rorschach virtuosos of the 1950s.

First, it's possible that Klopfer, Hertz, and the others were geniuses of a sort. Perhaps some people possess a special aptitude for Rorschach interpretation. Drawing on this unique talent and their experience with thousands of patients, they develop an uncanny skill that allows them to extract insights from inkblots.[39]

Of course, this is the view that Bruno Klopfer and Rorschach devotees have always preferred (see Chapter Three).[40] It can be traced to Hermann Rorschach's colleague Emil Oberholzer, who believed that his friend's "experience with the test . . . combined with the acute psychological insight and scientific talent with which Rorschach was endowed, made it possible for him to bring the interpretation of the results to a remarkably, almost dizzily, high state of refinement."[41]

However, this venerable belief in Rorschach geniuses is difficult to reconcile with the revelations of research. As we discussed earlier, when the supposedly extraordinary insight of Rorschach experts has been tested in rigorously controlled studies, results have been disappointing.[42] For example, when Bruno Klopfer, Zygmunt Piotrowski, and Molly Harrower tried to identify potential personality disturbances in the study by Holtzman and Sales, they flopped completely, performing no better than chance.[43] Why had their wizardry suddenly forsaken them? It's true that in some studies of global interpretation, Rorschach experts performed better than chance. However, even then their performance was notably short of wizardry.

Furthermore, there's serious reason to question the old belief that Rorschach experts grow increasingly skillful as they accumulate years of experience with the test. In 1966, the *Journal of Projective Techniques and Personality Assessment* published a startling article by Dale R. Turner based on a dissertation he completed at the University of Portland under the supervision of Walter Klopfer. Turner gave the Rorschachs of psychiatric inpatients to highly experienced Rorschach experts, graduate students, and undergraduates.

The accuracy of the judges' Rorschach-based ratings was evaluated by comparing them with ratings by physicians, psychologists, and other individuals who knew the patients. The results were unexpected: No group of Rorschach judges was significantly more accurate than another. The highly seasoned Rorschach experts with many years of experience didn't perform significantly better than graduate students or even undergraduates. The experts' experience with hundreds or thousands of Rorschachs apparently added nothing to their accuracy.

Given the weight of such research findings, it's unlikely that the Rorschach wizards of the 1950s were true geniuses. Thus we have to consider a second explanation for their extraordinary performances: Maybe they were frauds.

Thanks to the shrewd article by J. R. Wittenborn and Seymour Sarason that we discussed earlier, there's little question that some Rorschachers of the 1940s and 1950s used techniques that lent the test a false impression of infallibility. Apparently the phenomenon was sufficiently common that these two authors felt the need to comment.

However, it's extremely unlikely that all Rorschach wizards of the era were conscious frauds. For instance, Marguerite Hertz was well-known for her astonishing blind analyses using the Rorschach. However, she was also a dedicated scientist and not the sort of person to encourage mumbo-jumbo. In fact, unlike other proponents of the test, Hertz was unusually frank, sometimes even blunt, when dissecting the Rorschach's shortcomings. That someone with her honesty and character would consciously stoop to cheap trickery is not credible.

Thus we're led inexorably to a third explanation: The uncanny Rorschach wizards of the 1950s were really cold readers who, like Denis Dutton's self-deluded astrologer, were deceived by their own performances.

The Rorschach Wizard as Cold Reader

If blind diagnosis with the Rorschach was really just cold reading, how could it have worked? A Rorschach wizard about to give a blind analysis usually has access to much more information than most fortune tellers ever obtain. First, a Rorschach protocol usually contains valuable clues regarding a patient's intellectual capacity, likely educational level, and possible presence of schizophrenia or other psychotic disorders. Furthermore, many protocols provide hints regarding the patient's interests or occupation. As an interesting example, the Rorschach protocol of Nobel prize–winning molecular biologist Linus Pauling has recently been published. Here are a few of his responses to the blots:

> There is enough symmetry between the two pairs of white spots to indicate there might be a symmetrical translation that might produce an infinitely long figure. . . .
>
> The two little central humps at the top suggest a sine curve. . . .
>
> This reminds me of blood and the black of ink, carbon and the structure of graphite. . . .
>
> I'm reminded of Dali's watches. . . .[44]

Even non-wizards can guess that the person who produced these Rorschach responses was intelligent, well-educated in mathematics ("infinitely long figure," "sine curve") and chemistry ("the structure of graphite"), and probably had broad cultural interests (the reference to artist Salvador Dali). Furthermore, we can infer that the person probably has science "on the brain," so that even when discussing nonscientific subjects such as inkblots, he's likely to introduce allusions to chemistry or math.

Besides the clues contained in the Rorschach protocol, other sources of information are often available to the wizard. For example, the protocol may have been submitted by a therapist who tends to work with certain types of patients (for example, patients with an anxiety disorder). If it has been submitted by an intern, this too may be a clue, because interns are frequently assigned to treatment units in which the patients share a particular diagnosis or type of problem.

Finally, the fact that a protocol comes from a particular clinic or hospital can be informative. For example, if a protocol comes from an inpatient psychiatric unit, the chances are high that the patient is suicidal or out of touch with reality. In contrast, if it comes from an outpatient clinic, the level of disability is likely to be less severe.

Thus the Rorschach wizard who undertakes a blind diagnosis is often in possession of a wealth of information that would make a palm reader envious. In the early part of the diagnostic performance, this information can be fed back to the listeners in classic cold reading style. For example, with the Linus Pauling protocol, the reading might begin, "Hmmm. This is obviously a very bright individual. Well educated, a 'cerebral' type. Focuses on thoughts, probably avoids reacting to events in a purely emotional way. I have the impression of a scientist rather than a businessperson or artist, though I do see some artistic tendencies. If there's any psychological impairment, it's only in the moderate range. A psychotic disorder is unlikely."

If the protocol comes from a particular source—for example, a therapist who usually works with outpatients—the Wizard can use "group-specific" Barnum statements. For instance, here are three fairly safe statements that fit virtually all outpatients one way or another:

- This patient's emotions "tend to be inconsistent in terms of their impact on thinking, problem solving and decision making behaviors. In one instance . . . [the patient's] thinking may be strongly influenced by feelings. . . . In a second instance, even though similar to the first, emotions may be pushed aside and play only a peripheral role."[45]

- This patient has "a potential for frequent experiences of affective disruption. . . ." He is likely to "complain about recurring bouts of depression, moodiness, tension or anxiety, although many patients with this pattern *do not* report periodic episodes involving negative emotional experiences."[46]

- This patient probably tends to be "more obvious or intense in expressing feelings than the average individual. This is not necessarily a negative finding for an adult, especially if there are no difficulties with controls. However, it can be a significant liability for those with interpersonal or reality testing problems and/or those experiencing forms of emotional disruption. Any of these conditions can give rise to situations in which the magnitude of emotional expression is likely to be inappropriate for the circumstance."[47]

We consider these three statements to be Barnum statements, even though they are based closely on quotes from a recent Rorschach book by John Exner, and they appear to be saying something important and specific. In fact, they apply to virtually all patients.

For example, the first statement, which sounds like it came straight out of Bertram Forer's famous horoscope book, says that the patient's thoughts sometimes control her feelings, but that her feelings sometimes control her thoughts. Most patients and many normal individuals would agree with this statement. The second statement says that the patient has some depression, tension, moodiness or anxiety (most patients do), but an escape clause adds that many patients don't openly show these emotions. Such "double-headed" statements are used frequently by cold readers.[48]

The third statement may be the most interesting of all. It *seems* to say that the client has problems expressing emotion. However, if read carefully, it actually says that *if* the patient has interpersonal, psychotic, or emotional problems, his emotional expression is likely to be "inappropriate." Of course, this statement is bound to be true. Inappropriate expression of emotion is virtually *always* present in individuals experiencing interpersonal conflicts and psychotic or emotional disorders.

Such Barnum statements are apparently still taken seriously by many psychologists today, judging from the large number of Exner's books that are purchased by professionals. We can be fairly sure that when Rorschach wizards of the 1950s spouted similar phrases during blind analyses, their colleagues thought something important was being said.

Once the listeners were "warmed up" by such apparently profound insights, the Rorschach wizard's job became much easier. Abandoning any initial skepticism, listeners probably began giving subtle or not-so-subtle feedback by nodding, smiling, or looking puzzled. The wizard could use this feedback as a guide for making increasingly precise statements. In all likelihood, wizards probably used something like the Push, which we described earlier. For instance, here's how the Push could be used Rorschach-style:

WIZARD: There are signs of a very severe trauma, it could be recent. Perhaps a rape? Or a violent assault?

LISTENER: No. She . . .

WIZARD: This trauma may have happened in her teen years or even earlier. She may be repressing it so she doesn't remember.

LISTENER: She was in a severe car accident when she was only eight.

WIZARD: I think that may be it. She and people she loved were badly injured?

LISTENER: Yes.

As this example shows, the Push places the Rorschach wizard in a win-win situation. If the long-shot guess is correct—for example, the patient has actually been raped or assaulted—then the accuracy of the wizard's prediction may seem miraculous. In contrast, if the guess is incorrect, the wizard can usually reinterpret it so that it seems close to something that really happened, or claim that the trauma occurred, but that the patient has repressed the experience.

Although a few Rorschach interpreters may cynically use cold reading techniques to create a false impression of uncanny insight, we doubt that most psychologists who use blind analysis intend any deception. As Denis Dutton and Ray Hyman pointed out, a cold reader can be entirely sincere.

Many Rorschach wizards of the 1950s probably developed their cold reading skills without realizing what they were doing. When they made certain statements about patients (for example, Barnum statements), they often met with the agreement, approval, or even astonishment of their listeners. When they made certain highly intuitive guesses about patients (actually, the Push), they found that they were often "close" to the truth, and that their listeners were highly impressed. Reinforced by positive feedback from their colleagues, the wizards gradually became skilled cold readers, believing that their remarkable insights had come from the Rorschach.

THE RORSCHACH UNDER HEAVY FIRE

For about ten years—1945 to 1955—the Rorschach enjoyed a grace period. Although the test's worth hadn't yet been demonstrated in rigorous scientific studies, most clinicians and researchers expected that the results would be favorable when the studies were eventually published. During this era of good feelings, the list of Rorschach researchers included some of the most prominent names in twentieth-century American psychology, including J. P. Guilford, Lee J. Cronbach, Albert Bandura, Donald Fiske, Joseph Zubin, Hans Eysenck,

Figure 7.1.   Lee J. Cronbach.
One of the twentieth century's leading psychologists in testing and
measurement. Cronbach was an enthusiastic Rorschach researcher
in the 1940s but became disenchanted with the test by 1955.
Source: Stanford University News Service. Used by permission.

Julian Rotter, Seymour Sarason, Richard Lazarus, and (almost) Paul
Meehl.[49]

Not until the mid-1950s did a pessimistic tone intrude into psychological journals. The shift in opinion began with Joseph Zubin, the
well-known researcher and long-standing proponent of the test, who
shocked his colleagues in 1954 with a jarring litany of the Rorschach's
"failures." Lee J. Cronbach, Arthur Jensen, and Hans Eysenck soon followed with similar negative appraisals.[50] Even Marguerite Hertz,
whose faith in the test never wavered, suggested that the Rorschach
was in need of overhaul.[51] By the mid-1960s, the scientific verdict was
nearly unanimous. Aside from the members of the Society for Projective Techniques, few prominent psychologists held the Rorschach
in esteem.

Lee J. Cronbach: Friend Turned Critic

The most outspoken and persistent critic of the Rorschach in the
1950s was Lee J. Cronbach of Stanford, one of the leading educational
psychologists of the twentieth century and father of "Cronbach's
alpha," a statistic familiar to every graduate student who has taken a

testing course. Cronbach's criticisms carried special weight, not only because of his stature as a researcher and statistician but because like Joseph Zubin he'd once been enthusiastic about the Rorschach.

After serving in the Navy during World War II, Cronbach joined the faculty of the University of Chicago. There he conducted an ambitious Rorschach study on Ruth Munroe's Inspection Technique (see Chapter Five).[52] Munroe had reported positive findings for the Inspection Technique in a study at Sarah Lawrence College, but Cronbach found that the technique was of little use for predicting students' success.

This disappointing experience didn't noticeably dampen Cronbach's enthusiasm for the Rorschach. He was deeply interested in global interpretation, the supposed ability of Rorschach experts to integrate the meaning of several different scores to arrive at an interpretation. During the war Cronbach had served as an instructor at a Navy sonar school.[53] Sonar listening was a difficult art that somewhat resembled Rorschach interpretation. Trainees had to learn to differentiate submarines from schools of fish and other underwater objects on the basis of subtle, often indescribable sounds. As a sonar instructor, Cronbach knew that global interpretation of underwater sounds was a genuine skill that could be taught. That the same might be true for the Rorschach struck him as plausible.

In the late 1940s Cronbach published several articles that explained how the validity of global interpretation could be studied by researchers.[54] His sophisticated research designs were light-years beyond the horse-and-buggy studies then being conducted on the Rorschach. His most important Rorschach article from this period, "Statistical Methods Applied to Rorschach Scores: A Review," appeared in the prestigious *Psychological Bulletin*.[55]

Cronbach's *Psychological Bulletin* article was intended to provide guidance to Rorschach researchers by identifying inappropriate statistical methods and suggesting alternatives.[56] To illustrate his discussion, Cronbach pointed out that many Rorschach research articles (including studies by Marguerite Hertz, Zygmunt Piotrowski, and David Rapaport) contained glaring statistical errors. In a passage that dismissed most of the findings reported by Rorschachers, Cronbach said: "So widespread are errors and unhappy choices of statistical procedures that few of the conclusions from statistical studies of the Rorschach test can be trusted. . . . Perhaps ninety per cent of the conclusions so far published as a result of statistical Rorschach studies are unsubstantiated—not necessarily false, but based on unsound analysis."[57]

Rorschach researchers could hardly have been pleased by Cronbach's catalogue of their blunders, even though he ended his article on a positive note: "The question whether the test has any merit seems adequately answered in the affirmative by studies. . . . Supplemented as these are by the testimony of intelligent clinical users of the test, there is every reason to treat the test with respect. . . . With improvements . . . we can look forward to impressive dividends."[58]

Perhaps because Cronbach wasn't particularly diplomatic in pointing out the bloopers in Rorschach research, the excellent statistical advice in his article seems to have been generally ignored by the test's proponents. Many of the elementary errors that he identified in 1949 are still being repeated by Rorschach researchers today.

After publishing this article, Cronbach's enthusiasm for the Rorschach seems to have waned. Within a few years, he arrived at two insights that he lacked in 1949. First, as the negative research findings began to accumulate in the early 1950s, Cronbach realized that the Rorschach couldn't possibly be as powerful as its proponents claimed.[59] Second, he came to see that for all their lip service to science, many of the test's advocates really didn't care what the research said.

Reviewing a new volume of *Rorschach's Test* in 1953, Cronbach noted with exasperation that Samuel Beck had simply ignored the scientific literature on the test: "He does not reverse any earlier interpretations. We have now had thousands of research studies, some well conducted, which have failed to establish validity of many interpretations commonly made. One would expect such evidence to be used in revising the interpretative scheme."[60]

Similarly, reviewing *Developments in the Rorschach Technique* by Bruno Klopfer and his colleagues a year later, Cronbach noted that none of the authors "considers for a moment abandoning a hypothesis. In twelve years, no element of Klopfer's system has been eliminated. If a study proves that some score does not measure what was claimed for it, the score is retained, and the interpretation is rephrased so that the negative data no longer apply. No one goes to the trouble of testing the modified hypothesis before announcing it. To respond to negative evidence by bringing forth new hypotheses which people are expected to use daily in clinical practice and for which there is no weight of public evidence, is inexcusable."[61]

Apparently assuming that Rorschachers were empiricists like himself, Cronbach had addressed his 1949 statistical article to them as if they were fellow scientists. By the mid-1950s he recognized his mistake.[62] From that time onward he was noticeably less charitable toward the Rorschach, and by 1956 he reached three conclusions about the test that he maintained for the remainder of his long and productive life. First, Cronbach said, some interpretations based on the Rorschach had "validity greater than chance." Second, the validity of these interpretations tended to be weak, so that very little confidence could be placed in them. Third, the traditional interpretations of many Rorschach variables were in error and should be discarded.[63]

In a widely cited statement in the 1956 *Annual Review of Psychology*, Cronbach summed up his new view, which would eventually be adopted by nearly everyone save Rorschach devotees: "It is not demonstrated that the test is precise enough or invariant enough for clinical decisions. The test has repeatedly failed as a predictor of practical criteria. . . . There is nothing in the literature to encourage reliance on Rorschach interpretations."[64]

Marguerite Hertz: A Critical Friend

Marguerite Hertz had been busy since the late 1930s, when she, Klopfer, and Beck had gone their separate ways following the great schism described in Chapter Three.[65] Working at the Brush Foundation and Western Reserve University in Cleveland, Hertz developed her own scoring system and published an impressive number of Rorschach studies.[66] Of the three pioneers, she was the most sophisticated researcher. For example, she developed impressive Rorschach norms for several groups of children and adolescents. In contrast, Klopfer never used norms at all, and Beck published norms that were based on limited, unrepresentative samples.

Although Hertz's system had a much more extensive research base than either Klopfer's or Beck's, it was never very popular. There were two reasons for its lack of success. First, most of Hertz's research dealt with children and adolescents, and her norms were for these groups. But in the Rorschach boom after World War II, most clinical psychologists were working with adults. Hertz's system was better suited for the old child-oriented clinical psychology than for the new profession that was spreading through the VA hospital system and elsewhere.

Figure 7.2.   Marguerite Hertz, Circa 1971.
A staunch defender of the Rorschach but a persistent critic of its
scientific deficiencies. Toward the end of her life
she said, "I have been happily wedded to the Rorschach."
Source: Photo by Steve Cagan. Used by permission.

Second, the neglect of Hertz's system was also explained by the fact
that, unlike Klopfer and Beck, she never published a comprehensive
book on the Rorschach that could serve as a text for students.[67] A sad
story explains this failure. While at the Brush Foundation, Hertz collected and analyzed thousands of Rorschach protocols and almost
completed a book manuscript. However, the Foundation was closed

in 1942. Without notifying Hertz, university officials where the foundation had been quartered ordered the offices to be "cleaned." Her data and manuscript were thrown out by accident and burned as trash. Without the data Hertz decided not to rewrite the book.[68]

About every ten years from the 1930s through the 1980s, Hertz published a major review article in which she surveyed the current status of the Rorschach, evaluated the progress of researchers, and identified directions for future studies.[69] Her lively and well-written reviews usually adopted a "good news–bad news" format. In some sections of each review, Hertz spoke optimistically about the Rorschach's strengths and described recent scientific advances. In other sections, she sharply criticized the practices of Rorschach researchers and clinicians, pointing out the substantial gaps between what Rorschachers believed and what the scientific literature showed.

The most pessimistic of these reviews appeared in 1959, when attacks on the test were becoming frequent. Hertz began by strongly reaffirming her feeling that the Rorschach was a valuable clinical tool: "Those of us who work in the clinic, in the hospital, in the institution, in the school and college, or on the anthropological expedition, feel in the Rorschach we have an instrument which, *under the critical eye of the clinician,* tells us much about the personality structure and the dynamics underlying the behavior of an individual."[70]

However, Hertz frankly acknowledged that such feelings hadn't been confirmed by research. Quoting Lee J. Cronbach and a recent *Annual Review* chapter by Arthur Jensen, who had dismissed the Rorschach as "worthless,"[71] she called such challenges to the test "right and proper."

Then Hertz violated one of the great Rorschach taboos. In contrast to Beck and Klopfer, who had steadfastly declined to change their Rorschach systems in response to scientific evidence, she voiced the unspoken and heretical thought that was almost surely in the minds of all but her most fervent Rorschach listeners: "There are many features of the Rorschach method which may be and probably are invalid."[72]

Hertz didn't seriously believe that the entire Rorschach was invalid. However, she was ready to accept that some aspects of the test would have to be discarded. Furthermore, as the remainder of her article made clear, Hertz believed strongly that if the valid aspects of the test were to be demonstrated in research, then Rorschachers would have to begin mending their ways. In the remainder of her review, Hertz described the most serious problems with the Rorschach and suggested how to correct them. Her recommendations boiled down to the same three fundamental principles that she had championed during the great Rorschach schism twenty years previously: research, standardization, and norms.

With regard to *research*, Hertz named each of the most popular Rorschach books and criticized them for their lack of attention to scientific findings. For instance, she chided Bruno Klopfer for his 1954 textbook's approach to research: "The text . . . contains chapters on validating studies and on the crucial theoretical and practical problems but the presentation of the procedure, scoring and interpretation are not influenced by them. One must view with alarm the mathematical precision with which many scoring formulae are introduced with their respective interpretations without any validating evidence to support them."[73]

Hertz was only slightly kinder to Samuel Beck: "Beck's books adhere rather closely to orthodox Rorschach procedure and are invaluable for their penetrating analysis of cases. There are however few references to research findings."[74]

Hertz warned that so long as Rorschach books were devoted to unproven speculations and the arcane minutiae of scoring, the scientific status of the test would not be advanced.

With regard to *standardization*, Hertz vividly described the chaos that prevailed in the administration, scoring, and interpretation of the Rorschach. Not only were there several different American Rorschach systems, each with a distinct set of procedures, but many clinicians were adopting a mix-and-match approach, combining the various systems in whatever way they liked, or even dispensing with scoring altogether.

Finally, with regard to *norms*, Hertz pointed out that although there had been some improvement, "The problem of adequate norms for the various scoring categories still plagues us. . . . Unfortunately we do not have adequate norms for judging the records of many kinds of individuals, especially the 'normal' individual."[75]

Although Samuel Beck had developed norms based on a sample of 157 adults,[76] Hertz noted that they were all employees at the Spiegel Mail Order House in Chicago and not necessarily representative of American adults.

The scientific picture that Hertz painted was just as bleak as the one Lee J. Cronbach had depicted. However, given her own positive experiences with the test, she was more sanguine about the future: "Some of us are unwilling to share the extreme views of our critics, that the Rorschach is invalid because its validity has not yet been established. Rather, we prefer to reevaluate not only our method and its basic assumptions, but the procedures we are using and the people who are trying to do the validation."[77]

Hertz's provocative 1959 review, with its call for drastic reform, had no immediate effect on her colleagues in the Society for Personality Assessment. During the 1960s, neither Klopfer nor Beck altered his system to accommodate new research findings. Attempts to improve standardization and norms were minimal. Not until fifteen years later would a serious effort be made to implement her ideas by a young researcher named John Exner.

Critics in the Mental Measurements Yearbook

The grace period for the Rorschach expired around 1955. Following the publication of Zubin's and Cronbach's negative articles, the test faced a level of scrutiny that it had previously escaped. Distinguished critics began to ask hard questions: How strong was the scientific support for the common interpretations of Rorschach variables? How believable were its cherished assumptions, such as global interpretation?

A sample of the searching critiques of this era can be found in the *Mental Measurements Yearbook,* which was then the most highly respected reference book in the field of psychological testing.[78] First published in 1938 by Oscar K. Buros, then of Rutgers (he later moved to the University of Nebraska at Lincoln), the *"MMY"* appeared in a new edition every five or six years, with each update featuring pithy and up-to-date reviews by leading experts.

The 1959 and 1965 editions of the *MMY* included four sharply negative reviews of the Rorschach by unusually distinguished psychologists: Hans Eysenck of the University of London, Laurance Shaffer of Columbia University, Arthur Jensen of the University of California at Berkeley, and Raymond McCall of Marquette University.[79] After surveying the research literature these four reviewers arrived at very similar conclusions. First, they agreed, the scientific evidence for the Rorschach's validity was overwhelmingly negative. For example, McCall wrote: "The original interpretive suggestions of Rorschach were based on his analysis—which was, as we have pointed out, largely intuitive rather than controlled—of the records of some

288 Swiss mental patients and 117 normals. Though tens of thousands of Rorschach tests have been administered by hundreds of trained professionals since that time, and while many relationships to personality dynamics and behavior have been hypothesized, the vast majority of these interpretive relationships *have never been validated empirically.*"[80]

Second, the reviewers agreed that global interpretation of the Rorschach had been discredited. Most studies of global interpretation yielded negative results, and the few that reported positive results were unimpressive. As Laurance Shaffer wrote: "Global judgments fail to show either validity or reliability sufficient to the task of personality description or diagnosis."[81]

Third, all of the reviewers (except Eysenck, who argued that most positive findings on the Rorschach were the result of statistical mistakes or methodological errors) agreed that a handful of Rorschach scores, such as *M, F+%,* or *Z,* possessed at least some validity. However, they concluded, as had Cronbach, that the predictive validity of these scores was too weak to provide a basis for clinical decision making. As Arthur Jensen commented: "The fact that some of these studies have reported validity coefficients which, when significant at all, are generally in the range of .20 to .40, cannot be interpreted as supporting the clinical usefulness of the test. . . . Validity in this range is practically useless for individual assessment."[82]

In addition to these general points, each reviewer attacked specific chinks in the Rorschach's armor. For example, Eysenck ridiculed the idea of global Rorschach interpretation, which he considered a preposterous idea designed to shield the Rorschach from scientific examination:

It is claimed in favour of the Rorschach that it measures the whole personality rather than any particular aspect of it. This differentiates it sharply from scientific measuring instruments which are constructed specifically to measure one clearly identifiable attribute of reality at a time. No physicist would entertain for one minute the claims of a device said to measure the whole universe in all its salient aspects; in line with scientific tradition he relies on measuring instruments which are more restricted in their function. . . . By putting all his eggs in one basket as it were, the Rorschach expert makes certain that none of his hypotheses can in fact be verified because none can be tested along the orthodox lines of scientific practice.[83]

Raymond McCall derided Bruno Klopfer's claim that Animal Movement responses represent "impulses to immediate gratification" that "stem from the most primitive or archaic layers of the personality."[84] Klopfer's idea, said McCall, "represents a strenuous effort to find a place in the Rorschach for the Freudian id. . . . The suggestion that perception of animal movement is determined by 'animal impulses' in us is indeed fetching, if a little preposterous."[85]

McCall chided Klopfer for drawing simple-minded analogies between animal imagery and animal impulses, and between "diffuse" shading responses and "diffuse" anxiety. McCall thought such ideas represented a throwback to ancient ways of thought, assuming "a primitive isomorphism between Rorschach responses and mental state the like of which has not been seriously advanced by anyone since Empedocles in the 5th century B.C. ('For earth is known by earth in us; water by water.')"[86]

The most devastating of the reviews was published in the 1965 *MMY* by Arthur Jensen, who later became widely known for his controversial writings on the genetics of intelligence. Besides marshaling evidence of the Rorschach's poor reliability and validity, Jensen scathingly criticized what he called "the Rorschach culture." Rorschach devotees, said Jensen, with their reverence for "orthodoxy" and "authority," had created "an atmosphere that is philosophically quite alien to the orientation of modern psychology as it is now taught in the leading American and British universities." Whereas other psychologists tried to improve and develop their tests, Rorschachers clung to the same procedures that Rorschach had introduced nearly half a century earlier: "The Rorschach culture apparently has assumed that these 10 blots cannot be improved upon and that they alone are a sufficient foundation for building a science of personality diagnosis."[87]

Jensen poked fun at the literary efforts of Rorschach "artists," whose elaborate and scientifically baseless interpretations he compared to works of literary fiction by Marcel Proust and Henry James. He also made a crucial observation that previous reviewers either missed or left unspoken: Psychologists who continued to use the Rorschach weren't simply wasting time and money. They were actually doing harm. "The strong bias toward pathology in Rorschach reports on nonpsychiatric subjects can lead to harmful consequences in nonpsychiatric settings, such as in schools and in industry."[88]

At the end of his review, Jensen made the then-shocking recommendation that psychologists should abandon the Rorschach in clinical practice, and that graduate programs should stop teaching it. Probably anticipating that this proposal would outrage many of his readers, Jensen closed with a famous quip that would dog the Rorschach until the present day: "The rate of scientific progress in clinical psychology might well be measured by the speed and thoroughness with which it gets over the Rorschach."[89]

WHERE NEXT FOR THE RORSCHACH?

Jensen's review marked the culmination of scientific attacks on the Rorschach. Thereafter, criticisms would recur, but less often and with less ferocity. It wasn't that the critics had run out of steam or that the scientific status of the Rorschach had improved. To the contrary, as far as most psychological researchers were concerned the issues had been decisively settled. Since the 1960s, experimental psychologists have generally taken a jaundiced view of the Rorschach.

Only within the fields broadly defined as *clinical*—clinical psychology, counseling psychology, and school psychology—did discussion about the Rorschach continue. In journal articles and books during the 1960s and early 1970s, psychologists in these areas reacted to the scientific attacks on the Rorschach and pondered their options.

Old Believers

One way of responding to negative scientific evidence is simply to ignore it. This reaction, by no means rare, was exemplified by Bruno Klopfer, still executive editor of the *Journal of Projective Techniques*. In a new edition of his popular textbook published in 1962, Klopfer reassured his readers that although the research findings were negative, there was no need to be concerned: "The literature on validation highlights a few seemingly 'positive' findings in a context of many apparently 'negative' findings and contradictory results. Perhaps it is not necessary to be concerned with validity in the usual sense; or perhaps a new technique of validation is necessary."[90]

Klopfer didn't specify what "new technique of validation" might give better results. His position, though probably anathema to some of his more scientific contemporaries, at least had the virtue of candor. As a phenomenologist, Klopfer had never really liked the American empirical approach to psychology or cared about validity "in the usual sense" (see Chapter Three).

Klopfer's "What, me worry?" attitude seems to have been shared by his old adversary Samuel Beck, whose books and articles barely acknowledged the scientific problems besetting the Rorschach. For example, the same 1959 edition of the *MMY* that carried negative reviews by Eysenck, Shaffer, and McCall also included a pro-Rorschach review by Beck.[91] Beck almost completely ignored the scientific controversy raging around the test and irritably dismissed negative research findings as irrelevant: "All sorts of results have come out that have made no sense, either to the strict experimentalist or to the Rorschach test investigator. Let it be said at once and unequivocally that validation such as is sought in a laboratory experiment is not at present to be expected for whole personality findings, whether by the Rorschach test or by any other."[92]

Rejecting the Rorschach: Behaviorism and Community Psychology

While Bruno Klopfer, Beck, and their followers stood steadfastly by the Rorschach, some clinical psychologists wanted to usher it unceremoniously off the stage of history. By coincidence, the scientific assault on the Rorschach in the late 1950s and 1960s coincided with two other important developments within clinical psychology, what's often called the "behaviorist revolution" and the rise of community psychology.[93]

During the 1960s there was a surge of interest in behaviorism and the application of behavioral techniques to psychological problems.[94] Strongly influenced by B. F. Skinner, many clinical psychologists adopted the view that abnormal behavior is learned, maintained by environmental influences, and correctable by behavioral techniques that use principles of reinforcement. Such traditional psychological concepts as *thoughts, emotions,* and *motivation* came to be widely regarded as suspect and largely irrelevant to the task of behavioral change. The idea of *personality* was viewed as fuzzy-headed, because it seemed to imply that human behavior was somehow caused by inner factors, whereas behaviorist doctrine held that behavior is controlled primarily by reinforcement from the environment.

Clinical psychologists of a behaviorist bent had little patience with such hypothetical psychodynamic entities as the unconscious, the ego, and penis envy.[95] Nor did they see a need for the Rorschach or other forms of personality assessment. As Marguerite Hertz observed, "If, as some contend, behavior is merely a response to environmental stimuli, the individual's inner life has become irrelevant."[96]

The other new force in clinical psychology during the 1960s, community psychology, reflected broader changes in U.S. society. In a single decade, Americans witnessed the assassination of President John F. Kennedy and of Martin Luther King Jr., convulsive struggles over civil rights, the sexual revolution, widespread use of illegal drugs, the War on Poverty, and protests against the war in Vietnam. In this era of social upheaval, some clinical psychologists began to question the relevance of their profession as it had traditionally been practiced.

The idea grew that instead of focusing on the assessment and treatment of patients who were psychologically disturbed, clinical psychologists should concern themselves with changing the social and economic conditions that create and maintain psychological problems.[97] For example, instead of administering tests and psychotherapy to juvenile delinquents, clinical psychologists should be trained to identify and eliminate social problems that foster delinquency, such as poverty, unemployment, and prejudice. Instead of psychoanalyzing teen mothers, clinical psychologists should address the social factors that lead to teen pregnancy.

Such concerns, coinciding with funding changes by the federal government to promote "community mental health," gave rise to the field of community psychology. Community psychologists sought to understand the broad social, cultural, and economic forces that affect mental health, and to implement interventions that could improve the psychological well-being of entire communities or groups, not just single individuals. Community psychologists, like behaviorists, saw little worth in the Rorschach. The Rorschach and similar assessment techniques were viewed at best as irrelevant, and at worst as a diversion of money and professional effort from areas in which they could be put to better use.

Replacing the Rorschach:
The Holtzman Inkblot Test

Since the late 1940s, experts on psychological testing recognized that the Rorschach was a poorly constructed test, even aside from questions about its validity.[98] The test's worst psychometric flaw was the "problem of R," which we discussed in Chapter Six: The number of responses given by a patient can vary from less than ten to more than a hundred, with a substantial impact on most other Rorschach scores. For example, someone who makes a large number of responses is more likely to give at least one response that can be scored for psychopathological content. In addition, there was no satisfactory way to determine the stability of Rorschach scores over time (see Chapter Three). Test-retest reliability was questionable because a patient's responses at the second testing were likely to be affected by memory for responses at the first testing.[99] Alternate-form reliability was also problematic. With no well-accepted second set of inkblots, an alternate form of the Rorschach couldn't be administered to clients to determine if the results were similar for both forms of the test.

To overcome these problems, Wayne Holtzman (whose earlier research we described in Chapter Six) developed an inkblot test during the late 1950s that eliminated the worst psychometric features of the Rorschach. With the Holtzman Inkblot Test or HIT, patients were shown forty-five blots and asked to give a single response to each one. Thus R was always forty-five and the "problem of R" disappeared, so that fluctuations in R couldn't cause other scores to rise or fall. The HIT also included an alternate set of forty-five blots that could be used to retest patients.

In a book published in 1961, *Inkblot Perception and Personality*, Holtzman and his colleagues provided extensive information on the HIT, including norms for psychiatric patients, adults, children, and college students, and tables on scoring reliability and alternate-form reliability.[100] Detailed instructions were provided for the scoring of Color, Movement, Shading, Form Appropriateness, and other traditional inkblot variables. Furthermore, the HIT contained a measure of Deviant Verbalizations that could be used to help identify patients with schizophrenia.[101]

For all its virtues, though, the HIT never really caught on. When Lewis Terman had transformed Binet's crude intelligence test into the psychometrically sophisticated Stanford-Binet during the 1920s and 1930s, psychologists of the era eagerly embraced his innovations (see Chapter Three). In contrast, Wayne Holtzman's refined version of the Rorschach was generally ignored by clinicians.[102] Even today, it remains largely unknown outside the academic community.

There are probably several reasons why Holtzman's test never generated much enthusiasm. First, Holtzman published the HIT at about the same that Piotrowski and Bohm introduced their new approaches to the Rorschach (see Chapter Five). All three innovators faced the same problem: Most clinical psychologists of the era were already members of the Beck or Klopfer parties and uninterested in alternatives.

Second, most Rorschachers of the 1960s didn't really care about such niceties as norms and reliability, and many, like Bruno Klopfer, were openly disdainful toward psychometrics. Despite her continued efforts, Marguerite Hertz had failed to persuade her colleagues in the Society for Projective Techniques that standardization and norms were essential. In such a climate, the psychometric virtues of the HIT didn't constitute a major selling point.

A third reason is that some psychologists viewed the HIT as "cumbersome."[103] In fact, it's likely that anyone who gave this excuse never actually tried the test, because the HIT takes only about as long to administer, score, and interpret as the Rorschach.[104] Criticisms of the HIT may have revealed more about the speaker's own resistance to change than about the test itself.

The fourth and probably decisive reason for the HIT's commercial failure was its creator's unwillingness to promote it by making grandiose claims. As a Stanford graduate mentored by the hard-headed Ernest Hilgard, Holtzman was firmly grounded in the American empirical tradition and reluctant to make unproven claims for his test's validity, as Bruno Klopfer and other Rorschach promoters had been doing routinely since the 1930s. Holtzman didn't claim, for example, that the HIT provided a complete picture of an individual's personality, or that it was an x-ray of the psyche. Instead, he adhered closely to the scientific evidence and was modest in his claims. In the realm of inkblots, however, there were few rewards for those who were careful, scientific, and modest. When it came to the Rorschach, oversell had always been the key to success.

Reforming the Rorschach: New Approaches to an Old Test

Among clinical psychologists in the late 1960s and early 1970s, a respectable minority valued the Rorschach but realized that the scientific criticisms leveled against it were mainly correct. For example, in the 1965 and 1972 *Mental Measurements Yearbooks,* reviews by several pro-Rorschach psychologists forthrightly summarized the test's scientific failures but expressed the hope that it could be saved.[105]

Typical was the review by Richard Dana of the University of South Florida. Dana acknowledged: "In spite of our persistent efforts to convert the Rorschach into a psychometric instrument, we have failed. . . . Indeed we have come to the end of an era: preoccupation with the Rorschach as a test." Nevertheless, Dana argued, the Rorschach might be a valuable tool in the hands of a well-informed clinician: "It is clinician and not test which enables personality study. . . . For the psychologist who accepts his own inner resources as the instrument for putting together the pieces of someone else's experience, the Rorschach will continue to be a convenient touchstone."[106]

During this era several writers put forward suggestions about how the Rorschach could be reformed in a way that remained faithful to both clinical experience and scientific evidence. The first major proposal for change appeared in a 1965 book by Joseph Zubin, in collaboration with Leonard Eron of the University of Iowa and Florence Schumer. These authors concluded that although most traditional approaches to the Rorschach had yielded unsatisfactory results, there was some promise in approaches based on the analysis of content.[107] Zubin and his colleagues suggested that the Rorschach be regarded as an interview rather than a test, and that interpretation should focus on content.[108]

A 1971 book by Marvin Goldfried of the State University of New York at Stony Brook, George Stricker of Adelphi University, and Irving Weiner of the University of Rochester adopted a different approach. In a thorough review of the research literature, they identified several Rorschach indexes that had been repeatedly validated for specific clinical purposes. Their list turned out to be fairly short, consisting mainly of scores we've already mentioned, such as Deviant Verbalizations, the Piotrowski signs for organic brain damage, and the Rorschach Prognostic Rating scale.

Goldfried and his coauthors recommended that clinicians use a Rorschach index only if it had been well-validated, and if research had shown that its use could result in an overall improvement in clinical decision making: "If such research is unavailable, as it is for many Rorschach indices, it is best to restrict the index to continued research applications and not to rely on it for clinical purposes."[109]

Although such a recommendation might appear to be common-sensical, it represented a radical departure from well-established Rorschach custom. Rorschachers had always been willing to adopt poorly validated scales on the basis of clinical validation or the declaration of a semi-deified expert such as Rorschach or Bruno Klopfer. The idea that a Rorschach score should be validated before use, and that its demonstrated validity should be high enough to be clinically useful, was strong medicine indeed. If this recommendation were to be followed, the result would be a leaner, meaner Rorschach, trimmed down to a few well-validated scores.

A third, much different approach to the Rorschach was proposed in 1976 by Edward Aronow of Montclair State University and Marvin Reznikoff of Fordham University in their book *Rorschach Content Interpretation*. Based on a review of the research literature, these authors concluded (as had Zubin and his colleagues) that although the Rorschach's structural scores had generally performed poorly in scientific studies, content scales had received some scientific support (for a discussion of content versus structural approaches, see Chapter Five).[110] Within the category of content, these authors included Deviant Verbalizations and the Elizur scales for Anxiety and Hostility.

However, Aronow and Reznikoff didn't recommend that the content scales be used in clinical work, because their reliability tended to be low and "personality characteristics are likely to be measured with a relatively low degree of precision."[111] Instead, they proposed what they called a "content oriented" and "idiographic" approach to the Rorschach. Aronow and Reznikoff's basic idea was to approach the Rorschach analogously to dream interpretation.[112] The psychologist showed the blots to the patient and asked questions after each card to elicit personal associations: "What does that image make you think of?" "What does that bring to mind?"[113] Interpretations of Rorschach symbolism often arose spontaneously in the testing session and sometimes came from the patients themselves.

Aronow and Reznikoff tried this procedure with about a hundred adult patients and found it had two advantages. First, the authors reported that patients' associations to the inkblots sometimes revealed important "unconscious dynamics." Second, patients often "opened up" during the Rorschach session and revealed some of their most important thoughts and feelings.[114] Aronow and Reznikoff freely conceded that their approach didn't allow a psychologist to score such traditional determinants as *M* and *WSumC*. However, in their opinion this didn't constitute a serious drawback, because they considered *M* and *WSumC* to be clinically uninformative.

Aronow and Reznikoff's approach represented a creative and largely successful attempt to remain loyal to two long-standing traditions within clinical psychology: the psychometric approach to tests and psychodynamic thinking. If psychologists wanted an inkblot *test,* these authors suggested, they should use the Holtzman Inkblot Test, which was psychometrically superior to the Rorschach.[115] But if they wanted a psychodynamically helpful technique, analogous to dream interpretation, they should use the content approach to the Rorschach. By maintaining a clear distinction between *testing* and *psychodynamic exploration,* Aronow and Reznikoff seemed to show that psychologists could keep their Rorschach cake and eat it too.

Thus in the early 1970s several paths appeared open to scientifically oriented clinical psychologists who remained loyal to the Rorschach. One option was to switch to the Holtzman Inkblot Test, with its superior psychometric properties. A second possibility was to retain the Rorschach, but limit interpretation to a few well-validated scores, as Marvin Goldfried and his colleagues suggested. A third option was to adopt Aronow and Reznikoff's content approach, abandoning the Rorschach as a test but retaining it as an aid to exploration in psychotherapy.

All these options shared a common drawback: Psychologists would have to seriously change how they conceptualized and used the Rorschach. As it turned out, none of these painful possibilities would have to be faced. Instead, a new and much more appealing choice appeared unexpectedly in 1974, when a relatively unknown scholar, John Exner, published his new Comprehensive System for the Rorschach. According to Exner, it was a mistake to believe that the Rorschach had serious psychometric problems, or that most of its scores lacked validity. Psychologists could keep using the Rorschach in much the same way they always had. With a collective sigh of relief, Exner's readers welcomed the news that they wouldn't have to change their ways after all. This is the story we'll tell in the next chapter.

CHAPTER EIGHT

New Life for the Rorschach

John E. Exner's Comprehensive System

The Rorschach is quietly disappearing from the professional psychology scene.

—George W. Albee,
"The Uncertain Future of Clinical Psychology," 1970

There is no denying that Exner's work has injected new life into the aging Rorschach and may have extended its life potential to well beyond three score and ten.

—A. I. Rabin, *"The Rorschach: A New Lease on Life," 1980*

As the quotes introducing this chapter indicate, the 1970s witnessed a dramatic and unforeseen resurgence of popularity for the Rorschach Inkblot Test. When George Albee gave his presidential address to the American Psychological Association at the beginning of the decade, the Rorschach seemed to be slowly but surely lumbering toward the Elephant Graveyard. Some pundits predicted its imminent demise, whereas others expected it soon to be replaced by the psychometrically superior Holtzman Inkblot Test.

By 1980, however, the Rorschach had made such a remarkable comeback that a prominent expert on projective techniques, A. I.

Rabin, declared that it had been given a "new lease on life." The Rorschach's scientific credibility had been patched up and its critics had fallen conspicuously silent. The reason for this miraculous comeback can be traced almost exclusively to one man: John Exner.

JOHN E. EXNER AND THE IDEA OF AN INTEGRATED RORSCHACH SYSTEM

For the past quarter century, a single individual has stood astride the world of the Rorschach. As a 1998 commendation from the American Psychological Association stated, with only slight exaggeration, "John E. Exner's name has become synonymous with this test."[1] No other individual, with the possible exception of Bruno Klopfer, has exerted such an enormous influence on how American psychologists use the Rorschach.

Early Career

Born on April 18, 1928, John Ernest Exner Jr. grew up in Syracuse and Buffalo, New York. As a young man he joined the U.S. Army Air Force, serving as a crew chief and flight engineer during World War II and the Korean War. In the early 1950s he entered Trinity University in San Antonio. At first he intended to pursue a career in law, but after taking an undergraduate course in abnormal psychology he changed his mind. Earning a B.S. and M.S. in psychology from Trinity, Exner then attended Cornell University in Ithaca, New York, where he received his Ph.D. in clinical psychology in 1958.[2]

Exner's first academic appointment was at DePauw University in Indiana.[3] He later served as director of training in clinical psychology at Bowling Green State University in Ohio, and at Long Island University in Brooklyn.[4] During the late 1960s he also worked briefly for the Office of Selection of the Peace Corps.[5]

While a graduate student at Cornell, Exner became passionately interested in the Rorschach. At the urging of his professors, he visited Samuel Beck in Chicago, then Bruno Klopfer in California. As he reported later, "I fell in love with *both* those guys. They were like godfathers to me."[6] Eventually he established friendly relations with the other Rorschach "systematizers," including Marguerite Hertz and Zygmunt Piotrowski (but not David Rapaport, who died at a relatively young age in 1960).

Exner said that, soon after earning his Ph.D., he developed a "delusion of grandeur" and tried to arrange a meeting between Beck and Klopfer, so that these two old foes could resolve their differences and present a common front to critics of the Rorschach.[7] Even though Exner obtained a grant to pay for these Rorschach "peace talks," Beck and Klopfer rejected the olive branch.[8] Their animosity was too great to be erased by Exner's well-meaning efforts. Thereafter he explored other strategies for bringing the Rorschach systems together.

The Rorschach Systems and a Survey of Rorschach Users

During the late 1960s, Exner became preoccupied with the question of how the major Rorschach systems differed and how they might be unified. Although he published a few modest studies on the Rorschach, he seemed to be more strongly attracted to historical scholarship than scientific research.[9] In 1969 he published *The Rorschach Systems*, a minor Rorschach classic. The book's opening chapters described the early history of the Rorschach in America, including a portrayal of the personalities and issues involved in the great schism of the 1930s. The remainder of the book analyzed each of the five major American Rorschach systems—Beck, Klopfer, Hertz, Piotrowski, and Rapaport—painstakingly enumerating their differences with respect to administration, scoring, and interpretation.

The Rorschach Systems unequivocally demonstrated that there was no longer a single "Rorschach test."[10] In a series of detailed tables Exner showed that the five Rorschach systems used different procedures for administering the test, included diverse variables, and often scored and interpreted these variables in widely discrepant ways. As he later reflected: "What I had found was that there were five clearly different approaches to the 10 blots, often subtle, but generally so different that one could argue that there were five Rorschachs instead of one, or even more if the foreign proliferations of Rorschach's work were included."[11]

In *The Rorschach Systems*, Exner hinted that integration of the various systems would be a good idea.[12] Subsequently, he and his wife conducted a mail survey of 395 clinical psychologists to determine how the Rorschach systems were being used in clinical practice. The survey results, published in 1972, indicated that about 55 percent of Rorschachers primarily used the Klopfer system, and approximately

35 percent primarily used the Beck system.[13] The remaining three systems were far less popular.

Such findings weren't novel: Prior surveys found that the Klopfer and Beck systems were dominant.[14] However, Exner's survey presented intriguing new information. Over 20 percent of psychologists responding to the survey indicated that they didn't ordinarily score the Rorschach.[15] Apparently they relied on an intuitive approach to the blots rather than a formal system. Furthermore, among the remaining psychologists, 75 percent reported that they personalized their scoring by adding scores borrowed from other systems or derived from their own experience.[16]

In 1959 Marguerite Hertz criticized her Rorschach colleagues for combining various Rorschach systems in a way that made no scientific sense (see Chapter Seven). And in 1968 Samuel Beck observed: "The Rorschach scene is at present a chaos of sights and a cacophony of sounds, with very little sign of real order. With few exceptions . . . everyone using the test does that which is right in his own eyes."[17]

Exner's 1972 survey confirmed these impressions: A substantial proportion of Rorschachers took a mix-and-match approach to the test. He ended his article in much the same way he concluded his book, by hinting that it would be desirable if "only one approach to the technique were taught and used."[18]

UNIFYING THE SYSTEMS

In 1974 Exner published the first volume of *The Rorschach: A Comprehensive System*, a groundbreaking work that proposed to unify the five major Rorschach systems into one "comprehensive" system that preserved the best features of each. No Rorschach book quite like it had ever been published before. Unlike Bruno Klopfer's texts, it included norms. Unlike Samuel Beck's texts, it was replete with references to the scientific literature.

Exner devoted page after page to discussions of research methodology, standardization, and validity. He appeared to be a tough-minded psychologist in the mold of Marguerite Hertz, combining a passionate devotion to the Rorschach with an abiding respect for psychometrics. Most exciting of all, in his reviews of the scientific literature, Exner concluded that the Rorschach *worked*—that it yielded valid and clinically useful results if used "intelligently"—that is, according to the Comprehensive System.[19]

In a second volume published in 1978 Exner presented norms for children and adolescents and reported test-retest reliability results for the most important variables in his system. And in a third volume, published in 1982 with Irving Weiner, he provided additional normative and test-retest information for children and adolescents. All of these volumes presented new research evidence in support of the Comprehensive System's validity. In addition, Exner began publishing a series of "Workbooks" with scoring rules and exercises for students.[20] Since the early 1980s, he has periodically generated new editions of all these volumes.[21]

In 1968, several years before he began publishing his books on the Comprehensive System, Exner established the Rorschach Research Foundation, which soon became known as the Rorschach Workshops Inc. Supported in part by grant money from the National Institute of Mental Health, Exner and his coworkers at the Workshops carried out three ambitious projects over six years.[22] First, they conducted several mail surveys to identify the Rorschach procedures and scores most commonly used by clinicians. Second, they reviewed the published research literature to identify those features of each Rorschach system with the strongest scientific support. Third, they carried out more than 150 studies on the administration, scoring, and validity of the Rorschach.[23]

These surveys, literature reviews, and research projects provided Exner with guidance as he decided which administration procedures and Rorschach variables to retain in the Comprehensive System. As he published a stream of books over the next twenty years, the Workshops continued to generate hundreds of studies that provided a seemingly impregnable scientific foundation for the Comprehensive System.[24] In the following sections we'll describe the features of the System that seemed finally to establish the Rorschach as a psychometrically sound test.

Administration

Since the 1940s, administration procedures for the Rorschach had been a divisive topic among the test's American proponents. For example, Samuel Beck recommended that the psychologist sit behind the patient and hand the cards one by one over a shoulder (Hermann Rorschach's procedure). Before beginning the test, the psychologist should provide a short explanation and instruct patients to "be sure to tell the examiner everything that you see."[25] Beck's instruction to "tell everything" was modeled on a similar injunction ("the fundamental rule") that Freudian psychoanalysts give to their patients.[26]

However, Bruno Klopfer objected to Beck's procedures.[27] According to Klopfer, Beck's instruction to "tell everything you see" placed a "restriction" on patients and overemphasized the importance of producing a large number of responses. Instead, Klopfer recommended that the psychologist sit beside and slightly behind patients, and accompany the first card with the simple question that Hermann Rorschach had used: "What might this be?"[28]

The disagreements over Rorschach administration weren't only between Beck and Klopfer. Marguerite Hertz, Zygmunt Piotrowski, and David Rapaport each developed different procedures for administering the test. All five systematizers produced arguments in favor of their approach and against the others.

In his first book on the Comprehensive System, Exner weighed the arguments of the systematizers and chose Klopfer's seating and introductory procedures. Thus in the Comprehensive System the psychologist sits beside the patient and begins the testing procedure by asking "What might this be?"

Other details of Comprehensive System administration tend to be consistent with Klopfer's approach. During the first part of the test, called the "Response" phase, the patient goes through the cards one at a time and makes responses to each. In general, psychologists allow patients to give as many or as few responses as they please at this stage.[29] The average number of responses given by patients to all ten cards tends to be around twenty-three (somewhat more than two responses per card).[30]

After a patient has completed the Response phase, the "Inquiry" phase begins. The psychologist goes through the cards again one by one, reading back the patient's statements from the Response phase. The purpose of the Inquiry is to understand the patient's earlier responses so that they can be scored accurately. For example, the psychologist may need to clarify where in the blot the patient saw an image, or whether Color played a role in the response.

The Inquiry is the most delicate part of Rorschach administration. Exner called it the "soft underbelly of the test."[31] The psychologist must gather enough information to score responses accurately, but avoid asking suggestive questions that might unduly influence the patient's answers. In general, Exner recommended a conservative approach: "Brevity should be the rule and the questions must be nondirective."[32]

Although the administration procedures for the Comprehensive System require training and good judgment, Exner reassured his readers that "the task of administering the Rorschach is not simple, but it is not difficult to learn."[33] In fact, he indicated that the task is straightforward enough to be learned by individuals with only limited education:

> More than 600 examiners have participated in the many projects [of the Rorschach Workshops] to date. Some have been professional psychologists or psychology graduate students, but more than half come from more varied backgrounds, ranging from a professional musician and a retired tailor, to an extremely talented high school senior. Other examiners have included physicians, dentists, nurses, social workers, educators, homemakers, and a few very adept secretaries who discovered that administering the Rorschach can sometimes be as boring as typing letters. The ability of these laypeople to learn to collect Rorschach data in a standardized format has been among the very reassuring aspects of the system.[34]

Norms

Probably no feature of the Comprehensive System was more impressive than its norms (see Chapter Three for a discussion of norms and their importance to psychological tests). In his 1974 volume introducing the System, Exner presented only minimal normative information.[35] However, each succeeding volume added more numbers for more groups. By the early 1990s, each of Exner's books provided more than fifty densely printed pages of normative tables.[36] For practically every Rorschach variable, extensive norms were presented for nonpatient adults, children, and psychiatric patients.

The most important norms were those of nonpatient adults.[37] By 1986, Exner had amassed a pool of 1,332 Rorschach protocols of adults who never had psychiatric hospitalizations or received extended psychotherapy.[38] He randomly selected seven hundred protocols from this pool to form his normative sample. Tables describing the age, gender, marital status, education, and socioeconomic level of subjects indicated that the sample had been successfully "stratified to represent the U.S. census."[39]

Exner stressed that the adults in his nonpatient sample were "not necessarily normal" and that they ranged from "strange to sturdy."[40] Thus, his norms weren't to be interpreted as a snapshot of psychological health. Rather, they provided a yardstick to measure a patient's similarity to run-of-the-mill Americans. By comparing patients' Rorschach scores with the norms, psychologists could readily determine whether a patient fell above or below average on every Rorschach variable, and whether the scores were so deviant from normal as to suggest psychopathology.

Scoring Reliability

As psychologists learned from the controversies over intelligence testing in the 1920s, two experts who score exactly the same test responses sometimes make substantially different ratings (see Chapter Three). "Scoring reliability" (also known as "interrater reliability") can be a potential problem for many tests. However, because the scoring of a questionnaire like the MMPI-2 requires almost no individual judgment (particularly if scoring is done by a computer), questionnaires are relatively foolproof compared with intelligence tests like the WAIS or projective tests like the Rorschach.[41]

The scoring reliability of the most commonly used modern intelligence tests is .90 or higher.[42] For purposes of illustration, Graph A in Figure A.3 (in the Appendix) shows the hypothetical scores of two psychologists who have scored intelligence tests from the same patients with a reliability of .90. Each dot represents the intelligence test score of a single patient. The patient's score as determined by Psychologist 1 is plotted along the x-axis (at the bottom) and the score as determined by Psychologist 2 is plotted along the y-axis (at the side). As Graph A shows, intelligence test scores assigned by the two psychologists tend to be fairly similar when reliability is .90, although striking discrepancies occasionally occur.

Research on the scoring reliability of the Rorschach was rare before Exner.[43] The few studies on the topic suggested that scoring reliability might be very good for some Rorschach variables but very poor for others.[44] Before publishing his books, therefore, Exner initiated studies at the Rorschach Workshops to examine the reliability of all the variables he was considering for inclusion in the Comprehensive System. Ultimately, he decided to include Rorschach variables in his System only if the correlation between scorers was .85 or higher.[45] In his 1978 and 1986 volumes on the Comprehensive System, Exner reported that the Rorschach Workshops had conducted two additional studies of scoring reliability, which had verified that the reliability of all scores in the Comprehensive System was .85 or higher.[46]

Graph B in Figure A.3 shows the hypothetical scores of two psychologists who have scored the same Rorschach variable from the same patients with a reliability of .85.

As the graph shows, the Rorschach scores assigned by the two psychologists tend to be similar when reliability is .85, though not quite as similar as the intelligence test scores in Graph A.[47] Psychologists generally accepted Exner's minimum standard of .85 reliability as adequate.[48] The reliability figures reported in his books appeared to justify the confident statement of his coauthor Irving Weiner: "All of the variables coded in the Comprehensive System can be coded with substantial interrater reliability."[49]

Test-Retest Reliability

The controversies regarding intelligence testing in the 1920s and 1930s also taught psychologists the importance of test-retest reliability: If patients are given a test twice, their scores should generally be consistent from test to retest. Because there are drawbacks to giving *exactly* the same test twice to the same patients (for example, patients may remember their answers from the first testing), it's generally better to use two *parallel* versions of the test, an approach known as alternate-form reliability. (See Chapter Three for a discussion of test-retest and alternate-form reliability. Of course, consistency in scores is not expected if the characteristic being measured is unstable, and the time between test and retest is relatively long. Chapter Three also provides a more detailed discussion of this and related issues.)

The alternate-form reliability approach has been applied to modern intelligence tests. Researchers have reported that when the same subjects are given the Stanford-Binet Intelligence Test and the Wechsler Adult Intelligence Scale (WAIS), the scores correlate about .88.[50] For all intents and purposes, this number serves as an estimate of the tests' alternate-form reliability. For purposes of illustration, Graph A in Figure A.4 shows the hypothetical scores of fifty subjects who have taken both the Stanford-Binet and the WAIS, with a correlation of .88 between the two tests. As the graph shows, the results from the two tests are generally similar.

In his books on the Comprehensive System and several journal articles, Exner reported extensive test-retest data for dozens of important Rorschach variables. His numbers indicated that the average test-retest reliability of Rorschach scores is about .80 if the retest occurs within a few days or weeks of the original test.[51] Graph B in Figure A.4 shows the hypothetical Rorschach scores of fifty adults who have taken the Rorschach twice within a short time interval.

As psychologists have known for over half a century, however, test-retest coefficients for the Rorschach can be artificially inflated by memory effects, particularly if the interval between test and retest is brief.[52] Patients may remember and repeat their earlier responses, making the correlation between test and retest scores look deceptively impressive. Alternatively, a few patients may feel compelled to change their answers the second time they take the test.

To minimize such problems, Exner conducted additional studies in which the time between test and retest was one to three years. Memory effects presumably are reduced with these longer time intervals, because subjects are less likely to remember their responses from the first test. Remarkably, even in these studies Exner found that the average test-retest reliability of Comprehensive System scores was consistently above .75, and sometimes as high as .82.[53] These numbers were at least as good and probably even better than the test-retest reliability coefficients for the MMPI and MMPI-2.[54]

Saving the Best of the Old Scores

In the 1950s and 1960s, such prominent critics as Lee J. Cronbach, Arthur Jensen, and Hans Eysenck had concluded that the validity of Rorschach scores is generally either poor or nonexistent (see Chapter Seven). Eysenck denied that *any* Rorschach score had well-demonstrated validity.[55] Cronbach, Jensen, and other critics expressed a more moderate view, concluding that the validity of a few Rorschach scores was above zero, but too weak to be useful in clinical work.

When Exner published *The Rorschach Systems* in 1969, he agreed with the critics' negative evaluation of the research findings: "It is probably true, as many critics proclaim, that a true statistical validity has not been demonstrated for the Rorschach regardless of the fact that more than 3,000 books and articles concerning the instrument have been published."[56]

However, by the time he began disseminating his books on the Comprehensive System, Exner had apparently concluded that validity could be statistically demonstrated. Contrary to his earlier views, he maintained that the Rorschach included many "empirically sturdy elements."[57] The Comprehensive System preserved commonly used Rorschach scores, added new ones, and gradually expanded to include more than 180 variables.[58]

Exner salvaged virtually all of the scores that Hermann Rorschach introduced in 1921. Human Movement (*M*), Color (*WSumC*), and the Experience Balance (*EB*) were all included in the Comprehensive System. So were White Space responses (*S*), Whole Card responses (*W*), and Details (*D*) (see Chapter Two).

After safely stowing Hermann Rorschach's scores within the Comprehensive System ark, Exner led aboard a menagerie of variables from the Beck and Klopfer systems, including Beck's mystic *EA*, which supposedly embodied "the present total inner force with which the patient operates" (see Chapter Five).[59] Although Exner adopted a few scores from Hertz and Piotrowski, his new system was far more heavily indebted to his two Rorschach godfathers.

One of Exner's most ticklish choices involved the scoring of Form Quality. Beck had retained Rorschach's *F+%*, whereas Klopfer had abandoned it in the 1940s and developed his own cumbersome approach to Form Quality (see Chapters Two and Three).[60] Exner adopted Beck's approach, but with modifications.[61] The Comprehensive System eventually included four measures of "good" form quality (*F+%*, *X+%*, *XA%* and *WDA%*), one measure of "poor" form quality (*X-%*), and one measure of "unusual" form quality (*Xu%*).

Exner also found room for a modified version of David Rapaport's Deviant Verbalizations (see Chapter Five). Exner called these verbalizations "Special Scores." By combining six Special Scores, he created an overall index of thought disorder called "*WSum6*."[62]

Although Exner welcomed a broad range of old Rorschach scores into the Comprehensive System, he kept some out. For example, he rejected Color Shock and the traditional interpretation of the Mother and Father cards, on the grounds that they were never validated.[63] Surprisingly, he also excluded several indexes—Klopfer's Rorschach Prognostic Rating Scale, the Piotrowski signs for organic brain damage, the Elizur content scales for Hostility and Anxiety (see Chapter Seven), and the Rorschach Oral Dependency scale (a measure of dependency developed by Joseph Masling)[64]—even though they performed well in validity studies. The Comprehensive System wasn't barren of indexes, however, because Exner energetically developed his own.

Exner's New Indexes

The idea of Rorschach indexes first became popular in the early 1940s, when it was known as the sign approach (see Chapter Five).[65] The underlying principle was straightforward: Several Rorschach scores could be added or subtracted from each other to yield a single overall measure of depression, stress, or some other psychologically important characteristic.

Exner was to become the most prolific inventor of indexes in the Rorschach's history. Table 8.1 lists his innovations. The Egocentricity Index, his first creation, was discovered accidentally in a 1969 study that examined Reflection and Pair responses in four groups—homosexuals, sociopaths, depressed patients, and college students.[66] (A Rorschach response is scored as a Reflection if it refers to a mirror image or reflection, such as "trees reflected in a lake," and as a Pair if it refers to two of the same objects, such as "two bears" or "two lobsters.")

Exner found that the homosexuals and sociopaths in the study produced an exceptionally high number of Reflection responses. The findings regarding Pair responses were less clear-cut. He concluded: "Subjects characterized as highly narcissistic [homosexuals and sociopaths] offered significantly greater numbers of reflection type responses than do other subjects. This finding seems consistent with the psychoanalytic conception of narcissism as self-love in that preoccupation with 'self-likeness' as manifest in reflection or mirror image occurs."[67]

According to Greek myth, the beautiful Narcissus fell in love with his own image reflected in a pool. Exner's findings suggested that the ancient story conveys a deep truth, and that individuals with an excess of "self-love" exhibit a preoccupation with mirrors and reflecting surfaces. At the time that Exner published his study, many psychoanalytic thinkers would have found such an idea plausible. Many would have also accepted without objection his extremely dubious assumption that homosexuals are a narcissistic group that can be lumped together with sociopaths. Thus, although there's no reason to believe that Exner was homophobic, his ideas concerning reflection responses were par-

Table 8.1.   Sample Indexes of the Comprehensive System
for the Rorschach.

Name	Symbol	Common Interpretations
Egocentricity Index	*3r+(2)/R*	Self-focus, self-concern, self-esteem (low score can indicate depression)
Depression Index	*DEPI*	Depression or other major affective disorder
Schizophrenia Index	*SCZI*	Schizophrenia or other psychotic disorder (eliminated from system around 2001)
Suicide Constellation	*S-CON*	Imminent risk of suicide or suicidal preoccupations
Obsessive Style Index	*OBS*	Obsessiveness, perfectionism
Hypervigilance Index	*HVI*	Mistrust, guardedness, vulnerability to paranoia
Coping Deficit Index	*CDI*	Immaturity, difficulty sustaining relationships
Perceptual Thinking Index	*PTI*	Impaired Perception or Thinking (revision of *SCZI*)
Experience Actual	*EA*	"Available resources"; "Capability to initiate deliberate action in coping situations"
Experienced Stimulation	*es*	Uncontrolled "demands" from within (impulses and emotions) or without (environmental stressors)
D Score		Score less than 0 indicates insufficient inner "resources" to cope with current "demands."
Adjusted D		Score less than 0 indicates chronic control problems and long-standing difficulty coping with demanding situations.

tially based on questionable assumptions regarding the personality characteristics of homosexuals.

On the basis of these findings, some additional Rorschach Workshops studies, and an article in the Japanese journal *Rorschachiana Japonica*, Exner included Reflection and Pair responses in the Comprehensive System.[68] Reflections are rare, he said, and indicate narcissism. If even a single Reflection response appears in a Rorschach protocol, a psychologist can conclude that "a nuclear element in the subject's self-image is a narcissistic-like feature that includes a marked tendency to overvalue personal worth. . . . This inflated sense of personal worth tends to dominate perceptions of the world."[69]

By combining Reflection and Pair responses, Exner created the Egocentricity Index. A patient's score on the index is calculated by tripling the number of Reflection responses, then adding the number of Pair responses, and finally dividing this sum by the total number of Rorschach responses.[70] Reflection responses are tripled, Exner said, because they're rare.[71]

Exner reported several unpublished studies from the Rorschach Workshops that seemed to demonstrate the validity of the Egocentricity Index as a measure of self-esteem and self-focus. For example, in one study, scores on the Index were related to the number of times that subjects used the words *I, me,* and *my,* and the amount of time that they spent looking in a mirror.[72]

As the years passed, Exner developed additional indexes to identify psychological symptoms and disorders. One of the most important was the Depression Index, better known as the *DEPI* (rhymes with "peppy").[73] According to Exner, a high score on the *DEPI* "correlates very highly with a diagnosis that emphasizes serious affective problems."[74] Another was the Schizophrenia Index or *SCZI* (rhymes with "dizzy").[75]

Exner also developed other indexes. He invented the Suicide Constellation to identify patients who have suicidal preoccupations or are at risk for attempting suicide, the Obsessive Style Index as an index of obsessiveness and perfectionism, the Hypervigilance Index to measure mistrust, guardedness, and vulnerability to paranoia, and the Coping Deficit Index to identify social immaturity and difficulty sustaining relationships.[76] His latest innovation, the Perceptual-Thinking Index, is said to measure aberrations in thinking and perception typically seen in schizophrenia and other psychotic disorders.[77]

In addition, Exner introduced three important indexes that supposedly measure patients' stress tolerance and capacity for self-control. First is *es* (Experienced Stimulation), ostensibly an index of uncontrolled "demands" acting on the individual.[78] These "demands" may come from within (unruly impulses or depressive thoughts) or without (environmental stressors).

The second index is the *D Score.*[79] A *D Score* below 0 supposedly indicates that a patient's "resources" are insufficient to deal with current "demands." In more ordinary terms, we'd say that the patient is "stressed out" and unable to cope.

The third index is *Adjusted D.*[80] An *Adjusted D* below 0 supposedly indicates that a patient has chronic problems in coping. According to Exner, a low *Adjusted D* score is also an indicator of "control problems" and a tendency to malfunction in demanding situations.[81]

If Exner's readers felt any doubts about these innovations, they could take solace from the extensive research supporting his new indexes. The unpublished studies of the Rorschach Workshops summarized in Exner's books provided a scientific foundation for the Egocentricity Index, the Depression Index, *Adjusted D,* and his other indexes. The highly positive results seemed to vindicate the rugged old faith of Klopfer and Beck: If approached in a fashion that was sufficiently subtle and complex, the Rorschach could yield remarkable insights into the human psyche.

THE TRIUMPH OF THE COMPREHENSIVE SYSTEM

Although Exner's first book on the Comprehensive System represented an enormous effort, its treatment of basic psychometric issues was incomplete. The norms presented in his 1974 volume were sketchy, and crucial information on scoring reliability and test-retest reliability was absent.[82] However, his second volume, published in 1978, filled these gaps and gave the Comprehensive System "psychometric respectability."[83] By the mid-1980s, Exner's approach to the Rorschach had become more popular than any of the five systems it displaced.[84] In the next sections we'll describe developments in the profession of clinical psychology during this era, and then chronicle the Comprehensive System's stellar rise to success.

The Changing Character of Clinical Psychology

The profession of clinical psychology has experienced extraordinary growth since its birth in the years following World War II (see Chapter Four). In the late 1940s there were only about 20 graduate programs in clinical psychology. By the mid-1970s the number increased to 100, and by 1995 it rose to over 175.[85] A similar growth pattern can be seen in the membership rolls of the American Psychological Association, which rose from about 7,000 members in 1950 to 39,000 in 1975, and to 79,000 in 1995.[86] As the figures indicate, the number of psychologists doubled between 1975 and 1995, the period when the Comprehensive System was rising to prominence.

When David Shakow and his colleagues adopted the "scientist-practitioner model" of clinical training at the Boulder Conference in 1949, they anticipated that future graduates of clinical psychology programs would work in such institutional settings as universities, hospitals, and clinics, and that their primary duties would be to conduct research and perform psychological testing.[87]

These assumptions turned out to be only partly correct. Although the large majority of clinical psychology graduates during the 1950s and 1960s entered positions in universities or the public sector,[88] by the mid-1970s a sizable minority (20–25 percent) were working in full-time private practice rather than in institutions.[89] Contrary to what the participants in the Boulder Conference hoped, only about 25 percent of clinical graduates published any research except their Ph.D. dissertation.[90] And most new clinicians preferred to provide psychotherapy rather than administer psychological tests.[91] Because of widespread demand for psychotherapy, psychologists from the 1950s to the present have been much more likely to work as therapists than as psychological diagnosticians and testers.[92] By the early 1970s, it was clear that the field of clinical psychology was assuming a different shape than its founders had anticipated.[93]

In the middle and late 1960s, some psychologists, particularly practitioners, began to express dissatisfaction with the scientist-practitioner model.[94] Why should students receive training in research, asked critics, if they were never going to work as researchers? Doctoral programs, the argument went, should emphasize training in clinical skills such as testing and psychotherapy.[95]

In the 1950s, Adelphi University established a psychodynamically oriented clinical psychology program based on what was called the "scholar-practitioner" model. Research training wasn't emphasized. For their dissertations, Adelphi students could write theoretical papers or describe individual case studies, rather than conduct formal studies with statistical analyses.[96]

In the late 1960s and early 1970s, similar scholar-practitioner programs began to spring up throughout the country.[97] In most cases they offered the Psy.D. degree (Doctor of Psychology), rather than the Ph.D. (Doctor of Philosophy). The Psy.D. was viewed as analogous to the M.D., and indicated that the recipient had been trained primarily as a service-providing professional rather than as a scientist.[98]

Prominent among these new "professional schools" was the California School of Professional Psychology (CSPP), founded in 1969 under the leadership of Nicholas Cummings, an Adelphi graduate who also founded American Biodyne, an innovative company specializing in the provision of mental health services.[99] By the end of the 1970s, professional schools such as CSPP accounted for about 25 percent of all new doctorates awarded in clinical psychology nationwide. By the end of the 1980s the number had risen to 39 percent.[100] At present the figure is higher than 50 percent.[101]

As professional schools have proliferated and graduate training has placed less emphasis on the development of research skills, the membership and character of the American Psychological Association (APA) have changed dramatically. Until 1975 the list of APA presidents was a virtual "Who's Who" of psychology's most eminent researchers. After that date the names of practitioners predominated, and in 1996 a psychologist with a Psy.D. was elected APA president for the first time.[102] The past several years provide some suggestion that the trend may be beginning to reverse, as several prominent researchers have recently been elected to the APA presidency. However, it's too early to tell whether this trend signals a more long-term change in the nature of APA leadership.

As the leadership of the APA has changed, so has its direction.[103] The APA Board of Professional Affairs (which represents "professional" psychologists) has come to play an increasingly important role in the organization's politics. Since the mid-1970s, the APA has vigorously promoted the financial interests of practitioners. For instance, the APA was instrumental in disseminating a "model licensing law" for psychologists in the late 1980s and early 1990s,[104] and has fought to ensure that psychologists are eligible for reimbursement by insurance companies and other third-party payers.[105] More recently, the APA has supported controversial "prescription privilege" laws that would allow psychologists to prescribe medications.[106]

Although the balance of power in the APA has shifted from scientific psychology to professional psychology over the past twenty-five years,[107] it would be an exaggeration to say that the organization has become entirely "anti-scientific." Many respected researchers have retained their membership in APA (though a substantial number defected to the more research-oriented American Psychological Society in 1988), and the association continues to publish several highly respected scientific journals.

Nevertheless, in the present climate the APA has tended to be tolerant—some would say overly tolerant—of clinical practices that lack a sound scientific basis. For example, APA offers continuing education credits to practitioners who take workshops in such questionable techniques as calligraphy therapy, sand play therapy, rebirthing, and psychological theater therapy.[108] APA even offers credits for techniques such as crisis debriefing (administered to survivors of the terrorist attacks of September 11th, 2001) that have been found to be harmful in several controlled studies.[109]

Some critics contend that APA has abdicated its responsibility to science and the public by failing to combat unvalidated clinical practices.[110] Unlike the American Medical Association,[111] the APA doesn't require its members to restrict their practice to empirically validated techniques. Instead, a laissez faire attitude prevails.

Laxness toward scientifically dubious techniques is not a new phenomenon in clinical psychology, of course. In Chapter Four we described the 1950s fad for projective techniques. Clinical psychology has long been a teeming carnival in which some booths hawk unsound practices and questionable theories. Although many clinical psychologists restrict their work to scientifically sound practices, a substantial number have always been attracted to bizarre tests and treatments.

Nevertheless, some critics argue that the gap between clinical science and practice has widened over the past few decades, and that APA's permissive attitude is less justified now than it was half a century ago.[112] In the 1950s, research on psychotherapeutic and assessment techniques was in its infancy. The evidence is considerably more plentiful today, so that a lax attitude toward nonscientific practices is less defensible.

The Comprehensive System rose to popularity in the easygoing and permissive era of the 1980s and 1990s. During those decades, popular practices included the use of anatomically detailed dolls in sexual abuse evaluations; the use of hypnosis, drugs, or dream interpretation to recover memories of childhood abuse; and Eye Movement Desensitization and Retraining (EMDR). The first two are unsupported by good scientific evidence. The third has support as a treatment for posttraumatic stress disorder, but has not been shown to be more effective than other treatments, despite the claims of its promoters. Its adherents often make preposterous and unsubstantiated claims for its effectiveness for treating other mental disorders. Unlike these techniques and some of the others we've mentioned, however, the Comprehensive System presented hard numbers and research findings to support its claims. In this respect, Exner's work appeared to have a firmer scientific basis than many other popular psychological practices of the time.

Praise and Popularity: The Comprehensive System in the 1980s and 1990s

By the time the Comprehensive System first rose to prominence in the 1980s, the conflicts and ideologies that had divided clinical psychology during the 1960s had subsided (see Chapter Seven). In the 1960s, the Rorschach had been criticized by behaviorists because it purported to measure "personality" (a suspect concept) and by community psychologists because it was considered "irrelevant." But by the 1980s many behaviorists had mellowed into "cognitive behaviorists" and accepted the idea that thoughts ("cognitions") can influence behavior.[113] Although still skeptical about personality tests, cognitive behaviorists weren't interested in renewing the controversy over the Rorschach. Community psychologists were similarly disinclined, having turned their attention to issues far removed from projective tests.

In fact, the Rorschach's popularity had never seriously declined. Despite predictions that the test's demise was imminent (see George Albee's quote at the beginning of this chapter), practitioners had shown no sign of abandoning their inkblots in the 1960s and 1970s. As mentioned earlier, psychological testing had generally decreased in importance as psychologists devoted more of their time to therapy. However, testing was an important part of most psychologists' identity, and the Rorschach remained their favorite test. Surveys up until the end of the 1970s showed that, despite the warnings of Cronbach, Jensen, and other naysayers, practitioners prized the Rorschach more highly than any other personality test.[114] Not until the 1980s did it slip slightly, and only then into second place behind the MMPI.[115]

If the Comprehensive System was to succeed, it would have to win the acceptance of the many practitioners who still clung to the Beck and Klopfer systems in stubborn defiance of scientific evidence. Nor would the new system's psychometric virtues necessarily gain it many adherents. Loyalties to the old systems ran deep and were largely resistant to arguments based on research and psychometrics. As the fate of the Holtzman Inkblot Test had shown, it was possible to throw a psychometrically lavish inkblot party and have nobody show up.

However, the Comprehensive System was to be far more successful than Holtzman's test, in part because it soon won warm endorsements from leaders in the Rorschach community. One of the earliest commendations came from A. I. Rabin, a respected expert on projective tests and close friend of Samuel Beck. In a review in *Contemporary*

Psychology titled "The Rorschach: A New Lease on Life," Rabin praised Exner for accomplishing a "Herculean task" in giving the Rorschach "psychometric respectability."[116] Rabin commented favorably on Exner's "impressive" normative tables and his studies of test-retest reliability. In particular, Rabin commended Exner's "mini-experiments" (the Rorschach Workshops studies). These studies, said Rabin, "offer solid support to a number of Rorschach theoretical assumptions and have bolstered many of the psychometric aspects of the method."[117]

As noted earlier, approximately every ten years since the mid-1930s, Marguerite Hertz had published a half-laudatory, half-critical review of recent Rorschach developments. In what was to be the last of these classic articles, published in 1986, Hertz praised the Comprehensive System, describing it as "the bright spot on the horizon" for the Rorschach. In a personal tribute she said: "The research studies that have emanated from the Rorschach Workshops since their inception represent for me the first serious and systematic attempt to confront some of the unresolved issues that have plagued us through the years. . . . Best of all, Exner and his colleagues have brought discipline into our ranks and a sense of optimism to our field."[118]

Although few Rorschachers used Hertz's system, her integrity and critical intellect were widely respected. She was, moreover, the last surviving Rorschach "pioneer" (Bruno Klopfer having died in 1971 and Samuel Beck in 1980).[119] The scientific status of the Comprehensive System was greatly enhanced by the endorsement of this doughty Rorschach champion, who for forty years had upheld the cause of standardization, norms, and research.

Praise for the Comprehensive System poured in from experts outside the Rorschach fold as well. In a popular 1982 textbook on psychological testing, Robert Kaplan and Dennis Saccuzzo of San Diego State University praised Exner's "heroic effort" and predicted: "If Exner's goal of providing a standard administration and scoring system can be realized, the 21st century may find the Rorschach elevated to a position unimaginable 20 years ago."[120]

Exner's work even received kind words from one of the most respected authorities in psychological testing, Anne Anastasi of Fordham University.[121] A staunch upholder of the psychometric approach, Anastasi usually had little favorable to say about projective tests. However, in the 1982 and 1988 revisions of her classic textbook, she praised the Comprehensive System for its standardized administration, well-defined scoring rules, and extensive norms. Echoing A. I. Rabin, Anastasi compared Exner to a healer who'd injected new vitality into the decrepit Rorschach: "The availability of this system, together with the research completed thus far, has injected new life into the Rorschach as a potential psychometric instrument."[122]

The warm praise from Rorschach experts, textbook authors, and psychometric experts—which was virtually unanimous from 1980 to 1995—quickly won over a sizable minority of practicing psychologists. By the mid-1980s, survey data indicated that approximately 35 percent of psychologists who used the Rorschach had adopted the Comprehensive System.[123] By the end of the decade the number was 40 percent, approximately twice as high as the numbers for either the Klopfer or Beck system.[124]

Most important, the Comprehensive System soon gained approval from the majority of professors teaching the Rorschach in clinical psychology graduate programs. As we mentioned in Chapter Seven, textbooks have always been integral to Rorschach success. Popular textbooks helped to make Klopfer more influential than Beck, and Beck more influential than Hertz. Thus it was significant that a survey of graduate instructors in the mid-1980s reported that Exner's books were used more frequently in assessment courses than those of all his competitors combined.[125] When asked to list the individual who made the most important contributions to the Rorschach technique, these instructors named John Exner more often than Bruno Klopfer, Samuel Beck, and even Hermann Rorschach himself![126]

With success came personal recognition and influence. In 1980 Exner received the Society for Personality Assessment's highest honor, the Bruno Klopfer Distinguished Contribution Award (formerly known as the Great Man Award, it had been renamed in Klopfer's memory following his death).[127] In 1986 Exner's coauthor Irving Weiner assumed the editorship of the influential *Journal of Personality Assessment*.[128] Weiner was Exner's long-time friend and colleague, and had worked with him at the Rorschach Workshops.[129] From 1986 until the present, all editors of the journal have been staunch advocates of Exner's Comprehensive System.

New Opportunities and Honors

By the 1990s, Exner had clearly prevailed. According to a survey in the early part of the decade, the Comprehensive System was taught in about 75 percent of graduate courses on the Rorschach. The Klopfer and Beck systems had sunk virtually out of sight.[130]

Figure 8.1.   John Ernest Exner.

A 1998 commendation from the American Psychological Association
lauded his work on the Rorschach and stated, "John E. Exner's
name has become synonymous with this test."

Source: Nell Redmond. Used by permission.

In 1984, at the age of fifty-six, Exner (Figure 8.1) left Long Island
University and moved the Rorschach Workshops to Asheville, North
Carolina.[131] Although founded in 1968 as a research enterprise, the
Workshops began to offer intensive five-day training seminars in the
early 1970s, even before Exner published his first book on the Comprehensive System.[132] Instructors in the early years included Exner,
Irving Weiner, and Marguerite Hertz.[133] By the 1990s, the list of Workshops instructors had expanded to include some of the most prominent experts on the Comprehensive System, such as Donald Viglione
and Philip Erdberg of the California School of Professional Psychology and Barry Ritzler of Long Island University. These training Workshops continue to be offered at Asheville and other locations
throughout the United States, Japan, and Europe, currently charging

$650 per participant.[134] They've been attended by thousands of psychologists and have contributed substantially to the spread of the Comprehensive System.[135]

The Comprehensive System has also benefited from the expansion of a lucrative new market for psychological testing: forensic assessments. Over the past twenty years, an increasing number of clinical psychologists have extended their practices into the legal arena.[136] For example, many forensic psychologists act as evaluators in custody disputes to determine which parent of a divorced couple is best suited for custody of a child. Psychologists also evaluate the sanity, legal competence, and potential for violence of criminal defendants, the extent of psychological harm in personal injury suits, and the suitability of applicants for police training.[137] In many cases, such evaluations are mandated by courts.

In the early 1980s, Irving Weiner called the attention of his colleagues in the Society for Personality Assessment to the growing demand for forensic evaluations,[138] and in 1982 he and Exner published a case history illustrating how the Rorschach could be used to evaluate children and parents involved in a custody dispute.[139] In the years since then, the Comprehensive System has become highly popular among forensic psychologists, in part because Exner's and Weiner's writings can be used in court to defend the method's scientific validity.[140] As we discussed in Chapter One, between 30 percent and 35 percent of psychologists routinely use the Rorschach whenever they conduct assessments in legal cases, such as custody evaluations, child abuse assessments, and criminal evaluations. Although exact figures are unavailable, the large majority of these evaluators apparently use the Comprehensive System.[141]

Such impressive success would probably never have occurred were it not for Exner. By the early 1970s, the test had become an embarrassment, a bad habit that psychologists refused to relinquish. But by the mid-1990s, thanks to Exner's tireless efforts, the Rorschach seemed to be more secure and scientifically sound than most tests in psychology.

When the Comprehensive System was beginning its ascent to fame, A. I. Rabin and Anne Anastasi likened Exner to an amazing healer who rejuvenated the Rorschach. Two decades later, when his system had attained national renown, the Board of Professional Affairs of the American Psychological Association apparently found the old metaphor insufficient to describe Exner's achievement. In a tribute published in the *American Psychologist* in 1998, the Board called upon religious imagery that evoked Jesus' raising of Lazarus in the New Testament: "Exner has almost single-handedly rescued the Rorschach and brought it back to life. The result is the resurrection of perhaps the single most powerful psychometric instrument ever envisioned."[142]

The use of such language by a scientific organization would have been exceedingly unusual. However, it was not a scientific group but the APA Board of *Professional* Affairs that honored Exner in this way. In fact, the Board's tribute ignored a fierce scientific controversy over the Comprehensive System that had begun in the mid-1990s and been gathering in intensity. This is the story we tell in the next chapter.

CHAPTER NINE

The Unraveling of the Comprehensive System

The reliability and validity of the Comprehensive System have been greatly overstated. . . . Exner's efforts to systematize the Rorschach and to meet professional standards for psychological tests are laudable, but the Comprehensive System does not yet meet these standards.

—John Hunsley and Michael Bailey,
"The Clinical Utility of the Rorschach:
Unfulfilled Promises and an Uncertain Future," 1999

Comprehensive System . . . reliability, validity, normative, and other problems may indicate not so much that the edifice was built incorrectly as that the edifice defied such construction in the first place.

—Edward Aronow, "CS Norms, Psychometrics, and Possibilities for the Rorschach Technique," 2001

By the early 1990s, John Exner had seemingly established a Peaceable Kingdom where the Rorschach lion could lie down beside the psychometric lamb. His accomplishments equaled or even surpassed those of Bruno Klopfer, who had carved out a Rorschach realm in the 1940s by means of more warlike tactics.

Surrounded by a cultish band of followers, Klopfer had crossed swords with Samuel Beck and declared war on the American psychometric approach to tests (see Chapters Three and Four). Exner's style was much different. Whereas Klopfer had been controversial, charismatic, and prone to hyperbole, Exner was a consensus builder, prosaic and cautious. His declared aim was not to overturn the psychometric tradition but to demonstrate that the Rorschach could be molded into a psychometrically sound test.

Exner's "both-and" approach to the Rorschach and psychometrics was well-suited to the tolerant mood of clinical psychology in the 1980s and 1990s. Devoted Rorschachers welcomed his work because it finally conferred scientific legitimacy on their beloved test. Psychologists with a more tough-minded attitude were impressed because he seemed to share their dedication to scientific principles.

However, in an ironic déjà vu of Rorschach history, the popularity of Exner's Comprehensive System was to generate its own problems. During the Rorschach's first heyday in the 1950s, eager researchers churned out hundreds of dissertations and articles on the test. Unexpectedly, these studies revealed the test's weak validity and tendency to overpathologize, eventually discrediting it in the eyes of scientifically oriented psychologists. Forty years later, the widespread acceptance of the Comprehensive System was to set in motion a similar chain of events.

From 1974 until the late 1980s, scientific information on Exner's system had emanated from virtually a single source. If psychologists or graduate students wanted to examine the scientific evidence for his claims, they consulted the many volumes of *The Rorschach: A Comprehensive System*. Around 1990, however, studies of the Comprehensive System by other researchers began to accumulate, and by the middle of the decade, a respectable number of dissertations and new articles were appearing each year. The story they told often differed sharply from that in Exner's books.

In this chapter we'll describe how fundamental problems with the Comprehensive System surfaced in the late 1990s and early 2000s, setting off a controversy that swept through psychology's leading journals and onto the pages of the *New York Times* and *Scientific American*. But before telling that story, we'll look back with benefit of hindsight at what seemed to be the triumphal period of the Comprehensive System in the 1980s and early 1990s.

EARLY WARNING SIGNS

Even before the controversies of the late 1990s, clues were surfacing that the foundation of the Comprehensive System might not be as sturdy as many psychologists assumed. Warning signs were scattered throughout Exner's books and the scientific literature, although they generally went unheeded.

The Unpublished Studies of the Rorschach Workshops

When published research on a Comprehensive System score was scarce or negative (and it often was), Exner's books often filled the gaps by reporting studies from his Rorschach Workshops. According to information sent out by the Workshops, more than a thousand studies were undertaken there from 1968 to 1990—an average of more than forty per year.[1] If this number is accepted at face value, Exner's team generated an average of one study every nine to ten days, and sustained this astounding pace for over twenty years.

Exner's books were thickly strewn with scholarly citations to studies on the Comprehensive System.[2] However, if readers took the trouble to consult the list of references at the end of a chapter, they discovered that the large majority of Exner's citations regarding the system were to unpublished studies by the Rorschach Workshops.

The Workshops Studies appeared in other guises as well. For example, Exner often described studies (presumably from the Workshops) without providing any citation at all. Or he supported his points by providing citations to his previous books, which in turn reported additional unpublished studies. Anyone who tried to locate the scientific research underpinning the Comprehensive System soon found that all trails led to the Rorschach Workshops, and that the overwhelming majority of the Workshops Studies had never been published.

Several features of the Workshops Studies probably should have given pause to Exner's readers in the 1980s and early 1990s. First, his descriptions of the studies tended to be brief and vague, omitting critical information about research procedures and data analyses. For example, his explanation of how and when he collected his norms was so lacking in detail that it apparently failed to meet the minimum standards set forth in the *Standards for Educational and Psychological Testing* of the American Psychological Association (See Exhibit 9.1).

In addition, Exner's descriptions of his studies sometimes revealed errors in research design and statistics.[3] Furthermore, when he reported the same Workshops Study in different places, his numbers sometimes changed inexplicably from one book to the next.[4] They sometimes changed even within the same book.[5]

Such lapses probably should have reminded Exner's readers that most of his research had never been subjected to the scientific peer review process, and that hardly any of his findings had been replicated by independent researchers. It's worth pausing for a moment to discuss these two important issues—peer review and independent replication—because they play such an important role in the everyday workings of science and in the controversies that eventually engulfed the Comprehensive System.

When a scientist submits a research report to a journal, the editor typically sends out copies to several experts ("peers"), who are asked to comment on the study's strengths and weaknesses and recommend whether it should be published. This "peer review process" helps to keep obviously flawed research from being published and can eliminate bias or error in studies that are otherwise of good quality. Even when reviewers recommend the publication of an article, they usually point out how it can be improved. Thus, peer review, although rarely perfect, provides researchers with corrective feedback about the shortcomings and biases of their work.[6]

Dissertations go through a similar process. Before undertaking a dissertation project, a graduate student must meet with a committee of professors, describe the project, and solicit their comments and suggestions. In some cases, the initial proposed research design may be drastically modified or even rejected. When the project has been completed, the dissertation manuscript is again submitted to the committee for review and approval.

Considering that the Comprehensive System's scientific credibility depended on the Workshops Studies, and that few of these had been peer reviewed, it was especially worrisome that most of Exner's findings had never been replicated by independent researchers. Replications (studies that try to reproduce the findings of earlier research) provide another important quality control mechanism in science. For example, the relationship of Rorschach scores to intelligence has been examined in numerous studies. Similarly, the global validity of the

Exhibit 9.1.   American Psychological Association Standards.

These standards are relevant to evaluation of the Exner nonpatient adult norms:

4.4. Reports of norming studies should include the year in which normative data were collected, provide descriptive statistics, and describe the sampling design and participation rates in sufficient detail so that the study can be evaluated for appropriateness.

4.3. Norms that are presented should refer to clearly described groups. These groups should be the ones with whom users of the test will ordinarily wish to compare the people who are tested.

Source: American Psychological Association, 1985, p. 33.

Rorschach was studied in the 1950s by a variety of researchers (see Chapter Six).

The results of a single study can be misleading. Perhaps the researcher who conducted it made a mistake in experimental procedure or statistical analysis. In rare instances, the data may have been fabricated or fudged, as apparently happened in the case of the famous (now notorious) psychologist Sir Cyril Burt, whose findings on the genetics of intelligence were apparently padded with nonexistent subjects.[7] In other cases, the results from a single study may represent an isolated fluke. This situation is surprisingly common in psychological research, especially when investigators test multiple hypotheses within the same study. However, when many well-designed studies have examined the same topic and produced similar findings—as with the relationship between Rorschach scores and intelligence—then considerably more confidence can be placed in the results.

There's no fixed rule about how many replications are necessary to establish the validity of a test score. Four or five well-done studies may be enough, if they've been conducted by independent researchers and yielded similar results. However, if the results from different researchers are at odds, ten or fifteen replications may be necessary to resolve the discrepancies. And under rare circumstances, only one or two studies may be necessary. For example, when a long-established and well-validated test, such as the Beck Depression Inventory or the Wechsler Adult Intelligence Scale, is revised, only a few independent studies may be necessary to verify that the new version works as well as the old one.

Replication becomes particularly important if a test is used to make important decisions about people's lives. When the stakes are high, reliance on the work of a single revered expert is risky and can lead to disastrous consequences (see the story of Henry Goddard and intelligence tests in Chapter Three). It's therefore striking that in the 1980s and early 1990s the Comprehensive System was adopted enthusiastically by psychologists in mental health clinics, schools, and legal settings, even though most of its scores had not been adequately replicated by independent researchers. In fact, the few well-designed replications of Exner's work often reported results strikingly different from his.

Disturbing Dissertations

Before the mid-1990s, only a handful of scholars publicly raised any objections to the Comprehensive System.[8] Even then, the disagreements tended to be mild and narrowly focused. For example, in the late 1970s, Charles Fonda, an expert on White Space responses, pointed out that there was little support for Exner's interpretation of Space responses as an indicator of hostility.[9] In the early 1990s, James Kleiger of the Menninger Clinic argued that the logic underlying the Experience Actual (see Chapters Five and Eight) was inconsistent, and that the few studies on the score had yielded discouraging results.[10]

Both dissenters had compelling evidence on their side, yet neither met with a favorable response. Exner never addressed Fonda's criticisms and dismissed Kleiger's.[11] The interpretation of Space responses and the Experience Actual in Exner's books remained unchanged.

Meanwhile, independent research on the Comprehensive System was beginning to accumulate, although the results often appeared where few psychologists thought to look—the dissertations of graduate students. Three dissertations from the 1980s were particularly important, although their implications weren't widely recognized at the time.

The first was completed in 1980 by Lewis Aron, a graduate student at St. John's University in New York. Using the Comprehensive System, Aron administered the Rorschach to two groups of college students. Students in one group had experienced a high number of stressful events during the previous year, whereas students in the other group had experienced few such events.

Aron's dissertation seems to have been the first independent attempt to replicate Exner's two indexes, Experienced Stimulation (*es*) and the *D Score* (see Chapter Eight).[12] Because these two indexes ostensibly measure the presence of stressors and individuals' ability to cope with them, Aron expected the scores of the high-stress and low-stress students to differ markedly.

But neither of Exner's indexes performed as expected. The high-stress and low-stress students in Aron's study didn't differ significantly on either *es* or the *D Score*,[13] although the high-stress group exhibited higher scores on another Rorschach variable, the Elizur Anxiety Scale (see Chapter Six).

Aron presented his findings at a symposium organized by Exner.[14] Subsequently the dissertation was published as an article, but for whatever reason, it reported only the positive results for the Elizur Anxiety Scale, without mentioning the negative results for *es* and the *D Score*.[15] Aron's troubling findings regarding the two Comprehensive System indexes were forgotten. Exner didn't mention these results in his books, and no one else seems to have noticed them again until 2001.[16]

A dissertation by William Whitehead of the University of Texas Southwestern Medical School in Dallas also yielded important results. Whitehead conducted a study of global judgment modeled on research that had been popular in the 1950s and 1960s (see Chapter Six). The MMPI and Rorschach were administered to two groups of back pain patients (depressed and nondepressed), and two groups of patients with psychotic disorders (schizophrenia and bipolar disorder). The test results were distributed to experienced psychologists and highly trained graduate students, who were asked to make diagnostic judgments.

The results of Whitehead's study, completed in 1985 using the Comprehensive System, were virtually the same as those reported in the 1950s and 1960s using the older Rorschach systems. When the judges relied on either the MMPI or the Rorschach, they were able to discriminate back pain patients from psychotic patients at a level of accuracy that was better than chance. However, accuracy was higher for the MMPI than for the Rorschach. Furthermore, judges who used the MMPI and Rorschach together were slightly *less* accurate than judges who used the MMPI alone.[17]

Whitehead also examined whether the judges could discriminate between depressed and nondepressed back-pain patients. He found that judges who used the MMPI performed at a level above chance, but that those who used the Rorschach did not. Apparently, the Comprehensive System was not useful to clinicians in the identification of depression.[18]

Whitehead's study confirmed an old truism: Although the Rorschach can identify psychotic patients at a level above chance, it's usually unsuccessful at identifying other disorders, and generally doesn't increase accuracy beyond what can be obtained from the MMPI (see Chapter Six). However, Whitehead's dissertation was never published and went unnoticed by Rorschach scholars until 2000.[19]

A third significant dissertation from the 1980s was completed in 1989 by Gregory Meyer at Loyola University of Chicago. In retrospect, Meyer's dissertation is especially fascinating because it reported three crucial findings that foreshadowed the Rorschach controversies of the late 1990s.

First, using a sophisticated statistical technique known as factor analysis, Meyer examined the old "problem of R" in Exner's Comprehensive System. As Fiske and Baughman had shown in the early 1950s, R (the number of responses that a patient gives to the test) is the tide on which other Rorschach scores rise and fall (see Chapter Six). Meyer's factor analysis of Rorschach scores from 265 undergraduates showed that R continued to be a problem for the Comprehensive System, just as for earlier systems: "The great preponderance of the variability within the Rorschach data is simply due to the fact that subjects can give as many or as few responses to each card as they like. . . . [It] can be concluded that the traditional use of the Rorschach, where a subject can give as many or as few responses as desired, seriously compromises the validity of the test."[20]

In a second part of his dissertation, Meyer examined the relationship of the Rorschach to questionnaires. For example, several Comprehensive System scores are supposedly related to stress and painful emotions. Meyer hypothesized that these scores would be correlated with questionnaires that measure negative moods and depression. However, when he compared scores from the Rorschach and the questionnaires, he found no significant relationship. He concluded that the Rorschach "does not measure the fundamental dimensions of mood and personality that over the course of the past 20 years have become the most widely accepted paradigm for the study of personality and mood."[21]

Meyer's third major finding was unexpected. While preparing his data, he routinely computed simple descriptive statistics, including means and standard deviations, for the Rorschach variables. He discovered that the scores of the students in his sample were highly discrepant from Exner's norms, so that the students generally appeared sick: "For virtually every variable the variances and/or the means were significantly different across the two samples. . . . In general, and in contrast to the objective data. the Rorschach data indicated that the current sample was more 'pathological' than the standardization sample."[22]

Meyer carefully rechecked the scoring of the Rorschach protocols. He also examined the possibility that his sample of undergraduates was abnormal. He concluded that "there were no clear problems with the present sample in terms of Rorschach scoring or in terms of its comparability to a typical college population." Meyer concluded that his data indicated "problems" with Exner's norms.[23] It was the first harbinger of a controversy that would engulf the Comprehensive System ten years later.

Having uncovered three significant flaws in the Comprehensive System, Meyer seemed disenchanted. He minced no words when discussing the shortcomings in Exner's work: "Much of Exner's data remains unpublished, or non-refereed (in his books) and somewhat sloppy or contradictory when it is published."[24]

Meyer published his findings about the "problem of R" in the *Journal of Personality Assessment* in 1992.[25] It was a daring act, because at the time public criticisms of the Comprehensive System were rare. His article drew a rejoinder from Exner, who minimized the importance of the problem of R, calling it a "ghost of the past."[26] Meyer also published his finding that the Comprehensive System failed to correlate with questionnaires.[27]

However, Meyer's most explosive results were never published. His discovery that the Comprehensive System norms tend to make normal people appear "pathological" lay dormant in his dissertation until it was unearthed a decade later.[28] By that time Meyer had become the Comprehensive System's most prominent defender, disavowing the disturbing conclusions in his dissertation and energetically defending Exner's norms.[29]

THE CONTROVERSY OVER
THE COMPREHENSIVE SYSTEM

By the mid-1990s, the Comprehensive System was being taught to thousands of students in clinical psychology programs throughout the United States.[30] Doubts about the Rorschach were considered largely passé.[31] As Exner's co-author Irving Weiner expressed it: "Those who currently believe the Rorschach is an unscientific or unsound test with limited utility have not read the relevant literature of the last 20 years; or, having read it, they have not grasped its meaning."[32]

The "relevant literature," many psychologists thought, could be found in the various editions of Exner's books.

Another literature was slowly taking shape, however, as the number of dissertations and articles on the Comprehensive System increased. A substantial number of independent attempts to replicate Exner's findings had been unsuccessful, although few commentators noticed. Flaws in his research procedures had occasionally been noted, though no one yet grasped how important they were.

In 1995 and 1996 the first serious critiques of the Comprehensive System appeared. As new evidence emerged in the following years, heated debates erupted in clinical psychology's leading journals over the very aspects of the system that had established its psychometric respectability—scoring reliability, norms, and validity.

In this controversy, a key role has been played by the Rorschach Research Council,[33] a group of seven scholars organized by John Exner to promote research and development of the Comprehensive System. With few exceptions, articles published in defense of the system over the past several years have been written by members of the council, including Exner, Gregory Meyer (now at the University of Alaska at Anchorage), Mark Hilsenroth (Adelphi University), and Donald Viglione (California School of Professional Psychology of Alliant International University, San Diego). Exner's coauthor, Irving Weiner (University of South Florida), has also contributed to the debate.

The authors of this book have been among the most active critics of the system. Also outspoken in the Rorschach debate have been John Hunsley (University of Ottawa), Michael Bailey (Northwestern University), William Grove (University of Minnesota), and Robyn Dawes (Carnegie-Mellon University). However, virtually all of the research casting doubt on the system has come from psychologists favorably disposed toward the Rorschach and the Comprehensive System.

As we describe the controversy over the Comprehensive System, we'll inform readers about both sides of the debate and offer our own perspectives. In our view, the fundamental flaws in the system are obvious, although the debate about them threatens to go on interminably.

Scoring Reliability:
How Well Do Psychologists Agree?

There's no doubt that psychologists sometimes differ when scoring the Rorschach. One author of this book has observed amusing disagreements among his colleagues. In one instance, a graduate student asked how he should score the response of a patient who reported a "bra" in one of the blots. A male psychologist said that it should be scored as a "Sex" response, whereas several female psychologists insisted that it was a "Clothing" response. In this case, the scoring may have constituted a projective test for the psychologists as much as for the patient!

In the early 1990s such disagreements were assumed to be rare and inconsequential. Since 1978 Exner had assured readers that the scoring reliability of all variables in the Comprehensive System was .85 or higher.[34] Textbooks on psychological testing cited the number unquestioningly, and psychologists generally accepted Irving Weiner's claim that "all of the variables coded in the Comprehensive System can be coded with substantial interrater reliability."[35]

THE PROBLEM WITH PERCENTAGE OF AGREEMENT   In 1996, however, two articles (published almost simultaneously) pointed out the same problem.[36] Although the reliability of psychological tests is usually measured by a correlation coefficient, the .85 figure that Exner reported for Rorschach scores wasn't a correlation coefficient at all.[37] Apparently it was something quite different, namely "percentage of agreement."

In his classic 1965 critique of the Rorschach, Arthur Jensen warned against the use of percentage agreement as a measure of scoring reliability: "A word of caution concerning improper estimation of Rorschach reliability: these often consist of reporting the *percentage of agreement* between two or more judges. It should be clear that percentage agreement is not a legitimate measure of reliability and tells us none of the things we want to know when we ask about the reliability of a test."[38]

The problem with percentage of agreement, Jensen explained, is that it can make reliability appear higher—often *much* higher—than it really is.[39] To understand the problem, consider two psychologists who score the same Rorschach protocol. The protocol includes twenty responses, and each psychologist has randomly scored one response as Texture (a Texture response involves the sense of touch, for instance "a fuzzy rug"). The scores of the two psychologists are shown in Table 9.1. As can be seen, Psychologist A has randomly chosen to score the first response as Texture, and Psychologist B has chosen the eleventh.

Because each psychologist has deliberately scored at random, we'd expect the scoring reliability to be very low. In fact, if we calculate the correlation between the two scorers, we arrive at −.05, which correctly indicates very poor reliability (see Chapter Three).[40]

However, if we compute percentage of agreement, we get 90 percent, which seems to be very impressive. How can it be that the two psychologists achieved 90 percent agreement if they scored randomly? Notice that for eighteen out of twenty responses *both* psychologists scored *no* Texture response. These eighteen responses count as agreements. Thus the percentage of agreement is 18/20 = 90 percent!

As the example shows, percentage of agreement can be very high even if a Rorschach protocol is scored *completely at random*. For this reason, many psychometrically sophisticated psychologists have long considered percentage of agreement to be misleading as a measure of reliability.[41]

Exner, neglecting these problems, reported that he used percentage agreement to evaluate the scoring reliability of the Comprehensive System. Because he described the minimum reliability of his scores as ".85" instead of "85 percent,"[42] textbook writers and psychologists often interpreted the number as if it were a correlation coefficient, assuming that the reliability of the system must be high.

REEXAMINING THE SCORING RELIABILITY OF THE COMPREHENSIVE SYSTEM   When the problems with Exner's reliability figures were publicized in 1996, he explained in a comment in the journal *Psychological Science* that he didn't calculate "percentage of agreement" in the usual way: "Possibly I may have misled some members of the measurement community because I have used the label 'percentage of agreement,' rather than some other term to describe the procedure used. Possibly I should have labeled this approach 'percentage correct,' and I apologize if my negligence in the selection of wording has created a misconception."[43]

Although Exner proceeded to explain how he calculated "percentage correct," his explanation was ambiguous, creating confusion in the psychological journals.[44] In any event, it was clear that the reliability

Table 9.1. Correlation and Percentage of Agreement Between Two Psychologists Who Have Randomly Scored the Same Twenty Rorschach Responses for Texture.

Response No.	Psychologist A	Psychologist B
1	Yes	No
2	No	No
3	No	No
4	No	No
5	No	No
6	No	No
7	No	No
8	No	No
9	No	No
10	No	No
11	No	Yes
12	No	No
13	No	No
14	No	No
15	No	No
16	No	No
17	No	No
18	No	No
19	No	No
20	No	No

Correlation = −.05
Percentage of Agreement = 90 percent

Note: Yes = It's a Texture Response. No = It's Not a Texture Response.

figures in his books weren't correlation coefficients. Contrary to what psychologists had assumed for years, the scoring reliability of Comprehensive System scores remained unknown.

Several researchers favorably disposed toward the Comprehensive System undertook the task of determining its scoring reliability. In an article published in the *Journal of Personality Assessment* in 2000, Marvin Acklin and his colleagues reported correlation coefficients for Rorschach scores in two groups, patients and nonpatients. They found that more than 50 percent of Comprehensive System scores had reliabilities below .85, the standard established by Exner.[45] These results might have been devastating, except that Acklin and his colleagues proposed to lower the standard, arguing that a reliability of .61 or higher was "acceptable." Even by this lower standard, however, 12 percent of Rorschach scores had "unacceptable" reliability.[46]

It may be helpful to take a moment to consider the findings of Acklin and his colleagues in a broader context. For purposes of comparison, Graph A in Figure A.5 (in the Appendix) shows the scoring reliability of modern intelligence tests. This graph depicts the hypothetical scores of two psychologists who have scored fifty intelligence tests from the same patients. Each dot represents the intelligence test score of a single patient. The patient's score as determined by Psychologist 1 is plotted along the x-axis (at the bottom) and the score as determined by Psychologist 2 is plotted along the y-axis (at the side). The correlation between the two psychologists in Graph A is .90, which is the *minimum* scoring reliability of modern intelligence tests (see Chapters Three and Eight).[47]

Graph B shows the hypothetical scores of two psychologists who have scored Rorschachs from the same patients with a reliability of .85. Until the mid-1990s, psychologists generally believed that this was the *minimum* reliability of all scores in the Comprehensive System. However, Acklin and his colleagues found that fewer than half of Comprehensive System scores meet this standard.

Graph C shows the hypothetical scores of two psychologists who have scored Rorschachs from the same patients with a reliability of .61. As can be seen, the disagreements between the two psychologists are often extreme. For example, one child received a score of 105 from Psychologist 1, but a score of 72 from Psychologist 2. This difference is the equivalent of two psychologists assigning IQ scores of 105 (slightly above average) and 72 (borderline retardation) to the same child based on the same test results. Reliability this poor would be considered abominable for an IQ test, but Acklin and his colleagues considered it "acceptable" for the Rorschach.

Other studies on Comprehensive System reliability soon appeared. Lisa Nakata, a graduate student at the Pacific School of Professional Psychology, reported findings very similar to those of Acklin and his colleagues. In a dissertation completed in 1999, Nakata found that 45 percent of Comprehensive System scores fell below Exner's .85 standard of reliability, and that 10 percent fell below .61.[48]

Further results, reported in 1999 by Thomas Shaffer, Philip Erdberg, and John Haroian of the California School of Professional Psychology at Fresno, were even more discouraging. Their study was important because one of the scorers—Philip Erdberg—was a former instructor of Exner's Rorschach Workshops. These researchers found that reliability was below .85 for 84 percent of Rorschach scores, and below .61 for 44 percent.[49]

Vincent Guarnaccia and his colleagues at Hofstra University took a different approach to the same issue in 2001. They created a scoring test based on Rorschach responses in Exner's books. The test was administered to two groups—graduate students who had received instruction in the Comprehensive System, and licensed psychologists who used the system in their work. Both groups performed poorly. Guarnaccia concluded, "In general, accuracy scores for both students and professionals were below acceptable levels. The results suggest that high levels of scoring errors may exist in the field use of the Comprehensive System."[50]

However, an article published in the *Journal of Personality Assessment* reported much more encouraging results. In a study that included several samples of psychiatric patients, Gregory Meyer and his collaborators (including John Exner and Mark Hilsenroth) found that the reliability of Comprehensive System scores was much better than in other studies.[51] For example, a centerpiece of Meyer's article was a table reporting correlation coefficients for 171 separate scores.[52] In contrast with other studies, reliability was below .85 for only 20 percent of Rorschach scores, and below .61 for only one score.[53] Meyer argued that a reliability of .60 was "good," and a reliability of .74 was "excellent."[54] (Graph D in Figure A.2 depicts reliability of .74.)

Meyer and his colleagues suggested that other researchers had arrived at inappropriately low estimates of Rorschach reliability because they used small samples of subjects. In support of this opinion, the Meyer article showed that reliability coefficients can be underestimated if a Rorschach variable is rarely scored, and if sample size is small. Meyer and his colleagues concluded that previous negative findings may have been due to researchers' biases: "Claims of poor reliability may have emerged from negative attitudes toward the Rorschach as a method of assessment rather than from an understanding of the instrument and an appreciation of the available empirical literature."[55]

OUR PERSPECTIVE ON SCORING RELIABILITY   It's ironic that carefully conducted reliability studies on the Comprehensive System didn't appear until the late 1990s, many years after its acceptance in training programs and clinical practice. The issue of scoring reliability is not merely academic, because reliability is necessary for validity. If some scores in the Comprehensive System lack adequate scoring reliability, there's little possibility that they can predict important psychological characteristics. However, once such researchers as Acklin, Nakata, and Shaffer began to focus on the topic, they arrived at similar findings: All reported that reliability was below .85 for more than 50 percent of Rorschach scores.

The article by Meyer and his colleagues has cast some doubt on these figures, but by no means has it resolved the problem of Comprehensive System scoring reliability. Meyer and his colleagues made a compelling argument that the reliability of certain rarely scored Rorschach variables can be underestimated in small studies.[56] However, the fact remains that Acklin, Nakata, Shaffer, and their colleagues consistently reported low reliability for variables that are *not* rarely scored (for example, the Schizophrenia Index, the Suicide Constellation, and *Adjusted D*).[57]

Furthermore, the study by Meyer and his colleagues contains serious flaws of its own. These authors reported that when their article was submitted to another journal, questions were raised about its statistical approach.[58] Although Meyer and his colleagues rejected the criticisms, there are good reasons to believe they should have listened. The reliability figures in their article are almost certainly overestimates, inflated by statistical error.[59]

When replication studies yield conflicting results, there's often no way to resolve the inconsistencies except to carry out more studies. Of course, confusion will only increase unless the new studies use sound methodology and statistics. See Exhibit 9.2 for our methodological recommendations for future research on Comprehensive System scoring reliability.

In our opinion, it's vital that researchers use a sound standard to evaluate the performance of Comprehensive System scores. We disagree strongly with Acklin and Meyer's claims that Rorschach scoring reliability of .61 is "good," and that reliability of .74 is "excellent." As the graphs in Figure A.5 show, serious errors can occur when standards are set this low.[60] For this reason, experts have recommended a much higher standard of .80 or .90 for tests used in clinical or forensic settings.[61] Because the Rorschach can affect important decisions about people's lives, adherence to high standards is essential. We recommend that the Rorschach's scoring reliability be evaluated against either the .85 standard proposed by Exner or the .90 standard applied to intelligence tests.

Exhibit 9.2. Researching Comprehensive System Reliability.

Regarding interrater reliability studies of the Comprehensive System, we suggest the following guidelines:

1. All protocols in a sample should be randomly sampled from the same population (for example, all the protocols administered in a certain clinic over a certain time period). If two populations are studied (for example, clinical versus nonclinical, clients from clinic A versus clients from clinic B), the samples should be kept separate.

2. Although a sample size of twenty can be informative, a sample size of fifty or a hundred is preferable because it provides more stable estimates of the correlation coefficients.

3. Although two scorers are sufficient, studies that use three or more scorers are preferable, because they allow the researcher to explore whether disagreements are caused by the unreliability of a variable or the unreliability of individual scorers.

4. All scorers should score *all* protocols in a sample. Although it may seem more convenient to let one pair of scorers score half the sample while another pair scores the other half, such a design can create extremely complex statistical problems regarding calculation of the intraclass correlation coefficient (ICC).

5. Scoring should be independent and autonomous (that is, while the study is still under way, scorers must be unaware of the scoring by other scorers, and should not consult any other person about scoring). It is acceptable, however, for scorers to consult appropriate books or course notes.

6. Scorers should not practice scoring together before initiating a reliability study. Otherwise, they may develop their own set of idiosyncratic scoring conventions that allow them to achieve higher reliability than they could by using the regular set of scoring rules. Similarly, to avoid the effect of such idiosyncratic conventions, it's undesirable for a teacher-student pair to participate as raters in the same reliability study. The best situation (which is not always practical) is for raters to be well-trained, but by different teachers.

7. If the purpose of the study is to examine the interrater reliability of a Rorschach score, the data should be analyzed with the two-way random effects form of the ICC, which is available in SPSS.

8. Reliability should be estimated for ratios (for example, *EB, FC:CF + C, W:M*), not just the separate variables that make up these ratios. The reliability of ratios can be considerably different from the reliability of their component scores (Cronbach, 1949c). Similarly, reliability should be estimated for indexes (for example, *DEPI, Adjusted D*) and percentages (*X+%, F%*). The study by Acklin et al. (2000) provides a relatively good model for which variables to include.

9. If the sample of protocols is small (that is, less than fifty), then it may be inadvisable to calculate the reliability of scores with low base rates (that is, scores that occur in fewer than 1 percent or 2 percent of responses).

10. If the reliability of low-base-rate scores is of interest, then a large number of protocols should be scored (a hundred or even two hundred). To reduce the burden on scorers, it may be possible to design the study so that they are asked to score *only* the low-base-rate scores, while ignoring other scoring categories.

In the meantime, can anything conclusive be said regarding the scoring reliability of the Comprehensive System? Our reading of the studies by Acklin, Nakata, Shaffer, and their colleagues suggests several consistent findings, many of which can't be attributed only to small sample size. In Table 9.2, we present a brief selection of important Comprehensive System scores that have consistently demonstrated either high (.85 or above) or low (lower than .80) reliability in these studies.[62] We suspect that future studies will confirm the general picture presented in Table 9.2. Until several independent researchers have arrived at consistent results, however, the scoring reliability of the Comprehensive System will remain murky, just as it has been since the 1970s.

Still Overpathologizing:
The Comprehensive System Norms

In the 1950s, psychologists' tendency to overdiagnose psychopathology on the basis of the Rorschach was well-documented (see Chapter Six). For example, in a study at Berkeley, psychologists relying on the test diagnosed two-thirds of adolescents in a community sample as "maladjusted."[63] Similarly, when a researcher at the University of Chicago gave psychologists the Rorschach of a normal man he called David, they tended to describe him less accurately and as much sicker than he really was.[64]

By the 1990s, however, the Rorschach's tendency to overpathologize normal people was virtually forgotten. If the old studies had been remembered, they probably would have been dismissed as irrelevant to the Comprehensive System. Psychologists took it for granted that Exner's norms provided a benchmark of normality. According to those norms, few normal adults ever produce a Reflection response or receive a high score on the Schizophrenia Index. Thus, when an individual received one of these scores, it was regarded as rare and deviant.

Anyone reading Exner's books couldn't fail to be impressed by the dozens of dense pages filled with numbers. Means, standard deviations, and other statistics were reported for over a hundred Rorschach variables in normal adults, psychiatric patients, and children.[65] So massive were the norms of the Comprehensive System, so impressive the effort that had created them, it was virtually impossible to imagine that they might be wildly wrong.

Table 9.2.   A Selection of Comprehensive System Scores That Probably Have High and Low Scoring Reliability.

High reliability (.85 or above)

R	WSumC	PER
W	Lambda	COP
D	Zf	Human content
Dd	Zsum	Active movement
S	Blends/R	
EA	Affective Ratio	
M	Egocentricity Index	
FM	Reflections	

Low reliability (below .80)

Schizophrenia Index	WSum6	FC: CF + C
Suicide Constellation	All Special Scores	Sum V
Coping Deficit Index	Level 2 Special Scores	Sum T
Adjusted D		Sum Y
		Passive movement

THE LID BLOWS OFF   It was at an international Rorschach conference in Amsterdam in the summer of 1999 that the news first broke upon an audience of bewildered listeners. In a symposium with the bland title "Rorschach Nonpatient Data: Findings from Around the World," Philip Erdberg, Thomas Shaffer, and colleagues from Mexico, Portugal, France, Italy, and Finland presented the results of an international collaborative project. Whereas most Rorschach studies focus on individuals with psychological problems, the researchers in the symposium presented findings on nonpatients—people living in the community with no obvious psychological disorders.

The results of this seemingly innocuous project would dramatically alter the way that many psychologists viewed the Comprehensive System. There were two central findings. First, the researchers reported that the Rorschach scores of individuals in Europe, Central America, and the United States were often very similar. This finding was welcome to many listeners. It suggested that the Comprehensive System could be disseminated successfully in countries outside the United States without being seriously affected by cultural or linguistic differences.

The second finding was disconcerting. Although the scores from the various countries resembled each other, they didn't resemble the Comprehensive System norms. For one Rorschach variable after another, striking differences from the norms emerged. In all the countries, including the United States, nonpatient subjects looked pathological when compared with the numbers in Exner's books.

Following the conference, word quickly rippled across the Internet. "So what do you think?" asked one member of a discussion group for psychologists. "Are Exner's norms off or is this evidence for the decline and fall of western civilization?"[66]

Within a few months, Shaffer and Erdberg published the study of American adults that they presented in Amsterdam.[67] Their subjects were college students and volunteer donors at a blood bank who were administered the WAIS-R, MMPI-2, and Rorschach—and it should be noted that these blood bank donors were *volunteers* who gave their blood, not individuals who sold their blood for money. At the time of the study, it was illegal to sell blood in California. The group scored above average in intelligence and looked normal on the MMPI-2. However, according to the Rorschach they were seriously disturbed. About one in six scored in the pathological range on the Schizophrenia Index. Nearly 30 percent gave a Reflection response (Exner claimed such responses were rare and invariably indicated narcissism; see Chapter Eight). On these scores and many others, this apparently normal group of American adults appeared severely pathological when compared with the Comprehensive System norms.

Other articles with similar results followed. In 2000, Mel Hamel, collaborating with Erdberg and Shaffer, reported a study of a hundred children in California. According to behavioral histories and ratings by parents, the children were quite healthy. However, on the Rorschach they appeared deeply disturbed. Hamel and his colleagues commented: "If we were writing a Rorschach-based, collective psychological evaluation for this sample, the clinical descriptors would command attention. In the main, these children may be described as grossly misperceiving and misinterpreting their surroundings and having unconventional ideation and significant cognitive impairment. Their distortion of reality and faulty reasoning approach psychosis. These children would also likely be described as having significant problems establishing and maintaining interpersonal relationships and coping within a social context. They apparently suffer from an affective disorder that includes many of the markers found in clinical depression."[68]

The authors of this book also published an article on the Comprehensive System norms. Searching the scientific literature back to 1974, we identified thirty-two studies that had administered the Comprehensive System to nonpatient adult Americans (many of these studies had focused on patients with psychological disorders, but used nonpatients as a comparison group). When we combined the nonpatient results across studies, we found that they were markedly discrepant from the Exner norms but very similar to the numbers reported by Shaffer and Erdberg. For example, we found that 29 percent of adults gave a Reflection response—the same figure reported by Shaffer and Erdberg, but four times as large as the 7 percent reported in the Exner norms. We concluded, "The norms for important Comprehensive System scores do not currently represent American nonpatient adults and probably never did. Whether the Rorschach is interpreted by itself or in combination with other data, the possibility of overdiagnosing psychopathology is likely to increase if these norms are used. We recommend that psychologists not use the norms in clinical or forensic work, with either children or adults."[69]

As is often the case with discoveries, the startling findings reported in 1999 and the following years weren't *entirely* new. Earlier researchers had identified problems with the Comprehensive System norms, although the findings had attracted little attention. We've already mentioned Meyer's 1989 dissertation, which concluded that there were "problems" with the norms.[70] Similarly, a 1993 chapter by Robert Kelly and Sharon Ben-Meir of the University of California at Los Angeles noted that Exner's norms seemed to overpathologize normal children.

Ironically, Exner's books provided probably the most striking illustration of the Comprehensive System's tendency to overpathologize.[71] In a study in the early 1980s, Beatrice Mittman of Long Island University distributed packets of Rorschach protocols to ninety alumni of the Rorschach Workshops under Exner's guidance.[72] The psychologists were asked to assign the protocols to several diagnostic categories, including "normal." Although most protocols came from psychiatric patients, some were from nonpatient adults.

Mittman's findings were troubling. Overall, psychologists using the Comprehensive System diagnosed more than 75 percent of apparently normal individuals as disturbed. The incorrect diagnoses most likely to be assigned were depression, other mood disorders, and personality disorder. For example, the psychologists classified 12 percent of the nonpatient protocols as "major affective disorder," 23 percent as "reactive depression," and 43 percent as "personality disorder." These results are reminiscent of the studies from the 1950s that first exposed psychologists' tendency to overpathologize when using the Rorschach.

Exner published a summary of Mittman's findings. However, he didn't discuss the possibility that the Comprehensive System might overpathologize. Instead, he concluded that the results reflected bias in the psychologists who participated in the study: "It seems clear that the 90 judges . . . were set or disposed to find pathology or psychological liabilities."[73]

THE NORMATIVE SAMPLE AS "HEALTHIER THAN AVERAGE"   The disconcerting revelations about Exner's norms that first surfaced at the 1999 Amsterdam conference set off a fierce controversy in the psychological journals. Articles reached widely divergent conclusions. Commentators without ties to the Comprehensive System unanimously concluded that the norms were probably in error.[74] In contrast, defenders of the system denied that a problem existed. Exner and Weiner questioned the findings of Shaffer and Erdberg, speculating that the subjects in their study may have been unusually defensive, or that the Rorschach had been administered incorrectly.[75] Gregory Meyer vigorously criticized our review of thirty-two studies of nonpatient American adults. He asserted (despite the findings of his dissertation) that "the Comprehensive System norms do not overpathologize." Meyer rejected the findings of his dissertation on the grounds that the administration and scoring of Rorschach protocols may have been inadequate.[76]

One of Meyer's arguments was particularly influential among defenders of the Comprehensive System. He claimed that other groups looked sick compared with the Exner norms because the norms were based on an unusually healthy group of nonpatients.[77] Meyer noted that many subjects in the Comprehensive System normative sample were recruited either through their work, or through such social organizations as the PTA, Audubon Society, and bowling leagues. Consequently, he contended, they demonstrated "positive evidence of functioning and health." Because the members of the normative sample were "healthier than average," Meyer argued, it was hardly surprising that other groups of nonpatients appeared pathological when compared with them.[78]

Because Meyer's argument was echoed by Weiner and other advocates of the Comprehensive System, we'll take a moment to examine it in detail.[79] First, we should note that Exner's books provided little information about the mental health of subjects in the normative group. He stated merely that "none have any admitted psychiatric history" and that "the subjects are not necessarily normal; they are simply not patients."[80]

The members of the normative sample apparently weren't interviewed in depth to exclude individuals with a history of psychological symptoms, alcohol abuse, or criminal activity.[81] Nor were they administered the MMPI or other questionnaires to measure their psychological health. Although some subjects in the normative sample were recruited from their jobs or clubs, Exner reported that others were recruited through social service agencies, apparently to ensure that the sample included a wide variety of individuals.[82]

Exner's books provided no solid evidence—for example, from diagnostic interviews or personality questionnaires—to support Meyer's picture of the normative sample as substantially "healthier than average." Thus Meyer was forced to rely on indirect evidence to support his views—for instance, when he conjectured that membership in such groups as the Audubon Society and bowling leagues constituted "positive evidence of functioning and health."[83] Furthermore, Meyer ignored Exner's straightforward statement in 1991 that members of the normative sample were *not* necessarily normal: "The only element common to all subjects is the absence of psychiatric history. The subjects are not necessarily normal; they are simply not patients. As such they represent a vast array of individual differences, with dimensions ranging from introversive to extratensive, well controlled to poorly controlled, gregarious to isolated, strange to sturdy, and so on."[84]

In fact, the notion that Exner's normative group was "healthier than average" didn't surface until *after* the norms became controversial. The norms were first published in 1989.[85] Not until ten years later, following the Amsterdam conference and its startling revelations, did Meyer, Weiner, and other defenders of the Comprehensive System begin to claim that its norms represented unusually healthy individuals.

Until 1999, psychologists who used the Comprehensive System were under the impression that its norms represented "average" nonpatients. This was the view encouraged by Exner's books and dis-seminated by his followers. As Barry Ritzler, a professor at Long Island University and instructor for Exner's Rorschach Workshops, stated: "I have often made the claim that the Exner norms represented people at 'average' levels of psychological functioning. . . . I do not see the Exner norms as 'high' functioning. At least, not the highest. Not the lowest either. These are regular folks who represent the middle range of psychological effectiveness."[86]

CONSTERNATION ON THE INTERNET: THE 221 DUPLICATE PROTOCOLS   By early 2001, the controversy over the Comprehensive System norms had attracted widespread attention in scientific journals and even the *New York Times*.[87] In the midst of this debate, a stunning new revela-tion appeared unobtrusively in the fifth edition of *A Rorschach Work-book for the Comprehensive System*, written by Exner and published by the Rorschach Workshops at the end of February 2001.

In the middle of a paragraph on page 172 of the *Workbook*, Exner discussed his new normative tables. These tables were based on six hundred nonpatient adults, although in his previous books the same tables had been based on seven hundred adults. Exner explained this discrepancy in two sentences: "The reduced number results from the fact that when the sample of 700 nonpatients was selected, using strat-ification criteria, more than 200 duplicate records were included. Once detected, those records were deleted from the sample and most have been replaced to constitute the sample used here."[88]

Exner thus notified psychologists that the Comprehensive System normative sample of seven hundred subjects described in his books since 1989 didn't really contain seven hundred subjects after all.[89] Instead, it consisted of only 479 subjects.[90] A subset of these—221— had somehow been duplicated and then added to the original 479, yielding an illusory sample of 700 subjects. Psychologists had been using this flawed set of norms for over ten years.

When news of the error began to spread though the Internet, reac-tions on psychology discussion lists included disbelief and outrage. Joel Dvoskin of the University of Arizona College of Medicine asked: "Is this a hoax? . . . Even if one assumes arguendo that the new norms are diagnostically valid, how many people were misdiagnosed during the past 11 years? This boggles the mind."[91]

Ray Hays of the University of Texas–Houston Medical School said: "What about ten years and hundreds of patients who were perhaps diagnosed incorrectly? Why should we pay for new norms? I want my money back for the hundreds of dollars I spent . . . and the thousands of hours I wrestled trying to make data fit together in some comprehensible form in psychological reports."[92]

However, Gregory Meyer came to Exner's defense on the lists: "I'm not sure what the important news is. Is it just that 'something' happened? Or is the important thing that it can be made to sound bad? Or is it congratulations to Exner for discovering and correcting a potential problem?"[93]

In the ensuing Internet discussions, many psychologists expressed understandable curiosity about how an error of such enormous magnitude could have occurred and remained undetected for more than a decade.

Exner didn't participate in the Internet discussions, nor to our knowledge has he ever publicly explained how the errors in the normative sample occurred. However, Barry Ritzler posted the following explanation: "John Exner told me that a technician who worked for him a number of years ago was responsible for entering the normative data. He actually entered 700 DIFFERENT cases, but pushed the wrong button and got a re-entering of the PREVIOUS 200 cases rather than 200 new ones. So 700 separate cases were prepared for entry into the norms, but only 500 got in, 200 twice."[94]

The person who discovered that the norms were based on hundreds of duplicate cases was apparently Gregory Meyer. On an Internet list in March 2001, he stated that he found the errors in spring 1999—two years before Exner acknowledged them in his *Workbook*: "I believe I was the one who discovered the problem. It was at a convention meeting in the course of running some analyses on a laptop. . . . The convention was the spring before last. Exner was present at the meeting and I told him about it then."[95]

Thus, it seems, when Shaffer and Erdberg presented their unsettling research on the norms at Amsterdam in the summer of 1999, Meyer and Exner probably already knew about the flaws in the normative sample.[96] However, neither mentioned the problem in their published defenses of the norms.[97]

WHICH NORMS ARE THE "REAL" ONES? Psychologists who use the Comprehensive System now face an uncomfortable quandary: Which norms, if any, are the "real" ones? Which can be used confidently with clients?

Many psychologists are currently using the "revised" norms published in Exner's 2001 *Workbook*. He constructed these norms by retaining the 479 unduplicated protocols from the "old" norms, then adding 121 more from his pool of Rorschach protocols, to bring the total to 600.

However, these revised norms have problems almost as serious as the old ones. Most important, the revised and old norms are very similar, and both differ strikingly from the numbers reported by Shaffer and his colleagues, the international studies presented at the Amsterdam conference, and our article. If the old norms are in error, probably the revised ones are too. Both apparently overpathologize normal people.

In addition, Gregory Meyer recently reported that the protocols used for Exner's norms (including the 2001 norms) have probably been scored incorrectly for Form Quality since the mid-1980s.[98] Apparently the norms for several important Rorschach scores (the Schizophrenia Index, $X+\%$, $X-\%$, $M-$, $S-\%$) have been seriously in error for more than fifteen years.

As can be seen, there are weighty reasons for psychologists *not* to use the revised norms that Exner published in 2001. Although he hasn't acknowledged that either the old or the revised norms are inaccurate, Exner has recently reported that he's collecting an entirely new sample of protocols and constructing a new set of norms.[99] However, preliminary results indicate that these new norms are similar to the old ones, and often discrepant from what Shaffer and other researchers have found. So long as Exner's results continue to differ markedly from those of other researchers, questions about the accuracy of his norms are bound to linger.

Meanwhile, Shaffer has proposed that psychologists adopt an alternative set of norms that he developed based on his research with Erdberg.[100] The advantage of these "Shaffer and Erdberg" norms is that they agree with what other researchers have reported. The disadvantage is that, in their currently published form, they're based on only 123 California adults, rather than a large national sample.[101] However, Shaffer and Erdberg have apparently been enlarging their sample and intend to publish updated numbers.

Until the dilemma of the Rorschach norms is resolved, psychologists face the difficult choice of deciding between the Exner norms and the Shaffer and Erdberg norms. Many patients who appear seriously disturbed according to one set of norms appear normal according to the other. As one psychologist, Kim McKinzey of San Francisco, remarked on the Internet, "Reminds me of when we had two popes."[102]

OUR PERSPECTIVE ON THE COMPREHENSIVE SYSTEM NORMS   As readers will have surmised, the authors of this book believe that the norms of the Comprehensive System are seriously in error and tend to make normal individuals appear pathological. In Table 9.3, we present a brief selection of important Comprehensive System scores that probably overpathologize normal individuals. This list is based on the Exner norms of 1991, 1993, and 2001, the research of Shaffer, Erdberg, and their colleagues, and our review of the literature.[103]

The defenders of the Comprehensive System have yet to address several grave issues, which loom large for those who question the norms. For example, what are psychologists' legal and ethical obligations toward patients who may have been misidentified as pathological by the Exner norms during the past fifteen or twenty years? What is the status of legal cases in which the Rorschach and its flawed norms have played a role? Published articles by Exner and his closest colleagues do not even acknowledge that these problems exist.[104] Psychologists are apparently on their own when facing such dilemmas.

Table 9.3.   A Selection of Comprehensive System Scores That Probably Overpathologize Due to Inaccurate Norms.

Depression Index	Ambitent *EB* Style	*Blends*
Schizophrenia Index	*Space*	*Blends/R*
Coping Deficit Index	*Sum Y*	Affective Ratio
X–%	*Sum T*	Reflections
X+%	*Populars*	Human responses
F+%	*Lambda* (*F%*)	Morbid responses
WSum6	*FC:CF+C*	Pure Color responses
Level 2 Special Scores	*WSumC*	Cooperative movement

Recently developed scores that may overpathologize:

WDA%

XA%

Perceptual Thinking Index

A few years ago, Jim Wood, first author of this book, was approached at a conference by a psychologist who regularly uses the Rorschach in legal cases. If the Comprehensive System's norms are in error, the psychologist asked, what could he use instead?

Jim suggested that, for a start, he should compare his Rorschach findings with Erdberg and Shaffer's numbers.

"I've tried that," the psychologist replied.

"And what did you find?" asked Jim.

The psychologist shrugged his shoulders and seemed uncomfortable. "Everybody comes out looking normal," he said.

What Does It Measure—Really? The Problem of Validity

In the 1980s and 1990s, the Rorschach was promoted for a remarkably wide variety of purposes. Exner, Weiner, and other proponents of the Comprehensive System claimed that it could identify such psychiatric disorders as depression, schizophrenia, and posttraumatic stress disorder.[105] It was said to reveal the presence of distressing emotions, and to detect a large number of undesirable personality characteristics including egocentricity, impulsiveness, and antisocial tendencies.

As the system grew, its advocates made ever bolder claims. Exner's former student Donald Viglione argued that the Rorschach was useful for predicting new crimes by murderers and rapists.[106] Gregory Meyer claimed at one point in his career that it could identify sexually abused patients and even predict the occurrence of cancer.[107]

Starting in the mid-1990s, however, critics of the Comprehensive System began to look more closely at the expansive claims of its promoters. The critics, including the authors of this book, concluded that most claims regarding the system's validity either lacked solid scientific support or were contradicted by research. But before providing a detailed discussion of Comprehensive System validity, we'll pause to discuss the standards we have used to evaluate it.

EVALUATING RORSCHACH VALIDITY: THREE CRITERIA   In a debate with Exner published in 1996, we proposed three criteria for identifying a well-validated Rorschach score.[108] Although our focus was on the Comprehensive System, these criteria can be applied to any psychological test:

1. The score's relationship to a particular psychological disorder or symptom has been examined in studies by *several unrelated researchers or research groups.*

2. The studies are *methodologically sound.*

3. Their results are *consistent.*

These three criteria emphasize the importance of independent *replication,* which, as we explained earlier in this chapter, is one of the most important quality control mechanisms in science. A single study by a single researcher or group of collaborators can yield misleading results due to mistakes or chance. In addition, a research team may replicate its own findings by making the same methodological errors across studies. However, when *several independent researchers or research groups* using *methodologically sound* procedures arrive at *consistent* results, the findings can be accepted with considerable confidence.

According to these criteria, studies from Exner's Rorschach Workshops are insufficient to establish the validity of the Comprehensive System. Several other researchers must examine the scores independently and report similar findings. Replications for the Comprehensive System are especially important for reasons that we'll explain in the next two sections.

FAILED REPLICATIONS: THE DEPRESSION INDEX AND EGOCENTRICITY INDEX   During the past decade, two serious problems with Exner's Rorschach Workshops Studies have become apparent. The first is that the findings from the Workshops often can't be replicated by other researchers. In fact, some of the most extensively studied indexes in the Comprehensive System have performed so poorly in replication studies that the positive findings originally reported by Exner appear to be anomalous.

For example, based on findings from the Rorschach Workshops, Exner reported that scores on the Depression Index correlate highly with diagnoses of depression.[109] However, this claim has been undermined by independent studies.[110] Out of fourteen attempted replications, eleven found no significant relationship between the Depression Index and diagnoses of depression, two reported mixed results, and only one yielded unmixed positive results.[111]

Similarly, Exner claimed that scores on the Egocentricity Index are related to self-focus and self-esteem, and that low scores on this index are related to depression. However, the large majority of independent attempts to replicate Exner's findings regarding the Egocentricity Index have been unsuccessful.[112] Contrary to the claims in his books, the Egocentricity Index seems to bear little or no relationship to self-focus, self-esteem, or depression.

The gaps between Exner's results and those of other researchers are sometimes puzzling. For example, in one unpublished Workshops Study, interviews of job candidates were tape recorded and scored for the number of times each candidate used the words *I, me,* or *my*.[113] Exner reported an astounding correlation of .67 between candidates' use of these pronouns and their scores on the Egocentricity Index. Furthermore, candidates with high Egocentricity scores spent significantly more time looking into a mirror while waiting to be interviewed than did candidates with low scores.

However, when other researchers tried to replicate these impressive findings, they came away empty-handed. They found that Egocentricity Index scores were not significantly related either to the use of first-person pronouns or to mirror inspection.[114]

The failure of the Egocentricity Index in replication studies was summarized in a 1995 review by two authors of this book.[115] Struck by the marked discrepancies between Exner's findings and those of other researchers, we began to wonder whether the Workshops Studies contain methodological or statistical errors that could explain the anomalies. Accordingly, we wrote to Exner requesting copies of some of the unpublished research cited in his books. This led us to discover the second problem with the Rorschach Workshops Studies.

THE INACCESSIBILITY OF THE WORKSHOPS STUDIES AND EXNER'S DATA   As we've mentioned, the descriptions of the Workshops Studies in Exner's books tend to be vague and brief. Exner commonly buttressed these short summaries by inserting scholarly citations to the unpublished studies of the Rorschach Workshops. We assumed, as many psychologists probably did, that these citations referred to written reports that provided further detail about his research methodology and results.

However, when we wrote to Exner in 1993 to request some of his unpublished studies on the Egocentricity Index, we received a reply from an administrative assistant informing us that they were unavailable.[116] In a follow-up, we wrote Exner and requested other Workshops Studies, stating that we'd be happy to pay for any copying or mailing expenses. Again the assistant replied by telling us that the works we requested were "not available in a form that can be easily copied and forwarded to you."[117] She wrote, "Dr. Exner has asked that I respond to your letter of February 5 requesting copies of some of our unpublished work. During the period from 1968 to 1990 more than 1000 studies were undertaken at Rorschach Workshops to address various issues. The majority of these are not written in a publishable form. Instead, they usually include a brief statement concerning the methodology of the study."

The assistant added that the Rorschach Workshops could provide raw data related to specific questions, but that we might have to pay for computer costs.

We subsequently recounted our experience with the Rorschach Workshops in several journals.[118] In one article we wrote: "Many readers of *The Rorschach: A Comprehensive System* are probably under the impression that the Workshops Studies are actual documents that can be examined by other scholars. However, this impression is often mistaken."[119]

In another we said: "It is important that research papers and data be made accessible. Certainly, if unpublished studies demonstrated that the Rorschach is invalid, Rorschach advocates would be unhappy if they could not obtain copies of the Method and Results sections for those studies."[120]

Exner published a reply to one of our articles, offering his own version of the facts: "They requested copies of more than 20 studies and were informed that, while most were not written in a form that could be released, they could obtain statements concerning the designs if those in various volumes were not clear, plus the raw data matrices, plus any tables relating to the data analyses still available, or the analyses could be regenerated provided they would assume the cost of downloading the data from a mainframe computer and/or the costs of any technician time."[121]

As can be seen, Exner generally confirmed our accounts. However, he introduced a few new details. Contrary to his assertions, neither he nor his assistant ever offered to send us any "statements concerning the designs" or "tables."

Years later, we again entered into a correspondence with Exner. Our article on the apparent errors in the Comprehensive System norms was accepted at *Clinical Psychology: Science and Practice* in summer 2000.[122] One of the reviewers of that article suggested that we write

Exner and ask to examine his normative data. Accordingly, we mailed a request to him, offering to pay expenses. We were somewhat hopeful because, in the published statement just quoted, Exner indicated that "raw data matrices" were available.

When Exner wrote back, he said that he felt some hesitation about sharing his data with us, but would discuss the matter with the members of the Rorschach Research Council.[123] A few months later he wrote again, saying that our request had been presented to the Council, which had rejected it. In his letter Exner stated: "That data have been analyzed and re-analyzed several times and it seems extremely unlikely that data errors might account for some of the discrepancies between these data and other published samples."[124]

Three months after we received this letter, Exner's new *Workbook* appeared.[125] In it he revealed that the 700 subjects in his normative sample actually consisted of 479 subjects, plus 221 duplicates.

WHICH COMPREHENSIVE SYSTEM SCORES ARE WELL-VALIDATED?   Readers should now appreciate our insistence that the scores of the Comprehensive System be validated by several independent researchers, and not simply by the Rorschach Workshops. Which of the system's scores have been well-validated, according to the three criteria we've described?

In Table 9.4, we've listed the variables in the system that, according to our review of the scientific literature, possess well-established validity.[126] We've tried to err on the side of generosity. For example, to the best of our knowledge, the relation between *R* (number of responses) and intelligence has not been well-validated using the Comprehensive System. However, because studies in the 1950s repeatedly demonstrated this relationship, we've included *R* in our list.

As can be seen, the Comprehensive System's validity is not much different from that of older Rorschach systems. Valid Comprehensive System variables fall into two broad categories. First, several scores bear a modest relationship to intelligence. People with higher intelligence are likely to give more responses to the test (*R*), and their responses tend to be complex (Blends/R, *Lambda*), well-organized (*DQ+, Zf, W*), and appropriate to the shape of the blots (*F+%, X+%, X−%*). Furthermore, people with higher intelligence are more likely to report human figures in the blots (Human responses), particularly figures in movement (*M*). These conclusions are parallel to what researchers reported in the 1950s using older Rorschach systems (see Chapter Six).

Table 9.4.   Comprehensive System Scores That Are Probably Valid.

Related to intelligence:

Number of responses (*R*)
Organizational activity (*Zf, DQ+, W*)
Complexity (low *Lambda*, low *F%, Blends/R*)
Form Quality (*X+%, F+%*, low *X–%*, probably *XA%* and *WDA%*)
Human figures (No. of Human responses, *M*)

Related to schizophrenia, other psychotic disorders, thought disorder, schizotypal personality disorder, and borderline personality disorder:

Form Quality (low scores on *X+%, F+%*; high scores on *X–%, M–*)
Deviant Verbalizations (*WSum6*)
Schizophrenia Index
Perceptual Thinking Index

Second, Comprehensive System measures of Form Quality (*X–%, X+%, F+%*) and Deviant Verbalizations (*WSum6*) are related to schizophrenia, psychotic disorders, and thought disorder. As we discussed in Chapter Six, research in the 1950s confirmed that poor Form Quality and Deviant Verbalizations are related to schizophrenia. Recent research suggests that Deviant Verbalizations are also related to bipolar disorder (formerly known as manic-depressive illness), and probably to schizotypal personality disorder and borderline personality disorder (conditions that sometimes involve thought disorder).

Exner combined several Rorschach scores for Form Quality and Deviant Verbalizations into the Schizophrenia Index. As would be expected, this index bears a well-demonstrated relationship to schizophrenia.[127] The Schizophrenia Index was recently discarded and replaced with the Perceptual-Thinking Index or PTI. The PTI has not yet been adequately validated.[128] However, considering its close resemblance to the Schizophrenia Index, we would be surprised if the PTI failed to show a relationship to schizophrenia, other psychotic conditions, and thought disorder.

Other than the scores listed in Table 9.4, we've been unable to identify any Comprehensive System scores with well-established validity. Some scores possess validity as measures of *cognitive ability* (intelligence) or *cognitive impairment* (thought disorder and psychosis). Otherwise, the Comprehensive System doesn't appear to bear a consistent relationship to psychological disorders or symptoms, personality characteristics, potential for violence, or such health problems as cancer.

Of course, it's possible we've overlooked something. Thus, in our debate with Exner in 1996, we invited him to publish a list of all additional Comprehensive System scores that meet our three well-defined criteria for validity, with citations to the supporting research.[129] Seven years have since passed, but as of this writing (October 2002), neither Exner nor any other advocate of the Comprehensive System has published such a list.

VALIDITY FOR DIAGNOSTIC OR FORENSIC PURPOSES   The Rorschach is used routinely in clinical and legal settings for diagnostic decision making. It's sobering to consider that the test lacks well-established validity for this purpose, with the few exceptions noted in Table 9.4. In an article published in 2000, we reviewed hundreds of studies regarding the relationship of psychiatric diagnoses to the Rorschach. We concluded: "Despite a few positive findings, the Rorschach has demonstrated little validity as a diagnostic tool. The Rorschach has not shown a well-demonstrated relationship to Major Depressive Disorder, Posttraumatic Stress Disorder (PTSD), anxiety disorders other than PTSD, Dissociative Identity Disorder, Dependent, Narcissistic, or Antisocial Personality Disorders, Conduct Disorder, or psychopathy."[130]

In a rare but welcome occurrence, several Rorschach proponents concurred with our opinion. For example, Robert Bornstein of Gettysburg College wrote, "The Rorschach Inkblot Method is not a diagnostic tool." Irving Weiner made the same point, but even more emphatically: "The Rorschach Inkblot Method is not a diagnostic test, it was not designed as a diagnostic test, it is not intended to be a diagnostic test, and it does not in fact work very well as a diagnostic test."[131]

Weiner's opinion represented a significant shift in his position, because only two years previously he had made claims that were considerably more optimistic regarding the Comprehensive System's diagnostic powers: "At present the Rorschach Comprehensive System provides indices for schizophrenia (*SCZI*) and depression (*DEPI*) that can prove helpful in identifying these two conditions. . . . In addition, although further documentation is needed, accumulating data indicate that there are on the horizon adequately conceptualized and empirically valid Rorschach indices for bipolar disorder, borderline and schizotypal personality disorder, and acute and chronic stress disorder."[132]

In recent years, there appears to be increasing recognition, even among Rorschach proponents, that the Comprehensive System has limited usefulness as a measure of psychological disturbance. Meanwhile, the validity of the system for forensic purposes has also come into question.

In the early 1990s, the application of the Comprehensive System in legal settings was given a strong boost by Carl Gacono, then at Atascadero State Hospital in California, and J. Reid Meloy of the University of California at San Diego. In a study of prison inmates based on Gacono's dissertation, these investigators identified several Rorschach scores that seemed to differentiate psychopaths (individuals who are emotionally cold, manipulative, and remorseless) and nonpsychopaths.[133] For example, Gacono and Meloy reported that psychopaths produced more Reflection responses (supposedly indicating narcissism) than did nonpsychopaths.

Because psychopathic individuals have a high rate of criminal recidivism and have generally been found to be poor risks for rehabilitation, these findings aroused considerable interest among forensic psychologists.[134] In 1994 Gacono and Meloy published a book on their work, *The Rorschach Assessment of Aggressive and Psychopathic Personalities,* and presented workshops throughout the United States on the evaluation of psychopaths. Their methods were widely adopted by psychologists who evaluate criminals for courts or in correctional settings.

However, in a pattern distressingly common for the Rorschach, most other researchers were unable to replicate Gacono and Meloy's findings. For example, ten replication studies examined the relationship between reflection responses and psychopathy.[135] Nine of the ten found no significant relationship.[136] Similar negative findings were reported for the other "psychopathic" Rorschach indicators identified by Gacono and Meloy.[137]

Interestingly, Gacono and Meloy's original positive findings may have been due to the same methodological error—contamination—that deceived Hermann Rorschach and Henry Goddard more than seventy years earlier (see Chapters Two and Three). Gacono reported in his dissertation that the same researcher who administered the Rorschach to prisoners also rated their levels of psychopathy.[138] As we explained in Chapter Two, such a procedure is vulnerable to confirmation bias, because the researcher's ratings of psychopathy may be unconsciously influenced by the Rorschach responses. In any case, it now seems clear that Gacono and Meloy's findings are not replicable, and that decisions made in forensic settings (for example, by parole boards) should not be informed by results from the Comprehensive System.[139]

COPING WITH NEGATIVE FINDINGS   In the face of mounting negative evidence, Exner and his colleagues have not abandoned their expansive claims regarding the validity of the Comprehensive System. For example, Exner has shown no indication of retiring the Depression Index, despite its multiple failures in replication studies. To the contrary, in a book published in 2000, he reaffirmed that high scores on the Index indicate "a significant and potentially disabling affective problem."[140]

Similarly, Weiner told the *New York Times* in 2001 that there are "plenty of studies" to support the Rorschach as a measure of depression.[141] Meyer took a more creative approach. The Depression Index fails to correlate with diagnoses of depression, he argued, because it measures "implicit" depression.[142] The nature of "implicit" depression was left unclear by Meyer, but it's apparently a sufficiently subtle phenomenon that it can be detected only by the Rorschach, not by diagnostic interviews or the MMPI-2.

Meyer also advanced a broader argument in support of Rorschach validity.[143] He correctly pointed out that the average or global validity of the Rorschach is about .30, meaning that across numerous studies, Rorschach scores correlate approximately .30 with psychological characteristics. The same is true of the MMPI. Because the two tests possess approximately equal overall validity, Meyer contended, "there is no reason for the Rorschach to be singled out for particular criticism or specific praise."[144]

We find at least some merit in Meyer's argument concerning global validity, and so we'll conclude our discussion of Comprehensive System validity by addressing the issues he has raised. Meyer's numbers regarding the global validity of the MMPI and Rorschach were taken from several meta-analyses published over the past twenty years.[145] Meta-analysis is a widely used statistical technique that averages the results from several studies to obtain a big picture of their findings.[146]

For example, in one meta-analysis, Harvard graduate student Jordan Hiller and his colleagues combined the results from thirty Rorschach articles randomly selected from the published literature.[147]

The topics of these articles were extremely diverse. For instance, three articles examined the correlation of Form Quality scores with learning disabilities.[148] Another examined the correlation of the Rorschach Prognostic Rating Scale with improvement after psychotherapy (see Chapter Six).[149] When the results from these and the remaining articles were combined, the average correlation was .26. When results from thirty MMPI articles were similarly combined, the average correlation was .37.[150] Although the MMPI showed a slight advantage over the Rorschach, this difference was not statistically significant.

Other meta-analyses have yielded broadly comparable results. If the findings of published articles are averaged, the global validity of the Rorschach is generally about .30, and the global validity of the MMPI is about .30 or perhaps slightly higher.[151]

If these numbers are accepted as roughly accurate, what should we make of them? Three points seem especially relevant. First, it's important to note that global meta-analyses of psychological instruments are informative—but only up to a point. Such analyses tell us only how well the average variable on a test performs across many studies for a wide range of purposes. They do not tell us much, if anything, about the validity of specific variables for specific clinical applications. Nor do they tell us whether findings for specific variables have been consistently and independently replicated.

In the case of the Rorschach and MMPI, global comparisons of these two instruments gloss over key differences. As we've already noted, only a handful of the more than 150 variables in the Comprehensive System have exhibited consistent validity across studies by independent researchers. In contrast, most or all of the ten major clinical scales of the MMPI (for example, Depression, Schizophrenia) have repeatedly been shown to relate to important psychological characteristics in studies by independent investigators. For example, across numerous investigations, Scale 4 (Psychopathic deviate) of the MMPI has been found to be associated with antisocial and criminal behaviors, as well as with substance abuse.[152]

A second point to consider when comparing the Rorschach and MMPI is the relative cost and efficiency of the two tests. In comparison with the Rorschach, the MMPI requires no special training to administer, can be scored much more quickly and easily, and is far less prone to scoring errors. Consequently, if the two tests are about equally valid overall, the MMPI seems to have the clear advantage.

Of course, it's possible, at least in principle, that the Rorschach may add important information when used in conjunction with the

MMPI. For example, perhaps the Rorschach is better than the MMPI at capturing certain forms of subtle emotional distress, and therefore can contribute unique information. In such a case, psychometricians would say that the Rorschach possesses "incremental validity" above and beyond the information provided by the MMPI.[153]

However, studies of the Comprehensive System's incremental validity have been disappointing. For example, in several studies, the addition of variables from the system has contributed little or nothing beyond MMPI variables in the detection of depression, schizophrenia, or conduct disorder. In the few cases in which Comprehensive System scores have exhibited incremental validity beyond more easily administered measures, the absolute amount of such incremental validity has been meager.[154]

Moreover, even if a few variables from the Comprehensive System could be shown to possess slight incremental validity beyond the MMPI, it's doubtful whether clinicians could use this information effectively. In several studies, accuracy actually *decreased* when clinicians who had access to the MMPI and other information were provided with Rorschach protocols (see Chapter Six and the discussion of Whitehead's dissertation earlier in this chapter).

The third point to consider when evaluating the global validity of the Rorschach is the *size* of that validity, namely, .30. A validity of only .30 is very discouraging if a test is used to assess individual clients in clinical and forensic settings. As an example, consider one of the Rorschach's best validated scores, Human Movement responses. As we discussed earlier, the number of Human Movement responses (M) is related to intelligence. Figure A.6 in the Appendix depicts the relationship between M and intelligence in a hypothetical group of clients when the correlation is .30, a figure consistent with existing research.

As can be seen, there's a definite trend to the data in Figure A.6: IQ scores *generally* increase from left to right. However, the trend is far too weak to predict the IQ of individual clients. For example, among clients who give four Human Movement responses, the IQ scores range from 72 (borderline mental retardation) to 123 (high intelligence).

As the example shows, a validity of .30 is hardly a cause for rejoicing if we intend to use a test score to make judgments about individual clients. If the average validity of the MMPI and Rorschach is only .30, this means that most published studies must be finding relationships that are quite small and unlikely to be useful in clinical work.

Does this mean that both tests are clinically useless? Not at all. Because the figure of .30 represents an *average*, some MMPI and

Rorschach scores may possess particularly good validity for certain purposes. But which scores are the winners?

For the MMPI-2, many psychologists have taken a hard-nosed view of the test. For example, in one book, based on extensive reviews of relevant research, Roger Greene of the Pacific Graduate School of Psychology specifies which MMPI-2 scales possess well-demonstrated validity for particular purposes, and which do not. If research evidence is weak or fails to support the validity of an MMPI-2 score, Greene isn't reluctant to tell readers.[155]

Until now, no similar book has existed for the Comprehensive System for the Rorschach. In contrast to Greene's textbook, none of the textbooks for the Comprehensive System distinguish clearly between those scores that are scientifically supported and those that are not. However, in this chapter we've attempted to make up for this deficiency by identifying the scores in the Comprehensive System that demonstrate well-established validity. We hope that users of the Comprehensive System will consult our book in the same way that MMPI-2 users consult Greene's.

To some extent, we agree with Meyer that "there is no reason for the Rorschach to be singled out for particular criticism or specific praise."[156] After all, the Rorschach is merely a test, with a few strengths and many limitations. Nevertheless, because the Rorschach remains widely used—with children, in courts, and with psychiatric patients—and because the test's proponents have overstated its strengths and denied its limitations for more than half a century, assertions regarding its validity must be examined closely.

In concluding this chapter, we'll note that the controversy over the Comprehensive System is still raging and shows little sign of abating. In recent years, acrimonious debates between critics and defenders of the system have enlivened the pages of numerous scientific journals and spilled over into such outlets as *Scientific American,*[157] *Skeptical Inquirer,*[158] and the *Harvard Mental Health Letter.*[159]

In the face of the scientific challenge and negative publicity that now beset the Comprehensive System, will psychologists abandon the Rorschach? If the past is any indication, the most likely answer is "No, not anytime soon." In the next chapter, we address the question: Where is the ever-resilient Rorschach likely to go from here?

CHAPTER TEN

Still Waiting for the Messiah

The Future of the Rorschach

It would accord with scientific ethics to abandon the Rorschach test, save in research studies, until such time as the true and the false hypotheses are much better distinguished.

> —Lee J. Cronbach, "Review of the Book Developments in Rorschach Technique," 1955

I am calling for a moratorium on the use of the Rorschach Inkblot Test in clinical and forensic (but not research) settings. This moratorium should last until we have determined which Rorschach scores are valid and which ones are invalid.

> —Howard N. Garb, "Call for a Moratorium . . ." 1999

Before the appearance of John Exner's Comprehensive System, the Rorschach was a test sick almost unto death. Its unhealthy condition was first diagnosed in 1954 by Joseph Zubin in his famous article, "Failures of the Rorschach Technique." His grim judgment was confirmed by Lee J. Cronbach, Arthur Jensen, and others (see Chapter Seven).

In light of the Rorschach's moribund state, Exner's resuscitation of the test in the 1980s seemed almost miraculous. Anne Anastasi and

A. I. Rabin compared him to a healer who had "injected new life into the aging Rorschach." The Board of Professional Affairs of the American Psychological Association went even further, crediting Exner with the Rorschach's "resurrection" (see Chapter Eight).[1]

However, it now seems clear that Exner was not the Messiah that some took him to be. The infirmities that plagued the Rorschach in the 1950s and 1960s—problematic scoring reliability, low validity, lack of adequate norms, and a tendency to overpathologize—were not miraculously healed by the Comprehensive System (see Chapter Nine).

In this chapter, we reflect on the future of the Rorschach. We begin by taking stock of the Rorschach's failures, summarizing the main lessons that can be extracted from its history and the scientific literature.

WHAT'S WRONG WITH THE RORSCHACH?

When Zubin enumerated the "failures" of the Rorschach in 1954, he based his opinions on what was still a scanty scientific literature. However, subsequent research confirmed most of his hunches. From the limited evidence available, Zubin correctly inferred that the test had serious problems concerning scoring reliability, that global validity was a failure, and that the Rorschach was unrelated to most psychiatric diagnoses.[2]

In the present section, we update Zubin's list of Rorschach failures, drawing on an additional fifty years of research and history. Following his example, we begin by discussing the failures of the Rorschach as a technique. Afterward, we describe what Arthur Jensen called the "Rorschach culture." As Jensen recognized, the Rorschach is more than a technique. It's a belief system that mimics a minor religion. The perennial controversies regarding the Rorschach probably have less to do with its well-known shortcomings as a psychometric test than with the unique customs and habits of thought that its followers have cultivated.

Failures of the Rorschach as a Technique

Most of the Rorschach's weaknesses as a psychometric test were evident by 1960. However, for the past twenty-five years many psychologists have labored under the illusion that the Comprehensive System rectified these problems and placed the test on a firm psychometric footing.

Figure 10.1.   Joseph Zubin.
One of the twentieth century's leading researchers
in clinical psychology. His famous 1954 paper, "Failures of the
Rorschach Technique," ignited a scientific controversy that
has lasted nearly half a century.
Source: Veterans Administration Healthcare System.

LACK OF GOOD NORMS   As we discussed in Chapter Three, norms are essential to a psychometric test. The test scores of a client are meaningless unless they can be compared with the scores of other individuals.

Norms constitute the most obvious failure of the Rorschach. Although the test is more than eighty years old and has been administered to millions of Americans, it has never possessed an adequate set of adult norms. Bruno Klopfer denied that norms were necessary (see Chapter Three). Samuel Beck's norms were based on employees at a Chicago mail order house, and David Rapaport's on an all-male group of Kansas State Highway Patrolmen.[3] Exner was given credit for creating the first nationally representative Rorschach norms. However, the problems with his numbers are now increasingly apparent (see Chapter Nine).

With respect to children's norms, the Rorschach is in even worse shape now than it was half a century ago. In the 1940s and 1950s, Louise Ames, Mary Ford, and other researchers provided norms for diverse groups of children and adolescents.[4] However, those norms are now outmoded. The Exner and Weiner norms that replaced them appear to be seriously inaccurate (see Chapter Nine).

OVERPATHOLOGIZING   The tendency of the Rorschach to overpathologize is its second failure. Research suggests that the Comprehensive System misidentifies about 75 percent of normal individuals as emotionally disturbed (see Chapter Nine, Table 9.3). The error rate of older Rorschach systems appears to be similar (see Chapter Six). The Rorschach's tendency to make normal people appear sick is a reason for concern in the assessment of children, who may be mislabeled as emotionally disturbed. Furthermore, if the Rorschach is used in custody evaluations, it's likely to misidentify a substantial number of psychologically healthy parents as pathological.

UNRELIABLE SCORING   Results from recent research are conflicting. However, most studies indicate that a substantial number of important Comprehensive System variables cannot be scored with sufficient reliability for clinical and forensic purposes (see Chapter Nine, Table 9.2).

LACK OF RELATIONSHIP TO PSYCHOLOGICAL DIAGNOSES   A few Rorschach scores are helpful for the evaluation of thought disorder (see Chapter Nine, Table 9.4). For this reason, they can provide useful information for the diagnosis of schizophrenia, bipolar disorder, borderline personality disorder, and schizotypal personality disorder. Furthermore, the Elizur Anxiety scale (a content scale from the 1950s) is related to anxiety (see Chapter Six). Otherwise, the Rorschach lacks a well-demonstrated relationship to psychological disorders and symptoms. Even Bornstein, a major proponent of projective tests, acknowledges, "The Rorschach Inkblot Method is not a diagnostic tool."[5]

LACK OF INCREMENTAL VALIDITY   Research has shown that when psychologists already possess detailed biographical information and MMPI scores, the addition of the Rorschach is unlikely to improve their ability to make diagnoses or evaluate clients' personalities. To the contrary, some studies have found that psychologists tend to become *less* accurate with the addition of the Rorschach (see Chapter Six).

THE PROBLEM OF *R*   In the 1950s, it was recognized that Rorschach scores can be unduly influenced by the total number of responses that a client gives to the blots (*R*). This Rorschach "failure" has not been eliminated by the Comprehensive System. As Meyer wrote, "*R* is the primary entity being measured by the structural data of the test" (see Chapters Six and Nine).[6]

The Shortcomings of the "Rorschach Culture"

Proponents of the Rorschach often seem baffled by the harsh criticism it attracts. For example, a recent textbook on the Comprehensive System commented, "Why one test instrument so inflames controversy is somewhat puzzling." The authors speculated that the Rorschach may awaken opposition because it is "unique."[7]

In fact, the unique character of the Rorschach was its strongest selling point in the 1940s and 1950s, when such hard-headed researchers as Lee J. Cronbach, Albert Bandura, and Julian Rotter pursued its intriguing possibilities (see Chapter Seven). The great Rorschach controversy that erupted soon afterward was due not to stodgy psychologists who despised the test's unique qualities, but to two other factors.

First, by 1960, research revealed that the Rorschach was a flawed test, inappropriate for most of the purposes for which it was used. Second, the test's proponents denied or ignored negative findings (see Chapter Seven).

This second factor—the refusal of Bruno Klopfer, Samuel Beck, and most leading Rorschachers to acknowledge the test's shortcomings—created irritation and eventually disgust among many research-oriented psychologists. The heat of the Rorschach controversy was generated not by negative research findings—after all, dozens of psychological tests have proven unfruitful—but by the refusal of the Rorschach's proponents to acknowledge its obvious flaws.

By the mid-1960s, some thoughtful observers realized that the Rorschach constituted a belief system for many of its adherents, a quasi-religious set of assumptions resistant to disconfirming evidence. Arthur Jensen discerned a "Rorschach culture," dominated by "orthodoxy" and "tradition" and enveloped in "an atmosphere that is philosophically quite alien to the orientation of modern psychology as it is now taught in the leading American and British universities."[8]

This distinctive "Rorschach culture" probably accounts for much of the distrust that research psychologists have felt toward the test during the past forty years. Reflecting the long-standing tensions between romanticists and empiricists noted by Paul McHugh (see Chapter Four), there's still a widespread perception in many quarters of psychology that Rorschach proponents don't "play by the rules" that generally guide scientific investigation and discourse.

Before describing the most problematic aspects of "Rorschach culture," we want to emphasize that they do *not* apply to all psychologists who use or conduct research on the test. Many of these psychologists play by the same rules as the rest of psychology. However, the characteristic features of "Rorschach culture" are so distinctive that they will quickly be recognized by anyone who has had repeated dealings with the test's enthusiasts.

PERSISTENT OVERSTATEMENT   As this book has documented, proponents of the Rorschach have persistently made stunning overstatements concerning its powers. For example, consider this array of comments from many of the test's most prominent advocates, extending over nearly half a century:

> "The Rorschach method does not reveal a behavior picture, but rather shows—like an x-ray picture—the underlying structure which makes behavior understandable." Bruno Klopfer, 1940[9]

> "Twenty-one years of routine research have proven more than ninety per cent of [Rorschach's] assumptions correct." Bruno Klopfer, 1943[10]

> "Rorschach produced more than an experiment or a test. He created a new, systematic, independent, and comprehensive science." Zygmunt Piotrowski, 1957[11]

> "[The Comprehensive System for the Rorschach is] perhaps the most powerful psychometric instrument ever envisioned." Board of Professional Affairs, American Psychological Association, 1998[12]

"All of the variables coded in the Comprehensive System can be coded with substantial interrater agreement." Irving Weiner, 1998[13]

"A Depression Index [score] of 6 or 7 correlates very highly with a diagnosis that emphasizes serious affective problems. . . . Subjects having these values in the *DEPI* are almost always diagnosed as having some significant affective problems." John Exner, 1991[14]

"Studies have demonstrated the ability of the Rorschach or the TAT to differentiate . . . patients who have experienced physical or sexual trauma from those who have not." Gregory Meyer et al., 1998[15]

"Research has clearly documented the value of [projective] assessment methods for predicting medically related outcomes. . . . With respect to cancer, Rorschach data provided incremental information that could not be obtained from other sources, predicting cancer occurrence over and above other risk factors such as smoking history, serum cholesterol level, and time elapsed since baseline testing." Gregory Meyer et al., 1998[16]

"The Rorschach is a test that has consistently proved . . . to have been accepted without question in clinical training institutions." Barry Ritzler et al., 2002[17]

This tradition of "over-sell" apparently originated with Bruno Klopfer. Following in his footsteps, the habit of exaggeration seems to have become a permanent fixture of the "Rorschach culture," perhaps because it proved highly successful. Many clinical psychologists gullibly swallowed claims that the test was like an x-ray, that it could identify depression, predict cancer, or detect sexual abuse. Realistic descriptions of the Rorschach's powers would have elicited far less enthusiasm.

Although overstatements have enhanced the Rorschach's popularity, they've also tended to discredit it among psychologists with a scientific orientation. The exaggerated claims of its proponents have often lent the Rorschach an unsavory reputation.

UNWILLINGNESS TO ABANDON DISCREDITED HYPOTHESES   The Rorschach's leading proponents have seldom been willing to surrender their expansive claims, even in the face of overwhelming negative evidence. For example, as Cronbach noted with exasperation in the 1950s, Beck failed to change his interpretation of Rorschach scores in response to disconfirming evidence.[18] Klopfer magisterially dismissed a decade of negative findings in a single sentence: "Perhaps it is not necessary to be concerned with validity in the usual sense; or perhaps a new technique of validation is necessary" (see Chapter Seven).[19]

As we discussed in Chapter Nine, similar patterns can be observed among contemporary proponents of the Comprehensive System. The Depression Index provides a striking example. Despite an avalanche of negative findings, Exner and Weiner continue to assert that the Rorschach is useful for identifying depression.[20]

Meyer now contends that the Index measures "implicit" depression.[21] Cronbach's comment from the 1950s, quoted in Chapter Seven, still seems to apply to the contemporary Rorschach: "If a study proves that some score does not measure what was claimed for it, the score is retained, and the interpretation is rephrased so that the negative data no longer apply. No one goes to the trouble of testing the modified hypothesis before announcing it. To respond to negative evidence by bringing forth new hypotheses which people are expected to use daily in clinical practice and for which there is no weight of public evidence, is inexcusable."[22]

GREAT MEN   Adulation of heroes is one of the enduring features of "Rorschach culture." As we discussed in Chapter Five, the Society for Personality Assessment—without a trace of irony—bestowed its "Great Man Award" on Bruno Klopfer in 1966.[23] John Exner has been similarly lionized.[24] Gregory Meyer shows signs of becoming the next towering figure on the Rorschach landscape.

The idolization of Rorschach leaders presents a striking contrast to mainstream clinical psychology, which is democratic, egalitarian, and sometimes almost anarchistic. Robert Holt, a prominent advocate of the Rapaport system for the Rorschach, summed up the difference in the 1960s: "The culture of clinical psychology is strongly anti-authoritarian, a value incompatible with the traditionalism and respect for authority that are required for the transmission of an art like psychodiagnosis."[25]

INTOLERANCE TOWARD OPPOSING VIEWPOINTS   Rorschachers' nasty infighting was legendary in the early days of clinical psychology. Until the 1960s, they directed their missiles mainly toward each other. The

feud between Beck and Klopfer began in the 1930s and was still striking sparks in the 1960s (see Chapters Three and Seven).

In the current controversy over the Comprehensive System, intolerance has assumed a different form, as the test's proponents have
taken to questioning the personal integrity and competence of its critics. For example, in an interview with the *New York Times,* Gregory
Meyer likened three of the authors of this book to believers in creationism.[26] He also published an article that accused some of us of
knowingly publishing falsehoods.[27] Carl Gacono, whose work on psychopathy we discussed in the previous chapter, publicly compared
Rorschach critics to "assassins" and "terrorists."[28] Irving Weiner,
assuming a more dignified tone, disparaged Rorschach critics as outsiders who lack experience in personality assessment: "In considering
obstacles to our achieving the scientific and professional status that
we believe personality assessment should enjoy, we have had little difficulty recognizing that they reside mainly outside of our house, and
not under our own roof. These obstacles take the form mainly of critics who demean the psychometric respectability and practical utility
of personality assessment. . . . Typically these critics are not assessment
psychologists themselves, do not conduct any assessment research of
their own, and do not apply personality assessment methods in their
work."[29]

LACK OF SCIENTIFIC OPENNESS   Scientists generally maintain a tradition of openness regarding the sharing of data and other information.
For example, the Ethical Principles of Psychologists published by the
American Psychological Association urge researchers to make their
data available for scrutiny by others.[30] This fundamental dictate permits scientists to cross-check each other's work and identify errors or
biases when they occur.

The culture of the Comprehensive System is strikingly lacking in
such openness. As we reported in Chapter Nine, when we asked Exner
for copies of the unpublished Rorschach Workshops Studies that form
the scientific foundation of his system, we were informed that they
were unavailable. Similarly, when we asked to examine the normative
data for the Comprehensive System, Exner consulted the members of
the Rorschach Research Council, who rejected our request (see Chapter Nine).

The decision of the council is particularly striking, because it suggests a general failure among the Rorschach's leading defenders to rec-

ognize the importance of openness in science. In a posting to the Internet, Gregory Meyer defended Exner's failure to release his data: "Collecting data is not like going to the store to buy some chips for a Super Bowl party. With the chips, you probably wouldn't care who had a taste, what they did with the chips, or whether they shared them with someone else without your permission. Data is more like having a daughter. If some respectable guy who seemed to have reasonable intentions wanted to take her out, you'd probably feel fine about it. However, you'd feel very different if he mistreated her or if he believed he was now free to pass her on to any other guy who asked."[31]

Meyer's ideas concerning the sharing of data seem much different from the position set forth in the Ethical Principles of Psychologists: "After research results are published, psychologists do not withhold the data on which their conclusions are based from other competent professionals who seek to verify the substantive claims through reanalysis and who intend to use such data only for that purpose, provided that the confidentiality of the participants can be protected and unless legal rights concerning proprietary data preclude their release."[32]

DISREGARD FOR REPLICATION   As discussed in Chapter Nine, replication of research findings is one of the most important quality control mechanisms in science. Replication is especially vital when findings are likely to affect people's lives, as is the case with test scores used in clinical and forensic settings. For this reason, we've urged that Rorschach scores be accepted as well-validated for a particular purpose only after they've been found valid by several independent researchers using sound methodology.

The need for independent replication has been largely ignored by Rorschach proponents, sometimes with disturbing consequences. For example, on the basis of his unreplicated findings, Exner claimed that scores on the Depression Index are highly correlated with depression. Accepting this assertion without demur, many psychologists have confidently used the Index from the 1980s until the present. It's sobering to reflect on the consequences in light of the many replication studies that have failed to find a significant relationship between the Index and depression (see Chapter Nine).

Similarly, Gacono and Meloy claimed to have identified several Rorschach indicators of psychopathy. They then began to teach these purported indicators to trainees at well-attended workshops. Soon many forensic psychologists began to use the scores to evaluate felons in court cases and prisons. Meanwhile, numerous replication studies failed to confirm the validity of Gacono and Meloy's indicators (see Chapter Nine).

As a final example, we note a recent statement published by the Psychological Assessment Work Group (PAWG), a committee with close ties to the Rorschach community, that was commissioned by the American Psychological Association's Board of Professional Affairs. PAWG concluded that "studies have demonstrated the ability of the Rorschach or the TAT to differentiate among Axis II conditions like borderline, antisocial, narcissistic, and schizotypal personality disorders and Axis I conditions like schizophrenia, major depression, conduct disorder, and panic disorder."[33]

This broad claim regarding the Rorschach's diagnostic power, which conflicts sharply with our own review of the literature (see Chapter Nine), was based largely on isolated research findings and unreplicated studies.[34] Contrary to PAWG's conclusions, the Rorschach does not possess a well-demonstrated relationship to most of these disorders.[35]

FAILURE TO ADOPT HIGH STANDARDS FOR RESEARCH AND PRACTICE   In a recent review, we concluded that research on the Rorschach often exhibits striking methodological and statistical flaws.[36] We won't enumerate these problems here, except to note that they're sufficiently serious to cast doubt on many, if not most, positive findings reported in recent years. As an example, we can mention Gacono and Meloy's research on the Rorschach and psychopathy, some of which was marred by what researchers call "criterion contamination" (see Chapter Nine). As even Exner acknowledged: "The paucity of contemporary interest in Rorschach research methodology should be cause for concern because future research could easily repeat some of the disasters of the past if certain guidelines are not firmly in place."[37]

The low standards that characterize much research on the Rorschach are sometimes matched by low standards for practice. For example, as we noted in Chapter Nine, some Rorschach advocates now argue that a scoring reliability of .61 is "good," and that a reliability of .74 is "excellent."[38] Such standards are dramatically lower than those expected of intelligence tests, and are contrary to the recommendations of many respected experts concerning tests used in clinical and forensic settings (see Chapter Nine).

Some Rorschach advocates also seem willing to accept a lowered standard for validity. For example, in a recent article, Meyer suggested that psychologists should be "rather satisfied" with a validity as low as .11, and "pleased" with a validity of .26.[39] Although a test score with a validity this low is generally useless for assessing individual clients in clinical or forensic settings (see Chapter Nine), Meyer suggested that by combining two or more tests with low validity, psychologists can achieve higher validity.

However, in practice, it's difficult, if not impossible, to combine test information in the way suggested by Meyer.[40] For example, even though some Rorschach scores bear a modest relationship to psychotic disorders, clinicians' ability to identify such disorders doesn't generally improve when the test is added to other sources of information (see Chapters Six and Nine). Thus, although the idea of combining two or more "weak" tests to attain "strong" validity is attractive, it is generally impractical.[41]

CIRCLING THE WAGONS

Because the failures of the Rorschach technique and Rorschach culture have been resistant to change over the past half century, only an optimist would expect major reforms in the near future. In the 1950s, Marguerite Hertz bluntly informed her fellow Rorschachers that scientific criticisms of the test were "right and proper," and that drastic changes were necessary (see Chapter Seven). In the current controversy over the Comprehensive System, no courageous figure like Hertz has emerged. To the contrary, the system's proponents seem concerned mainly with fending off and denying the legitimacy of criticisms. A fortress mentality has prevailed, as the Rorschach's defenders have mobilized the resources of the Society for Personality Assessment and the American Psychological Association on their behalf.

The Society for Personality Assessment

The Society for Personality Assessment (SPA) started its existence as Bruno Klopfer's Rorschach Institute (see Chapter Three). Not surprisingly, in recent years it has risen energetically to the defense of the Comprehensive System.

In 1999, the SPA established a quarter-time paid position for an "Assessment Advocacy Coordinator."[42] Irving Weiner now fills this role.[43] His responsibilities include "responding to misinformation and denigration of assessment" and lobbying the American Psychological Association.[44] Since assuming these duties, Weiner has repeatedly debated critics of the Comprehensive System in public forums, including the *New York Times*,[45] the *Harvard Mental Health Letter*,[46] and National Public Radio.

The SPA's official publication, the *Journal of Personality Assessment (JPA)*, has also become active in the battle on behalf of the Comprehensive System. Originally produced on a hand-cranked mimeograph as the *Rorschach Research Exchange, JPA* has evolved into a well-respected scholarly journal, publishing numerous high-quality studies on a variety of tests. However, true to its origins, *JPA* continues to accord special treatment to the Rorschach, publishing a substantial number of research reports, case studies, and theoretical articles on the test.

Most major psychology journals rotate editorial positions among scholars who represent diverse backgrounds and viewpoints. In contrast, the helm of *JPA* has been occupied exclusively by Rorschachers who adhere to either the Klopfer or the Exner systems. Bruno Klopfer himself held the editorship from 1936 to 1971. He was succeeded by his son Walter, who served until his untimely death in 1985. Since then, the editorship has been held exclusively by adherents of the Comprehensive System: Irving Weiner, Bill Kinder (Weiner's colleague at the University of South Florida), and now Gregory Meyer.

Such an arrangement has not been conducive to neutrality in the current Rorschach controversy. In recent years, *JPA* has become something of a battleship, with its guns trained directly on critics of the Rorschach. Many issues of the journal now carry one or more articles by members of the Rorschach Research Council that buttress the Comprehensive System against criticism.

Some of these "battleship" articles feature grim speculations on the motives of Rorschach critics.[47] Others contain significant statistical or methodological flaws. For example, a striking undetected error appeared in a 2001 study by Gordon Presley, Candy Smith, Mark Hilsenroth, and Exner that concluded that the scores of African Americans and White Americans on the Comprehensive System are very similar.

The problem with this study is that it composed its subjects from "the Exner (1993) Comprehensive System normative sample (N = 700)."[48] However, as explained in the previous chapter, this sample is known to have been seriously flawed. Specifically, it contained hundreds of duplicate records, as Exner has known since 1999.[49] Despite this difficulty, the study by Presley, Smith, Hilsenroth, and Exner was published in *JPA* in 2001 without any mention of the problem.

The American Psychological Association

In light of the Rorschach's recent vicissitudes, some readers might expect the American Psychological Association (APA) to launch an investigation of the Comprehensive System or take other actions to protect the public. Psychologists administer the Rorschach to hundreds of thousands of Americans each year. If the normative sample of the Comprehensive System was seriously flawed for ten to twenty years (as Exner has verified), and if its norms make most normal individuals appear pathological (as research overwhelmingly indicates), there seems little doubt that use of the test has contributed to the mislabeling of many normal children and adults as abnormal. One might hope that, at the least, a blue ribbon APA panel would be investigating the matter.

To the best of our knowledge, no such investigation is being planned or even discussed. To the contrary, as the controversy has intensified, the APA has worked closely with advocates of the Comprehensive System to polish the Rorschach's tarnished image.

As already mentioned, in 1997 the APA Board of Professional Affairs bestowed its Award for Distinguished Professional Contributions on Exner, enthusiastically extolling the Comprehensive System as "perhaps the most powerful psychometric instrument ever envisioned."[50] At about the same time, the Board of Professional Affairs, working with the SPA, established a committee known as the Psychological Assessment Work Group (PAWG), commissioning it to write a series of reports to "demonstrate the efficacy of psychological assessment services in clinical practice."[51] The materials prepared by PAWG were to be used "to lobby lawmakers" and "work with managed care gatekeepers."[52] In other words, the PAWG reports were intended to be used for advocacy—persuading governmental and institutional decision makers to pay for psychological testing.

Had PAWG approached its mission with scientific neutrality, its work would have been uncontroversial. However, from the outset, the group had strong ties to the Rorschach community. Three PAWG members (including Gregory Meyer) were well-known Rorschach proponents, and a fourth was a long-time associate of John Exner.[53] In contrast, the committee included only a single expert on the MMPI, one expert on neuropsychological assessment, and one expert on occupational assessment.[54] Not only was PAWG stacked heavily in favor of the Rorschach, but its work—although carried out under the auspices of the APA—received indirect financial support from Exner's Rorschach Workshops and the Society for Personality Assessment.[55]

Given this background, it's not surprising that PAWG resoundingly endorsed the Rorschach's value, not only in mental health settings but also in the medical arena. In 1998, in a ninety-page report distributed without charge to APA members, Meyer and his PAWG colleagues claimed that the Rorschach could identify victims of sexual abuse, predict the occurrence of cancer, and identify a large number of psychological disorders (we've quoted several of these claims earlier in this chapter). For reasons that are unclear, the PAWG report failed to mention the existence of any scientific controversy concerning the Rorschach. Most strikingly, it failed to discuss negative findings regarding the Rorschach's validity, although such findings are plentiful. Only positive findings for the Rorschach were mentioned in the PAWG report.

An article by PAWG, with Meyer as first author, appeared in 2001 in the flagship journal and official organ of the American Psychological Association, *American Psychologist*.[56] In an overstatement that could have come straight from the 1940s, Meyer and his colleagues claimed that the validity of the Rorschach and other psychological tests is "comparable" to that of medical tests.[57] The grandiosity of the claim was striking, considering that some medical tests have near-perfect accuracy, whereas no Rorschach score has ever consistently demonstrated validity above .44.[58] Even in the twenty-first century, it seemed, Rorschach advocates were still only a step away from Bruno Klopfer, who likened the test to an x-ray (see Chapter Three).

There seem to be three reasons why APA has sponsored PAWG and published its expansive claims. First, the lobbying efforts of Weiner and other representatives of the SPA appear to have been successful in establishing a close relationship between the two organizations.[59] Second, it seems that the APA Board of Professional Affairs, with its emphasis on practice rather than science, failed to ensure that PAWG represented a broad spectrum of scientific opinion, or that its reports accurately reflected the scientific literature.

Third and probably most important, the zeal of the APA leadership to promote practice appears to have largely overcome a focus on scientific accuracy and social responsibility. If the PAWG reports were commissioned for the express purpose of advancing the economic interests of psychologists, the reports fulfilled their purpose admirably. To put it bluntly, they were "good for business." Thanks to PAWG, practitioners who used the Rorschach could approach managed care gatekeepers and government decision makers with articles that extolled the test's value for psychological diagnosis, detection of sexual abuse, and even prediction of cancer.

In the long run, however, APA's decision to help promote the Rorschach may prove detrimental even to the narrow financial interests of psychologists in practice. APA's long-term future success in expanding the income of its members—for example, by obtaining prescription privileges for psychologists—will depend in large measure on the scientific and moral credibility of the profession. Although many psychologists continue to deceive themselves concerning the Rorschach's great value, the public and its leaders may not prove equally gullible. Legislators may hesitate before granting prescriptive authority to psychologists who are still basing their diagnoses, even in part, on inkblots.

THE RORSCHACH AND THE PUBLIC GOOD

Because the APA and many psychologists continue to promote the Rorschach despite its numerous flaws, the American public is left to fend for itself. There's little doubt that many psychologists will continue to use the test to assist in making diagnoses, conducting custody evaluations, and investigating allegations of sexual abuse. Furthermore, the reports and articles sponsored by the APA will predictably be used to introduce the Rorschach into court and to coax managed care gatekeepers into paying for the test. In the present section, we reflect briefly on the implications for three areas: the welfare of children, the legal system, and managed care.

The Rorschach and Children

The Rorschach is a tempting instrument to use with children. Because it resembles a game, children resistant to other tests may respond to it favorably. Furthermore, unlike questionnaires, it can be used with individuals whose reading ability is limited or nonexistent.

Attractive as the test might seem, its use with children is likely to do harm because of the danger of overpathologizing. As discussed in

Chapter Nine, a study of psychologically healthy children by Mel Hamel and his colleagues in 2000 found that the Comprehensive System drastically overestimated the presence of psychopathology. When compared with the Exner norms, the somewhat above-normal children in Hamel's study appeared to be suffering from "significant cognitive impairment," "distortion of reality and faulty reasoning [that] approach psychosis," and "significant problems establishing and maintaining interpersonal relationships."[60]

Because the Comprehensive System often yields distorted results, its use can produce substantial negative consequences for a child's life. In the worst case, a psychologist may naively accept the pathological test results as accurate. If this false information is passed on to parents, teachers, or physicians, a child who is normal or has minor emotional problems may come to be regarded as seriously disturbed. In some cases, the misinformation may cause the child to be treated with psychotropic medications or other inappropriate interventions.

Harm can arise even if the test results are recognized as inaccurate. A psychologist on an Internet list recently recounted his experience with a boy whom the Comprehensive System misidentified as extremely pathological. The psychologist wisely discounted the findings, but added, "Unfortunately, a social worker got hold of the [Rorschach] printout and raised questions about his being schizophrenic—a complete mess."[61]

It's impossible to say how many children over the past twenty years have been misidentified as disturbed by the Comprehensive System. Nor can we guess what damage it has done to their lives. At least as serious are the consequences of using the test with children suspected of having been sexually or physically abused.

As reported in Chapter One, one survey indicated that about 35 percent of psychologists who evaluate children in abuse and neglect cases use the Rorschach.[62] If the Comprehensive System is used in such evaluations, the results can be highly misleading. Because the test overpathologizes, it's likely to indicate that a child suffers from emotional and social problems. An evaluator who treats the scores as valid may well misinterpret them as evidence of familial problems or inappropriate parental behavior.

Even setting aside the problem of overpathologizing, the use of the Rorschach in abuse evaluations is almost impossible to justify because no Rorschach score has been well-validated as an indicator of sexual or physical abuse in children.[63] In fact, even Gregory Meyer (apparently abandoning his position in the PAWG reports) recently condemned use of the test for such a purpose: "Because it is impossible to determine whether a specific historical event actually did or did not happen from Rorschach responses, clinicians should not draw positive or negative conclusions about sexual abuse from the Rorschach. . . . To optimally serve patients, no less is required. Beyond their potential to harm patients, undisciplined or incorrect inferences discredit tests and the profession more generally."[64]

The Rorschach and the Legal System

Despite its flimsy scientific basis, the Rorschach plays a role in a surprisingly large number of legal cases. As already mentioned, the test is often used in custody and sexual abuse evaluations. Many prison psychologists use it when evaluating convicts for parole. In addition, courts throughout the United States often maintain "clinics" in which the Rorschach and other tests are used to evaluate juvenile and adult offenders prior to sentencing.

The widespread use of the Rorschach in the legal system arose in large part from the test's energetic promotion as a forensic tool. As early as 1982, Exner and Weiner published a case study to demonstrate how the Comprehensive System could be used to evaluate adults and children in custody cases (see Chapter Eight).[65] In the following years, Weiner edited two books on forensic assessment and published such articles as "Is the Rorschach Welcome in the Courtroom?" and "Authority of the Rorschach: Legal Citations During the Past 50 Years."[66] Similarly, Carl Gacono and J. Reid Meloy actively promoted their Rorschach "psychopathy indicators" for use with prisoners (see Chapter Eight).

Because lawyers and judges have generally been unaware of the controversy surrounding the Rorschach, its use in courts has gone virtually unchallenged until very recently. However, news about the Comprehensive System's problems has begun to spread. Attempts to introduce it into legal proceedings are likely to face increasing difficulties as the Rorschach's shortcomings become better known.

The authors of this book adopt the position that the Rorschach should rarely if ever be allowed into court because it lacks validity for most of the purposes for which it's used in civil and criminal cases.

For example, the Rorschach is generally worthless in custody cases because it bears no demonstrated relationship to parenting ability or (except in cases of extreme psychopathology) to personality characteristics that make one parent more suitable than another. Similarly, in the sentencing phase of criminal cases, the test is potentially misleading because it bears no demonstrated relationship to dangerousness, potential for violence, likelihood of recidivism, or suitability for rehabilitation.

Proponents of the Rorschach sometimes claim that the test is uniquely valuable in legal settings because it is difficult or impossible to fake. For example, Meloy and Gacono have strongly recommended the Rorschach for forensic evaluations and claimed that the test is "particularly suited to studying antisocial populations because it has very low face validity (i.e., it is an ambiguous stimulus) and partially bypasses volitional controls. Unlike self-report measures, which Hare (1991) has argued are inherently unreliable with psychopaths, the Rorschach is uniquely situated to empirically 'map' the psychostructure and psychodynamics of these subjects."[67]

As can be seen, Rorschach proponents still hold forth the hope—first promoted by Bruno Klopfer in the 1940s—that the test can function like an x-ray, allowing psychologists to peer deep inside the hearts of felons, even if they are resistant or actively deceptive.

However, such claims regarding the Rorschach's unique x-ray powers run contrary to the scientific evidence and amount to little more than urban legend. Most Rorschach scores lack validity even among individuals who are being honest. There's no evidence that the test performs any better among individuals who are being deceptive. For example, as we described in Chapter Nine, Gacono and Meloy's indicators of psychopathy have generally failed in replication studies.

Furthermore, as David Schretlen of Johns Hopkins University pointed out in a recent comprehensive literature review, the Rorschach's susceptibility to faking of psychopathology has been known for nearly half a century: "Although several studies during the 1950s and 1960s reported evidence of its susceptibility to faking, some proponents still contend that the Rorschach and other projective measures cannot be faked. Recent findings render this contention nearly impossible to defend. What remains unclear is not whether individuals can distort their Rorschach results, but whether such distortion can be detected."[68]

For example, numerous studies have found that schizophrenia can be faked on the Rorschach.[69]

Individuals being evaluated in forensic settings sometimes answer questionnaires deceptively or withhold important information that's diagnostically important. However, this problem can't be solved by turning to the Rorschach. In such circumstances, the better solution is to gather additional biographical and observational data.

For example, psychologists who suspect that a person is withholding information can conduct collateral interviews with reliable informants who have known the person over a long period of time. Another useful strategy is to gather extensive historical data from the person being evaluated, including detailed chronological information regarding employment, education, important relationships, criminal activities, and mental health history. Furthermore, information provided by the person being evaluated can be supplemented with independent data from case files and other documentary sources.

In short, if deception is suspected in a forensic evaluation, evaluators are ill-advised to rely on the Rorschach's dubious x-ray powers. Instead, they should seek information from more reliable sources that have long been recognized as helpful by both psychologists and attorneys. In the final chapter of this book, we'll further discuss these and other issues that may prove useful to attorneys who confront Rorschach-based expert evidence in court.

The Rorschach and Managed Care

During the past decade, psychologists in practice have been tightly squeezed in the vise of managed care, often reporting reduced income and burdensome paperwork.[70] The effect on testing practices is unclear. However, some psychologists have apparently responded to the pressures of managed care by using tests less frequently. Chris Piotrowski of the University of West Florida, an expert on testing practices among psychologists, has predicted that "the traditional test battery . . . will become a moribund clinical activity, at least where third-party and managed care constraints are an issue."[71]

Within this context, the APA and PAWG have made their recent push to promote the Rorschach and test batteries to managed care. However, if one examines the Rorschach dispassionately, it's difficult to see why managed care should be willing to pay for its use.

First, the most popular version of the test, the Comprehensive System, appears to be valid for very few purposes (see Chapter Nine, Table 9.4). Second, the test is extremely time-consuming and expensive, requiring approximately two and a half hours of a Ph.D.-level psychologist's time for administration, scoring, and interpretation.[72]

In contrast, the MMPI-2 typically takes between an hour and an hour and a half for patients to complete. It can generally be given to a small group of individuals with a clerical worker present. Scoring is usually done by a computer, and the results can be interpreted by a psychologist in approximately thirty minutes. Third, because of the Rorschach's tendency to overpathologize, its use may increase the incidence of misdiagnoses, with attendant liability problems.

In their attempts to make the test attractive to managed care, Rorschach proponents commonly point out that it possesses well-demonstrated validity as a predictor of treatment outcome.[73] This claim is true. The Rorschach Prognostic Rating Scale (RPRS), developed by Bruno Klopfer in the 1950s, has well-established validity for this purpose, although its predictions regarding individual patients are likely to be highly fallible.[74]

However, the RPRS is of more historical interest than practical importance. The difficulty is that the RPRS was created for use with the obsolete Klopfer system for the Rorschach, which adopted a much different approach to test administration and scoring than does the Comprehensive System.[75] There's no evidence that the RPRS would be valid if used in conjunction with the Comprehensive System, assuming that the two are compatible at all, which is doubtful. Nor is it practical to use the RPRS with the Klopfer system, which is outmoded and devoid of norms. Thus, although the RPRS represents a tantalizing curiosity from the Rorschach's past, its relevance to the concerns of modern managed care is virtually nil.

RECOMMENDATIONS FOR OUR COLLEAGUES

As we've already indicated, clinical psychology has traditionally been a democratic and antiauthoritarian profession, with a few notable aberrations. We hope that our colleagues will accept our recommendations regarding clinical practice and graduate training in the spirit in which they're offered—as a starting point for democratic discussion, debate, and reflection.

The Rorschach in Clinical Practice

It may surprise some readers that we have only a single recommendation to offer regarding use of the Rorschach in clinical practice:

WHEN USING THE RORSCHACH FOR CLINICAL OR FORENSIC
ASSESSMENT, PSYCHOLOGISTS SHOULD NOT INTERPRET
SCORES UNLESS THEY CAN BE RELIABLY SCORED, HAVE BEEN
WELL-VALIDATED, AND POSSESS ACCURATE NORMS.

In earlier chapters, we've indicated how we would define these terms. We believe that to be useful in clinical practice, a score should possess a minimum scoring reliability of .85 and a validity coefficient of at least .30. In fact, this standard for validity may well be too low for a measure used to assess individual clients.[76] A minimum validity of .40 or .50 may be more appropriate. We leave it to our colleagues to decide the issue.

If our recommendation is accepted as reasonable, clinical psychologists face several options. We'll evaluate each in turn.

ABANDON THE RORSCHACH Because so few Rorschach scores possess well-demonstrated validity, some psychologists may decide that the test is simply not worth using.

DECLARE A MORATORIUM ON THE RORSCHACH Howard Garb, one of the authors of this book, recently proposed that a moratorium be placed on clinical and forensic uses of the Rorschach. This moratorium would not be lifted unless and until the validity and invalidity of the test's scores are better established. As the quotes at the beginning of this chapter indicate, Lee J. Cronbach made virtually the same proposal half a century ago. His recommendation was obviously disregarded. Psychologists now have an opportunity to reconsider Cronbach and Garb's proposal in light of fifty years of additional scientific evidence.

USE A STRIPPED-DOWN RORSCHACH Because a few Rorschach scores do possess well-demonstrated validity—most notably, form quality scores and indexes of thought disorder—psychologists may elect to retain the test but use only these scores. As it happens, Edwin Wagner, creator of the Hand Test, recently published a manual entitled *The Logical Rorschach* that describes such a stripped-down approach to the test.[77] Wagner's version of the Rorschach requires further development. Its norms are limited and the evidence of its validity is still preliminary. However, the early research on the Logical Rorschach is encouraging.[78] We encourage researchers to energetically explore the reliability and validity of this new Rorschach mini-system.

TRY THE COMPREHENSIVE SYSTEM WITH THE SHAFFER AND ERDBERG NORMS Exner's Comprehensive System has provided a lingua franca for Rorschach users and researchers, and some psychologists may decide to retain it. In our view, it's highly risky to use the Exner norms. The norms being developed by Shaffer and Erdberg appear far more promising, although they're still under construction (see Chapter Nine).

If psychologists retain the Comprehensive System, they may prefer to take a more efficient approach to scoring. As we've indicated, many Comprehensive System variables lack well-demonstrated validity and are cumbersome to score. For example, although the news may shock some of our colleagues, Color and Shading probably bear minimal relation to personality or psychopathology. Furthermore, Shading variables are difficult to score reliably. By simply eliminating the scoring of Shading and Color, psychologists can reduce much of the agony and hairsplitting of the scoring process. Similarly, because Developmental Quality, Z scores, and Lambda appear to be highly correlated, it's probably unnecessary to score all three. Psychologists may decide it's necessary to score only one of these scores (for example, scoring all responses as either $DQ+$ or not $DQ+$).

SWITCH TO THE HOLTZMAN INKBLOT TEST The Holtzman Inkblot Test (HIT) is a promising psychometric treasure that has been unjustly neglected by psychologists (see Chapter Seven). It's more efficient to score than the Comprehensive System and contains all the "good things," including scales for Form Appropriateness (equivalent to Form Quality), Pathognomic Verbalization (a measure of Deviant Verbalizations), and Integration (closely related to Developmental Quality and Z scores). Furthermore, the scores for Form Appropriateness and Pathognomic Verbalization can be combined into an index that appears to function much like the Comprehensive System Perceptual Thinking Index.[79]

The HIT has three main drawbacks. First, its norms, though excellent, are old and may need to be updated. Second, further validation studies are needed, although the existing findings are encouraging. Third, the blots, now marketed by the Psychological Corporation, are prohibitively expensive (although this situation may change if psychologists begin to show interest in the test). Despite these problems, we believe the HIT is worthy of close attention.

USE THE RORSCHACH AS A PSYCHOTHERAPEUTIC TECHNIQUE As readers may have noted, our (single) recommendation regarding the Rorschach concerned only its use as an *assessment* tool. The use of the Rorschach as a *psychotherapeutic technique* is a separate issue. Marvin Reznikoff and Edward Aronow have long argued that although the Rorschach is a failure as a psychometric test, it possesses great value as an adjunctive technique in psychotherapy (see Chapter Seven). These authors advocate a content-oriented, idiographic approach to the Rorschach that has much in common with dream interpretation.

Psychologists interested in using the Rorschach within the context of psychodynamically oriented therapy may wish to explore the writings of Reznikoff and Aronow, which are refreshingly down to earth and nondogmatic. These authors are definitely not members of the "Rorschach culture." However, if psychologists adopt the Reznikoff and Aronow approach, we suggest that they bear three points in mind.

First, to minimize the influence of confirmation bias, psychologists should *actively* look for evidence that *disconfirms* their Rorschach interpretations, as well as evidence that confirms them. Second, it's probably advisable to wait until one has become reasonably familiar with a client (for example, after four or five therapy sessions) before administering the Rorschach. In this way, the insights derived from Rorschach interpretations are more likely to enrich and expand the therapist's already-formed intuitions than to replace them. Third, it's important to remember that the usefulness of the Rorschach as a psychotherapeutic technique has not been empirically demonstrated, although research on this topic is of considerable importance.[80]

The Rorschach in Graduate Training

Just as we made only one recommendation concerning the use of the Rorschach in clinical practice, we'll make only one concerning its place in graduate education:

GRADUATE PROGRAMS IN CLINICAL, COUNSELING, AND SCHOOL PSYCHOLOGY SHOULD ELIMINATE TRAINING IN THE COMPREHENSIVE SYSTEM FOR THE RORSCHACH FROM THEIR ASSESSMENT CURRICULUMS.

Our recommendation does not preclude instructors from covering material on the Comprehensive System in their graduate courses.

To the contrary, we believe that graduate students should know something about the system's principal indexes and their interpretation. In addition, because students are likely to encounter the Rorschach during their training experiences, they should be able to distinguish between Comprehensive System scores that are empirically supported and those that are not. Moreover, the history of the Rorschach affords an opportunity to educate students about the potential hazards of illusory correlation, confirmation bias, and other cognitive traps that can persuade clinicians that test scores are valid when in fact they are not.

Teaching students about the Comprehensive System is much different from *training* them in its use. To oversimplify matters only slightly, teaching about the test encourages students to become scientific and appropriately critical thinkers, whereas training encourages them to join the ranks of technicians who all-too-frequently interpret Rorschach scores with a worrisome blend of certainty and credulity.

Our recommendation that training in the Comprehensive System be discontinued, although certainly justified in light of the evidence, will undoubtedly outrage a subgroup of our colleagues. We know of more than one doctoral program in which faculty members carefully tiptoe around a single professor (often the assessment instructor) who becomes apoplectic at any mention of displacing the Rorschach.

Despite possible anguish, graduate programs cannot forever ignore the vicissitudes of the Comprehensive System. Besides, there are ways to approach the topic without shedding blood. In one graduate program, the director took a private survey of clinical faculty. The sentiment was in favor of dropping the Rorschach. Accordingly, it was replaced in the assessment course by other topics. In this concluding section of the chapter, we share our own reflections on the Comprehensive System and graduate training.

TIME REQUIREMENTS An enormous investment of time and effort is required to learn the Comprehensive System at a level adequate for professional use. A recent study examined the scoring accuracy of doctoral students who had received about twenty-five hours of classroom instruction and practice in the system (a typical amount of time compared with other training programs). The researchers found that the students' level of scoring proficiency was "well below what could be deemed acceptable in research or clinical practice. . . . It is likely that most graduate training in the Comprehensive System is inadequate. Clearly graduate students need much more instruction and scoring practice than can be achieved in the usual time allotted in graduate training programs."[81]

Thus, although the Comprehensive System already requires much more instructional time than other tests typically covered in assessment courses, even *more* time is required if students are to reach minimal scoring proficiency. Beyond that, there's the time required to learn interpretation and report writing. As two of the system's leading proponents concluded, "at least two courses are necessary to teach the Rorschach, one to teach administration and scoring, and at least one more to teach interpretation, diagnosis, and an integration of both into an assessment report."[82]

Graduate training programs face three options. First, they may continue to devote a relatively large proportion of time (twenty-five hours on average) to the Comprehensive System, knowing that this level of training is inadequate. Second, they may devote a larger amount of time to the test (one or two semesters), as some Rorschach proponents have advised. Or third, as we suggest, they may eliminate it from the curriculum, devoting the course time thereby made available to topics more likely to benefit students, such as fundamental issues in psychometrics and test construction, the strengths and weaknesses of clinical judgment and prediction, the use of structured interviews in psychiatric diagnosis, and the differences between scientifically supported and unsupported assessment techniques.

A MAZE OF SYMBOLS In 1937, Marguerite Hertz commented unfavorably on the complexities that Bruno Klopfer introduced into Rorschach scoring: "The writer [Hertz] has on many occasions felt that Klopfer's group was refining the scoring to the extent of becoming involved in a maze of symbols."[83]

More than sixty years later, the situation has grown worse than Hertz could have anticipated. The number of Comprehensive System scores has expanded, at last estimate, to more than 150. The intricacies of Rorschach scoring now begin to approach those of the U.S. tax code, so that devotees attend weeklong seminars, like accountants, to master the latest subtleties.

In the context of graduate education, the most serious objection to the Comprehensive System's elaborate scoring is that it diverts a great deal of mental energy into what is essentially a clerical activity, when instead students could be learning to think more deeply, abstractly, and critically about the fundamental issues of clinical assessment.

For example, a recently published graduate textbook on the Comprehensive System devoted more than seventy pages to the intricacies of scoring. The test's psychometric properties were covered breezily and uncritically in less than ten pages. The current controversy over the system was not directly mentioned, except for one citation that appeared in a bibliography at the back of the text.[84]

Such a book—which represents, we fear, the typical instructional approach to the Comprehensive System—is the antithesis of what graduate education should be. As a counterexample, we mention Roger Greene's famous book on the MMPI-2, which teaches students how to evaluate the psychometric properties of test scores and draw balanced inferences from the scientific literature. Such in-depth instruction is far more likely to benefit students than scoring dozens of Rorschach responses or mastering the subtle rules for Form-Dimension.

SENDING UNSPOKEN MESSAGES TO THE NEXT GENERATION OF PSYCHOLOGISTS   We know of many graduate programs in clinical psychology in which the Comprehensive System is still taught, even though most of the faculty regard it with grave reservations. In some cases, such a situation develops because faculty are reluctant to confront a colleague who is an ardent believer in the system. In other instances, the rationale provided is that students will need to know the Rorschach when they go on their required clinical internships.

A similar "fractured" situation pervaded clinical psychology during the 1950s and 1960s. Donald Routh of the University of Miami described a typical scenario from that era: "Perhaps my own experience in graduate school at the University of Pittsburgh was not unusual. We basically had one graduate course in how to use projective techniques, and in another required course they taught us why these procedures were 'no good.'"[85]

Although such a situation has its humorous side, it's worth reflecting on the unspoken message that it sends to students. In effect, the psychologists of tomorrow are being told that although science is well and good, it can be safely disregarded in the real world of clinical practice. Researchers in psychology often express bafflement at the willingness of many clinical practitioners to adopt unscientific procedures. However, the practitioners' attitude is often neither strange nor difficult to explain: *They learned it in graduate school!*

When graduate faculty consider whether they should continue to provide training in the Comprehensive System, they should carefully reflect on the implicit messages they may give to students. Besides signaling that it is acceptable to use unscientific procedures, a decision to provide training in the system can convey other attitudes. As indicated in our discussion of the "Rorschach culture," the test sometimes carries along with it a whole set of customs and habits of thought— hero worship, overstatement, resistance to disconfirming evidence, and intolerance of criticism. These faults are by no means characteristic of *all* psychologists who use the test, nor are they unique to the Rorschach. Nevertheless, they are sufficiently common to be a cause for concern to faculty members who want their students to absorb other values.

Graduate programs that continue to provide training in the Comprehensive System while minimizing or excusing its recent problems are delivering a large number of unspoken messages to students:

- It's acceptable to buttress scientific arguments with citations to studies that have never been written up and are unavailable for public scrutiny.

- It's acceptable to withhold one's data from examination by other scientists, even though the data may contain serious errors.

- It's acceptable to market a poorly studied depression scale for clinical use, and to claim that the scale is valid even after it has failed in numerous replications.

- It's acceptable to introduce assessment scores into courts of law even though these scores have not been replicated by independent research teams.

- It's acceptable to wait years before announcing that there are problems with one's test norms, even though they're being used with thousands of patients each day.

We hope that we won't be seen as too extreme when we suggest that better models of professional and scientific conduct should be held up for the next generation of clinical psychologists.

CHAPTER ELEVEN

Clinging to the Wreck

Why Some Psychologists Won't Let Go

When ideas go unexamined and unchallenged for a long time, certain things happen. They become mythological, and they become very, very powerful.

—E. L. Doctorow

Some psychologists believe that the Rorschach is completely worthless. Others, like us, believe that it's somewhat useful for a few purposes but is vastly overrated. Yet other psychologists, like a friend of ours, freely acknowledge the test's serious problems but retain considerable affection for it. In all that manure, quips our friend, there must be a pony somewhere.[1]

Many reasonable people find the Rorschach intriguing. Indeed, the present authors would not have written this book had they not found the Rorschach mystique fascinating in many ways. Nevertheless, the deep devotion of many Rorschachers to their cherished blots has struck outsiders as a trifle strange for more than half a century. The devotees of the test were thought to be cultish in the 1940s and orthodox in the 1960s. Today, it's difficult to overlook the passion with which some enthusiasts disclaim the test's seemingly undeniable problems, meanwhile denouncing its critics as "assassins" and "terrorists."[2]

Besides such Rorschach true believers, many middle-of-the-road psychologists continue to use the test, although with less fervor. For example, when accepting an award from the American Psychological Association, a distinguished clinician recently defended his continued use of the Rorschach on the grounds that it "gives information that I have found to be useful."[3]

The passionate faith of true-blue Rorschachers and the unwavering loyalty of more moderate psychologists present something of a puzzle in view of the Rorschach's many shortcomings. From the mid-1950s to the mid-1970s, the verdict of leading psychometric experts was almost uniformly negative, yet the Rorschach remained clinicians' favorite test. Despite the current controversy regarding the Comprehensive System, the Rorschach remains popular among practicing psychologists, although the past decade has apparently witnessed a modest decline in its use.[4]

Such phenomena are easier to understand, however, if the Rorschach is regarded as not merely a test but a sociological belief system (see Chapter Ten). Like many belief systems, it attracts a relatively small and insular group of fervent believers, as well as a mass of loyal but less ardent adherents.

THE TRAPS OF LOGIC AND EXPERIENCE

In this chapter, we discuss the reasons that many psychologists still cling to the wreckage of the Rorschach with such tenacity. Moreover, we address a question that has surely crossed the minds of many thoughtful readers by this point: "If the Rorschach is so scientifically problematic, why do so many clinicians continue to use it?" Some readers may privately go even further: "Isn't it possible that Rorschach proponents are picking up on something that the research is missing? Couldn't the clinical intuitions of these proponents be more valid than the research findings?"

These are legitimate questions that merit thoughtful responses. Before addressing these issues, we should make clear that the underlying psychological processes that account for the Rorschach's continuing popularity are by no means unique to the Rorschach community. Indeed, as we will point out throughout this chapter, all of us are susceptible to the kinds of cognitive traps and errors that underpin much of the Rorschach's popularity. These traps and errors are difficult to resist because they are subjectively compelling and involve deeply ingrained patterns of thinking.

Indeed, a number of scientists and science writers, such as Alan Cromer and Lewis Wolpert, have pointed out that the scientific method, which can be viewed as a toolbox of skills designed to protect researchers from mistakes, does not come naturally to the human species.[5] The propensities toward confirmation bias, illusory correlation, and the other cognitive errors we have discussed in this book are shared by all humans, not merely Rorschach proponents. This fact probably helps to explain why the scientific method did not emerge in full bloom until the eighteenth-century Age of Enlightenment. For most of recorded history, and almost certainly prior to recorded history, people have relied on their intuitions to distinguish truth from falsehood.

If the history of science teaches us anything, it's that common sense and intuition can be undependable barometers of the truth. Good scientists have learned this crucial fact. Through experiences in daily life, all of us have learned to trust our intuitions. In certain domains, like love and friendship, such intuitions are often a reasonable (although by no means foolproof!) guide to behavior. But when it comes to evaluating the merits of a psychological test, intuitions can prove sadly misleading. The scientific method, which Alan Cromer has described as "uncommon sense," provides an essential safeguard against this and other all-too-human pitfalls.[6]

In addition to explaining why many psychologists cling to the flotsam of the Rorschach despite its sinking scientific reputation, we hope in this chapter to warn readers against the superficially appealing but fundamentally flawed defenses of the Rorschach that have been advanced by some of its vocal proponents. We also intend to dispel commonplace logical fallacies to which some Rorschach proponents have fallen prey in their impassioned defenses of the test.

As we discuss different cognitive errors and traps that help to sustain widespread allegiance to the Rorschach, we will revisit a number of themes from earlier chapters. If the reader experiences an uncanny sense of what New York Yankee catcher Yogi Berra called "déjà vu all over again," we hope that we will be forgiven. Many of the psychological processes we delineate in this chapter are well-illustrated by recurrent practices that dot the historical landscape of the Rorschach movement.

Faith in Authority

"I have learned to respect my elders."

Faith in respected authorities is an indispensable element of education. Much of what we "know" was first learned from an authority (Mom, a fourth-grade history book, a college professor). However, authorities and self-proclaimed experts can sometimes be mistaken.

An important aim of higher education—and of scientific education in particular—is to help students outgrow the ingrained habit of intellectual subservience to authority. Yet the Rorschach has always had a problem in this regard, as astute observers have remarked for more than half a century (see Chapter Four). As recently as 2001, Edward Aronow—by no means an enemy of the test—chided his colleagues for treating the Rorschach as a faith and its leaders as nearly divine: "Too much has been taken on faith by Rorschachers over the years, with primary contributors almost deified, beginning with Rorschach himself."[7]

Aronow's observation that Rorschach heroes are "almost deified" is scarcely an exaggeration. Recall, for example, the quasi-religious undertones of the American Psychological Association's tribute to Exner in 1997 (see Chapter Eight).

Psychologists must beware of falling prey to their propensities toward hero worship. Logicians term this kind of error the "argument from authority," which is the fallacy of assuming that a claim is likely to be correct merely because it was advanced by a respected or experienced authority figure.[8]

An amusing illustration of Rorschachers' deference to their venerable leaders appeared in a recent Internet message.[9] A forensic psychologist explained to his colleagues on a popular discussion list that he found critics of the Rorschach to be unpersuasive because they had fewer years of experience than did the test's defenders. He concluded his message with the statement: "I have learned (the hard way) to respect my elders, which is apparently unlike the Young Turks currently criticizing the Rorschach."

Several members of the discussion list responded to their colleague by pointing out that the truth of criticisms leveled against the Rorschach is unrelated to the age or experience of its critics. Tribal societies may believe that "older is better," but philosophers and scientists abandoned this view centuries ago. Moreover, by implying that the claims of Rorschach critics should be discounted because of their supposedly limited clinical experience with the test, this psychologist fell prey to the "genetic fallacy," the error of evaluating a claim's truth in terms of its origins (the characteristics of the individuals making the claim).

Social Proof

"Thousands of psychologists can't be wrong."

Faith in the Rorschach is further sustained by what social psychologist Robert Cialdini calls "social proof."[10] As Cialdini explains, people often decide what's true or appropriate by observing what other people say and do. Which foods are appetizing and which are disgusting? Which sexual practices are acceptable? Which groups of people are superior, and which are inferior or evil? Powerful emotions and deeply held convictions about such matters are often based on such social proof.

For the past sixty years, many professionals in the mental health fields, including psychiatrists, psychologists, and social workers, have been swept away periodically by faddish techniques and concepts. In the 1940s and 1950s, projective tests generated enormous enthusiasm. In the 1960s, Primal Scream Therapy (which was popular among celebrities, including Beatle John Lennon) held wide appeal. In the 1970s, the new byword was Codependency. The 1980s and 1990s saw the spread of Recovered Memory Therapy, a group of techniques that involved highly suggestive procedures (hypnosis, guided imagery, sodium amytal or so-called truth serum) to retrieve memories that had purportedly been repressed for decades.[11]

Social proof provides much of the impetus for such movements. In books, seminars, workshops, and (nowadays) Internet discussion groups, enthusiastic practitioners recount their success stories regarding the latest therapy or technique. A contagious mood of elation and confidence spreads, because it hardly seems possible that so many highly educated and intelligent professionals could be wrong. Such overreliance on social proof as a method of validation courts what logicians term the "ad populum" (bandwagon) fallacy, the error of assuming that a claim is likely to be correct because it's widely held.

Although social proof can be highly misleading, Rorschach promoters continue to cite it as evidence of the test's legitimacy. The practice goes back at least to 1939, when Morris Krugman, the first president of Klopfer's Rorschach Institute, promoted the test by citing "testimony from reputable workers in the various schools of psychology and in widely different situations as to the validity of the Rorschach."[12]

Nowadays Exner's coauthor Irving Weiner still points to the popularity of the test as evidence of its usefulness: "In the United States, mental health professionals use the Rorschach Inkblot Method to evaluate personality more than any other instrument except the Minnesota Multiphasic Personality Inventory. The Rorschach has survived and prospered because generations of psychologists in diverse cultures have found that it helps them help their clients."[13]

Here, Weiner appears to commit two logical errors. First, he lapses into the ad populum fallacy just discussed. Second, he falls victim to what logicians term the "ad antiquitem" fallacy, the error of assuming that a belief or technique is likely to be correct because it has survived for long periods of time. Many practices, including astrology and palm reading, have remained widely used for centuries even though they possess no validity.[14] We are not saying that Weiner did anything wrong by mentioning the popularity of the Rorschach. Rather, our point is that the test should be evaluated on the basis of scientific evidence, not on the basis of its popularity among practitioners.

Clinical Validation and Testimonials

"In my clinical experience . . . "

Naive faith in clinical validation has turned out to be one of Bruno Klopfer's most long-lasting and problematic legacies to clinical psychology. As history has shown, this reliance on clinical experience as an arbiter of the truth was a spectacularly bad idea. For example, Color Shock was widely accepted in the 1940s and 1950s on the basis of clinical experience, but was later shown to be useless.[15]

Clinicians who believe that they can evaluate the worth of Rorschach scores through personal observation are liable to be misled by a variety of cognitive illusions, as we'll discuss later in this chapter. The only dependable way to avoid such mental pitfalls is to rely on careful empirical studies—a point made over half a century ago by Marguerite Hertz and Donald Super (see Chapter Three).

Despite the lessons of history and the unanimous advice of experts on psychological testing, Klopfer's dubious legacy of clinical validation lives on among Rorschach devotees. If asked why they continue to use a particular score or index in the absence of scientific support, many Rorschachers respond with a personal testimonial. For instance, a psychologist recently justified his use of the Rorschach in custody evaluations as follows (notice his claim that the test works "without fail" and produces "exquisite correlates"): "I always use the Rorschach in custody evaluations. . . . It reveals psychopathology that is otherwise concealed. . . . Without fail I find exquisite correlates between Rorschach data on emotional controls, object relations and general judgment in response to life's difficulties and the obtained history of the person."[16]

Even mainstream psychologists fall prey to this superficially alluring trap. As noted earlier in this chapter, a distinguished clinician receiving an award from the American Psychological Association recently justified his use of the Rorschach by citing his personal experience. If enough of these clinical validations appear together—for example on an Internet discussion list—they can coalesce into social proof. A group of psychologists providing mutually reinforcing testimonials can persuade themselves and each other of the Rorschach's value.

Anecdotal Evidence

"Let me tell you about one of my cases . . ."

Memorable stories (scientists call them "anecdotes") play an important role in sustaining faith in the Rorschach. One such anecdote appeared recently in an article on the incremental validity of the Rorschach by Exner's coauthor Irving Weiner.

As we discussed in Chapter Six, the research literature on incremental validity shows that the Rorschach typically adds little or nothing to clinicians' accuracy beyond what can be gained from a thorough interview and the MMPI.[17] Instead of addressing this research literature, however, Weiner presented the "case study" of a mother and father who had been administered the MMPI and Rorschach as part of a custody evaluation. In Weiner's story, the MMPI failed to detect the parents' psychological defects, whereas the Rorschach uncovered their problems in considerable depth. Weiner concluded that his anecdote "unequivocally falsifies any statement that Rorschach assessment is without incremental validity or clinical utility."[18]

Because vivid stories of this kind are more compelling and memorable than statistics and research reports, they're often used by teachers and writers to make facts "come alive."[19] But although scientists are perfectly willing to use anecdotes as *illustrations* of important points, they usually take a dim view of such stories when they're presented as *evidence*. There are at least three reasons for this skepticism, which we'll briefly describe using Weiner's story as an example.

The first problem with anecdotes is that they may not be *typical*. For example, in the custody case presented by Weiner, the Rorschach seemed to add valuable information. However, prior studies on the incremental validity of the test, based on hundreds of people, have found something much different.[20] Weiner's Rorschach success story was almost certainly atypical.[21]

The second problem with anecdotes is their lack of good comparisons or *controls*. In Weiner's anecdote, the parents' Rorschach scores seemed fairly "sick." However, most normal people also appear disturbed on the test (see Chapter Nine). Had Weiner given the Rorschach to control subjects for purposes of comparison, their scores might not have been much different from the parents' scores. As Carnegie-Mellon psychologist Robyn Dawes noted, all good scientific research is *comparative*.[22] The question readers must always ask when evaluating a scientific finding is "Compared with what?" Lacking adequate comparisons or controls, anecdotes are often virtually uninterpretable because they do not permit a clear answer to this question.

The third problem with most anecdotes is their *vagueness*. In Weiner's anecdote, many crucial pieces of information were missing that would be required in a research article. Who gave the Rorschachs to the parents? When? Who scored the results? How accurate was the scoring?

Even some information that appears essential was missing from Weiner's anecdote. For instance, he never stated unequivocally that the test results were from real people. Weiner began his story by evoking an imaginary scenario: "So imagine, if you will, that you are consulting to a family court judge and have in front of you test protocols given by Mr. Able and Ms. Baker."[23] It seems unlikely that Weiner invented the mother, father, and their test scores as hypothetical examples of the Rorschach's incremental validity. However, his statements created an ambiguity that would be unacceptable in a research report.

As can be seen, a published anecdote like Weiner's can't be accorded much if any weight as a piece of scientific evidence. Even less faith can be placed in *unpublished* anecdotes, which tend to be more casual, impressionistic, and vague. Yet anecdotal evidence is regularly swapped among Rorschach enthusiasts in seminars and on the Internet. Such stories play an important role in sustaining confidence in the test. For example, one psychologist recently posted the following anecdote to the Internet regarding the meaning of Reflection responses (supposedly an indicator of narcissism). The psychologist described "a narcissistic student I saw many years ago who was in theology. She was great as long as she was helping, seen as being wonderful, loving, etc. If anyone ever challenged her opinions, she ALWAYS said they didn't understand God's word! . . . Her Rorschach—6 Reflections."[24]

Vivid Personal Experience

"I once had this incredible thing happen . . . "

Most clinicians who use the Rorschach on a regular basis can readily produce a vivid story from their own experience that seemingly illustrates the test's uncanny accuracy.

In this context, psychologists Daniel Kahneman and Amos Tversky referred to the "availability heuristic"—the tendency of information that is highly accessible in memory to exert an impact on our perception of the world.[25] Anecdotes that are vivid and dramatic are especially likely to exert an impact on our perceptions because they're so easy to recall. Moreover, they can lead clinicians to overestimate the value of a psychological test, because clinicians—who after all, are human—are more likely to remember the test's hits (its successful predictions and judgments) than its misses.

As an example, in a recent article, Donald Viglione recounted the memorable story of a twenty-five-year-old nurse who was admitted to a hospital with symptoms of depression. Her score on the Rorschach Suicide Constellation was elevated, but the treating psychiatrist ignored the finding and discharged her. Shortly afterward the nurse was found dead in a parked car, having "fashioned her own death through self-induced carbon monoxide poisoning."[26]

For readers, this story represents anecdotal evidence, with all the attendant problems we've discussed. But for the psychologist who administered the Rorschach to the unfortunate nurse, the episode is likely to constitute a compelling and memorable demonstration of the test's awesome power. As research has shown, such vivid personal experiences can be highly persuasive.[27] Moreover, these experiences lend themselves to the availability heuristic, because they tend to leave a powerful impression on our memories.

However, a vivid experience, no matter how impressive, may be atypical. The memorable instance in which the Rorschach scores a spectacular hit may be outweighed by many more instances, less well remembered, when it misses the mark entirely. Furthermore, almost any assessment method or fortune-telling system will have remarkable successes occasionally, if only by chance. As the proverb states, "Even a blind pig will find an acorn once in a while."

Some thoughtful readers may conclude that the psychiatrist in the Viglione anecdote was partly to blame. After all, the credo in clinical practice should be "better safe than sorry." But this superficially appealing logic points up another problem with vivid anecdotes (and anecdotes in general), namely, their vulnerability to *hindsight bias.*[28] As we all know, hindsight tends to be 20/20: once we're aware of an outcome, it's sorely tempting to tell ourselves that we "knew it all along." In this case, it's sorely tempting to conclude that "the psychiatrist should have known." But as the Nobel prize–winning physicist Niels Bohr noted wryly, "prediction is difficult, especially about the future."[29]

Cognitive Illusions

"I see it work every day . . . "

Conspiring to enhance the Rorschach's image are several mental illusions or "tricks of the mind" that can deceive unwary clinicians into believing that the test is much more powerful than it really is. Like visual illusions, these cognitive illusions are often subjectively compelling and difficult to dismiss.[30]

Such cognitive illusions help to explain why even well-educated and highly intelligent individuals can become persuaded of the validity of psychological tests despite overwhelming negative evidence. Nevertheless, with proper scientific training, clinicians can learn to become aware of cognitive illusions and overcome them. Although we've examined this topic already (see Chapters Six and Seven), we'll summarize the three most important issues here.

First, "confirmation bias" can mislead a clinician who attempts to evaluate the validity of a test through personal observation. If one begins with such a bias, evidence to support it can nearly always be found. For example, it's not difficult to find evidence for at least some indication of narcissism in a patient who produces numerous Reflection responses on the Rorschach, because narcissism is a highly inferential trait that is difficult to assess objectively—and virtually all people harbor at least a few narcissistic characteristics. To overcome confirmation bias, one must attend to both negative and positive findings.

Second is the phenomenon known as "illusory correlation," whereby clinicians come to believe that they've repeatedly seen a strong relationship between a test score and personality traits, even though no such relationship exists. This phenomenon helps to explain why rigorously controlled research studies are needed, because clinicians in daily practice may perceive that a Rorschach score is valid when it is not.

Third is what we term the "overpathologizing illusion." As explained in Chapter Six, a test such as the Rorschach that identifies many patients as sick can appear highly sensitive in clinical settings, even if it's completely invalid. In fact, clinicians may erroneously come to believe that such a test provides more profound insights than tests that do not overpathologize, because it tends to uncover pathology that better-normed tests do not.

Given the existence of such illusions, clinicians should be highly dubious of their impressions regarding the validity of the Rorschach, even if these impressions are subjectively compelling. Nevertheless, it can be exceedingly difficult for anyone to put aside intuitions when they conflict sharply with carefully controlled data. An otherwise intelligent psychologist recently told one of us, "I see the test provide clinically useful results every day."

But although "seeing is believing," scientific training demands a willingness to acknowledge that one's subjective perceptions regarding a test's value may be erroneous. To a substantial extent, scientific training involves the systematic inculcation of humility, the nagging but insistent sense that "Well, I might be wrong."

Reinforcement

"I've been highly successful with it . . . "

Psychologists have long recognized that if a behavior is rewarded, it's likely to recur. This simple principle of reinforcement probably accounts in part for clinicians' persistence in using the Rorschach. Of course, reinforcement principles help to explain a great deal of all human behavior, both scientific and nonscientific. The endeavors of great scientists are driven partly by reinforcement, because these individuals derive both extrinsic rewards (prizes, tenure, and promotion) and intrinsic rewards (intellectual mastery, the thrill of discovery) from their efforts. Nevertheless, when practices that are not grounded firmly in science are reinforced repeatedly, attitudes that are not conducive to scientific thinking may result.

The reinforcement of Rorschach behavior typically begins in graduate school, when the budding psychologist is rewarded with approval and high grades for mastering the test's intricacies. The reinforcement may continue on through internship, because some internship sites prize students who are experienced with the test.

After graduation, the psychologist receives financial reinforcement for administering the Rorschach. Furthermore, use of the test is likely to deliver its own implicit rewards. As Florence Goodenough observed shrewdly more than half a century ago, "It is flattering to the ego to feel that one has found a key that gives quick and easy access to the secrets of his neighbors' minds."[31] Finally, if the psychologist becomes a virtuoso with the test, social reinforcement (adulation from colleagues) may soon follow.

Self-Consistency

"It's impossible I've been wrong all these years . . ."

The role of "self-consistency" as a central motivator of behavior is one of the most significant findings of modern social psychology. Cialdini, whose views on social proof we discussed earlier, has said: "Once we make a choice or take a stand, we will encounter personal and interpersonal pressures to behave consistently with that commitment. Those pressures will cause us to respond in ways that justify our earlier decision. We simply convince ourselves that we have made the right choice, and no doubt, feel better about our decision."[32]

This principle may help to explain why psychologists who begin using the Rorschach seldom abandon it, even in the face of overwhelming negative evidence. By remaining consistent in their support for the test, they can "feel better" about their past actions.

In contrast, if clinicians were to acknowledge the Rorschach's shortcomings, they'd be forced to confront an array of potentially unpleasant realizations. For example, if the Comprehensive System is invalid for most purposes, psychologists who use it have squandered an enormous amount of time and energy pursuing a will-o-the-wisp. Worse yet, in using it to help make important decisions—about children, parents in custody cases, prisoners seeking parole—they may have inadvertently done serious harm.

In the nineteenth century, when Pasteur, Lister, and Semmelweis introduced their ideas about germs, sepsis, and infection, they encountered serious resistance from some physicians. Many doctors couldn't accept the devastating news that, by failing to observe adequate sanitary practices, they'd probably been harming many of the very patients they were trying to help. Similar forces are probably operating with some psychologists today, who are understandably reluctant to recognize how deluded they may have been about the Rorschach.

Lack of Alternatives

"Nothing else seems to work."

The Rorschach purportedly measures a remarkable number of personality characteristics, including egocentricity, problem-solving style, susceptibility to stress, resilience, empathy, and flexibility. Without the Rorschach, many psychologists would feel that they lack a good all-purpose measure of such qualities. Of course, a central point of this book is that psychologists *already* lack such a measure, although they haven't yet realized it.

Some psychologists turn to the Rorschach because they feel that they need a deep measure of personality. The information yielded by the MMPI and standard personality questionnaires is often clinically helpful, but can be unsatisfying for clinicians who want to understand what really makes a patient tick.

From the 1930s to the present, the Rorschach and other projective techniques have proven attractive precisely because they seem to offer a deeper understanding of clients than can be obtained from questionnaires. The authors of this book are in heartfelt sympathy with psychologists' desire for such understanding. However, it's now evident that the Rorschach—at least as commonly used—is not the answer. To the contrary, use of the Rorschach may often interfere with valid insight. By attending to its invalid scores, psychologists are distracted from other sources of information (interviews, collateral contacts, biographical data) that can provide a better understanding of clients.

Social Role Demands

"I have to say something . . . "

Psychologists frequently assume roles in which they're expected to offer opinions, even though uncertainty is enormous and the scientific knowledge base is extremely limited. For example, in custody evaluations that involve reasonably normal individuals, it's often impossible to know which parent will provide a child with a better environment. Research in this area is limited, and there are few or no well-validated procedures for arriving at recommendations.

After a comprehensive review of the research literature, William O'Donohue and April Bradley of the University of Nevada at Reno concluded that "currently mental health professionals [who conduct custody evaluations] may have little accurate information or warranted recommendations to offer."[33] Nevertheless, the lawyers and judges in such cases often press psychologists for a firm opinion.

Under such demands, psychologists sometimes resort to unvalidated procedures. The reasoning seems to be that any test, even one of dubious validity, will perform better than merely flipping a coin. Our view, however, is that use of the Rorschach in such circumstances is highly inadvisable because it can muddy the waters by providing false or misleading information.

The Romantic Tradition

"Who really cares what the research says?"

Finally, some proportion of Rorschachers continue to use the test because they strongly distrust the empirical side of clinical psychology and identify almost entirely with its romantic side (see Chapter Four). For example, we've participated in Internet discussions with psychologists who cavalierly dismiss the negative scientific findings on the Rorschach. They often argue that the studies are meaningless and that researchers have merely failed to tap the test's unique powers.

Such a point of view is not new. In the 1940s, Klopfer and his followers claimed that ordinary research on the Rorschach was meaningless (see Chapter Three). And in the 1950s, when the research findings turned out to be overwhelmingly negative, Klopfer simply dismissed them. However, we've sometimes wondered if present day psychologists who similarly dismiss research are equally frank when they testify in court or seek reimbursement from insurers. After all, the willingness of courts to listen to psychologists, and of insurers to reimburse their services, is presumably based on the assumption that psychologists' practices are justified by scientific findings.

KEEPING THE FAITH: A RECENT EXAMPLE FROM THE SOCIETY FOR PERSONALITY ASSESSMENT

In the current controversy, it's informative to observe how advocates of the Comprehensive System uphold the "Rorschach faith" by falling prey to the cognitive errors described in this chapter. Below we quote a recent message from the president of the Society for Personality Assessment, Stephen Finn, to its members.

Finn notes that "personality assessment" (by which he seems mainly to mean projective techniques) has recently come under attack from critics and third-party payers. He tells his readers that "we must actively bolster each other" and then suggests how they can sustain their "faith." As an interesting exercise, readers might wish to see how many themes identified in this chapter appear in Finn's recommendations to his fellow Rorschachers:

> It would be easy for us to begin interjecting these distorted messages [from critics of "personality assessment"] and lose faith in our work or a sense that anyone else sees its value. We can guard against this possibility by actively reminding each other of the power and impact of personality assessment. We must share stories, case examples, empirical data, and success experiences: of clients whose lives have been transformed by assessment, colleagues who recognize and treasure the work we do, studies that demonstrate the validity of our instruments, and successes we have had finding markets for our skills.
> Stephen E. Finn
> President of the Society for Personality Assessment
> 2002[34]

In Table 11.1, we list the themes that we've been able to identify.

Finn's message may have served to "rally the Rorschach troops," but we wish that he had encouraged practitioners to heed criticisms of the test and place greater emphasis on scientific research.[35]

Table 11.1.   Analysis of Stephen Finn's Recommendations.

Quote from Finn	Motivation or Evidence Being Evoked
"Lose faith"	Self-consistency
"Actively reminding each other of the power and impact of personality assessment"	Social proof
"Share stories"	Anecdotal evidence; Clinical validation
"Case examples"	Anecdotal evidence; Clinical validation
"Empirical data"	Research
"Success experiences"	Anecdotal evidence; Reinforcement
"Clients whose lives have been transformed"	Anecdotal evidence; Clinical validation
"Colleagues who recognize and treasure the work we do"	Social proof; Reinforcement
"Studies that demonstrate the validity of our instruments"	Research
"Successes we have had finding markets"	Reinforcement

CHAPTER TWELVE

Objection, Your Honor!

Keeping the Rorschach Out of Court

If a professional psychologist is "evaluating" you in a situation in which you are at risk and asks you for responses to ink blots or to incomplete sentences, or for a drawing of anything, walk out of that psychologist's office. Going through with such an examination creates the danger of having a serious decision made about you on totally invalid grounds. If your contact with the psychologist involves a legal matter, your civil liberties themselves may be at stake.

—*Robyn Dawes,* House of Cards:
Psychology and Psychotherapy Built on Myth, *1994*

This chapter has a different objective from the preceding ones. Specifically, it's primarily intended as a "self-help" resource for lawyers, forensic psychologists, and other individuals who confront Rorschach-based evidence in legal settings. In addition, it's likely to be of considerable interest to members of the general public who want to understand the implications of the use of the Rorschach for real-life cases in criminal and civil courts.

Our stance in prior chapters has been primarily research-oriented. In this chapter, we take a more practical, nuts-and-bolts approach. As stated in Chapter Ten, we believe that the Rorschach should rarely if ever be allowed into court. Here we provide suggestions and tips that may be helpful in challenging the test in legal proceedings, or even keeping it out of court entirely. We are not lawyers, and our ideas should not be construed as legal advice. However, we hope that our insights will prove useful.

We assume that many lawyers will pick up our book and quickly flip to this chapter for practical guidance. Thus we make no assumption that readers of this chapter are familiar with prior chapters. Furthermore, we sometimes repeat points that have been covered in earlier parts of the book (with apologies to readers who will find some of this material all too familiar). Readers who find this chapter irrelevant to their interests may want to skip ahead to the Epilogue that follows it.

THE RORSCHACH IN LEGAL SETTINGS: A PAPER TIGER?

The Rorschach pops up surprisingly often in the legal system, in both civil and criminal cases. We'll mention a few real-life examples from our own experience:

- An African American policeman sued his department for civil rights violations, alleging that he'd been subjected to racial discrimination. A psychologist called by the defense testified that the policeman's Rorschach revealed paranoia and a tendency to distort reality when under stress.
- The plaintiff in a tort case allegedly suffered from Dissociative Identity Disorder (known formerly as Multiple Personality Disorder). However, an expert witness for the defendant testified that the plaintiff's Rorschach results were inconsistent with such a diagnosis.
- A custody evaluator testified in court, mainly on the basis of the Rorschach, that a mother was "narcissistic"—extremely self-centered and unlikely to feel genuine concern for her children.
- A prison psychologist concluded from a prisoner's Rorschach that he lacked adequate "controls" and was likely to function poorly if released to the community. Due largely to the psychologist's report, the prisoner was denied parole.
- A forensic psychologist evaluated a death row inmate using the Rorschach and concluded that he was suffering from an

undiagnosed psychotic disorder. The inmate's attorneys filed an appeal of his conviction, arguing that at trial his psychiatric illness had gone undetected.

As can be seen, the Rorschach can play an important role in legal cases, even those that are literally a matter of life and death.

In the mid-1990s, use of the Rorschach was seldom challenged in court.[1] Attorneys sometimes attempted to rebut one expert's Rorschach interpretations by calling an expert who offered alternative interpretations for the test results.[2] Otherwise, challenges to the test seem to have been rare.

In recent years, however, the situation has changed. Word is percolating through the legal community that John Exner's Comprehensive System for the Rorschach is in serious scientific trouble. The authors of this book have been contacted by several attorneys seeking to rebut Rorschach-based expert testimony.

Judging from these cases, the Rorschach may be highly vulnerable to attack from even a moderately well-informed attorney. Here are a few real-life examples of how different lawyers have proceeded.

- A psychologist gave testimony based on the Comprehensive System during a pretrial hearing. Quoting from recently published articles, the opposing attorney asked the witness if he was aware of the many criticisms of the system. Admitting that he was unaware of these criticisms, the psychologist conceded that they might alter his opinions. The side that had hired the psychologist decided not to have him testify at trial.

- During deposition, an attorney closely questioned a psychologist about the scientific basis of her Rorschach-based opinions. When the psychologist began providing citations to Exner's books, the attorney asked her if these studies were peer-reviewed, had been replicated by other researchers, and were available for scrutiny by other psychologists. Unaccustomed to defending Exner's work, the psychologist floundered. The side that had hired her decided not to present her as a witness at trial.

- In a civil case, a psychologist had given the Rorschach to a plaintiff whom he diagnosed as seriously disturbed. The plaintiff's attorney demonstrated that the psychologist had violated the standardized administration and scoring procedures described in Exner's books. Although the psychologist tried to claim that his deviations from standardized procedures were inconsequential, he was easily refuted by quotes from the books.

• A psychologist conducting a custody evaluation concluded on the basis of Rorschach results that a mother suffered from thought disorder (a condition often associated with psychosis). The mother's attorney hired another psychologist to rescore the mother's Rorschach. The second psychologist did *not* find evidence of thought disorder. Through comparison with the scoring rules in Exner's books, it was possible to establish that the first psychologist had made serious scoring errors.

Three important themes seem to recur in these admittedly anecdotal examples. First, Rorschach-based testimony often turns out to be a paper tiger. If an opposing attorney puts up a fight, experts who have based their testimony on the Rorschach frequently retreat or are discredited. Second, if Rorschach-based testimony is vigorously opposed in depositions or pretrial hearings, it may never be introduced at trial. Finally, because the Rorschach is cumbersome and complicated, psychologists who use it sometimes cut corners, committing significant errors in administration or scoring that can be effectively challenged in court.

THE RORSCHACH IN LEGAL CASES: FUNDAMENTAL ISSUES

Attorneys can proceed along many avenues when dealing with Rorschach-based expert testimony. In the remainder of this chapter, we outline fundamental issues that should prove helpful.

The Rorschach Is Scientifically Controversial

From the mid-1950s until the late 1970s, the Rorschach was highly controversial in the scientific community (see Chapters Six and Seven). However, from the early 1980s to the mid-1990s, disagreements regarding the test virtually disappeared, thanks to John Exner's Comprehensive System. Exner was thought to have placed the test on a solid scientific footing (see Chapter Eight). Since 1996, however, the Comprehensive System has become the subject of heated criticism (see Chapter Nine). At present, the Comprehensive System and virtually all other Rorschach approaches used in forensic settings can be regarded as scientifically controversial at best, and scientifically questionable at worst.

The forensic implications of such controversy seem clear: Even if the Rorschach is admissible into the courtroom under current legal rules (an issue we discuss later in this chapter), expert witnesses' credibility may be undermined if they are shown to have relied on it. No longer can psychologists take the Rorschach into court and claim honestly that the test is widely accepted by the scientific community.

The following list outlines some of the evidence that demonstrates that the Rorschach is scientifically controversial. A number of the debates listed here directly involved the authors of this book. Although some Rorschach proponents have maintained that the controversy is limited to a small number of academic critics, including ourselves, this assertion is clearly inaccurate. It's critical to emphasize that the scientific controversy concerning the Rorschach is widespread in the psychological research community, as evidenced by the large number of eminent commentators who have raised questions concerning its validity and other psychometric properties (see Chapters Seven and Nine).

- In 2001, the leading Rorschach journal, the *Journal of Personality Assessment,* included a section titled "Special Series: More Data on the Current Rorschach Controversy."[3]

- *Psychological Assessment,* a journal of the American Psychological Association, has published two issues (1999 and 2001) with a total of eleven articles debating the merits and demerits of the Comprehensive System and other Rorschach approaches.[4]

- In 1999, the journal *Assessment* published a four-way debate among proponents and critics of the Comprehensive System.[5]

- In recent years, debates between critics and proponents of the Rorschach have appeared in other prominent journals and newsletters, including the *Journal of Clinical Psychology,*[6] *Clinical Psychology: Science and Practice,*[7] *Psychological Science,*[8] and the *Harvard Mental Health Letter.*[9]

- Critiques of the Comprehensive System have also recently appeared in *Psychological Science in the Public Interest,*[10] *Professional Psychology: Research and Practice,*[11] and *Scientific American.*[12]

- A 2002 chapter in the *Annual Review of Psychology* included a section titled "The Controversy over the Comprehensive System for the Rorschach."[13]

- In 2001, the *New York Times* carried an article on the Rorschach controversy, with the headline "What's in an Inkblot? Some Say, Not Much."[14]

Nearly All Rorschach Scores Lack Well-Demonstrated Validity

The authors of this book adopt the position that the Rorschach should generally be kept out of court because it lacks well-demonstrated validity for most of the purposes for which it is used in civil and criminal cases. As we explained in Chapter Ten, the Rorschach is usually of little or no value in custody cases because it rarely reveals valid information concerning parental qualities. Similarly, the test is potentially misleading in criminal cases because it bears no demonstrated relationship to such characteristics as dangerousness or suitability for rehabilitation.

This book reviews the validity of the Rorschach in several places. The validity of the "early" Rorschach systems is discussed in Chapter Six in the section titled "Seemingly Positive Findings," and in Chapter Seven in the section titled "Critics in the Mental Measurements Yearbook." The validity of Exner's Comprehensive System is discussed in Chapter Nine in the section titled "What Does It Measure—Really? The Problem of Validity."

In cases that involve the Comprehensive System, Table 9.4 in Chapter Nine is likely to be particularly useful. It shows all Comprehensive System scores that have been well-validated. If a score does not appear in Table 9.4, it has not been well-validated and is almost certainly irrelevant in legal proceedings.

Expert witnesses who use the Comprehensive System sometimes claim that scores other than those shown in Table 9.4 are well-validated. Any such assertion should be closely scrutinized: What studies can the expert cite in support of the scores' validity? Have any studies yielded negative findings? Do the supporting studies have any methodological problems? In nearly all cases, it will turn out that the expert is relying on unpublished and unreplicated studies described in Exner's books (see Chapter Nine to understand why this is a serious problem), citing unreplicated or methodologically questionable studies, or ignoring studies with negative findings.

The Rorschach Often Makes
Normal Individuals Appear Sick

One of the oldest and most serious problems with the Rorschach is its tendency to *overpathologize,* that is, to make normal people appear sick. For example, research evidence suggests that more than 25 percent of normal individuals are identified as "narcissistic" by the Comprehensive System. More than 50 percent are identified as having "poor reality testing" or "distorted thinking." Approximately 15 percent are identified as "depressed."[15]

For a thorough discussion of the Comprehensive System's tendency to overpathologize normal individuals, see the section titled "Still Overpathologizing: The Comprehensive System Norms" in Chapter Nine. Table 9.3 in Chapter Nine is particularly useful, because it lists the scores in the Comprehensive System that are most likely to make normal individuals appear sick.

It should be understood that *most normal individuals tested using the Comprehensive System will appear pathological.* The most effective way to refute mistaken diagnoses is to obtain a copy of the 1999 article titled "Current Nonpatient Data for the Rorschach, WAIS-R, and MMPI-2" by Shaffer, Erdberg, and Haroian, which appeared in the *Journal of Personality Assessment.* This article lists the average Rorschach scores of 123 nonpatient adults who were tested using the Comprehensive System. Clients who appear sick using the Comprehensive System often appear entirely normal when compared with the numbers in this article.

For instance, in one case we mentioned earlier, a policeman was said to "distort reality" because he scored .50 on X+% and F+%—two Rorschach scores that supposedly reflect reality testing. Compared with the numbers in Exner's books, the policeman's scores appear very low and seem to indicate serious cognitive problems. However, compared with the numbers reported by Shaffer and his colleagues, the scores of .50 are simply "average."[16]

Similar numbers for children can be found in "A Study of Nonpatient Preadolescent Rorschach Protocols" by Hamel, Shaffer, and Erdberg, which appeared in the *Journal of Personality Assessment* in 2000. The subjects in this study were a hundred preteen children whose mental health was slightly above average. Children who appear disturbed when compared with the numbers in Exner's books often appear normal when compared with the numbers reported by Hamel and his colleagues.

Another article highly relevant to the Comprehensive System's tendency to overpathologize is "The Misperception of Psychopathology: Problems With the Norms of the Comprehensive System for the Rorschach" by Wood, Nezworski, Garb, and Lilienfeld, which appeared in *Clinical Psychology: Science and Practice* in 2001.

The Rorschach Is Generally Useless as a Diagnostic Test

Although the Rorschach is commonly used in diagnosis, it has very little utility for this purpose. The only clear-cut exception involves conditions marked by thought disorder, such as schizophrenia and related disorders. Exner's coauthor Irving Weiner has recently declared: "The Rorschach Inkblot Method is not a diagnostic test, it was not designed as a diagnostic test, it is not intended to be a diagnostic test, and it does not in fact work very well as a diagnostic test."[17]

Even Exner has downplayed the Rorschach as a diagnostic tool: "If you're interested only in some diagnostic labeling, I don't know that the Rorschach is worth doing, not simply because of time but because you're flooded with information that you're not going to use."[18]

Regarding the general failure of the Comprehensive System as a diagnostic tool, see Chapter Nine, the section titled "What Does It Measure—Really? The Problem of Validity," especially the subsection titled "Validity for Diagnostic or Forensic Purposes." Also helpful is the article by Wood, Lilienfeld, Garb, and Nezworski, "The Rorschach Test in Clinical Diagnosis," which appeared in the *Journal of Clinical Psychology* in 2000. If a diagnosis of psychopathy, antisocial personality disorder, or conduct disorder is at issue, consult also "Coming to Grips With Negative Evidence for the Comprehensive System for the Rorschach" by Wood, Lilienfeld, Nezworski, and Garb, which appeared in the *Journal of Personality Assessment* in 2001.

Regarding the general failure of earlier Rorschach systems for diagnostic purposes, see the sections titled "Positive Findings: Diagnosing Psychosis and Estimating IQ" and "Seemingly Positive Findings" in Chapter Six.

Rorschach Scores Are Frequently Contradictory

Many variables in the Comprehensive System behave in a quasi-random fashion. In a striking understatement, a recent textbook declared that the interpretations generated by the system are "complex and sometimes contradictory."[19]

Ironically, the Rorschach's tendency to contradict itself may account partially for its excellent reputation among psychologists. As J. R. Wittenborn and Seymour Sarason of Yale noted half a century ago, the Rorschach's self-contradictions sometimes make it appear omniscient. No matter what a client is like, something in the Rorschach scores is bound to fit.[20]

Within a legal context, such self-contradictions provide fertile territory for cross-examination of experts who have relied on the test. When a psychologist offers an opinion based on Rorschach results, other results from the test are likely to contradict or at least be inconsistent with that opinion. For example, in the case mentioned earlier involving the African American policeman, the psychologist offered an opinion based on the Rorschach that the policeman was "paranoid." However, the opposing attorney pointed out that several Rorschach scores were inconsistent with paranoia, although the psychologist had ignored them. Cross-examination not only undermined the psychologist's testimony but exposed him as extremely biased in his interpretation of the test results.

Attorneys who wish to pursue this strategy will need to engage in considerable preparation. First, they will need to obtain through subpoena all the documents and computer files that the psychologist generated in administering, scoring, and interpreting the Rorschach. Because many psychologists enter Rorschach results into a computer and generate computerized reports, it's important to subpoena such materials, as well as paper documents. Because of ethical considerations, many psychologists are unwilling to release test materials to nonpsychologists, even under subpoena. To avoid prolonged wrangling, attorneys who subpoena such materials should probably arrange for them to be handed over to a psychologist hired for the purpose.

Second, attorneys will need to acquaint themselves with the standard interpretation of Rorschach scores. Chapters One, Eight, and Nine of this book will be of some assistance. A fuller explanation of Rorschach scores and their interpretation can be found in the *Hand-*

book of Psychological Assessment (third and later editions only) by Gary Groth-Marnat. Another useful resource is *Principles of Rorschach Interpretation* by Irving Weiner. The index of Weiner's book is exceptionally useful. It enables readers to quickly locate the sections of the book that deal with a specific score. Weiner is Exner's coauthor and a former editor of the *Journal of Personality Assessment,* and his book thus carries special authority.

Third, attorneys will usually benefit from consultation with a well-informed psychologist. A psychologist familiar with the Comprehensive System can often point out the Rorschach scores that are inconsistent with a particular opinion. Fourth, it's often helpful to reenter the original Rorschach results into one of the widely available computerized interpretation programs. The two most popular programs are "Rorscan" and the "Rorschach Interpretation Assistance Program" (RIAP). We recommend Rorscan, which can be purchased by psychologists (but not attorneys) through the Internet. In our experience, interpretive statements generated by Rorscan can be very helpful in identifying Rorschach results that an expert has ignored or brushed aside.

Many Important Rorschach Scores Cannot Be Scored with Adequate Reliability

For many years, Exner maintained that all scores in the Comprehensive System can be scored with a reliability of .85 or higher—a reasonably high level of reliability. Many psychologists continue to parrot this figure in court. However, several recent studies indicate that many important Comprehensive System scores possess scoring reliability below .85 and cannot be scored with the accuracy required for adequate clinical or forensic work (see Chapter Nine, the section titled "Scoring Reliability: How Well Do Psychologists Agree?" and Table 9.2, which lists Comprehensive System scores with high and low scoring reliability).

Setting aside the issue of whether a Comprehensive System variable *can* be scored with adequate reliability by highly trained experts, there remains the question of whether a *specific* psychologist has scored a *specific* Rorschach protocol correctly. Readers are referred to a fascinating case that is reported in detail on the Internet at http://home.earthlink.net/~rkmck/vault/Rorinterscor/McKCam02ab.html.

In this study, psychologists Kim McKinzey and Victoria Campagna sent a Rorschach protocol from a real-life death penalty case to thirty psychologists and asked them to rescore it. The differences in scoring were impressive and led to divergent conclusions regarding the psychological condition of the defendant.

Attorneys can adopt different approaches to the issue of scoring reliability, depending on the amount of time and money available. One option is to raise the issue in general terms, based on the results of the studies completed thus far. Another option—far more compelling—is to have the Rorschach protocol rescored by a second psychologist who is well-trained in the Comprehensive System and unaware of the previous psychologist's scores (we recommend that the second psychologist be one who has attended the Advanced Training seminar at the Rorschach Workshops).

Other options may arise according to the specific circumstances of the case. In one case with which we're familiar, the Rorschach had been administered twice to the same individual. As commonly happens, he gave precisely the same responses to some blots both times. His attorney was able to show that the psychologist had sometimes scored the same response differently the second time around.

Rorschach Scores Can Reflect Situational Factors and Examiner Effects

Psychologists typically interpret Rorschach scores as if they reflect personality characteristics of the examinee. However, research in the 1950s and 1960s demonstrated that Rorschach results can be influenced by situational factors and by the actions and personality of the *examiner* (see the section titled "The Rorschach Is an Interpersonal Situation" in Chapter Six).

It's commonly asserted—and widely believed by psychologists—that the Comprehensive System largely eliminated such influences. However, there has been surprisingly little research on this topic, aside from unpublished studies by Exner reported in his books. In our opinion, the Comprehensive System is probably vulnerable to many of the situational and examiner effects identified by researchers in the 1950s.

In forensic settings, it can be important to confront experts who interpret Rorschach scores without taking situational factors into account. As has been known since the 1950s, people change their scores on the Rorschach depending on why they're being tested. For example, people are likely to alter their responses to the test and be more careful in what they say if they believe they're being evaluated for a serious emotional disturbance, as is often true in forensic settings.[21] Furthermore, if distrust or hostility has arisen between the examiner and examinee, the Rorschach results can be affected.

Such effects should not be glibly attributed to negative personality traits, such as "defensiveness" or "guardedness" in the examinee. Instead, they may reflect the influence of the situation. It can be difficult or impossible to sort out personality from situational effects in a given individual. Expert witnesses who attempt to do so should be vigorously challenged to justify their reasoning.

Psychologists Who Use the Rorschach Often Deviate from Standardized Procedures

In our consultations with attorneys, we've been surprised to learn that psychologists are often sloppy about following the standardized procedures for the Comprehensive System. Exner has been very outspoken regarding the importance of adhering to standardized procedures: "It is vitally important that the test be used appropriately. Factors such as seating, instructions, recording responses, and Inquiry all become critical to generating the data bank from which many conclusions will be reached. . . . The procedures employed with the inkblots can often dictate whether a protocol is truly valid or whether it should be reduced to the level of a free-wheeling interview."[22]

In our experience, three violations of standardized procedure are most common.

INAPPROPRIATE INSTRUCTIONS   Exner advises that after establishing rapport, the examiner should introduce the test in a straightforward way, saying, "Now we are going to do the inkblot test."[23] Except under exceptional circumstances, the examiner should then hand the examinee the first blot and ask, "What might this be?"

Exner allows that with children or unusually anxious subjects, it may be appropriate to explain how the inkblots are made, or to explain that "people see all sorts of things in the blots."[24] However, he discourages even such minimal additions to the instructions: "This kind of commentary should be avoided whenever possible and, more specifically, it *should not* include any reference to card turning, right or wrong answers, or any statement that might create a set about the quantity of answers to be given."[25]

Although Exner's guidelines are clear-cut, some psychologists disregard them. For example, in one case with which we're familiar, the psychologist told an examinee about to take the Rorschach, "Just have fun with it. Use your imagination." Such a statement is in clear violation of the Comprehensive System administration rules, because it inappropriately frames the Rorschach task as a game that involves fantasy. Not surprisingly, the examinee gave an unusually large number of fanciful responses.

Because psychologists don't typically tape-record Rorschach testing sessions, such procedural errors can go undetected. When clients are administered the Rorschach, we suggest that attorneys question them soon afterward (preferably the same day) regarding how the test was introduced and the instructions that were given. A non-leading approach is likely to be most fruitful: "I'd like to know everything that the psychologist said and did when introducing the Rorschach. Start at the beginning, and tell me everything the psychologist said and did." Such an open-ended approach can be very fruitful, because the client may spontaneously report idiosyncratic deviations from standardized procedure that would not emerge under more focused questioning.

INAPPROPRIATE SEATING ARRANGEMENT   Exner explicitly describes the seating arrangement to be used with the Comprehensive System and explains why it is important: "The preferred seating arrangement for Rorschach administration is where the subject and examiner *sit side-by-side.* . . . There are two reasons for the side-by-side seating. The first, and most important is to reduce the effects of inadvertent and unwanted cues from the examiner that may influence the subject. Second, the side-by-side position affords the examiner a much better view from which to see the features of the blot as they are referred to by the subject."[26]

Exner follows this statement with a lengthy discussion of "examiner" effects on Rorschach scores, and concludes, "It would be folly to assume that the side-by-side seating eliminates all examiner influence, but it does reduce the prospect of the subject being influenced inordinately by the nonverbal behaviors of the examiner."[27]

Despite such warnings, some psychologists cavalierly disregard Exner's instructions and administer the Rorschach face-to-face or seated across a table. In one recent case, a psychologist freely admitted having done so, but claimed that there was no problem with such a procedure. He was soon deflated by the opposing attorney, who confronted him with the relevant passages from Exner's books.

INAPPROPRIATE RECORDING OF RESPONSES   Exner emphasizes that psychologists must write down every word that a client says while taking the Rorschach: "*All responses must be recorded verbatim.* . . . There are two reasons that responses must be recorded verbatim. First, the examiner must be able to read them later to decide on the coding (scoring) for the response. . . . Responses that are not recorded verbatim cannot be coded accurately, and the record will not be valid. Second, the verbatim recording creates a permanent record of the test so that others can know *exactly* what the subject said" (emphases in original).[28]

Exner states explicitly that the record of responses must be "legible." He continues with a very precise format for recording responses, and states that "the format for recording responses should not vary from examiner to examiner."[29]

Despite Exner's statements, we have encountered several legal cases in which the record of Rorschach responses was illegible, obviously not *verbatim,* or arranged in a nonstandardized and potentially misleading format. As an example, we refer readers again to the death penalty case discussed online at http://home.earthlink.net/~rkmck/ vault/Rorinterscor/McKCam02ab.html. The psychologist who administered the Rorschach in this case (a university instructor and widely recognized expert on the test) failed to number the responses or to record each Response side-by-side with its corresponding Inquiry, as required by Exner's format. The psychologist's failure to follow standardized procedures created considerable confusion when other psychologists attempted to rescore the test. As we discuss shortly, failure to follow standardized procedures or maintain adequate records can raise important ethical issues.

The Rorschach Is Not Like an X-Ray

Proponents often imply that the Rorschach has an advantage over questionnaires because it can measure underlying personality characteristics, even in an individual who is *unaware* of these characteristics or is *unwilling* or *unable* to report them. In the 1940s, this notion was advanced by Bruno Klopfer, who likened the Rorschach to an "x-ray" of the psyche (see Chapters Three and Six). Nowadays, Rorschach proponents similarly claim that the test measures "implicit" or "underlying" characteristics.[30]

There's a (very small) grain of truth to such claims with respect to intelligence and thought disorder. A few Rorschach scores bear a modest relationship to intelligence. These scores may be related to intelligence even among individuals who are *unaware* of their IQ level.[31] Similarly, a few Rorschach scores can detect disordered thinking, perhaps even in individuals who are *unwilling* or *unable* to report their psychotic cognitions.[32]

Nevertheless, broad claims that the Rorschach is like an x-ray are fanciful and misleading, as even the test's proponents seem to concede nowadays.[33] There are three important ways that the Rorschach does *not* resemble x-rays.

It's far easier to fake the Rorschach than an x-ray. It's difficult to fake a cracked rib or broken leg on an x-ray (unless the x-ray technician is in collusion!). However, it's relatively easy to fake thought disorder on the Rorschach, as we'll discuss in the next section.

The information provided by the Rorschach tends to be imprecise and fuzzy. Although x-rays can sometimes be ambiguous, the information they provide tends to be much more precise than the information produced by the Rorschach. Put another way, in general there is considerably more "error" in Rorschach results than in x-ray findings.

The Rorschach is routinely used for purposes that lack scientific support. This may be the most important difference between x-rays and the Rorschach. Physicians rarely if ever use x-rays for purposes for which they have no demonstrated usefulness. A doctor who used x-rays to detect diabetes or diagnose high blood pressure would be considered a quack. In contrast, many psychologists routinely use the Rorschach for purposes that lack good scientific support. For example, the Comprehensive System lacks demonstrated validity as a measure of depression, anxiety, narcissism, or coping skills, yet many clinicians commonly use it for these purposes.

Modern Rorschach proponents contend that they long ago stopped comparing the test to an x-ray. However, when they claim that the Rorschach detects "implicit" or "underlying" characteristics, they're only one step away from Bruno Klopfer and his old x-ray analogy. For this reason, attorneys should be acutely sensitive when experts testifying on the Rorschach claim that it can detect *underlying, implicit, hidden, disguised, undetected,* or *masked* psychopathology. Such words evoke the old x-ray myth. They convey the subtle message that although an individual may appear normal on the surface, the Rorschach can uncannily reveal the underlying truth.

Experts who openly or covertly suggest that the Rorschach is like an x-ray should be vigorously confronted with evidence of the test's nonexistent validity for most purposes. Furthermore, attorneys can present evidence that even in the few instances in which the test is valid (for example, as a measure of thought disorder), the Rorschach rarely if ever increases clinicians' accuracy when it's added to such mundane sources as detailed biographical information and MMPI results. (For related issues, see section titled "Using the Rorschach with Other Information: Does It Add Anything Worthwhile?" in Chapter Six.)

The Rorschach Can Be Faked

The notion that the Rorschach can't be faked is little more than an urban legend (see the section titled "The Rorschach and the Legal System" in Chapter Ten). Numerous studies have shown that individuals with a minimal amount of coaching can fake schizophrenia on the Rorschach.[34] Furthermore, research indicates that patients with depression and posttraumatic stress disorder are indistinguishable on the Rorschach from individuals who are faking.[35] In other words, clinicians using the Rorschach cannot distinguish fakers from individuals who genuinely suffer from these disorders. For an excellent review on the topic, see "Dissimulation on the Rorschach and Other Projective Measures" by Schretlen.[36]

It's well-established that individuals can malinger or fake bad on the Rorschach. However, only a few studies have examined the question of whether it's possible for individuals with psychological problems to fake good on the test, thereby making themselves appear healthier than they are. After surveying the scientific literature on the topic, Schretlen concluded: "No well-controlled Rorschach studies of defensiveness were found. However, the available data suggest that Rorschach test results are susceptible to distortion as a result of deliberate attempts by subjects to conceal psychopathology or present themselves in the best possible light."[37]

A recent study by Linda Grossman of the University of Illinois at Chicago and her colleagues, published in the *Journal of Personality Assessment,* reached far more sanguine conclusions regarding the

Rorschach's resistance to faking good, particularly in comparison with the MMPI: "Although the MMPI has been demonstrated to be useful in the detection of minimization, the assessment ends at that point, and one cannot measure the actual psychopathology experienced by the minimizer in those cases. This article suggests that the Rorschach is less vulnerable to participants' attempts at minimization and therefore can help assess the extent and possibly the type of emotional disturbance present in a participant attempting to appear free from such disturbance."[38]

However, because this study suffered from several methodological problems, its conclusions must be treated with considerable caution.[39]

Interestingly, there's one strategy for faking the Rorschach that is usually ignored in the scientific literature: An individual who plans to fake the test can memorize in advance an entire Rorschach protocol! Meloy and Gacono reported such a case: "John Cochran, Ph.D. . . . administered the Rorschach to a subject in a criminal setting. When he studied the protocol, it sounded vaguely familiar. He found the same verbatim protocol in *The Rorschach: A Comprehensive System Volume 2* (2nd edition)! The subject had memorized the responses to the entire protocol, one of the many he could choose from in his Rorschach 'library' that Dr. Cochran eventually observed in his prison cell."[40]

As this case illustrates, rote memorization is a relatively easy strategy for beating the Rorschach. In fact, it's probably much easier to memorize twenty Rorschach responses (with cues from the cards) than to memorize the answers for the 567 questions of the MMPI-2.

The prisoner discussed by Meloy and Gacono was detected because he borrowed his protocol from a well-known book, and because Dr. Cochran had both the good memory and the diligence to track down the "vaguely familiar" responses. However, other intelligent malingerers may succeed where this prisoner failed, either because they memorize a less obvious protocol (say, one taken from an obscure book or supplied by an obliging accomplice), or because the psychologist who examines them is less alert than Dr. Cochran.

Perhaps we should conclude this section by pointing out what may already be obvious: We thoroughly disapprove of faking tests (including the Rorschach) and view such behavior as unethical and fraudulent. Furthermore, attempts to fake tests can easily backfire, and are therefore inadvisable as well as unconscionable. It is only the claim that the test can't be faked that we wish to dispute.

Legal Admissibility:
The Rorschach and Daubert

In 1993, the U.S. Supreme Court articulated the "Daubert criteria" for the admissibility of scientific evidence in federal courts (*Daubert* v. *Merrell Dow Pharmaceuticals,* 509 U.S. 579, 583, 1993). These criteria have been elaborated in subsequent decisions. Furthermore, they have been adopted by many state courts.

Considerable doubt exists whether the Rorschach (and specifically the Comprehensive System) is legally admissible under the Daubert criteria. To the best of our knowledge, no court has ruled on this issue. Although we lack sufficient legal training to explore this topic in the depth that it deserves, we will mention several relevant points.

First, scholars disagree on whether the Comprehensive System meets the Daubert standards. Joseph McCann, a nationally recognized psychologist and attorney in Binghamton, New York, argued in a 1998 article in the *Journal of Personality Assessment* that the system meets the Daubert criteria. However, William Grove of the University of Minnesota and Christopher Barden, a psychologist and attorney in Salt Lake City, reached the opposite conclusion in a 1999 article in *Psychology, Public Policy, and the Law* (a publication of the American Psychological Association that appears in legal data bases as a law review).

Furthermore, three articles on the Comprehensive System and Daubert appear in the October 2002 issue of *Psychology, Public Policy, and the Law.* Arguing *against* the admissibility of the system is "Failure of Rorschach Comprehensive System-Based Testimony to be Admissible Under *Daubert–Joiner–Kumho,*" by Grove, Barden, Garb, and Lilienfeld. Arguing *in favor* of admissibility are "Protecting the Integrity of Rorschach Expert Witnesses: a Reply to Grove and Barden (1999) Re: The Admissibility of Testimony Under Daubert/Kumho Analyses" and "A Final Reply to Grove and Barden: The Relevance of the Rorschach Comprehensive System for Expert Testimony," by Ritzler, Erard, and Pettigrew.

Second, it's very unlikely that Rorschach systems other than the Comprehensive System meet the Daubert criteria, or even the older Frye rule (*Frye* v. *United States,* 293 F.1013, 9th Cir. 1923), which requires that the technique has achieved general acceptance in the relevant scientific community. For example, although McCann adopted an optimistic view regarding the admissibility of the Comprehensive System, he was far less sanguine regarding other Rorschach systems, which tend to be outmoded and are used by only a small minority of present-day psychologists.[41]

Third, the Daubert criteria notwithstanding, many judges will probably continue to admit the Rorschach into court.[42] However, a hearing to determine a projective technique's admissibility under Daubert can still serve a useful purpose by alerting a judge to the problems described in this chapter. Furthermore, even if the Rorschach is admitted into court, it may prove a liability to the side that uses it. As we've indicated, the Rorschach is vulnerable to challenge on numerous grounds, and the expert who uses it may be highly vulnerable if cross-examined by a well-informed attorney.

Dealing with Psychologists Who Intend to Use the Rorschach

Attorneys who read this chapter may well conclude that it's not in their client's best interest to take the Rorschach. How might they proceed, then, in cases where a court-appointed psychologist plans to use the test?

We suggest beginning with a good-natured and collegial approach: Contact the psychologist, explain why the test is inappropriate, and offer to supply additional information. Such an approach is likely to be effective because many psychologists who use the Rorschach are reasonable individuals who simply haven't kept up with the scientific literature and therefore don't realize how scientifically controversial the test has become in recent years.

Furthermore, as we discuss later in the chapter, the Ethical Principles of Psychologists of the American Psychological Association require that psychologists maintain up-to-date knowledge regarding their techniques, and that they refrain from using tests for inappropriate purposes. In their desire to act ethically—and to avoid possible ethical complaints—many or most psychologists may be amenable to gentle persuasion by attorneys.

In the quotation that appears at the beginning of this chapter, Robyn Dawes at Carnegie-Mellon University advises that it's better to walk out of a psychologist's office than to take the Rorschach or other projective techniques. We're genuinely uncertain whether this advice is sound. Because the Rorschach tends to overpathologize normal individuals, the consequences of taking the test can be very negative. Nevertheless, the consequences of storming out of an evaluator's office can also be negative. Some evaluators could interpret such an action as evidence of impulsiveness, uncooperativeness, or personal defiance.

Probably the most prudent course is for an attorney to contact the evaluator beforehand and determine which tests will be administered. If the Rorschach is part of the test battery, the attorney can protest tactfully and attempt to educate the psychologist, as we've suggested. Such attempts at persuasion may prove successful. In any case, unwanted negative consequences for the client are likely to be minimized.

PSYCHOLOGISTS' ETHICS AND USE OF THE RORSCHACH

The Ethical Principles of Psychologists of the American Psychological Association are available online at http://www.apa.org/ethics. Several sections of the Ethical Principles are relevant to cases involving the Rorschach:

STANDARD 1.05 MAINTAINING EXPERTISE.

Psychologists who engage in assessment, therapy, teaching, research, organizational consulting, or other professional activities maintain a reasonable level of awareness of current scientific and professional information in their fields of activity, and undertake ongoing efforts to maintain competence in the skills they use.

STANDARD 1.06 BASIS FOR SCIENTIFIC AND PROFESSIONAL JUDGMENTS.

Psychologists rely on scientifically and professionally derived knowledge when making scientific or professional judgments or when engaging in scholarly or professional endeavors.

STANDARD 1.14 AVOIDING HARM.

Psychologists take reasonable steps to avoid harming their patients or clients, research participants, students, and others with whom they work, and to minimize harm where it is foreseeable and unavoidable.

STANDARD 2.02A COMPETENCE AND APPROPRIATE USE OF ASSESSMENTS AND INTERVENTIONS.

Psychologists who develop, administer, score, interpret, or use psychological assessment techniques, interviews, tests, or instruments do so in a manner and for purposes that are appropriate in light of the research on or evidence of the usefulness and proper application of the techniques.

These standards seem to require that psychologists who use the Rorschach maintain a "reasonable level of awareness" of recent scientific developments regarding the test, take this scientific evidence into account when using the test, adhere to standardized testing procedures, and take steps to avoid harming patients or clients.

What are psychologists' ethical obligations in light of the current controversy over the Comprehensive System? For example, in light of the overwhelming negative evidence from replication studies, is it ethical for psychologists to continue using the Depression Index in evaluating depression, or Gacono and Meloy's psychopathy "indicators" in evaluating prisoners? In light of findings on the Exner norms and their tendency to overpathologize, is it ethical to continue using the norms with clients, thereby potentially causing harm? Is it ethical to deviate in significant ways from the administration procedures for the system and then use the results for clinical or forensic decision making? We believe that the answer to all these questions is no, although we've been publicly criticized for suggesting that important ethical issues are at stake.[43]

The Ethical Principles contain a section titled "Forensic Activities." One of the standards in that section seems to hold special relevance for psychologists who use the Rorschach in legal cases:

STANDARD 7.04B TRUTHFULNESS AND CANDOR.

Whenever necessary to avoid misleading, psychologists acknowledge the limits of their data or conclusions.

In our opinion, this standard places an obligation upon psychologists in legal proceedings to *proactively* acknowledge the current scientific controversy over the Rorschach. It seems to us that forensic psychologists who use the Comprehensive System have an ethical duty to forthrightly inform judges and lawyers that the test is controversial and to explain what the most important issues are. We believe that psychologists are acting inappropriately when they withhold such information, or only grudgingly acknowledge it under cross-examination, as we've seen in some cases.

How are these ethical issues relevant to attorneys in cases that involve the Rorschach? As suggested earlier, attorneys are best advised to approach these issues with psychologists in a nonthreatening, educational way. In many cases, psychologists may be amenable to persuasion once they are properly informed regarding the problems of the Rorschach and the relevant ethical issues.

In some instances, knowledge of the ethics code may be useful to attorneys when cross-examining hostile expert witnesses. For example, we recently read a trial transcript in which a psychologist adamantly insisted on certain opinions based on the Rorschach. The opposing attorney then read Standard 7.04b to the psychologist, which concerns the responsibility of forensic psychologists to acknowledge the limits of their findings and conclusions. The tone of the psychologist's testimony changed abruptly. He twice stated for the record that the Rorschach was "not my first choice."

In extreme cases, attorneys may consider the advisability of filing formal complaints with the Ethics Office of the American Psychological Association or with state licensing boards. In our opinion, such a step should be taken only as a last resort, and with the understanding that such complaints are unlikely to be successful. To the best of our knowledge, ethics committees and licensing boards seldom if ever sanction psychologists for using the Rorschach.

However, such committees and boards may be more responsive under some circumstances. For example, in a recent case brought to our attention, a psychologist testified that he'd read about the problems of the Comprehensive System in a newspaper article but hadn't followed up by reading the relevant scientific articles. Furthermore, he admitted that the Rorschach had been administered—contrary to established practice—by a psychologist sitting across a table from the examinee. A licensing board might regard such lax behavior as irresponsible and issue a disciplinary letter.

In closing this chapter, we express our hope that attorneys and forensic psychologists will find its content helpful. In the Epilogue that follows, we take farewell of our readers.

Will the Rorschach Go On Forever?

I am not aware of any experienced or knowledgeable personality assessor who has been dissuaded by these critics from continuing to do assessments, nor do I know of any anti-assessment psychologist who has been persuaded either by compelling logic or substantial empirical data to think otherwise.

—*Irving Weiner, "Advocating for Assessment: Coordinators Report," 2002*

The story of the Rorschach has taken us into a mysterious realm of wizards and semi-deified heroes. We've seen how Hermann Rorschach's intriguing inkblots traveled to America, attracted cultish devotion, and became the emblem of a new and quickly expanding profession—clinical psychology. We've described the fierce loyalty of Rorschach adherents, and the equally fierce scientific controversy that has swirled around the test for nearly half a century.

The Rorschach saga is fascinating and at times humorous, but also troubling. As clinical psychologists, the authors of this book can hardly take pride in our profession's persistent gullibility regarding the test. Furthermore, we're distressed at the thought that many normal individuals have probably been misidentified as abnormal on the basis of the Rorschach, with incalculable harm.

Will psychologists ever relinquish their faith in the test? Or will the Rorschach mystique instead go on forever? Alas, no quick fix seems imminent, particularly considering the American Psychological Association's ongoing support for the test. As the quote at the beginning of this Epilogue indicates, Rorschach proponent Irving Weiner shares our sense that psychologists have reached a deadlock over the test. However, in closing we'll mention two factors that may lead to positive change.

First, although psychologists who presently use the Rorschach are unlikely to abandon it, the next generation of clinical psychologists may adopt a more skeptical attitude. If today's graduate students are taught to think critically and scientifically about the Rorschach instead of merely being indoctrinated in its use, the test's popularity may gradually decline. A great deal depends on the willingness of university instructors to alter their approach to the test.

There's at least some reason to be hopeful in this regard. In the late 1960s and early 1970s, clinical psychologists in universities, more than their colleagues in practice, grew disenchanted with projective techniques because of their increasingly obvious scientific flaws.[1] It's possible that the present-day controversy over the Comprehensive System will have a similar effect on university instructors.

The second cause for hope is the attitude of the American public toward the Rorschach. Until recently, the lengthy controversy over the test has been confined within the walls of academia. However, word is beginning to leak out—in newspapers, magazines, and even radio broadcasts.

In the past, it has been easy for Rorschach enthusiasts to brush aside the warnings of their scientific colleagues. However, this situation may change as the public learns more about the test's problems. As "consumer awareness" grows, psychologists may find that their reliance on the Rorschach creates unwelcome credibility problems.

For example, the authors of this book have recently encountered several legal cases in which psychologists testifying as expert witnesses suffered serious embarrassment because they relied on the Rorschach. We were impressed that nonpsychologists—in this case lawyers and judges—quickly saw through the specious arguments that are typically used to shore up the test's credibility.

Increased public awareness may be the key to ending psychologists' long infatuation with the Rorschach. One can imagine a day when the embarrassment of using the test becomes too great, and clinicians reluctantly consign their inkblots to the dustbin of psychometric history. But no one familiar with the test's remarkable story would confidently predict such an outcome. Indeed, for over half a century the Rorschach has remained psychology's "Teflon Test," impervious to even the most damaging criticisms. Only time will tell whether the demise of the Rorschach becomes a reality or whether, to paraphrase Mark Twain, the rumors of its death are greatly exaggerated.

Graphs on Psychometrics and the Rorschach

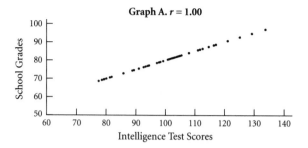

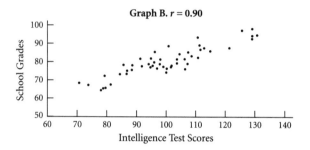

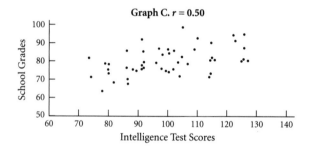

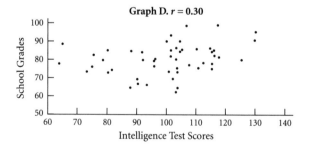

Figure A.1.
An Example of What Correlations Between 1.00 and 0.30 Look Like.

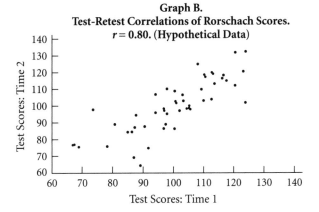

Graph A.
Test-Retest Correlations of Intelligence Test Scores.
$r = 0.90.$ **(Hypothetical Data)**

Test Scores: Time 2

Test Scores: Time 1

Graph B.
Test-Retest Correlations of Rorschach Scores.
$r = 0.80.$ **(Hypothetical Data)**

Test Scores: Time 2

Test Scores: Time 1

Figure A.2.
An Example of Test-Retest Correlations for Intelligence Test
and Rorschach Scores.

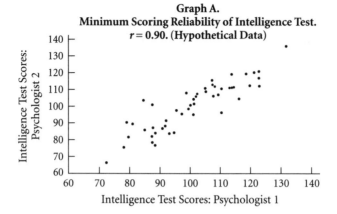

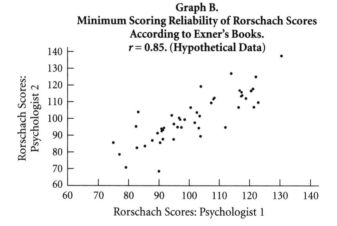

Figure A.3.
Example of Minimum Reliability Between Two Scorers.

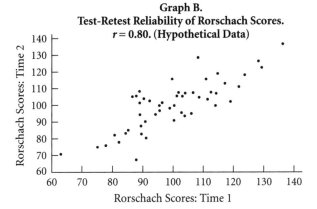

Figure A.4.
Illustrating the Test-Retest Reliability of
Intelligence Tests and the Rorschach.

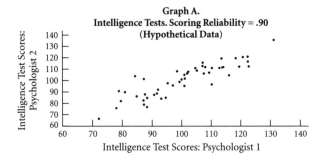

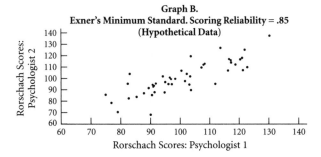

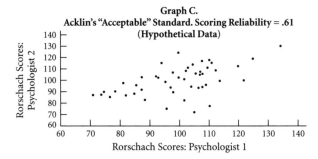

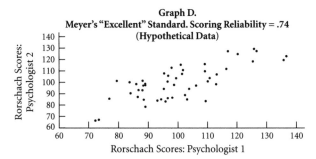

Figure A.5.
Examples of Different Levels of Scoring Reliability.

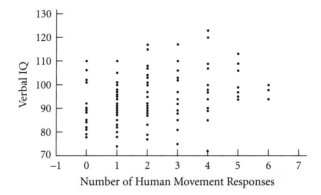

Figure A.6.

Correlation of .30 Between Human Movement Responses and Verbal IQ in a Hypothetical Data Set.

—⁓— Notes

Chapter One

1. Z. Piotrowski (1980), "CPR: The psychological x-ray in mental disorders"; see also B. Klopfer (1940, p. 26) "Personality aspects revealed by the Rorschach method."
2. Board of Professional Affairs, American Psychological Association (1998, p. 392).
3. Sutherland, 1992.
4. For example, see surveys by Camara, Nathan, and Puente (2000), Kennedy, Faust, Willis, and Piotrowski (1994), C. Piotrowski and Belter (1999), C. Piotrowski, Belter, and Keller (1998), and C. Watkins, Campbell, Nieberding, and Hallmark (1995). But see Archer and Newsom (2000), who found that among psychologists who work with adolescents, the Rorschach is more popular than the MMPI-A (the adolescent version of the MMPI).
5. "Cognitive impairment" and "distorted view of reality" are based on X-% of .23. For interpretation of this finding, see Exner's *Primer for Rorschach Interpretation* (2000, p. 176), and Weiner's *Principles of Rorschach Interpretation* (1998, pp. 113-114).
6. "Thoughtful" is based on pervasive introversive style and a high Zd score. For interpretations of these findings, see Exner's primer (2000, pp. 86 and 143).
7. The interpretation can be found in Exner's primer (2000, p. 263).
8. Specifically, $SumC$ is higher than $WSumC$. The interpretation of this finding can be found in Exner's primer (2000, p. 94).
9. The interpretation of an elevated $DEPI$ score can be found in Weiner (1998, p. 332) and Exner (2000, p. 80).
10. "Overly preoccupied with himself" is based on a large number of Pair responses (no Reflections), which elevated the Egocentricity Index. For the interpretation of this Index see Exner's primer (2000, p. 257) and Weiner's *Principles of Rorschach Interpretation* (1998, pp. 154-155). See also Exner (1974, p. 101).
11. "Angry" is based on a high number of Space responses. For the interpretation of this finding, see Exner's primer (2000 pp. 105-107).
12. For an interpretation of a high number of fictitious or part-human responses, see Exner's primer (2000, p. 267-268).
13. For the interpretation of Food responses, see Exner (1991, p. 184; 2000, pp. 313-314).
14. "Highly concerned about other people" is based on the high scores for Pure Human responses and Sum Human responses. For an interpretation of these findings, see Exner's primer (2000, p. 320). "Relates effectively" is based on $GHR > PHR$. For an interpretation of this finding, see Exner's primer (2000, pp. 322-324). "Regarded as likable

and outgoing" is based on $COP = 5$ and $AG = 0$. For an interpretation of this finding see Exner's primer (2000, pp. 329-330).

15. See reviews by Garb, Wood, Nezworski, Grove, and Stejskal (2001); Jorgensen, Andersen, and Dam (2000).

16. Although a full literature review regarding Morbid responses and depression cannot be given here, some important findings can be noted. In one study with positive results (Caine, Frueh, & Kinder, 1995), Morbid responses were significantly related to diagnoses of depression among adult females. However, in two studies with negative results (Archer & Gordon, 1988; and Archer & Krishnamurthy, 1997), Morbid responses were not significantly related to diagnoses of depression among adolescents. In one study the results were ambiguous (Lipovsky, Finch, & Belter, 1989): There was a striking trend toward a higher number of Morbid responses among depressed adolescents, but the effect was not statistically significant.

17. This study was conducted by Beatrice Mittman, working with John Exner, and is described by Exner (1991, pp. 432-433). For a critical discussion of these findings, see the recent article by Wood, Nezworski, Garb, and Lilienfeld (2001b).

18. Exner (2000, pp. 313-314).

19. For a single Food response indicating a high level of dependency, see Exner (1991, p. 184); for the comment about such findings being limited, see Exner (1997, pp. 44-45).

20. Rose, Kaser-Boyd, and Maloney (2000, p. 167).

21. Jorgensen, Andersen, and Dam (2000); Wood, Lilienfeld, Garb, and Nezworski (2000, pp. 398–399).

22. Shaffer, Erdberg, and Haroian (1999); Wood, Nezworski, Garb, and Lilienfeld (2001a).

23. Archer and Newsom (2000); C. Watkins et al. (1995).

24. Belter and Piotrowski (2001, p. 720).

25. Culross and Nelson (1997, p. 122).

26. C. Piotrowski et al. (1998, p. 444).

27. Hagen and Castagna (2001, p. 271).

28. Pinkerman, Haynes, and Keiser (1993, p. 9).

29. Borum and Grisso (1995).

30. B. Klopfer (1940, p. 26); Z. Piotrowski (1980).

31. Bornstein (2001).

32. Regarding the cultish reputation of Rorschach proponents in the 1940s, see the fascinating historical article by Aronow and Reznikoff (1973). See also Lindner as excerpted in Buros (1949, p. 140), and Bochner and Halpern (1942, p. ix).

33. Personal communication, Dr. William J. Stejskal, December 20, 1994.

34. Exner (1974, p. 3) states that "For at least two decades, the 1940s and 1950s, its name [the Rorschach] was almost synonymous with clinical psychology."

35. Zillmer, Harrower, Ritzler, and Archer (1995, p. xiv) state that their book is intended for psychologists and "for readers with a broad interest in Nazi Germany." The authors provide an extensive description of the test and its interpretation for readers who are unfamiliar with it.

36. Haller and Exner (1985).

37. Miale and Selzer (1975). Only the copies in the hardback version are in color. The copies in the paperback version are black-and-white facsimiles.

38. Poundstone (1983).

Chapter Two

1. Robert Todd Carroll, *The Skeptic's Dictionary,* "Fortune Telling." Available online: http://www.skepdic.com. (Access date: October 21, 2002.)
2. Carroll, *The Skeptic's Dictionary,* "Pareidolia."
3. Carroll, *The Skeptic's Dictionary,* "Our Lady of Watsonville."
4. Regarding the diabolic faces in the smoke from the World Trade Center, see http://www.tafkac.org/ulz/devil.html and http://www.snopes.com/rumors/wtcface.html. (Access date: October 21, 2002.) See also Janelle Brown (September 17, 2001); "Nostradamus called it! Internet conspiracy theorists are having a field day after the attacks" at http://www.archive.salon.com/tech/feature/2001/09/17/kooks.(Access date: October 21, 2002.)
5. Z. Piotrowski (1957, pp. 28-31); Zubin, Eron, and Schumer (1965, pp. 166-167).
6. Kerner's book is discussed by Ellenberger (1954, p. 196); Z. Piotrowski (1957, p. 31); and Zubin et al. (1965, p. 168).
7. For a discussion of psychological research before Rorschach that used inkblots, see Zubin et al. (1965, pp. 168-171).
8. Acklin and Oliveira-Berry (1996); Ellenberger (1954).
9. See Ellenberger (1954, p. 185).
10. Krugman (1940, p. 92).
11. Ellenberger (1954, p. 205); Gurvitz (1951).
12. According to Bruno Klopfer and Douglas Kelley (1946, p. 3) and Miale and Selzer (1975, p. 17); Rorschach experimented with "thousands" of inkblots, but Exner (1993, p. 5) says the number was forty.
13. The artistic process by which Rorschach created the inkblots has only recently been discussed in the United States, and the facts are still emerging. For clear statements that Rorschach altered the blots, see the essay by his colleague Walter Morganthaler (1954). On the cover of *A Primer for Rorschach Interpretation,* John Exner (2000) recently published what seems to be an early version of Card IX created by Hermann Rorschach. Simple examination of Cards VIII, IX, and X suggests that the medium used for many of the color and shading effects was probably watercolor. John Exner (2002b, p. 4) stated that Rorschach's blots were "hand-drawn figures."
14. For the details of Rorschach's struggle to print his book, see Morganthaler (1954).
15. The German title is *Psychodiagnostik.* An English translation was published in 1942 and reprinted in 1964.
16. Roemer (1967, p. 190).
17. Rorschach's friend Emil Oberholzer published it. Titled "The application of the form interpretation test," it appears as an addition at the back of most English editions of *Psychodiagnostics.*
18. Bleuler's quote was given by Walter Morganthaler on p. 1 of the English translation of *Psychodiagnostics.*
19. A thorough discussion of the effect of Mourly Vold's theories on Hermann Rorschach can be found in Ellenberger (1954, pp. 200-202). This article also appears as a chapter in Ellenberger (1993).
20. "Pure Color" is the current terminology for such responses. Rorschach called them "primary color answers."

21. Ellenberger (1954); p. 202.
22. Rorschach (1921/1964, p. 99).
23. For a similar critique of Rorschach's scientific justifications, see Rapaport, Gill, and Shafer (1946b, p. 238).
24. In *Psychodiagnostics*, pp. 81-83, Rorschach insisted, quite rightly, that his own concepts were not the same as Jung's. However, Jung later modified his own thinking, perhaps partly due to Rorschach's influence, so that the two men's ideas regarding introversion and extraversion became more similar. K. Bash (1955) provided a thoughtful discussion of these issues and argued compellingly that Rorschach's and Jung's ideas were actually much closer than might be thought from reading Rorschach's disclaimer in *Psychodiagnostics*. For further discussion of the connection between Rorschach and Jung, see Acklin and Oliveira-Berry (1996).
25. Rorschach's system for counting the number of Color responses weighted some types of Color responses more heavily than others. Specifically, "Pure Color" responses, which are discussed later in this chapter, were given a weight of 1.5, "Form-Color" responses a weight of 1.0, and "Color-Form" responses a weight of .5.
26. S. Carlson (1985).
27. Goldberg (1993); but see J. Block (1995).
28. Goldberg (1993).
29. In the 1940s and 1950s, Rorschachers often assumed that sociability and shyness were related to *EB* (for example, Bochner & Halpern, 1942, p. 40, and 1945, pp. 39-40; Phillips & Smith, 1953, p. 80).
30. For the Stanford study, see Holtzman (1950); "Validation studies of the Rorschach test: Shyness and gregariousness in the normal superior adult." For other early studies on the relationship of *EB* to social introversion/extraversion, see Thornton and Guilford (1936); Palmer (1956); and Wysocki (1956). For one study that did find a relationship between *EB* and social introversion/extraversion, see Allen, Richer, and Plotnik (1964); and for a study with mixed findings see Kunce and Tamkin (1981).
31. On the relationship of *M* responses to IQ, see Altus and Thompson (1949); Levine, Spivack, and Wight (1959), Lotsof (1953); Lotsof, Comrey, Bogartz, and Arnsfield (1958); and L. Williams and Lawrence (1953). Also, see the review by G. Frank (1979).
32. Reviews of research on *M* can be found in Dana (1968); Dana and Cocking (1968); J. Singer (1960); and J. Singer and Brown (1977).
33. For the relationship of *M* with activity level and slow writing with a pencil, see J. Singer and Herman (1954); J. Singer and Spohn (1954); and J. Singer, Wilensky, and McCraven (1956). For a failure to replicate this effect among college students, see Dana and Cocking (1968).
34. For a failure to replicate the pencil-writing findings among forty-five college students, see Dana and Cocking (1968). Although these authors reported that the observed correlation of .12 between writing speed and *M*% was statistically significant, in fact it was not. The authors mistakenly entered the same subjects into their analyses more than once.
35. See the review by Dana (1968) regarding *M* and fantasy. For more recent findings see Bonifacio and Schaefer (1969) and Boswell (1989).
36. See the review by Dana (1968) regarding *M* and time estimation.
37. G. Frank (1993b, pp. 1223-1224).
38. See reviews by Cerbus and Nichols (1963) and G. Frank (1976, 1993c). See also Fisher (1967).

39. See reviews by Bergman and Schubert (1974); Shapiro (1960).

40. See review by Cerbus and Nichols (1963).

41. Mann (1956).

42. See review by Cerbus and Nichols (1963). Interestingly, however, the number of Color responses (*WSumC*) is no longer included in the most widely used Rorschach index of depression, Exner's Depression Index.

43. The normative and reference data in Exner (1993) indicate that Color scores (*WSumC*) of depressed inpatients (M = 3.45) were lower than the scores of nonpatients (M = 4.52) and outpatients (M = 3.90) but higher than the scores of schizophrenic inpatients (M = 2.63) and patients with character disorders (M = 2.06). Also Exner (1986, p. 424) apparently found that *WSumC* did not discriminate depressed patients from other patients.

44. As Stevens, Edwards, Hunter, and Bridgman (1993, p. 348) have noted: "The [color-affect] hypothesis holds that a person's report of color on the Rorschach provides information regarding personal emotional life. Each Rorschach system, including Exner's Comprehensive System, has included some link between color and affect in the interpretive protocol. Curiously, however, a number of reviews have not yielded substantive empirical support for the color-affect hypothesis in the research literature. . . . " Stevens et al. call attention to negative reviews on the color-affect hypothesis by Benton (1950), Cerbus and Nichols (1963), G. Frank (1976, 1993c), Keehn (1953a, 1953b), and Norman and Scott (1952).

45. Dodge and Frame (1982); see also Dodge, Murphy, and Buchsbaum (1984); and Waldman (1996).

46. For a review, see McNally (1996).

47. A brief but helpful discussion regarding the influence of motivation, emotion, and personality on perception is provided by Hilgard (1987, pp. 161-163).

48. For Rorschach as genius, see Acklin and Oliveira-Berry (1996, p. 433); Ellenberger (1954, p. 173); and Z. Piotrowski (1957, p. 3).

49. Levine et al. (1959, p. 307).

50. Dawes (1994, p. 149).

51. For interpretations of *W, D,* and *Dd,* see Rorschach (1921/1964, Table V, p. 44).

52. Blatt and Allison (1963).

53. For interpretations of *S* responses, see Rorschach (1921/1964, p. 39).

54. Rorschach (1921/1964, pp. 199-200).

55. Fonda (1960, 1977).

56. G. Frank (1993d, p. 1113).

57. See letter by Sigmund Freud to Saul Rosenzweig, February 28, 1934: "My dear Sir, I have examined your experimental studies for the verification of the psychoanalytic assertions with interest. I cannot put much value on these confirmations because the wealth of reliable observations on which these assertions rest make them independent of experimental verification. Still, it can do no harm. Sincerely yours, Freud." As quoted in Shakow and Rapaport (1964, p. 129).

58. "As science has progressed, it has become increasingly concerned with quantification as a means of describing events" (Cowles, 2001, p. 2).

59. See Rorschach (1921/1964, Table VIII, pp. 50-51).

60. Gottesman (1991).

61. See the mean and median of *M* in a sample of 315 inpatient depressives reported by Exner (1993, p. 309).

62. *Psychodiagnostics* does not state how many of the manic-depressive patients were depressed or how many were manic.

63. A fifty-year-old textbook by psychologist Florence Goodenough (1949, pp. 34-36) discussed the problems of informal methods for estimating intelligence. Interestingly, her insightful remarks were based largely on work by Alfred Binet conducted thirty years previously.

64. See summaries of the research literature by Garb (1998) and Wood, Garb, Lilienfeld, and Nezworski (2002).

65. Faust (1984, pp. 64-69); Garb (1998); Nisbett and Ross (1980, pp. 169-172, 175-183).

66. Nisbett and Wilson (1977a, 1977b); T. Wilson and Nisbett (1978). See also the discussion by Nisbett and Ross (1980, pp. 195-227).

67. Sagan (1995).

Chapter Three

1. Several of Rorschach's Swiss colleagues continued to work on the test after his death, including Oberholzer, Walter Morganthaler, Hans Behn-Eschenburg, and Georg Roemer. Although all four of these men made important contributions to the development of the Rorschach Test, we confess (with apologies to our European colleagues) that we won't be discussing the European development of the test in any depth. Our focus is on the way the Rorschach developed in the United States.

2. Although prominent in the 1930s and 1940s, Levy is now seldom mentioned except for his relationship with Samuel Beck. Most books identify Levy as a psychiatrist, but Marguerite Hertz, who knew him personally, states that he was both a psychiatrist and a psychologist.

3. Hertz (1986, p. 398).

4. Hertz (1986, p. 398).

5. For example, see Beck (1955) for discussion of Freud, and Beck (1959, p. 274) for Rorschach; also see the review by Beck's associate Molish (1958, p. 189).

6. For a list of publications, see "Samuel Jacob Beck—Citation" (1965).

7. Exner (1981, p. 987).

8. Exner (1993, p. 10).

9. Biographical information about Bruno Klopfer in this section is taken from the following sources: Exner (1969b, pp. 7-89; 1993, pp. 8-14); Hertz (1970a); Reisman (1976, pp. 274-274); Skadeland (1986); Vorhaus (1960).

10. Exner (1993, p. 9).

11. Skadeland (1986, p. 359).

12. Rorschach (1921/1964, pp. 187-188).

13. Exner (1969b, p. 208). For early discussion of incomplete or cut-off wholes, see B. Klopfer (1937b, p. 143); see also B. Klopfer and Kelley (1946, pp. 83-84, 105).

14. Thornton and Guilford (1936); Z. Piotrowski (1937a); see also Hertz (1937, pp. 59-61).

15. This lecture appears at the back of all English editions of *Psychodiagnostics* under the title "The Application of the Form Interpretation Test." It also appears at the back of the second and all later German editions of the book (see remarks made in Walter Morganthaler's "Preface to the Second Edition" of *Psychodiagnostics* [Rorschach, 1921/1964, pp. 11-12]).

16. The responses called "Chiaroscuro" by Rorschach would be called "Shading" by later authors, who subdivided them into subcategories that included Vista, Diffuse Shading, and perhaps Texture and Achromatic Color. For an early discussion of the confusion that surrounded Chiaroscuro responses and their subcategories, see Hertz (1940).

17. "The Society for Personality Assessment" (1980, p. 661). Other writers have given the date for the founding of the Rorschach Institute as 1938 (Blatt, 1986, p. 343) or 1939 (Megargee & Spielberger, 1992a, p. 3).

18. Skadeland (1986, p. 359).

19. Handler (1994, p. 566).

20. Excellent book-length histories of clinical psychology have been written by Reisman (1976) and Routh (1994). A brief treatment is provided in a chapter by Hilgard (1987, pp. 615-661).

21. Routh (1994, p. 6).

22. Routh (1994, p. 25).

23. Hilgard (1987, pp. 493-494).

24. For negative comments on the self-report tests of that era, see L. Frank (1939b, 1948) and Hertz (1986, p. 397).

25. Henry Murray, as paraphrased by L. Frank (1939b, p. 395).

26. Hertz (1986).

27. Greene (2000, pp. 4-5).

28. Beck (1972, pp. 105-106).

29. L. Frank (1939a, p. 104).

30. B. Klopfer and Kelley (1946).

31. Zenderland (1998, p. 59).

32. Goodenough (1949, pp. 34-37).

33. Anastasi (1988, pp. 8-10).

34. Anastasi (1988, pp. 10-11).

35. Anastasi (1988, p. 11).

36. Goddard (1908, 1910); see also Hilgard (1987, pp. 463-466).

37. Although now well known to many psychologists, the Vineland Training School was "obscure" before Henry Goddard established its reputation (Zenderland, 1998, p. 2). Our discussion of Henry Goddard relies very heavily on Zenderland's book.

38. See, for example, Routh (1994, p. 8).

39. Zenderland (1998, pp. 202-203 and 232).

40. Goddard (1912). The full text of *The Kallikak Family* is available online at http://psych-classics.asu.edu/Goddard/. (Access date: October 21, 2002.)

41. Zenderland (1998, pp. 158-163, 321-323).

42. Goodenough (1949, p. 54); Zenderland (1998, p. 161).

43. As quoted by Zenderland (1998, p. 324).

44. As quoted by Zenderland (1998, p. 296).

45. For a fuller discussion of the debate on intelligence testing in the 1920s, see Zenderland, 1998, pp. 311-326.

46. Zenderland (1998, p. 321).

47. As quoted by Zenderland (1998, p. 276).

48. Zenderland (1998, p. 246).

49. Goodenough (1949, p. 57).

50. Goodenough (1949, p. 57).

51. An excellent summary of Lippmann's criticisms is provided by Zenderland (1998, pp. 312-315). Lippmann's articles, with replies by Lewis Terman, have been reprinted in *The I.Q. Controversy: Critical Readings* by N. Block and Dworkin (1976, pp. 2-44).

52. Walter Lippmann, "The mental age of Americans," in N. Block and Dworkin (1976, p. 4).

53. Lippmann, "The mental age of Americans," p. 4.

54. Lippmann, "The mental age of Americans," p. 8.

55. Walter Lippmann, "The abuse of the tests," in N. Block and Dworkin (1976, p. 20).

56. Re the Communist allegation, Terman wrote, "Now it is evident that Mr. Lippmann has been seeing red; also, that seeing red is not very conducive to seeing clearly" ("The great conspiracy: The impulse imperious of intelligence testers, psychoanalyzed and exposed by Mr. Lippmann," in N. Block and Dworkin, 1976, p. 32). The reference to Bryan is on p. 30 of the same source. For the comment of Leila Zenderland on this slur, see Zenderland (1998, p. 314).

57. Readers who would like to know more about these psychometric topics are urged to consult standard textbooks on psychological testing, such as those by Anastasi (1988) and Cronbach (1984).

58. Note that the present discussion applies exclusively to "norm-referenced tests," a category that includes all commonly used intelligence and personality tests. Some educational and occupational tests do not use norms, instead, they are "criterion-referenced," that is, they apply a predetermined scoring system. Because criterion-referenced tests are not pertinent to the subject of this book, they will not be discussed further here.

59. Cowles (2001, pp. 127-153).

60. Goodenough (1949, p. 57).

61. For example, see Exner (1993, p. 45) and Heilbrun (1992, p. 265).

62. Kaufman and Lichtenberger (1999, p. 12; 2000, p. 13).

63. See summary of Exner's test-retest coefficients in Viglione and Hilsenroth (2001, p. 455, Table 2). For further discussion of the test-retest reliability of scores in the Comprehensive System for the Rorschach, see Garb, Wood, Nezworski, Grove, and Stejskal (2001).

64. Anastasi (1988, p. 118).

65. Haller and Exner (1985).

66. For example, see Hertz (1937, pp. 63-64).

67. Anastasi (1988, p. 145).

68. The .50 figure comes from a task force established by the American Psychological Association (Neisser et al., 1996, p. 81). See also Jensen (1998, pp. 277-280), Cronbach (1984, pp. 243-244) and Anastasi (1988, pp. 254).

69. Kaufman and Lichtenberger (2000, p. 211).

70. Anastasi (1988, p. 239); Hilgard (1987, pp. 464-466).

71. Thurstone (1948, p. 471) wrote: "When the Binet tests were most in vogue, they were regarded as some sort of base criterion for judging all the other tests."

72. Aronow and Reznikoff (1973, p. 310).

73. For (more polite) comments regarding Bruno Klopfer's scientific background during the 1930s, see Handler (1994, pp. 566-567); Patterson and Davis (1985, p. 339).

74. Vorhaus (1960, p. 234).

75. He refers to his Freudian training in B. Klopfer (1961, p. 250).

76. Exner, (1969b, pp. 8-9); Handler (1994, p. 566); Skadeland (1986, p. 361); Hertz (1970a, p. xi). Phenomenological psychology emphasizes the role of the individual in creating

meaning and "co-constituting" the world of experience. It also stresses empathy as a means of understanding the experience of other individuals, and teaches that "parts" should be understood in the context of the "whole." The phenomenological psychology of the 1920s (in which Klopfer received his training) changed somewhat in response to existentialist thinking in the United States in the 1940s and thereafter (Churchill, 2000; Churchill & Richer, 2000).

77. Handler (1994, p. 566) summarizing a personal communication from John Exner (July 12, 1993).
78. Handler (1994, p. 566).
79. Hertz (1970a, p. xii).
80. No norms are provided in B. Klopfer and Kelley (1942, 1946) or in B. Klopfer and Davidson (1962). See also the remark by Morris Krugman in 1942 that "Klopfer seems to have little faith in tables of norms" (as excerpted in Buros, 1949, p. 178).
81. B. Klopfer and Kelley (1946, p. 21).
82. B. Klopfer (1939).
83. B. Klopfer (1939, pp. 52-54).
84. See the tables and decision rules in Exner (1990, 1991, 1993).
85. Exner (1981, p. 987).
86. B. Klopfer (1939, p. 53).
87. Exner (1993, p. 11).
88. Beck (1937a); for more details, see Exner (1993, p. 11).
89. B. Klopfer (1937b).
90. B. Klopfer (1937c); B. Klopfer and Davidson (1937).
91. Beck (1937b).
92. Following the order that they were printed in the journal, these comments were by Binder (1937a), Bleuler (1937), Benjamin (1937), Booth (1937), Hertz (1937), B. Klopfer (1937a), Z. Piotrowski (1937), Schachtel and Hartoch (1937), Guirdham (1937), and Loosli-Usteri (1937).
93. Guirdham (1937, p. 72).
94. Loosli-Usteri (1937, p. 74).
95. Benjamin (1937, p. 47).
96. Exner (1981, p. 987).
97. K. Bash (1982, p. 4).
98. See Note 16 for this chapter.
99. Rorschach (1921/1964, p. 195).
100. Rorschach (1921/1964, pp. 187-189).
101. Rorschach (1921/1964, p. 195; see also pp. 200-201).
102. Rorschach (1921/1964, p. 201).
103. See for example Hertz (1940, p. 123) and Beck (1944, p. 126).
104. Binder (1932); see also Binder (1937a, 1937b) and K. Bash (1982).
105. Exner (1969b, pp. 96-97).
106. Z. Piotrowski (1937a). Piotrowski's proposal for scoring animal movement (*FM*) was based on an idea proposed earlier by B. Klopfer and Sender (1936). However, Piotrowski's definition of *FM* was somewhat narrower than the definition proposed by Klopfer and Sender.
107. B. Klopfer (1939) as quoted by Exner (1969b, p. 76).

108. Beck (1937b, pp. 18-19).

109. Beck (1944, p. 155). General discussion of early Rorschachers' views of intellectual capacity is from B. Klopfer (1939); as summarized by Exner (1969b, p. 78).

110. Rorschach (1921/1964, p. 23).

111. Beck (1937b, pp. 15-16).

112. B. Klopfer (1937b, p. 144).

113. Exner (1969b, p. 36).

114. B. Klopfer and Davidson (1944).

115. Hertz (1937, p. 59).

116. Hertz (1937, p. 59).

117. Beck (1937b, p. 21).

118. Hertz (1937, p. 63). The quoted wording follows the original, including the use of "principals" and "extent of which."

119. Exner (1969b, p. 30).

120. B. Klopfer (1939, p. 47).

121. Krugman (1940, p. 94).

122. Haines (2002); McCoy (2000, pp. 71-94); J. Young (1967, pp. 137-142). For general histories of medical quackery in America, see the well-written books by J. Young (1961, 1967) and Holbrook (1959).

123. A 1945 review by Donald E. Super as excerpted in Buros (1949, p. 167).

124. Hertz (1942, pp. 550-551).

125. For example, see the remark by David Rapaport and his colleagues (1946a, p. v) that "it is better to present what experience teaches than to by-pass it for lack of statistical evidence."

126. L. Frank (1939a, 1939b).

127. Hertz (1942, pp. 529-531); see also B. Klopfer and Kelley (1946, pp. 12-13).

128. Hertz (1942, pp. 529-531).

129. B. Klopfer and Kelley (1946, p. 14).

130. B. Klopfer and Kelley (1946, pp. 16-17).

131. Klopfer's emphasis on configural interpretation seems to have been closely modeled on Zygmunt Piotrowski's "principle of interdependence of Rorschach components," which had been briefly described in an article in the *Rorschach Research Exchange* in 1937 (Z. Piotrowski, 1937a, p. 156).

132. Krugman (1949, p. 132).

133. The psychologist Robert E. Harris pointed out in 1943 that Klopfer's book on the Rorschach was self-contradictory regarding the configural approach: "That every record has unique configurational aspects is continually emphasized, but in spite of these recurring holistic strictures, Klopfer often seems to assume a one-to-one correspondence between a scoring category and a personality variable" (as excerpted in Buros, 1949, p. 176).

134. Wittenborn (1949, p. 133).

135. Beck (1937b, p. 21).

136. B. Klopfer and Kelley (1946, p. 22). Samuel Beck also believed that a minimum of three years' work was necessary to grasp the test "solidly." See his review in Buros (1949, p. 157).

137. B. Klopfer and Kelley (1946, pp. 21-22).

138. B. Klopfer and Kelley (1946, p. 18).

139. For example, see the reviews in Buros (1949) by Ralph R. Brown (p. 157), Lawson G. Lowrey (p. 150), Molly Harrower-Erickson (p. 151), and an anonymous reviewer (p. 158). See also Harriman (1946, p. 39).
140. Regarding "wizards," see Holt (1967b, p. 449).
141. Roustang (1982, pp. 1-16); Grosskurth (1991).
142. As Robert Holt, a psychoanalytic proponent of the Rorschach, wrote, "The culture of clinical psychology is strongly anti-authoritarian, a value incompatible with the traditionalism and respect for authority that are required for the transmission of an art like psychodiagnosis" (Holt, 1967b, p. 452).
143. Eugen Bleuler as quoted by Pichot (1984, p. 593).
144. L. Frank (1939b, p. 392); see also L. Frank (1948).
145. L. Frank (1939b, p. 395).
146. L. Frank (1939b, pp. 402-403).
147. L. Frank (1939b, pp. 402-403); B. Klopfer (1940, p. 26).
148. Reisman (1976, p. 221).
149. L. Frank (1939a).

Chapter Four

1. Regarding the cultish reputation of Rorschach proponents in the 1940s, see the fascinating historical article by Aronow and Reznikoff (1973). See also Goodenough (1949, p. 433).
2. From a 1946 review by Robert Lindner, excerpted in Buros (1949, p. 140). Lindner authored the book that was turned into the movie *Rebel Without a Cause.*
3. Bochner and Halpern (1942, p. ix).
4. Seymour Sarason at Harvard (Sarason, 1954), J. R. Wittenborn at Yale (Wittenborn, 1949; see p. 133 for reference to widespread teaching), and Lee J. Cronbach at the University of Chicago (Cronbach, 1950b).
5. Regarding the Rorschach's dominance in journal articles, see Aronow and Reznikoff (1973, p. 309). Regarding its dominance in dissertations, see Hilgard (1987, p. 516).
6. Wittenborn (1949, p. 133).
7. Bochner and Halpern (1942); for reviews, see Buros (1949, pp. 150-160).
8. A 1946 review by Edna Mann, as excerpted in Buros (1949, p. 150).
9. The title page of Bochner and Halpern (1945) indicates that both authors were M.A. level psychologists at the time of publication. Halpern eventually earned a Ph.D. and became well known for her participation in the U.S. civil rights movement in the 1960s (Routh, 1994, pp. 70-71).
10. Lee J. Cronbach stated "no book has had more influence on American Rorschach technique—and therefore on clinical diagnostic practice—than the Klopfer-Kelley book of 1942" (Buros, 1959, p. 1093).
11. B. Klopfer and Kelley (1946).
12. Exner (1969b, p. 32); Handler (1994, p. 570); Hertz (1970a, p. xi).
13. Lesser (1961, p. 181).
14. The first editions of the influential textbooks on psychological testing by Goodenough (1949) and Cronbach (1949a) did not appear until the end of the 1940s. The first

manual and book on the MMPI were published in 1951 (Hathaway & McKinley, 1951; Hathaway & Meehl, 1951).

15. Aronow and Reznikoff (1973, p. 309).
16. Meehl as excerpted in Buros (1949, p. 187).
17. Rosenzweig as excerpted in Buros (1949, p. 140); see also Lindner as excerpted in Buros (1949, pp. 139-140).
18. Harriman as excerpted in Buros (1949, p. 177).
19. B. Klopfer as excerpted in Buros (1949, p. 189).
20. Buros (1953, p. 237).
21. Buros (1949, p. 169).
22. For Klopfer's critical reaction, see Buros (1949, p. 169).
23. Hilgard (1987, p. 641); Reisman (1976, p. 61).
24. Hornstein (1992). According to Shakow and Rapaport (1964, p. 51), psychoanalytic theories were "foreign" to American psychologists in the behaviorist tradition. American psychologists in the functionalist tradition were more interested in Freud's ideas. However, these ideas do not appear to have been adopted by large numbers of psychologists until the late 1930s and 1940s.
25. Goggin and Goggin (2000).
26. Reisman (1976, pp. 228-230, 264-265).
27. Regarding the connection between a psychoanalytic orientation and Rorschach use, see the survey by Wade, Baker, Morton, and Baker (1978).
28. Beck (1939, p. 806).
29. B. Klopfer and Kelley (1946, p. 221).
30. Schachtel as excerpted in Buros (1949, p. 181).
31. Regarding the psychoanalytic nature of Bochner and Halpern's book, see Buros (1949, pp. 158-159).
32. Hertz (1951, p. 308).
33. Rorschach (1921/1964, pp. 123-124).
34. Wittenborn (1949, p. 133).
35. Hilgard (1987, p. 466).
36. Buros (1949, p. 159).
37. Harrower-Erickson and Steiner (1945); Harrower and Steiner (1951). (Molly Harrower published under the last name of "Harrower" and "Harrower-Erickson.")
38. Harrower-Erickson and Steiner (1945); Harrower and Steiner (1951).
39. A copy of the administration instructions, scoring form, and alternative responses for the Multiple Choice Rorschach Test were published in the journal *Psychosomatic Medicine* (Harrower-Erickson, 1943).
40. Buros (1949, p. 150).
41. J. Miller (1946, p. 181).
42. Carter (1950, p. 112); Hilgard (1987, pp. 633-634); J. Miller (1946, p. 182).
43. Hilgard (1987, p. 634); see also Carter (1950).
44. Baker and Benjamin (2000, p. 244).
45. Shakow (1965, p. 354).
46. Routh (1994, p. 126).
47. Routh (1994, p. 141).
48. Wright and Cummings (2001).
49. Routh (1994, p. 164).

50. McHugh (1994). The distinction between empiricists and romantics is closely correlated with the humorous but helpful distinction drawn by Paul Meehl (1956) between the "simpleminded" and the "muddleheaded." However, we prefer the terms *empiricists* and *romantics* because they reflect the positive aspects of both groups, place the groups in the context of intellectual history, and suggest that membership in one group or the other reflects broader social and cultural influences as well as the idiosyncrasies and foibles of individual people.

51. Our thanks to Richard McNally, who pointed out that the position McHugh calls "empiricist" actually represents a melding of the empiricist and rationalist positions, and is probably best described as *enlightenment*. We have retained McHugh's terminology, even though it's somewhat inaccurate, because it's consistent with the way that *empiricist* is used by most psychologists and will be more familiar to readers. For fascinating intellectual histories relevant to the romantic-empiricist distinction, see Barzun (1961), Berlin (1956, 1999), and Commager (1977).

52. See Shakow and Rapaport (1964) for a description of the tensions between Freudian and American empiricists in the first half of the twentieth century.

53. An amusing and instructional list of the complimentary and uncomplimentary names that empiricists and romantics apply to themselves and each other can be found in Meehl (1954, pp. 4-6).

54. "One finds the vanguard of the ink-blot movement still engaged in the generation-old conflict of intuitive versus empirical, clinical versus experimental, European versus American, and holistic versus atomistic" (J. Harris, 1960, p. 380).

55. Hilgard (1987, p. 473).

56. Hilgard (1987, pp. 473-474); Reisman (1976, pp. 215-216).

57. Hilgard (1987, p. 474).

58. Greene (2000, pp. 2-4).

59. Greene (2000, pp. 4-5).

60. The idea for the empirical approach to item selection came from E. K. Strong, whose highly successful Vocational Interest Blank had been developed using that approach. For an interesting discussion regarding the development of the MMPI, see Meehl (1989, pp. 349ff).

61. Wooten (1984); see also discussions in Greene (2000).

62. Megargee and Spielberger (1992b, p. 172).

63. Hilgard (1987, pp. 517-518).

64. Hilgard (1987, p. 634).

65. Hilgard (1987, p. 517).

66. Regarding the increased status that the Rorschach gave to clinical psychologists, see also the review by McCall in Buros (1959, p. 279), and the recollections of Albee (1970, p. 1075) and Cleveland (1976, p. 309).

67. Schafer (1954, p. 8).

68. Exner (1969b).

69. Thanks to Helge Malmgren, whose Web site provides information on Bohm and other prominent European experts on the Rorschach: http://www.phil.gu.se/fu/ro.html. (Access date: October 22, 2002.)

70. Hertz (1959, p. 35).

71. Hertz (1959, p. 42).

72. Phillips and Smith (1953, p. 146).

73. Phillips and Smith (1953, p. 147).

74. Albee (1970, p. 1075).

75. Beck (1959, p. 275).

76. Hertz (1951, p. 314).

77. B. Klopfer and Kelley (1946, p. 18).

78. Schafer (1954, p. 12).

79. Handler (1994, p. 566).

80. Rorschach's blind interpretation is titled "The Application of the Form Interpretation Test" and appears at the end of *Psychodiagnostics* (Rorschach, 1921/1964).

81. Emil Oberholzer in Rorschach (1921/1964, p. 185).

82. Emil Oberholzer in Rorschach (1921/1964, p. 184).

83. Hooker (1960, p. 240).

84. Beck (1960).

85. For example, Sacks and Lewin (1950, p. 481) reported, "Some Rorschach experts make a practice of giving demonstrations based on blind analysis and many Rorschach classes are taught to work with this approach."

86. Kaplan and Saccuzzo (1982, p. 379).

87. Kaplan and Saccuzzo (1982, p. 379).

88. Lisansky (1956, p. 311); Sacks and Lewin (1950, p. 481).

89. For scholarly surveys of the field of projective techniques as it existed in the 1950s and early 1960s, see Fisher (1967), W. Klopfer (1968), Murstein (1963), Rabin (1968; see also Rabin, 1981), and Rabin and Haworth (1960). For interesting early discussions of these techniques written in the late 1940s and early 1950s, see Anderson and Anderson (1951; also Rabin, 2001), Cronbach (1949a, pp. 433-451), and Goodenough (1949, pp. 415-441).

90. Kerman (1959).

91. Goodenough (1949, p. 427).

92. Buros (1959, p. 969).

93. Rabin (1963).

94. Reisman (1976, pp. 221-222); Goodenough (1949, pp. 437-438).

95. This description of the Tautophone, while not an exact quote, is closely modeled on Reisman (1976, pp. 221-222).

96. For discussions of the Szondi test, see Goodenough (1949, p. 438) and the influential article by Borstelmann and Klopfer (1953). The test was introduced into the United States by David Rapaport and widely disseminated among psychologists by Deri (1949). Some of the photographs of the Szondi test may be viewed on the World Wide Web at http://astro.ocis.temple.edu/~ruby/aaa/milton3.html or http://www.microcosms.ihc.ucsb.edu/gallery/gz-24.html. (Access date: October 22, 2002.)

97. For the U.S. reaction, see Cronbach (1960, p. 575); Borstelmann and Klopfer (1953). See also reviews by Ardie Lubin, Albert Rabin, Paul Meehl, Roy Schafer and Laurance Shaffer in Buros (1953, pp. 255-263). Nonetheless, a search of the World Wide Web using the Google search engine and the search term "Szondi test" reveals dozens of Web sites that still take the test seriously.

98. For recent discussions of the TAT, see Anastasi and Urbina (1997, pp. 419-423), Lilienfeld (1999a), and Lilienfeld, Wood, and Garb (2000).

99. Neuringer (1968, pp. 239-243); K. Newton (1959); Sappenfeld (1965).

100. Anastasi (1988, p. 611).
101. Machover (1949, see pp. 67, 56, and 79).
102. Goodenough (1949); Anastasi (1988, p. 304).
103. The wording of this sentence is not an exact quote, but is closely modeled on the wording of Anastasi (1988, p. 304).
104. Anastasi (1988, pp. 305-306). The Draw-a-Man test was updated in 1963 and renamed the Goodenough-Harris Drawing Test (D. Harris, 1963).
105. Anastasi (1988, pp. 609-610).
106. Viglione (1985); Wagner (1985).
107. Loevinger (1998).
108. Manners and Durkin (2001).
109. Although not a direct quote, this description is closely modeled on the explanation provided by Anne Anastasi (1988, p. 636).
110. Manners and Durkin (2001).
111. Manners and Durkin (2001). See also discussion in Lilienfeld et al. (2000).
112. See Reynolds and Sundberg (1976) regarding the striking contrast between the clinical popularity of the DAP and the research to support it.
113. Archer and Newsom (2000); Kennedy et al. (1994); M. Wilson and Reschly (1996).
114. For example, see Van Hutton (1994).
115. Anastasi (1988, p. 594).

Chapter Five

1. Munroe (1950). See also Goldfried, Stricker, and Weiner (1971, p. 255).
2. Goldfried et al. (1971, p. 255).
3. Munroe (1944, p. 46).
4. Munroe (1942, 1944, 1945, 1946, 1950).
5. Buros (1949, pp. 187-188).
6. See summaries by Goldfried et al. (1971, pp. 266, 274-275, 278-279), but for some positive findings see Goldfried et al. (1971, pp. 282-284).
7. Goldfried et al. (1971, p. 252).
8. Goldfried et al. (1971, pp. 301-303, 313-314, and 350-372).
9. Rorschach (1921/1964, p. 123).
10. See the article by Aronow and Koppel (1997), which argues that Hermann Rorschach was turning toward content interpretation toward the end of his life. We find the statements of Georg Roemer (1967) cited by Aronow and Koppel to be unconvincing. These statements were published forty-five years after Rorschach's death, and Roemer doesn't seem to have been a reliable reporter. On the other hand, we're more impressed by the quote from Rorschach and Oberholzer (1924, p. 369), in which Rorschach says that "such experiences have ... demonstrated that the content of the interpretations given to the experiment can be of some importance." However, this statement hardly constitutes a ringing endorsement by Rorschach of the content approach.
11. Bochner and Halpern (1942, pp. 61-62).
12. Bochner and Halpern (1945, pp. 61-62).
13. Bochner and Halpern (1945, p. 82).

14. F. Brown (1953, p. 265).
15. F. Brown (1953, p. 272).
16. For example, see the discussion by Phillips and Smith (1953, pp. 198-223) of "shock" on the various Rorschach cards, and the discussion by B. Klopfer, Ainsworth, Klopfer, and Holt (1954) regarding the interpretive meaning of each card.
17. F. Brown (1953, p. 257).
18. F. Brown (1953, p. 260).
19. F. Brown (1953, p. 262).
20. F. Brown (1953, pp. 267–277).
21. F. Brown (1953, p. 277).
22. Lindner (1946, 1950).
23. Lindner (1950, p. 83).
24. Lindner (1950, p. 88).
25. Lindner (1950, p. 81).
26. B. Klopfer et al. (1954, p. 376); see also the cautionary statement by Abt and Bellak (1950, p. 75). Lindner's work was published in 1946; see remarks by Abt and Bellak (1950, p. 75), and also the many references to Lindner's work in Phillips and Smith (1953).
27. Phillips and Smith (1953, p. v).
28. Cronbach as excerpted in Buros (1959, p. 1129).
29. For example, see critical comments on Phillips and Smith in an early review by Douglas Kelley (Buros, 1959, p. 1128) and a recent book by Weiner (1998, pp. 93-94, 189-191, 224).
30. Phillips and Smith (1953, p. 133).
31. Phillips and Smith (1953, p. 136).
32. Phillips and Smith (1953, p. 141).
33. Phillips and Smith (1953, p. 137).
34. Phillips and Smith (1953, p. 130).
35. A listing of the sexual images in the Rorschach that can readily be identified by ordinary people is given by Pascal, Ruesch, Devine, and Suttell (1950). See also related articles by Shaw (1948) and Charny (1959).
36. Phillips and Smith (1953, p. 150).
37. Phillips and Smith (1953, pp. 150-151).
38. Cronbach as excerpted in Buros (1959, p. 1130).
39. Kelley as excerpted in Buros (1959, pp. 1128-1129).
40. Kelley as excerpted in Buros (1959, p. 1128).
41. B. Klopfer et al. (1954). Kelley's review was published in 1955.
42. See also the statement by B. Klopfer and his colleagues (1954, p. 377) that many "hypotheses derived from projective techniques are not capable of being verified or discredited by knowledge of overt behavior."
43. For example, see an exchange on content analysis that appeared in the *Journal of Personality Assessment:* Acklin (1995), Aronow, Reznikoff, and Moreland (1995), Moreland, Reznikoff, and Aronow (1995), and Ritzler (1995).
44. B. Klopfer et al. (1954, pp. 376-402; reference to "Father" and "Mother" cards on pp. 393-396).
45. B. Klopfer et al. (1954, p. 376).
46. Z. Piotrowski (1937a); B. Klopfer and Kelly (1946, pp. 16–17). See our discussion in Chapter Three of this book.

47. Society for Personality Assessment Distinguished Contribution Award (1971); Pickren (2000).

48. Exner (1969b, pp. 121-123; 1993, p. 12).

49. Z. Piotrowski (1937b).

50. Goldfried et al. (1971, pp. 332-335).

51. See also a discussion of *Perceptanalysis* by DeCato (1993b).

52. B. Bricklin (2001, p. 195).

53. P. M. Bricklin (2001, pp. 201-202).

54. Z. Piotrowski (1957, p. 120). See also Z. Piotrowski (1960, 1977) and DeCato (1993a, 1993b).

55. Z. Piotrowski (1957, pp. 447-450).

56. Z. Piotrowski (1957, p. 141).

57. Z. Piotrowski (1957, p. 455).

58. Z. Piotrowski (1957, pp. 416-420).

59. Z. Piotrowski (1957, p. 427).

60. Z. Piotrowski (1957, p. 428).

61. Z. Piotrowski (1957, p. 428).

62. Z. Piotrowski (1957, p. 429).

63. Z. Piotrowski (1957, pp. 191, 196-197).

64. Z. Piotrowski (1957, p. 211).

65. Z. Piotrowski (1957, p. 212).

66. The insight that the timing of Piotrowski's book may have accounted for, at least in part, the relative unpopularity of his ideas is taken from Exner (1969b, pp. 36-44).

67. Hertz (1959, p. 36).

68. Wagner (1965); Wagner and Hoover (1971, 1972); G. Young and Wagner (1993).

69. Z. Piotrowski (1957, p. 3).

70. Molish (1958, p. 190).

71. Z. Piotrowski (1980, p. 85; 1982, p. 192; 1984, p. 148).

72. Z. Piotrowski and Biele (1986).

73. H. Piotrowski (2001, p. 204).

74. B. Bricklin (2001); P. M. Bricklin (2001); B. Bricklin and P. M. Bricklin (1987); H. Piotrowski (2001).

75. In our opinion, most books on the Rorschach tend to be tedious and intellectually narrow. Notable exceptions include *Perceptanalysis* by Zygmunt Piotrowski, *Psychoanalytic Interpretation in Rorschach Testing* by Roy Schafer, *An Experimental Approach to Projective Techniques* by Joseph Zubin, Leonard Eron, and Florence Schumer, *Rorschach Psychology,* edited by Maria Rickers-Ovsiankina, *Rorschach Content Interpretation* by Edward Aronow and Marvin Reznikoff, *Rorschach Handbook of Clinical and Research Applications* by Marvin Goldfried, George Stricker, and Irving Weiner, *Disordered Thinking and the Rorschach* by James Kleiger, *The Clinical Interaction With Special Reference to the Rorschach* by Seymour Sarason, *Psychodiagnosis in Schizophrenia* by Irving Weiner, and of course Hermann Rorschach's *Psychodiagnostics.* Whether or not one agrees with these authors, they were clearly thinking intensely and imaginatively about real data and important clinical issues.

76. Piotrowski called himself a "personologist," a European term. For his own discussion of his intellectual roots, see Z. Piotrowski (1984).

77. Z. Piotrowski (1957, p. x).

78. Molish (1958, p. 190).

79. Z. Piotrowski (1980). Excerpts from Piotrowski's Rorschach interpretation program are given by Exner (1969b, pp. 147-151).

80. Kleiger (1999, p. 30).

81. Eagle (2000); see also Kleiger (1993) and Holt (1967a).

82. Rapaport (1941); see also Holt (1967a, p. 10).

83. Rapaport et al. (1946a, 1946b).

84. Eagle (2000, p. 508).

85. The numbers are from McNemar as excerpted in Buros (1949, p. 899).

86. For criticisms of the statistical analyses in Rapaport's book, see the reviews by Quinn McNemar, Clare Wright Thompson, and D. R. Miller in Buros (1949, pp. 899-906).

87. Rapaport, Gill, and Schafer (1968).

88. Goldfried et al. (1971, p. 289).

89. James Kleiger (1999) provides an exceptionally clear and perceptive discussion of "Deviant Verbalizations" and the measurement of thought disorder using the Rorschach. The present section is heavily indebted to Kleiger's work.

90. Kleiger (1999, p. 48).

91. This is the D2 detail on Card III. See Exner (2001b, pp. 120-122).

92. Rapaport et al. (1946b, p. 338).

93. This description and the examples are taken from Kleiger (1993, pp. 49-50). See also Rapaport et al. (1946b, pp. 344-350).

94. For example, see the summary of validity studies on the Thought Disorder Index provided by Kleiger (1999, pp. 90-99).

95. Kleiger (1999, pp. 216-218).

96. Johnston and Holzman (1979); Solovay et al. (1986). For conflicting interpretations of recent research using the Thought Disorder Index, see Viglione (1999, pp. 254-255), Garb, Wood, Nezworski, Grove, and Stejskal (2001, pp. 438-439), and Viglione and Hilsenroth (2001, pp. 460-461).

97. The term *WSum6* is an abbreviation for "Weighted Sum of the 6 Special Scores." See Exner (1993).

98. Wagner (2001). See also the discussion of Wagner's work in Kleiger (1999, pp. 136-138).

99. Kleiger (1993).

100. V. Norris, personal communication, May 23, 1992, as quoted in Kleiger (1993, p. 200). See also Holt (1967a, pp. 12-15).

101. Kleiger (1993, p. 199); see also Schafer (1954).

102. Holt (1967a, p. 12).

103. The authors would like to thank Dr. Helge Malmgren, whose "Classical Rorschach Page" at http://www.phil.gu.se/fu/Europe was immensely helpful as we wrote this section on Evald Bohm and the European Rorschach tradition. (Access date: October 22, 2002.)

104. Bohm (1951/1958, p. 3; also see the "Translators' Preface" by Anne and Samuel Beck on pp. x–xi).

105. Loosli-Usteri (1938), as cited in Bohm (1951/1958, p. 106).

106. Bohm (1951/1958, pp. 97-100).

107. Bohm (1951/1958, pp. 95-104).

108. Samuel Beck in Buros (1959, p. 274).

109. For example, see Beck's reaction to the negative research evidence on Color Shock (Beck, 1952, p. 43), and Cronbach's comments in Buros (1959, p. 979).

110. Beck (1959, p. 275).
111. A 1946 review by Donald E. Super, as excerpted in Buros (1949, p. 76).
112. A 1953 review by Lee J. Cronbach, as excerpted in Buros (1959, p. 979).
113. Beck (1944, pp. 58-82).
114. Beck (1944, p. 69).
115. Beck simply called this variable "the sum of Z." The term "*Z sum*" comes from Exner (1993).
116. Beck (1945, pp. 12-13).
117. Hertz (1977, pp. 54-62).
118. Beck (1949, pp. 129, 128).
119. Regarding the greater importance of *EA*, see Beck (1960, p. 18).
120. Beck (1960, p. 16).
121. Beck (1960, p. 22).
122. For critical remarks concerning the theory and evidence underlying *EA*, see Kleiger (1992a).
123. Skadeland (1986, p. 359).
124. Handler (1994, p. 567).
125. Hooker (1960, p. 240).
126. Skadeland (1986, p. 360).
127. W. Klopfer (1971, p. 501); B. Klopfer et al. (1954); B. Klopfer (1956); B. Klopfer, Meyer, Brawer, and Klopfer (1970). For a recent, very favorable discussion of this three-volume series, see Handler (1994).
128. B. Klopfer (1957).
129. For striking examples of Klopfer's "magical" reputation, see Hooker (1960).
130. Vorhaus (1960, p. 232).
131. Great Man Award: Bruno Klopfer (1966).

Chapter Six

1. Goodenough (1949, pp. 435-436).
2. Aronow and Reznikoff (1973, p. 309); Hilgard (1987, p. 516).
3. Guilford (1948, pp. 8-9).
4. Guilford (1948, p. 9).
5. Guilford (1948, p. 9).
6. E. Kelly and Fiske (1950). The authors later provided a more detailed description of their study in a book (E. Kelly & Fiske, 1951). See also E. Kelly and Goldberg (1959). Two decades later, Rae Carlson (1969) published a reanalysis of the Kelly and Fiske data, claiming to have identified a Rorschach index that would have outperformed all other assessment devices in the study, if it had been used.
7. E. Kelly and Fiske (1950, pp. 403-404).
8. Claims for the usefulness of the Rorschach in vocational assessment and selection were made by Harrower (1950, pp. 152-155); Z. Piotrowski (1943a, 1943b, 1964); Snowden (1956); G. Williams and Kellman (1956); and Z. Piotrowski and Rock (1963). Barry Ritzler, a professor at Long Island University who teaches for John Exner's Rorschach Workshops, recently reported that the Rorschach has been used "for many years in

helping the Montreal Canadians and the Philadelphia Flyers draft players." Ritzler believes that it would be a good idea to use the Rorschach to evaluate Navy SEALS and the New York Giants (Message from Barry Ritzler to Rorschach Discussion List at rorschach@maelstrom.stjohns.edu, October 22, 2001). For reviews of the Rorschach's poor validity in vocational counseling, see Super and Crites (1962, pp. 560-575) and Ricciuti (1962).

9. Holtzman and Sells (1954, p. 485).

10. See discussion of this issue by Holtzman and Sells (1954, p. 488).

11. Molly Harrower, who participated in the study by Holtzman and Sells (1954), later published her own reflections on the findings (Harrower, 1954, p. 301).

12. Holtzman and Sells (1954, p. 487).

13. Correlation with psychiatrists' judgments of case history was .09. Correlation with diagnoses (*eta*) was .23. Neither correlation was significantly different from zero (R. Newton, 1954, p. 249).

14. In a study apparently based upon the same group of subjects, S. Cummings (1954) had psychologists rate each Rorschach card individually for "adjustment." When these individual card ratings were pooled, the adjustment ratings differentiated schizophrenics from normals and unhospitalized neurotics (but not from hospitalized neurotics) and differentiated hospitalized neurotics from normals (but not from schizophrenics). When put together, the results of S. Cummings (1954) indicate that the Rorschach did provide valid information regarding gross maladjustment, whereas the results of Newton (1954) indicate that clinicians were unable to use this information effectively when making global estimates of adjustment.

15. Grant, Ives, and Ranzoni (1952).

16. Chambers and Hamlin (1957, pp. 107–108.) The authors noted that the forced choice format made it easier for psychologists to make correct guesses, and that the task was not typical of the diagnostic situations faced by clinicians in their daily work.

17. Armitage and Pearl (1957).

18. The mean correlation of the judges with criteria was .29 when projective tests were used. The mean correlation expected by chance was .14 (Silverman, 1959, p. 12). The "incremental validity" due to using projective tests was thus .25.

19. Little and Shneidman (1959, p. 37).

20. Little and Shneidman (1959).

21. This was Test Subject 3. See Little and Shneidman (1959, pp. 3, 6).

22. The numbers in this paragraph are taken from Table 2 of Little and Shneidman (1959, pp. 6-10).

23. Little and Shneidman (1959, p. 26).

24. The present summary of research on incremental validity is based on the highly informative review by Garb (1984). See also Garb (1998).

25. B. Klopfer and Kelley (1946, p. 18).

26. The Rorschach experts correctly diagnosed a psychotic disorder in 7/12 (58 percent) cases. They misdiagnosed a psychotic disorder in nonpsychotic patients in 6/36 (17 percent) of cases. The corresponding numbers for the MMPI were 75 percent and 8 percent.

27. For example, see Bilett, Jones, and Whitaker (1982) and Chambers and Hamlin (1957). See also Cummings (1954); but see our remarks and footnotes earlier in this chapter on the study by R. Newton (1954).

28. Bilett et al. (1982).

29. Johnston and Holzman (1979, pp. 60-63). It's been suggested (but not demonstrated) that the Rorschach may be a better measure of thought disorder than intelligence tests, because the Rorschach is more ambiguous and therefore "a psychotic-like thought disturbance should freely emerge" (Armstrong, Silberg, & Parente, 1986).

30. Armitage, Greenberg, Pearl, Berger, and Daston (1955); Davis (1961); Trier (1958); see also Bialick and Hamlin (1954).

31. Three Rorschach variables (M, R, and P) showed the most consistent relationship to intelligence but their correlations with intelligence, averaged over studies, were .30 at best. For example, see Altus and Thompson (1949), Armitage et al. (1955), Hauser (1962/1963), Levine et al. (1959), Lotsof (1953), and Lotsof et al. (1958).

32. Abrams (1955); Armitage et al. (1955, pp. 323-324); Fielding and Brown (1956); Wysocki (1957).

33. Abrams (1955); Armitage et al. (1955, pp. 323-324); Fielding and Brown (1956); Taulbee (1955).

34. Davis (1961); Trier (1958); see also the dissertation of Russell Hauser (1962/1963).

35. Davis (1961, p. 156).

36. Thorndike and Lorge (1944).

37. We thank Edwin Wagner, whose insightful comments contributed substantially to our discussion of this topic. The books of John Exner and Irving Weiner on the Comprehensive System don't mention the work of Davis or Trier or the possibility of estimating intelligence from vocabulary. Neither does a recent nuts-and-bolts textbook on the Rorschach by Rose et al. (2000).

38. For a thoughtful review of the shortcomings of early Rorschach research, see Cronbach (1949c).

39. For case studies of serious Rorschach misses, see Sacks and Lewin (1950) and Wittenborn and Sarason (1949).

40. Hertz (1951, p. 312).

41. Brockway, Gleser, and Ulett (1954); Grant et al. (1952).

42. Arnett (1999); Offer (1969).

43. Soskin (1954a, 1954b, 1959).

44. Soskin (1959).

45. Soskin (1959, p. 77).

46. For similar findings, see Samuels (1952). The study by Samuels is reprinted in Murstein (1965, pp. 162-187).

47. Rosen (1973).

48. The quote is taken from a 1947 report reproduced by Shakow (1969, p. 106).

49. The problem of R had also been discussed in an earlier article by Cronbach (1949b).

50. The underlying problems are that the relationship of various Rorschach scores to R is often nonlinear, and that even when linear, the slope of the line is different for different variables (for example, W and D). For example, in Fiske and Baughman's study, Animal responses (supposedly an indicator of stereotyped thinking) correlated .50 with R. But if the number of Animal responses was divided by R, then the resulting score, $A\%$, correlated -.30 with R. For a thoughtful discussion, see Cronbach (1949b, pp. 409-417).

51. L. Frank (1939b, pp. 393–395).

52. L. Frank (1939b, pp. 402-403).

53. Masling (1960/1992, p.p. 634); see also the review by Zax, Stricker, and Weiss (1960).

54. Calden and Cohen (1953); Henry and Rotter (1956).

55. Hersen and Greaves (1971); Krasner (1958); Simkins (1960).

56. Gross (1959); Hersen and Greaves (1971); see also Wickes (1956).

57. Baughman (1951); Gibby (1952); Gibby, Miller, and Walker (1953); Lord (1950); D. Miller, Sanders, and Cleveland (1950); Sanders and Cleveland (1953); but see Berger (1954); Bernstein (1956); and Wickes (1956).

58. Lord (1950); see also Luft (1953).

59. W. Klopfer and Taulbee (1976, p. 546).

60. See reviews by Cerbus and Nichols (1963) and G. Frank (1976, 1993b).

61. Beck (1945, p. 37).

62. Beck (1945, pp. 37-41); B. Klopfer and Davidson (1962, p. 152).

63. Lazarus (1949, p. 512).

64. For a review of the studies on Color Shock and the effects of colored versus achromatic cards on Rorschach responses, see Baughman (1958).

65. Baughman (1954; 1959; see also Baughman, 1958, 1967, and Russell, 1967).

66. Baughman (1954); see also Baughman (1959).

67. Rorschach (1921/1964, p. 35).

68. "[Rorschach] found the color shock phenomenon essentially pathognomic for the neuroses. With slight modifications this opinion has been confirmed" (Beck and Molish, 1967, p. 16).

69. B. Klopfer and Davidson (1962, p. 24).

70. Regarding the relationship of IQ scores to M, R, P, W, and F+%, see Altus and Thompson (1949); Armitage et al. (1955); Hauser (1962/1963); Levine et al. (1959); Lotsof (1953); and Lotsof et al. (1958). Regarding the relationship to developmental level, see Goldfried et al. (1971, pp. 52-54). Regarding the relationship to organizational activity, see Hertz (1977, pp. 54-62, 65-67).

71. Regarding the relationship of serious mental disorders to F+%, see Korchin (1960); Korchin and Larson (1977, pp. 178-179); Mayman (1970, pp. 32-40). Regarding the relationship with measure of thought disorder, see Goldfried et al. (1971, pp. 288-305) and Kleiger (1999).

72. Ames, Learned, Metraux, and Walker (1952); Ford (1946/1975); Meili-Dworetzki (1956).

73. Goldfried et al. (1971, pp. 306-344).

74. Goldfried et al. (1971, pp. 350-372); Meyer and Handler (1997).

75. Elizur (1949).

76. Aronow and Reznikoff (1976, pp. 82-110); Goldfried et al. (1971, pp. 89-140).

77. The two most thoughtful and thorough reviews of Rorschach successes are Aronow and Reznikoff's *Rorschach Content Interpretation* and Goldfried et al.'s *Rorschach Handbook of Clinical and Research Applications*. In a few cases, we are less impressed than they are by particular scales. For example, we have not included Fisher and Cleveland's "Barrier" and "Penetration" scales among our list of successes, because virtually all the positive findings for these scales up through the 1970s came from Fisher and Cleveland and their colleagues, and had not been independently replicated.

78. J. Singer (1960); J. Singer and Brown (1977).

79. Eron (1965, p. 496).

80. "From the viewpoint of the Rorschach test's claim to scientific validity the present situation is one of chaos. The more publications, the more confusion" (Beck and Molish, 1967, p. 3).

81. Eron in Buros (1965, p. 495).

Chapter Seven

1. For a recent critique of clinical validation, see Meehl (1997).
2. Hastorf and Cantril (1954).
3. For discussions of confirmation bias, see Faust (1984, pp. 64-69); Garb (1998, pp. 87-88, 183, 185-186, 195-196); and Nisbett and Ross (1980, pp. 169-172, 175-183). There's also somewhat controversial evidence that confirmation bias can occur even in the absence of prior beliefs or preconceptions (see Higgins and Bargh, 1987, pp. 397-405).
4. Sir Francis Bacon, *First Book of Aphorisms,* Aphorism XLVI, as quoted by Nisbett and Ross (1980, p. 167).
5. B. Klopfer (1939, p. 47).
6. B. Klopfer and Kelley (1946, p. 22). Samuel Beck's 1942 review of *The Clinical Application of the Rorschach Test* as excerpted in Buros (1949, p. 157).
7. The phrase "true believers" is taken from Eric Hoffer's (1951/1963) book of that title.
8. Zubin (1954, p. 305).
9. Zubin et al. (1965).
10. Chapman and Chapman (1967, 1969). For independent studies that have replicated the illusory correlation effect, see Garb (1998, pp. 23-25); also see Golding and Rorer (1972); Lueger and Petzel (1979); and Waller and Keeley (1978).
11. Chapman and Chapman (1967, pp. 195-196).
12. Chapman and Chapman (1967, pp. 196-199).
13. Chapman and Chapman (1969).
14. Chapman and Chapman (1967, pp. 193-194) explicitly drew the analogy between visual illusions and illusory correlations.
15. Chapman and Chapman (1967, p. 200, Table 3).
16. Chapman and Chapman (1969, pp. 271-272).
17. A 1945 review by Donald E. Super as excerpted in Buros (1949, p. 167).
18. Zubin (1954, p. 305).
19. The story of Croesus as told in Herodotus' *History,* Book I.
20. Wittenborn and Sarason (1949, p. 22).
21. Wittenborn and Sarason (1949, p. 22).
22. Wittenborn and Sarason (1949, p. 22).
23. Forer (1949, p. 120).
24. Hyman (1981); Forer (1949).
25. The term "Barnum effect" was coined by Paul Meehl (1956, p. 266).
26. For scholarly reviews on the Barnum effect, see Dutton (1988); Furnham and Schofield (1987); Snyder, Shenkel, and Lowery (1977). For an accurate popularized account, see Snyder and Shenkel (1975).
27. These quotes are taken from Ulrich, Stachnik, and Stainton (1963, p. 833). Our thanks to Dutton (1988) for calling them to our attention.
28. S. Carlson (1985).
29. This passage on Gauquelin (1969) is paraphrased from Myers (2001). The quote comes from p. 507 of Myers' book.
30. Snyder et al. (1977, pp. 107-108); see also Richards and Merrens (1971).
31. Snyder (1974).
32. Dutton (1988); Hyman (1981); see also "Cold Reading and Psychics."
33. Earle (1995); see also Saville and Dewey (date unknown).

34. Many of the examples of Barnum statements in this section are based upon Saville and Dewey (date unknown).

35. See "The Psychic Frauds" at http://www.geocities.com/Omegaman_UK/frauds.html.

36. Hyman (1981, p. 81); Dutton (1988, p. 331).

37. Dutton (1988, p. 331).

38. Hyman (1981, p. 86).

39. Kaplan and Saccuzzo (1982, p. 379).

40. B. Klopfer and Kelley (1946, p. 18).

41. Emil Oberholzer in Rorschach (1921/1964, p. 184).

42. Some studies not discussed here (for example, Potkay, 1971; Symonds, 1955) reported strikingly better results for blind analyses. However, these studies generally lacked adequate controls or were otherwise seriously flawed.

43. Holtzman and Sales (1954).

44. Gacono, DeCato, Brabender, and Goertzel (1997, pp. 436-447).

45. Interpretation if *EB* is ambitent, that is, if *M* is approximately equal to *WSumC* (Exner, 2000, p. 87).

46. Interpretation if *DEPI* is 5 and *CDI* is less than 4 (Exner, 2000, p. 80).

47. Interpretation of high *FC:CF* + *C* (Exner, 2000, p. 101).

48. Hines (1988).

49. Guilford (1948); Thornton and Guilford (1936); Cronbach (1950b); Bandura (1954a, 1954b); Fiske and Baughman (1953); Zubin (1941a, 1941b); Eysenck (1945); Henry and Rotter (1956); Jensen and Rotter (1945); Sarason (1954); Lazarus (1949). Meehl's first ideas for a dissertation study involved the Rorschach or TAT (Meehl, 1989, p. 350).

50. For example, see Cronbach (1955, 1956); Jensen (1958); and a review by Eysenck in Buros (1959, pp. 276-278).

51. Hertz (1959).

52. Cronbach (1950b).

53. Cronbach (1989, pp. 70-71).

54. Cronbach (1948, 1949b, 1950a).

55. Cronbach (1949c).

56. Cronbach (1949c, p. 393).

57. Cronbach (1949c, p. 425).

58. Cronbach (1949c, pp. 426-427).

59. For a summary of the negative findings that had become apparent even by the end of the 1940s, see Schofield (1950).

60. A 1953 review by Cronbach, reprinted in Buros (1959, p. 979).

61. A 1955 review by Cronbach, reprinted in Buros (1959, p. 1094).

62. See "Report on a Psychometric Mission to Clinicia" by Cronbach (1954).

63. Cronbach (1956; 1960, p. 565; 1984, p. 554).

64. Cronbach (1956). Another *Annual Review* chapter of the same era by Arthur Jensen (1958, p. 296) was also sharply critical of the Rorschach.

65. For biographical information on Marguerite Hertz, see Ames (1970); Exner (1969b); Hertz (1986); and Kessler (1994).

66. For a listing of Hertz's publications up until 1970, see Ames (1970).

67. Exner (1969b, p. 157) pointed out that Rorschach history might have been different had Hertz published a comprehensive book on the test. See also Handler (1996, p. 656).

68. The story of the destruction of Hertz's data and manuscript are based upon her correspondence with John Exner, as reported in Exner (1969b, pp. 26-27, 157).
69. Hertz (1935, 1942, 1951, 1959, 1970b, 1986).
70. Hertz (1959, p. 33).
71. Jensen (1958).
72. Hertz (1959, p. 34).
73. Hertz (1959, p. 36).
74. Hertz (1959, p. 36).
75. Hertz (1959, p. 44).
76. Beck, Rabin, Thiesen, Molish, and Thetford (1950).
77. Hertz (1959, p. 34).
78. Cronbach (1949a, pp. 79-80); Hilgard (1987, p. 834).
79. Eysenck (1959); L. Shaffer (1959); Jensen (1965); McCall (1959).
80. McCall (1959, p. 279).
81. L. Shaffer (1959, p. 286).
82. Jensen (1965, p. 507); See also L. Shaffer (1959, p. 288): "The predictive or concurrent validity of the Rorschach is, in the areas of its best competence, perhaps of the order of .20 to .40."
83. Eysenck (1959, p. 278).
84. B. Klopfer et al. (1954, p. 265).
85. McCall (1959, p. 283).
86. McCall (1959, p. 281).
87. Jensen (1965, p. 502).
88. Jensen (1965, pp. 503, 509).
89. Jensen (1965, p. 509).
90. B. Klopfer and Davidson (1962, p. 24).
91. Beck (1959, pp. 273-276).
92. Beck (1959, p. 275).
93. For discussions of the attitudes toward the Rorschach generally held by behaviorists and practitioners of community psychology, see Hertz (1970b) and Weiner (1972).
94. Hilgard (1987, pp. 645-649).
95. Hilgard (1987, pp. 645-649).
96. Hertz (1970b, p. 453). Robert Archer (1999, p. 309) has made a similar remark: "If one challenges the utility of a concept like personality, it is not surprising that one would challenge the usefulness of personality assessment."
97. Albee (1968, 1970); Reisman (1976, pp. 389-391).
98. For a discussion of the Rorschach's psychometric flaws, see Holtzman, Thorpe, Swartz, and Herron (1961).
99. Cronbach (1949c).
100. Holtzman et al. (1961); for further information on the Holtzman Inkblot Test, see Hill (1972); Holtzman (1988, 2000); Holtzman, Díaz-Guerrero, and Swartz (1975); Holtzman and Swartz (1990); and Swartz, Reinehr, and Holtzman (1999). For reviews of the test, see Cundick (1985) and Dush (1985).
101. See Holtzman et al. (1961, pp. 214-221) and Holtzman (1988, pp. 583, 591-596).
102. Reisman (1976, p. 377).
103. Cleveland (1976, p. 316); Holtzman (1988, p. 597).

104. Holtzman (1988, p. 597).
105. Dana (1965); Eron (1965); Reznikoff (1972).
106. Dana (1965, p. 495).
107. W. Klopfer (1968, pp. 148-149) and Aronow and Reznikoff (1976) also concluded that content approaches yielded more promising research results than structural approaches.
108. Zubin et al. (1965, pp. 238-239).
109. Goldfried et al. (1971, p. 389).
110. Aronow and Reznikoff (1976, pp. 1-2).
111. Aronow and Reznikoff (1976, pp. 310-311).
112. Aronow and Reznikoff (1976, pp. 210-231, 264-296).
113. Aronow and Reznikoff (1976, p. 271).
114. Aronow and Reznikoff (1976, pp. 272-275).
115. Aronow and Reznikoff (1976, pp. 315-316).

Chapter Eight

1. Board of Professional Affairs (1998, p. 391).
2. Biographical information in this paragraph is taken from Exner's autobiographical statements in his dissertation (Exner, 1958, p. ii) and in a book by Trull and Phares (2001, p. 226).
3. Exner (1958, p. ii).
4. Exner (1969b, title page).
5. Exner (1969a, pp. 324, 330); Board of Professional Affairs (1998, p. 391).
6. John Exner as quoted by Handler (1996, p. 652).
7. Exner (1980, p. 564).
8. Handler (1996, p. 652).
9. For a list of Exner's publications up until 1980, see Exner (1980, pp. 576-577).
10. Previous writers, such as Marguerite Hertz (1959) and Zubin et al. (1965), had commented on the "chaos" that existed regarding Rorschach administration, scoring, and interpretation. Furthermore, Toomey and Rickers-Ovsiankina (1960) presented tables comparing the various scoring approaches.
11. Exner (1980, p. 565).
12. Exner (1969b, p. 261; see also p. 256).
13. Exner and Exner (1972, p. 404).
14. Jackson and Wohl (1966); Lesser (1961).
15. Exner and Exner (1972, p. 405).
16. Exner and Exner (1972, p. 405).
17. Beck (1968, p. 131).
18. Exner and Exner (1972, p. 408).
19. Exner (1974, p. 23).
20. Exner (1985, 1990, 1995b, 2001b); Exner, Weiner, and Schyler (1976).
21. Exner (1986, 1991, 1993); Exner and Weiner (1995). See also Exner (2000).
22. Exner (1974, pp. 16-17; 1986, pp. 20-24; 1993, pp. 20-24); Exner and Martin (1983, p. 409); Handler (1996, p. 654).
23. Exner (1993, p. 23).
24. Exner (1993, p. vii) gives the number of Rorschach Workshops studies as "more than

550." A letter from Exner's administrative assistant at the Workshops informed us that the number was "more than 1000" (personal communication from Patricia Greene to James Wood, dated March 11, 1994, as quoted in Garb et al., 2001, p. 443).

25. Beck (1944, pp. 2-3).
26. The injunction to "tell everything" is supposed to be followed during free association in the psychoanalytic session (Freud, 1933/1965, pp. 10-11).
27. B. Klopfer and Kelley (1946, pp. 31-34).
28. B. Klopfer and Kelley (1946, pp. 29-35).
29. There are a few exceptions to this general rule (Exner, 1993, pp. 67-72).
30. Exner (1993, p. 260).
31. Exner (1993, p. 78).
32. Exner (1993, p. 78).
33. Exner (1993, p. 81).
34. Exner (1986, p. x).
35. Exner (1974, p. 217). Exner (1974) didn't provide standard deviations for the Rorschach scores. Interpretation of an individual patient's scores is difficult or impossible unless norms are available both for mean (average) scores and standard deviations. Exner (1978, pp. 3, 5) stated that the standard deviations were omitted from his previous book because "the sample sizes were generally small, and because one or more of the samples might have consisted of an overly heterogeneous grouping."
36. Exner (1993, pp. 258-317).
37. Exner (1993, pp. 258-276).
38. Exner (1993, p. 259).
39. The table can be found in Exner (1993, p. 259). The claim that the normative sample was "stratified to represent the U.S. Census" was made by Exner's coauthor, Irving Weiner (1998, p. 27).
40. Exner (1991, pp. 460-461).
41. Even self-report questionnaires can be incorrectly scored, however (Allard, Butler, Faust & Shea, 1995; Allard & Faust, 2000).
42. For example, subtests on the Wechsler Adult Intelligence scales have a minimum scoring reliability of .91 and a median reliability in the upper .90s (Psychological Corporation, 1997).
43. See reviews by Jensen (1959, pp. 120-122) and Reznikoff, Aronow, and Rauchway (1982).
44. For example, see Houck and Dawson (1978); Lisansky (1956); Pope and Jensen (1957); J. Watkins and Stauffacher (1952).
45. Exner (1986, p. 23). Exner (1996, p. 11) confirmed that in these early studies, the .85 figure represented a correlation coefficient and not some other kind of reliability statistic: "It is true that during the early 1970s when the basic scoring-coding criteria were selected for inclusion in the system, I used two correlational methods (Pearson r and Spearman's rho) to evaluate interscorer reliability and did exclude any possible scoring categories that did not achieve a .85 level."
46. Exner (1978, p. 14; 1986, p. 23). Exner (1993, p. 91) revised the criteria for interrater reliability to "a minimum standard of 90 percent agreement among coders or a .85 intercorrelation."
47. The standard deviation is approximately 10, so the example illustrates that with a reliability of .85, scores between two raters can differ by as much as one standard deviation.

48. Subtests on the Wechsler Adult Intelligence scales have a minimum scoring reliability of .91 and a median reliability in the upper .90s (Psychological Corporation, 1997).
49. Weiner (1998, p. 25).
50. Kaufman and Lichtenberger (1999, p. 168).
51. See summary of Exner's test-retest coefficients in Viglione and Hilsenroth (2001, p. 455, Table 2). For further discussion of the test-retest reliability of scores in the Comprehensive System for the Rorschach, see Garb, Wood, Nezworski, Grove, and Stejskal (2001).
52. Cronbach (1949c, p. 422).
53. Exner (1993, 1999); Exner, Armbruster, and Viglione (1978).
54. See comparison of test-retest reliability coefficients for the MMPI, MMPI-2 and Comprehensive System in Viglione and Hilsenroth (2001, p. 455).
55. Although conceding that some validity studies of the Rorschach had yielded positive results, Eysenck (1959) rejected most of these studies on the grounds that they'd been statistically or methodologically flawed, or that they hadn't been adequately replicated by other researchers.
56. Exner (1969b, p. 248).
57. Exner and Martin (1983, p. 409).
58. In a recent article, Meyer (2002, p. 111) reports that he analyzed 188 different Comprehensive System variables.
59. Beck (1960, p. 20).
60. For a description of Klopfer's Form Level approach, see B. Klopfer and Davidson (1944).
61. Exner's use of four symbols (+, o, u, -) to score Form Quality was adapted from Marvin Mayman (1970; see Exner, 1993, pp. 150-155). However, a comparison of the two approaches shows that Exner substantially altered the meaning of these symbols. Furthermore, Mayman did not accept the use of Form Quality tables based on statistical frequency of responses. Instead, Mayman taught that the Form Quality of responses should be determined according to how well they met certain rationally defined criteria, such as veridicality, specificity, and imaginativeness (see Korchin & Larson, 1977; Lohrenz & Gardner, 1967; Mayman, 1970). In most important respects, therefore, the Comprehensive System's approach to Form Quality is closer to Beck's approach than to Mayman's.
62. Exner (1993, pp. 165-171, 182, 478-481).
63. Exner (1993, pp. 421, 515).
64. Masling, Rabie, and Blondheim (1967). For recent reviews of the Rorschach Oral Dependency Scale, see Bornstein (1996, 2001).
65. "Exner and his colleagues . . . have become the most thorough, instrumental, and contemporary representatives of the Rorschach's psychometric or sign approach" (H. Lerner & Lerner, 1987, p. 374).
66. Exner (1974, pp. 148-149 and 291, 1969a).
67. Exner (1969a, pp. 328-329).
68. For a discussion of the rationale behind the inclusion of Pair and Reflection responses, see Nezworski and Wood (1995).
69. Exner (1991, p. 173).
70. The formula for the Egocentricity Index is $3r + (2) / R$, where r equals the number of Reflection responses, (2) equals the number of Pair responses, and R equals the total number of responses in the protocol. (Exner, 1974, pp. 148-149; 1993, p. 188).

71. Exner (1974, p. 294).
72. Exner (1993, pp. 433-436). But for a critique, see Nezworski and Wood (1995).
73. Exner (1991, pp. 23-26; 1993, pp. 188-189, 359-363; 2000, p. 80).
74. Exner (1991, p. 146).
75. Exner (1991, pp. 22-23; 1993, pp. 353-359).
76. Regarding Suicide Constellation, see Exner (1991, p. 152; 1993, pp. 183, 342-345; 2000, pp. 342-343). Regarding Obsessive Style Index, see Exner (1991, p. 31; 1993, pp. 451-452; 2000, pp. 211, 253-254). Regarding Hypervigilance Index, see Exner (1991, pp. 29-31; 1993, pp. 439-441,452; 2000, pp. 211, 254). Regarding Coping Deficit Index, see Exner (1991, pp. 26-29; 1993, pp. 363-366; 2000, pp. 27-28, 80-82, 310-311).
77. Exner (2000, pp. 343-345).
78. Exner (1986, p. 344; 1993, p. 375).
79. Exner (1993, p. 185; 2001b, p. 95). Theoretically, *D Scores* can range between -5 to +5, inclusive. In practice, however, they nearly always fall between -3 and +3.
80. Exner (1993, pp. 184-185; 2001b, pp. 94-95).
81. Exner (2000, pp. 23-28).
82. Most important, Exner (1974) provided means for several Rorschach variables, but not standard deviations. Without standard deviations, norms are generally useless for clinical applications.
83. Rabin (1980).
84. C. Piotrowski, Sherry, and Keller (1985). See also C. Piotrowski and Keller (1989).
85. Routh (1994, p. 126).
86. The membership figures are available in the APA archives at http://apa.org/archives/yearlymembership.html. (Access date: October 25, 2002.)
87. Shakow (1965).
88. Hobbs (1963); E. Kelly and Goldberg (1959, p. 5).
89. Gottfredson and Dyer (1979, p. 89); Mills, Wellner, and VandenBos (1979, p. 120).
90. E. Kelly and Goldberg (1959, pp. 8-9); L. Levy (1962).
91. Holt (1967b); E. Kelly and Goldberg (1959, p. 7).
92. Shakow (1965, p. 358).
93. Routh (1994, pp. 128-129).
94. Routh (1994, pp. 128-129).
95. N. Cummings (2001, pp. 70-72).
96. Routh (1994, p. 132-133).
97. N. Cummings (2001); Dawes (1994, pp. 14-18); Routh (1994, pp. 133-135).
98. For a more detailed explanation of the difference between the Psy.D. and Ph.D., see the following Web page of the American Psychological Association: http://apa.org/ed/graduate/phd_psyd.html. (Access date: October 25, 2002.)
99. N. Cummings (2001); Routh (1994, pp. 133-134). Regarding Cummings's degree from Adelphi, see N. Cummings (2001, p. 94). In 2000 the California School of Professional Psychology changed its name to Alliant University, and in 2001, Alliant University and United States International University were joined to create Alliant International University (http://www.alliant.edu/about/history.htm and http://apa.org/monitor/sep00/cspp.html). (Access date: October 25, 2002.)
100. Pion (1992, p. 232), as cited in Dawes (1994, p. 16).
101. From July 1998 through June 1999, the number of graduates from traditional clinical

programs was 1,006, and the number from professional clinical programs was 1,185. (See the following Web page of the American Psychological Association: http://research.apa.org/gs00tab16.pdf. Access date: October 25, 2002.)

102. See listing of APA presidents at http://apa.org/about/paspres.html. (Access date: October 25, 2002.)

103. Routh (1994, p. 154) states, "The attitude of psychology organizations toward the independent practice of psychology has also undergone approximately a 180-degree turn."

104. Dawes (1994, pp. 175-177).

105. J. G. Wiggins (2001).

106. Foxhall (2000).

107. "By the 1970s, it was clear that the changing demographics of the APA meant that political control of the Association was shifting from the academic to the applied psychologist" (Fowler, 1992, p. 279).

108. Lilienfeld (1999b); see also Wood et al. (2002, p. 532).

109. For example, see Gist and Lubin (1999), Lilienfeld (1999b), and Mayou, Ehlers, and Hobbs (2000). See also Wood et al. (2002, p. 532).

110. For example, see Robyn Dawes's (1994, p. 162) criticism of the APA Council of Representatives for its permissive stance regarding the use of anatomically detailed dolls in sexual abuse evaluations. See also Lohr, Fowler, and Lilienfeld (2002), Lilienfeld (1999b), McFall (2000), Hayes (1989), and Sechrest (1992).

111. American Medical Association (1989, Principle 2.19).

112. Dawes (1994); Lilienfeld (1999b); Lohr et al. (2002).

113. Hilgard (1987, pp. 645-649).

114. Surveys by Lubin, Wallis, and Paine (1971); Sundberg (1961); Wade and Baker (1977); and Wade et al. (1978) found the Rorschach to be the most popular personality test. However, a survey by W. Brown and McGuire (1976) found the Rorschach and MMPI to be about equally popular in mental health settings, and Sell and Torres-Henry (1979) reported that the MMPI was substantially more popular than the Rorschach in college counseling centers.

115. Lubin, Larsen, and Matarazzo (1984). C. Piotrowski et al. (1985) found that the Rorschach was still the most popular test. However, C. Piotrowski and his colleagues sent their survey to the membership of the Society for Personality Assessment (formerly the Society for Projective Techniques), a group that was strongly inclined in favor of projective tests and unrepresentative of the entire profession of clinical psychology.

116. Rabin (1980, pp. 52-53).

117. Rabin (1980, p. 53). For another favorable review of Exner's work by prominent pro-Rorschach authors, see Lerner and Lerner (1987).

118. Hertz (1986, p. 404).

119. W. Klopfer (1971); Exner (1981).

120. Kaplan and Saccuzzo (1982, p. 386).

121. Anastasi (1982, 1988).

122. Anastasi (1982, p. 569; 1988, p. 599).

123. C. Piotrowski et al. (1985, p. 117).

124. C. Piotrowski and Keller (1989).

125. Ritzler and Alter (1986, p. 47).

126. Ritzler and Alter (1986, p. 47). See also Hilsenroth and Handler (1995).

127. Bruno Klopfer Distinguished Contribution Award (1980).

128. Weiner (1985) describes his plans for the journal.
129. Exner (1974, pp. xi-xii).
130. Hilsenroth and Handler (1995, p. 248).
131. Board of Professional Affairs (1998, p. 391).
132. An advertisement for a "Special Rorschach Tutorial and Annual Rorschach Workshop," offered on January 15-19 and 22-26, 1973, in Los Angeles and sponsored by the Rorschach Workshops Inc., appears on the page facing p. 403 in the *Journal of Personality Assessment*, 1972, volume 36.
133. The advertisement described in the preceding note lists Exner, Hertz, and Weiner.
134. Goode (2001).
135. Board of Professional Affairs (1998, p. 392).
136. Weiner (1983, p. 456); Wood et al. (2002).
137. Weiner (1983, p. 456).
138. Weiner (1983, p. 456).
139. Exner and Weiner (1982, pp. 375-376, 394-434).
140. McCann (1998).
141. Borum and Grisso (1995); Hagen and Castagna (2001, p. 271); Pinkerman, Haynes, and Keiser (1993, p. 9).
142. Board of Professional Affairs (1998, p. 392).

Chapter Nine

1. Patricia Greene, Administrative Assistant at the Rorschach Workshops, stated in a letter to us dated March 11, 1994: "Dr. Exner has asked that I respond to your letter of February 5 requesting copies of some of our unpublished works. During the period from 1968 to 1990 more than 1000 studies were undertaken at Rorschach Workshops to address various issues." No studies were forthcoming, however. Copies of this letter are available upon request from the first author of this book.
2. In Exner's most recent book documenting the research base of the Comprehensive System (Exner, 1993), we counted only twelve citations to works on the Comprehensive System that were *not* coauthored by Exner. Four of these were articles in peer-reviewed journals, four were dissertations, and the remainder were book chapters, conference presentations, or newsletter articles. In contrast, Exner cites 110 of his own works: 60 unpublished studies of the Rorschach Workshops, 24 articles in peer-reviewed journals, 10 of his own books, and newsletter articles, computer programs, conference presentations, computer interpretation programs, and book chapters.
3. For example, in one study Exner (1974, p. 29-30) found that the Rapaport method of administering the Rorschach elicited substantially more responses ($R = 36$) than did other methods of administering the test, including the Klopfer method ($R = 23.9$). However, subsequent research has shown that the Rapaport method elicits approximately the same number of responses as the method of administration used by Klopfer and Exner (Baldwin, 1998, p. 34; Blais, Norman, Quintar, & Herzog, 1995, p. 105). Exner's results differed sharply, probably because of poor methodology: His collection of protocols using the Rapaport, Klopfer, and other systems was from a "sample of convenience," assembled from protocols that had been donated by various clinicians (Exner,

1974, pp. 28-29) and from patients with various diagnoses. As a result, in Exner's study, the *type of patients* and *individual differences among clinicians* were confounded with the *method of administration*. Later studies have used random assignment to avoid these problems.

4. Regarding his famous study on Reflection responses, Exner (1974, p. 291) stated that "Reflections occurred in 17 of the 20 homosexual protocols and 15 of the 20 character disorder records. Conversely, they appeared in only three of the 20 depressive records and seven of the 20 control records." However, Exner (1986, p. 392; 1993, pp. 433-434) stated "Frequency data revealed that reflections appeared in more than 75 percent of the records of the homosexual and antisocial groups, but not at all among the depressives and in only three nonpatient records." As can be seen, in these two descriptions of the same study, the number of Reflection responses changed from 3 (15 percent) to 0 (0 percent) among depressives, and from 7 (35 percent) to 3 (15 percent) among nonpatient controls.

5. Exner (1993, p. 50) described an unpublished Workshops Study as follows: "Exner and Bryant (1974) found an average of nearly *four* texture responses in the records of 30 nonpatient adults who had recently separated from close emotional relationships. The subjects were retested approximately 10 months later. Twenty-one of the 30 reported that they had established new relationships or reconstructed the one that had been fractured earlier. . . . Conversely, the nine subjects who reported a continuing sense of loss all gave three or more texture responses in the second test." However, in the same volume, Exner (1993, p. 384) stated: "Exner and Bryant (1974) found that 30 recently separated or divorced subjects averaged 3.57 texture responses. . . . Twenty-one of the 30 separated or divorced subjects were retested after 6 months, at which time 14 reported having reconstituted or replaced the lost relationship." As can be seen, in these two accounts of the same study (a) the re-test period is given as 10 months and 6 months, (b) the number of subjects retested is given as 30 and 21, and (c) the number of subjects who had reestablished a new relationship or reconstructed the old relationship was given as 21 and 14. See also Exner (1978, p. 111): "Six of the nine subjects who were not retested after the six month interval refused further participation in the study, while the remaining three could not be located."

6. For a more thorough discussion of peer review, see Weller (2001).

7. Mackintosh (1995a, 1995b, 1995c); Tucker (1997). But in defense of Burt, see Fletcher (1991); Jensen (1995); and Joynson (1989). For other examples of fraud in science, see Kohn (1986) and Broad and Wade (1982). Also see the Web site of the Office of Research Integrity of the U.S. Department of Health and Human Services at http://ori.dhhs.gov. (Access date: October 28, 2002.)

8. Fonda (1977, pp. 135-136); G. Frank (1993a, 1993d); Greenwald (1990, 1991); Kleiger (1992a, 1992b); see also Greenwald (1999).

9. Fonda (1977, pp. 135-136); see also Fonda (1951, 1960).

10. Kleiger (1992a, 1992b).

11. Fonda's (1977) critique was published in the same well-known book as an essay by J. Singer and Brown (1977). Exner (1993, p. 447) cited the Singer and Brown essay, but not Fonda's. Exner (1992a) did address Kleiger's findings.

12. Aron (1980) called *es* "*ep*," in accordance with Exner's terminology at that time. He reported the *D Score* as "*ep–EA*."

13. Aron (1980, pp. 109, 109-115). Aron also reported no significant differences for Diffuse Shading, Shading, or Inanimate movement.

14. Aron (1982, p. 582, note).

15. Aron (1982).

16. Hunsley and Bailey (2001, p. 482).

17. Whitehead (1985, p. 28). The mean adjusted hit rate was 31 percent for the MMPI alone, 22 percent for the Rorschach alone, and 29 percent for the MMPI plus Rorschach. All these figures are statistically different from a hit rate of 0 percent ($p < .0001$). The difference between the MMPI *alone* and the MMPI and Rorschach *together* was not statistically significant.

18. Whitehead (1985, p. 29).

19. Lilienfeld et al. (2000).

20. Meyer (1989/1991, pp. 225, 229).

21. Meyer (1989/1991, p. 222).

22. Meyer (1989/1991, p. 167).

23. Meyer (1989/1991, p. 156-158, 172-175).

24. Meyer (1989/1991, pp. 71-72).

25. Meyer (1992a); see also Meyer (1992b, 1993).

26. Exner (1992b).

27. Meyer (1992b).

28. Wood, Nezworski, et al. (2001a).

29. Meyer (2001b, p. 394, footnote 3).

30. Hilsenroth and Handler (1995).

31. Shontz and Green (1992).

32. This quote appears in both Weiner (1995, p. 73) and Weiner (1996, p. 206).

33. Exner (2000, p. iv) lists the members of the Rorschach Research Council as Thomas Boll, S. Philip Erdberg, Mark Hilsenroth, Gregory Meyer, William Perry, and Donald Viglione.

34. Exner (1978, p. 14; 1986, p. 23).

35. Groth-Marnat (1990, p. 279; 1997, p. 397); Weiner (1998, p. 25).

36. McDowell and Acklin (1996); Wood, Nezworski, and Stejskal (1996a).

37. The most familiar form of the correlation coefficient, r, is discussed in Chapter Three. Since the 1930s, several other forms of the correlation coefficient have also been used by psychologists, including the intraclass correlation coefficient and *phi*. Both of these statistics are closely related to r. In fact, *phi* can be calculated by the same formula as r. The *kappa* statistic is often used to measure agreement among raters. Strictly speaking, *kappa* is not a correlation coefficient. However, it is very closely related to *phi*, so that the formulas for *kappa* and *phi* generally yield results that are very close.

38. Jensen (1965, p. 504).

39. Jensen (1965, pp. 504-505).

40. The reliability is -.05, whether we use r, *phi*, or *kappa*. As we noted earlier, these three statistics usually yield results that are very similar.

41. Cohen (1960); Fleiss (1981); Light (1971).

42. Exner (1978, p. 14; 1986, p. 23).

43. Exner (1996, p. 11).

44. Regarding the confusion surrounding Exner's method of calculating "percentage correct," see the exchanges between Wood, Nezworski, and Stejsakl (1996b, p. 14; 1997, p. 491) and Meyer (1997a, p. 481 and Footnote 2; 1997b, p. 497).

45. This summary of results is based on the intraclass correlation coefficients reported by Acklin, McDowell, Verschell, and Chan (2000, pp. 29-32).

46. Acklin et al. (2000, p. 35). For scoring of individual responses, Acklin et al. (pp. 34-35) reported that *kappa* was lower than .61 for 18 percent of Comprehensive System scores.

47. For all graphs in Figure A.5, the Pearson correlation coefficient (*r*) is equal to the intraclass correlation coefficient (ICC). That is, when the data presented in the graphs were used to calculate *r* and the ICC, identical values were obtained.

48. The 45 percent and 10 percent figures are for the combined clinical and nonclinical samples in Nakata's (1999, pp. 85-90). For scoring of individual responses, Nakata (pp. 71-82) found that 75 percent of CS scores had a *kappa* below .85, and 37 percent had a *kappa* below .61.

49. Thomas Shaffer, personal communication, January 10, 2000. In their article (T. Shaffer et al., 1999, p. 306) the authors offer to make their findings regarding interrater reliability available upon request. The numbers in their article are based on *kappa* rather than the intraclass correlation coefficient. However, Meyer, Hilsenroth, et al. (2002, p. 255) have reported that *kappa* and the intraclass correlation coefficient differ very little (mean difference = .02) for experienced Rorschach raters. Philip Erdberg and Thomas Shaffer would fall into this category.

50. Guarnaccia et al. (2001, p. 464, Abstract).

51. Meyer, Hilsenroth, et al. (2002). For an earlier article on scoring reliability, see Meyer (1997a, 1997c); but see Wood, Nezworski, and Stejksal (1997).

52. Meyer, Hilsenroth, et al. (2002, p. 239).

53. These figures from Meyer, Hilsenroth, et al. (2002) are for the intraclass correlation coefficient.

54. Meyer, Hilsenroth, et al. (2002, pp. 234-235).

55. Meyer, Hilsenroth, et al. (2002, p. 268).

56. According to the results reported by Meyer and his colleagues, the intraclass correlation coefficient can yield biased results when the base rate of a score is less than .05.

57. In Acklin et al. (2000) and Nakata (1999), the reliabilities of these scores are reported as follows: Schizophrenia Index—.45, .56, .77, .46; Suicide Constellation—.55, .67, .00, .00; Adjusted *D*—.53, .68, .77, .46.

58. Meyer, Hilsenroth, et al. (2002, pp. 230-232).

59. The main problem was that most of Meyer's "samples" were formed by combining several subsamples from different populations, with each of these subsamples scored by a different set of judges. For example, Sample 1 of Meyer, Hilsenroth, et al. (2002, pp. 223-224) was formed by combining two different subsamples. In the first subsample of twenty-three cases, Gregory Meyer and an undergraduate assistant scored all protocols. In the second subsample of forty-three cases (which came from a different population of protocols) three graduate students scored all protocols. Meyer combined these two subsamples into a single sample of sixty-six cases, with the effect that subsamples were confounded with scorers, and that scorers were correlated with each other (that is, if Meyer scored a protocol, so did his assistant). As a result, certain sources of variance that should have been independent were allowed to correlate, with resulting possibilities for inflation of the intraclass correlation coefficient (ICC). For example, if Meyer and his assistant both tended to score a Rorschach variable more liberally than the three graduate students (in the article, Meyer reported that he had taught the assistant to score), this systematic source of covariance would tend to inflate the numerator of the ICC. Similar considerations apply to the ICCs reported on p. 239 of the article by Meyer et al. Contrary to the claims of Meyer et al. (pp. 230-232), use of the Model 1 ICC does not elimi-

nate or control for such problems. If sampling strategy does not match the model, the ICC can yield distorted results. In a later note, we make specific recommendations for designing interrater reliability studies using the ICC.

60. For the graphs in Figure A.5, the intraclass correlation coefficient (ICC) is the same as *r*. For example, in graph C, *r* is .61 and the ICC is also .61. As we mentioned earlier, *r* and the ICC generally give similar results.

61. Heilbrun (1992), and Nunnally and Bernstein (1994). But see Cicchetti (1994), Cicchetti and Sparrow (1981), Fleiss (1981), and Landis and Koch (1977).

62. Because *XA%* is a relatively new variable, its reliability wasn't reported by Acklin et al. (2000) or Nakata (1999). However, *XA%* is equal to $(1 - X-\%)$, and its reliability is therefore the same as *X–%*.

63. Grant et al. (1952).

64. Soskin (1959).

65. Exner (1991, 1993).

66. Message from M. B. to the Rorschach Discussion and Information Group at rorschach@maelstrom.stjohns.edu, July 27, 1999. A copy of this message is available from the first author of this book upon request.

67. T. Shaffer et al. (1999).

68. Hamel et al. (2000, p. 291).

69. Wood, Nezworski, et al. (2001a, pp. 359, 362, 363).

70. Meyer (1989/1991).

71. Exner, 1991 (pp. 432-433). We wish to thank Dr. Kim McKinzey for calling this example to our attention.

72. Mittman (1983). Mittman (p. ii) states: "I would like to thank Dr. John E. Exner, Jr. for his academic guidance and support through the various stages of this project."

73. Exner (1991, p. 433).

74. Aronow (2001); Hunsley and Di Giulio (2001); Widiger (2001).

75. Exner (2001a, pp. 386-387); Weiner (2001b, p. 123).

76. Meyer (2001b, p. 394).

77. Gregory Meyer, Message to the Rorschach Discussion and Information Group at rorschach@maelstrom.stjohns.edu, April 6, 2000.

78. Meyer (2001b, p. 390).

79. Meyer and Archer (2001, p. 494); Viglione and Hilsenroth (2001, p. 457); Weiner (2001a, p. 426).

80. Exner (1993, p. 258; 1991, pp. 460-461).

81. Exner (2002a, p. 394).

82. Exner (1993, p. 258).

83. Meyer (2001b, p. 390).

84. Exner (1991, pp. 460-461).

85. Exner (personal communication, February 20, 2001) informed us that the adult nonpatient norms in his 1991 and 1993 books first appeared in the Rorschach Workshops *Alumni Newsletter* in 1989.

86. Barry Ritzler, messages to the Rorschach Discussion and Information Group at rorschach@maelstrom.stjohns.edu, March 12, 2001. Copies available from the first author of this book upon request.

87. Goode (2001); Lilienfeld et al. (2000); Lilienfeld, Wood, and Garb (2001a).

88. Exner (2001b, p. 172).

89. Exner (personal communication, February 20, 2001) informed us that the adult nonpatient norms in his 1991 and 1993 books first appeared in the Rorschach Workshops *Alumni Newsletter* in 1989.

90. John Exner, personal communication, March 23, 2001. Copy available from the first author of this book upon request.

91. Joel Dvoskin, message to the Law and Psychology Discussion List at psylaw-l@crcvms.unl.edu, March 1, 2001. A copy is available from the first author of this book upon request.

92. Ray Hays, message to the Law and Psychology Discussion List at psylaw-l@crcvms.unl.edu, March 1, 2001. A copy is available from the first author of this book upon request.

93. Gregory J. Meyer, message to the Society for a Science of Clinical Psychology at sscpnet@listserv.acns.nwu.edu, March 3, 2001. A copy is available from the first author of this book upon request.

94. Barry Ritzler, message to the Rorschach Discussion and Information Group at rorschach@maelstrom.stjohns.edu, March 7, 2001. Copies available from the first author of this book upon request.

95. Gregory Meyer, messages to the Society for a Science of Clinical Psychology at sscpnet@listserv.acns.nwu.edu, March 4 and 5, 2001. Copies are available from the first author of this book upon request.

96. In addition to Meyer's Internet message, Exner (2002a, p. 392) has stated that the duplicate records were "detected in 1999."

97. Exner (2001a); Meyer, (2001b).

98. Meyer and Richardson (2001). Copies are available from Gregory Meyer, Department of Psychology, University of Alaska at Anchorage.

99. Exner (2002a).

100. Thomas Shaffer presented a Continuing Education course on March 9, 2002, titled "New Variables, New Norms: An Update of the Comprehensive System." According to Kim McKinzey, a forensic psychologist who attended the course, "Shaffer will be publishing a set of CS norms based on his 1999 123 S study, enhanced by 149 more Ss and some 1800 Ss from a dozen other countries, all of which are (a) close to his USA norms and (b) **far** from Exner's. He hasn't started writing yet. So, we now have: Exner's repudiated norms, Shaffer's repudiated norms, Exner's unpublished (& likely to be repudiated) norms, and Shaffer's unwritten (& likely to be repudiated) norms." (Kim McKinzey, messages to the Law and Psychology Discussion List at psylaw-l@crcvms.unl.edu, December 10, 2001, March 11, 2002. Copies are available from the first author of this book upon request.)

101. T. Shaffer et al. (1999).

102. Kim McKinzey, message to the Law and Psychology Discussion List at psylaw-l@crcvms.unl.edu, March 11, 2002. Copies are available from the first author of this book upon request.

103. Exner (1991, 1993, 2001b); T. Shaffer et al. (1999); Wood, Nezworski, et al. (2001a); see also Hamel et al. (2000).

104. Exner (2001a); Meyer (2001b); Meyer and Archer (2001); Viglione and Hilsenroth (2001); Weiner (2001b).

105. For quotes and citations regarding the claims that Comprehensive System scores are related to diagnoses, see Wood et al. (2000b).

106. Viglione (1999, p. 258).
107. Meyer, Finn, et al. (1998, pp. 26, 29); see also Kubiszyn et al. (2000, p. 121, 123). It should be noted that in 2001, Meyer seemed to take a much different stance from his 1998 and 2000 statements: "because it is impossible to determine whether a specific historical event actually did or did not happen from Rorschach responses, clinicians should not draw positive or negative conclusions about sexual abuse from the Rorschach. . . . To optimally serve patients, no less is required. Beyond their potential to harm patients, undisciplined or incorrect inferences discredit tests and the profession more generally" (Meyer & Archer, 2001, p. 499). Thus, one year after claiming that projective techniques can discriminate physical and sexual abuse victims from nonvictims, Meyer said that to do so might harm patients and can discredit the Rorschach and the profession!
108. The criteria were proposed by two of the authors of this book and a collaborator (Wood, Nezworski, & Stejskal, 1996b).
109. Exner (1991, p. 146).
110. For reviews of validation research on the Depression Index, see Jorgensen et al. (2000); Wood, Lilienfeld, et al. (2000a); and Wood, Lilienfeld, et al. (2001). But see Ganellen (1996a, 1996b, 2001).
111. *No relationship:* Archer and Gordon (1988); Archer and Krishnamurthy (1997); Ball, Archer, Gordon, and French (1991); Caine et al. (1995); Carter and Dacey (1996); Lipovsky, Finch, and Belter (1989); Meyer (1993); Ritsher, Slivko-Kolchik, and Oleichik (2001); Sells (1990/1991); Silberg and Armstrong (1992); Viglione, Brager, and Haller (1988). But see Meyer (2000, 2001a). *Mixed results:* Ilonen et al., (1999); H. Singer and Brabender (1993). *Positive:* Jansak (1996/1997).
112. Nezworski and Wood (1995); but see Exner (1995a). For a positive finding regarding the Egocentricity Index, see Hilsenroth, Fowler, Padawer, and Handler (1997).
113. Exner (1993, pp. 434-345). But for a critique, see Nezworski and Wood (1995).
114. Calkins (1980/1981); Himelstein (1983/1984); and Jacques (1990/1991). The average sample size in these three studies was seventy. For a summary and discussion of these findings, see Nezworski and Wood (1995).
115. Nezworski and Wood (1995).
116. Patricia Greene, Personal Communication, November 2, 1993. Copies are available from the first author of this book upon request.
117. Patricia M. Greene, Personal Communications, March 11, 1994. Copies are available from the first author of this book upon request. This excerpt was also published in Garb, Wood, Nezworski, Grove, and Stejskal (2001, p. 443).
118. Nezworski and Wood (1995); Wood et al. (1996a); Garb et al. (2001).
119. Wood et al. (1996a, p. 8).
120. Garb et al. (2001, p. 443).
121. Exner (1995a, p. 205).
122. Wood, Nezworski, et al. (2001a).
123. John Exner, personal communication, September 14, 2000. Copy available upon request from the first author of this book.
124. John Exner, Personal Communication, December 8, 2000. Copy available upon request from the first author of this book.
125. Exner (2001b).
126. Some Rorschach scores not included in the Comprehensive System possess well-demonstrated validity (see Chapter Six). Most prominently, the Rorschach Oral

Dependency scale bears a well-demonstrated relationship to dependent behaviors, the Rorschach Prognostic Rating Scale is related to therapy outcome (see Chapter Ten), and the Elizur Hostility and Anxiety scales have repeatedly been found to bear a relationship to relevant criteria (see Chapter Six). Holt's Primary Process scales (a purported measure of primary process thinking), Fisher and Cleveland's Barrier and Penetration scales (supposedly related to the permeability of psychological boundaries), and Urist's Mutuality of Autonomy scale (supposedly a measure of object relations) may also possess validity (see Aronow & Reznikoff, 1976; Goldfried et al., 1971; Urist, 1977), although research support has been less clear-cut. For example, most of the supportive findings on Barrier and Penetration were published more than forty years ago by the scales' developers, whereas independent replication efforts have yielded ambiguous results.

127. See review by Jorgensen et al. (2000).

128. For the only peer-reviewed article on the PTI as of this writing (July 2002), see S. Smith, Baity, Knowles, and Hilsenroth (2001).

129. Wood, Nezworski, and Stejskal (1996b, p. 15).

130. Wood, Lilienfeld, et al. (2000b, p. 395); see also Garfield (2000); P. Lerner (2000); and Weiner (2000).

131. Weiner (1999, pp. 336-337).

132. Weiner (1997, pp. 10-11).

133. Gacono (1990); Gacono and Meloy (1991, 1992); Gacono, Meloy, and Berg (1992); Gacono, Meloy, and Heaven (1990). These studies all drew on the same sample of prisoners ($N = 30$ to 43) and therefore did not constitute independent replications.

134. Hare (1991).

135. Darcangelo (1996/1997); Egozi-Profeta (1998/1999); Loving and Russell (2000); Muntz (1998/1999); Murphy-Peaslee (1993/1995); Ponder (1998/1999); Siemsen (1999); A. Smith (1994/1995); Welsh (1999); M. Young, Justice, Erdberg and Gacono (2000). See also Loving (1998); A. Smith, Gacono, and Kaufman (1997, 1998).

136. The only one of the ten studies to find a statistically significant relationship was Loving and Russell (2000).

137. For a summary of attempts to replicate the findings of Gacono and Meloy, see Wood, Lilienfeld, Nezworski, and Garb (2001, pp. 52-53).

138. Gacono (1988/1989, pp. 99-100; see also Gacono, 1990, p. 592) states: "A Rorschach Test was then administered by one of the researchers (both advanced doctoral level clinical psychology students with training and experience in Rorschach administration). Once a subject completed the tests, he participated in a structured interview for the purpose of completing the Psychopathy Checklist. The interviews were conducted by one researcher and observed by the other. Checklist scores for each subject were rated independently by each researcher. An average of the researchers' scores represented the final Psychopathy Checklist Score." Gacono's procedure of averaging ratings from two researchers may have mitigated, though not entirely eliminated, the problem of contamination.

139. Wood, Lilienfeld, et al. (2000a); Wood et al. (2001). But see Gacono, Loving, and Bodholdt (2001).

140. Exner (2000, p. 80).

141. Goode (2001).

142. Meyer (1997b, p. 326).

143. Meyer (1997b); Meyer and Archer (2001).

144. Meyer and Archer (2001, pp. 491-492).

145. Meta-analyses comparing the global validity of the Rorschach and MMPI include Atkinson (1986), Garb, Florio, and Grove (1998), Hiller, Rosenthal, Bornstein, Berry, and Brunell-Neuleib (1999), Meyer and Archer (2001), and Parker, Hanson, and Hunsley (1988). See also Garb et al. (2001), Garb, Florio, and Grove (1999), Parker, Hunsley, and Hanson (1999), and Rosenthal, Hiller, Bornstein, Berry, and Brunell-Neuleib (2001).

146. For a guide to meta-analysis designed for nonscientists, see Hunt (1999). For useful introductions to the techniques of meta-analysis, see Durlak (1995), Hunter and Schmidt (1990), and Lipsey and Wilson (2001).

147. Hiller et al. (1999).

148. Cruz, Brier, and Reznikoff (1997); Harper and Scott (1990); Salyer, Holmstrom, and Noshpitz (1991).

149. Sheehan and Tanaka (1983).

150. We have given the weighted effect sizes for the Rorschach and MMPI in the meta-analysis by Hiller et al. The unweighted effect sizes for the same data set were .29 and .30. Virtually all textbooks on meta-analysis recommend the use of weighted effect sizes. For a debate on the relative merits of weighted and unweighted effect sizes, see Garb et al. (2001) and Rosenthal et al. (2001).

151. For criticisms of the methodology of some global Rorschach meta-analyses, see Garb, Wood, Nezworski, Grove, and Stejskal (2001); Hiller et al. (1999); and Wood, Nezworski et al. (2001a). But see Meyer and Archer (2001) and Rosenthal et al. (2001).

152. Greene (2000).

153. Regarding the concept of incremental validity, see Meehl (1956) and Sechrest (1963).

154. Lilienfeld et al. (2000).

155. Greene (2000). For a detailed list of instances in which Roger Green criticizes the validity of MMPI-2 scales, see Garb, Wood, Lilienfeld, and Nezworski (2002).

156. Meyer and Archer (2001, pp. 491-492).

157. Lilienfeld et al. (2001a).

158. Lilienfeld (1999a).

159. Lilienfeld et al. (2000); Weiner (2001c).

Chapter Ten

1. Board of Professional Affairs (1998, p. 392).

2. Zubin was wrong on some points, however. Most notably, he thought the Rorschach was a complete failure as a measure of intelligence.

3. Regarding the Beck norms, see Beck et al. (1950). Regarding the Rapaport norms, see a 1946 review by Clare Wright Thompson, as excerpted by Buros (1949, p. 902).

4. Ames et al. (1952); Ford (1946/1975); see review of children's norms in Hertz (1959, pp. 44-46).

5. Bornstein (2001, p. 44).

6. Meyer (1992a, p. 236).

7. Rose et al. (2000, p. 138).

8. Jensen (1965, p. 502).

9. B. Klopfer (1940, p. 26).

10. Bruno Klopfer in 1943, as excerpted in Buros (1949, p. 189).

11. Z. Piotrowski (1957, p. 3).
12. Board of Professional Affairs (1998, p. 392).
13. Weiner (1998, p. 25).
14. Exner (1991, pp. 25, 146-147).
15. Meyer, Finn, et al. (1998, p. 26); see also Kubiszyn et al. (2000, p. 121).
16. Meyer, Finn, et al. (1998, p. 29); see also Kubiszyn et al. (2000, p. 123).
17. Ritzler, Erard, and Pettigrew (2002a, p. 243).
18. A 1953 review by Cronbach, reprinted in Buros (1959, p. 979).
19. B. Klopfer and Davidson (1962, p. 24).
20. Exner (2000, p. 80); Goode (2001).
21. Meyer (1997b, p. 326).
22. A 1955 review by Cronbach, reprinted in Buros (1959, p. 1094).
23. Great Man Award: Bruno Klopfer (1966).
24. As a 1998 commendation from the American Psychological Association stated, "John E. Exner's name has become synonymous with this test." (Board of Professional Affairs, 1998, p. 391).
25. Holt (1967b, p. 452).
26. Goode (2001).
27. Meyer (2000, pp. 71-73) alleged, "Wood et al. . . . championed a formula they knew was incorrect," and "Wood et al. knew their statements were not true before they submitted their final article for publication." Meyer's allegations were false, and we replied to them in a subsequent article (Wood, Nezworski, Stejskal, & Garven, 2001).
28. Carl B. Gacono, messages to the Rorschach Discussion and Information Group at rorschach@maelstrom.stjohns.edu, April 18, 2001. Copies available from the first author of this book upon request.
29. Weiner (2002, p. 3).
30. Ethical Principles of Psychologists, Ethical Standard 6.25 (American Psychological Association, 1992).
31. Gregory J. Meyer, message to the Rorschach Discussion and Information Group at rorschach@maelstrom.stjohns.edu, January 31, 2000. Copy available from the first author of this book upon request.
32. Ethical Principles of Psychologists, Ethical Standard 6.25 (American Psychological Association, 1992).
33. Kubiszyn et al. (2000, p. 121).
34. Garb et al. (2002).
35. The TAT isn't valid for most of these purposes either. Wood et al. (2000a, 2000b); but see Garfield (2000); P. Lerner (2000); and Weiner (2000).
36. Wood, Lilienfeld, et al. (2000b).
37. Exner and Sendin (1997).
38. Meyer, Hilsenroth, et al. (2002, pp. 234-235).
39. Meyer, Finn, et al. (2001, p. 134).
40. Regarding the difficulty of combining different sources of information in clinical judgments, see Dawes (1994, pp. 75-105), Goldberg (1991), and Grove, Zald, Lebow, Snitz, and Nelson (2000).
41. Also relevant to the issue of combining "weak" tests to arrive at clinical judgments is the following statement in the *Standards for Educational and Psychological Testing* (American Psychological Association, 1999, p. 11): "A few lines of solid evidence regarding a

particular proposition are better than numerous lines of evidence of questionable quality."

42. Minutes of the Meeting of the Board of Trustees of the Society for Personality Assessment, September 18-19, 1999 (Society for Personality Assessment, 2000, p. 181). See also Gregory J. Meyer, position announcement sent to the Rorschach Discussion and Information Group at rorschach@maelstrom.stjohns.edu, November 17, 1999. Copy available from the first author of this book upon request.

43. Minutes of the Meeting of the Board of Trustees of the Society for Personality Assessment, March 23, 2000 (Society for Personality Assessment, 2001a, p. 585).

44. Society for Personality Assessment (2000, p. 181; 2001a, p. 585).

45. Goode (2001).

46. Weiner (2001c).

47. Meyer (2000, pp. 71-73); Meyer, Hilsenroth, et al. (2002, p. 268); but see Wood, Nezworski, Stejskal, and Garven (2001).

48. Presley, Smith, Hilsenroth, and Exner (2001, p. 491, Abstract).

49. Exner (2002a, p. 392) states that the duplicate records "were detected in 1999."

50. Board of Professional Affairs (1998, p. 392).

51. Kubiszyn et al. (2000, p. 120).

52. Society for Personality Assessment (2000a, p. 181).

53. Gregory Meyer and Stephen Finn have both published articles on the Comprehensive System. The late Kevin Moreland was an expert on the Rorschach, but was not affiliated with the Comprehensive System. Robert Dies, a member of PAWG, has been an associate of Exner since at least 1966 (see Exner, 1966, p. v) and is said to have carried out a study of scoring reliability for the Rorschach Workshops in the early 1990s.

54. The MMPI expert was Stephen Finn, whom we've also listed as an expert on the Comprehensive System. The neuropsychological testing expert was Gary G. Kay. The expert on occupational and employment testing was Lorraine D. Eyde.

55. A footnote to Kubiszyn et al. (2000, p. 119) states: "We are grateful to the many APA staff members who provided their support and assistance to the work group and to the Society for Personality Assessment and Rorschach Workshops for supporting Gregory J. Meyer to review much of the literature discussed here."

56. Meyer, Finn, et al. (2001). The description of *American Psychologist* as the "official organ" of the APA is from Richard McCarty, the journal's editor (see Lilienfeld, 2002a).

57. Meyer, Finn, et al. (2001, p. 128, Abstract).

58. Garb, Klein, and Grove (2002). But see Meyer, Finn, et al. (2002). Elsewhere, Meyer, Finn, et al. (2001, p. 141) report that the (now abandoned) Rorschach Prognostic Rating Scale has a mean validity across studies of .44. These authors do not report any other Rorschach score that has consistently shown a validity above .40.

59. Society for Personality Assessment (2000, p. 181; 2001a, p. 585; 2001b, pp. 393-394).

60. Hamel et al. (2000, p. 291).

61. B. M., message to the Rorschach Discussion and Information Group at rorschach@maelstrom.stjohns.edu, July 13, 2002. Copy available from the first author of this book upon request.

62. Pinkerman, Haynes, and Keiser (1993, p. 9).

63. Regarding the Rorschach as an indicator of sexual or physical abuse, see Garb et al. (2002); Garb, Wood, and Nezworski (2000); Lilienfeld, Wood, and Garb (2000).

64. Meyer and Archer (2001, p. 499).

65. Exner and Weiner (1982, pp. 375-376, 394-434).
66. Hess and Weiner (1999); Meloy, Hansen, and Weiner (1997); Weiner and Hess (1987); Weiner, Exner, and Sciara (1996).
67. Meloy and Gacono (1998, p. 96).
68. Schretlen (1997, p. 208).
69. Albert, Fox, and Kahn (1980); McDougall (1996); Mittman (1983; see also description in Exner, 1991, pp. 431-436); Netter and Viglione (1994); Perry and Kinder (1992); but see I. Bash and Alpert (1980); Seamons, Howell, Carlisle, and Roe (1981). See also reviews by Perry and Kinder (1990) and Schretlen (1997).
70. Phelps, Eisman, and Kohout (1998).
71. C. Piotrowski (1999, p. 792).
72. Ball, Archer, and Imhof (1994).
73. Kubiszyn et al. (2000, p. 124); Meyer, Finn, et al. (1998, p. 31).
74. Meyer and Handler (1997).
75. B. Klopfer et al. (1954, pp. 688-699); B. Klopfer, Kirkner, Wisham, and Baker (1951).
76. Regarding a validity coefficient of .30, see Mischel (1968); also see Garb (1998, pp. 20-22).
77. Wagner (2001). Wagner's "autisms" overlap with some of the "Deviant Verbalizations" identified by David Rapaport, but exclude some scores that Rapaport included.
78. Greaves (2000); Wagner (2001).
79. Holtzman et al. (1961, pp. 214-221).
80. Wood et al. (2002).
81. Guarnaccia et al. (2001, p. 472).
82. Hilsenroth and Handler (1995, p. 255).
83. Hertz (1937, p. 59).
84. Rose et al. (2000, p. 215).
85. Routh (1994, p. 111).

Chapter Eleven

1. Our friend was referring to the following joke: The mother and father of a little boy brought him to see a psychologist. "He's just too optimistic," they said. The psychologist claimed to have a technique that would cure the little boy of this problem. The psychologist locked the boy in a in a room filled with manure. Several hours later the psychologist and the parents returned to the room. They found the little boy eagerly shoveling manure with a broad smile on his face. "What are you doing?" asked the psychologist. The little boy answered, "In all this manure, there must be a pony somewhere!" We should add that the psychologist's treatment approach would be considered unsound by most psychologists.
2. Carl B. Gacono, messages to the Rorschach Discussion and Information Group at rorschach@maelstrom.stjohns.edu, April 18, 2001. Copies available from the first author of this book upon request.
3. Silver (2001, p. 1009).
4. Archer and Newsom (2000).
5. Cromer (1994); Wolpert (1992).

6. Lilienfeld (2002b).
7. Aronow (2001, p. 284).
8. For references to these and other logical fallacies, see Gray (1991) and Shermer (1997).
9. Dr. R. M., message to the Law and Psychology Discussion List at psylaw-l@crcvms.unl.edu, December 9, 2001. Copy available from the first author upon request.
10. Cialdini (1993, pp. 94-135).
11. Loftus (1993).
12. Krugman (1940, p. 94).
13. Weiner (2001c, p. 4).
14. Lilienfeld et al. (2001b).
15. Exner (1993, pp. 421, 515).
16. E. C., message to the Rorschach Discussion and Information Group at rorschach@maelstrom.stjohns.edu. May 3, 2002. Copy available from the first author of this book upon request.
17. Garb (1999); see also relevant sections of Garb (1998).
18. Weiner (1999, p. 338). Paradoxically, Weiner stated on the same page, "Let it not be said or thought that the two case examples of conjoint RIM-MMPI assessment in this article are put forth as sufficient documentation of the incremental validity of Rorschach assessment."
19. On the vividness and persuasiveness of anecdotal evidence, see D. Levy (1997, pp. 180-186); Stanovich (1998, pp. 59-67).
20. Garb (1984, 1999).
21. Weiner (1999, p. 338) seems to say that his anecdote is "representative," although he presents no evidence to support that assertion: "No matter how representative these two cases may be, they are merely illustrative and are not to be taken as systematic empirical validation of Rorschach validity. . . . The pattern of clinical and test findings they illustrate does in fact occur, and is known to occur widely in clinical practice." He presents no evidence that these findings are "known to occur widely in clinical practice."
22. Dawes (1994, pp. 43, 46-50).
23. Weiner (1999, p. 329).
24. A. H., message to the Rorschach Discussion and Information Group at rorschach@maelstrom.stjohns.edu, March 23, 2001. Copy available from the first author of this book upon request.
25. Tversky and Kahneman (1973). See also D. Levy (1997, pp. 180-186).
26. Viglione (1999, p. 257).
27. Tversky and Kahneman (1973). See also D. Levy (1997, pp. 180-186).
28. Fischoff (1975).
29. Kaplan (2001).
30. Piatelli-Palmarini (1994).
31. Goodenough (1949, p. 37).
32. Cialdini (1993, p. 91).
33. O'Donohue and Bradley (1999, p. 310).
34. Finn (2002, p. 1).
35. Finn (2002, p. 1) advised members of SPA to "non-defensively listen to our critics," but only "so that we can better understand their misconceptions."

Chapter Twelve

1. Weiner et al. (1996).
2. For an example of one expert rebutting another's Rorschach interpretation in a legal case, see Kaplan and Saccuzzo (1982, pp. 382-383).
3. See Table of Contents, *Journal of Personality Assessment*, August, 2001. See also Bornstein (2001), Gacono et al. (2001), Ganellen (2001), and Wood, Lilienfeld, et al. (2001).
4. Dawes (1999); Garb et al. (2001); Hiller et al. (1999); Hunsley and Bailey (1999, 2001); Meyer and Archer (2001); Rosenthal et al. (2001); Stricker and Gold (1999); Viglione (1999); Viglione and Hilsenroth (2001); and Weiner (2001a).
5. Acklin (1999); Garb (1999); Weiner (1999); Wood and Lilienfeld (1999). See also Archer (1999).
6. Garfield (2000); P. Lerner (2000); Weiner (2000); Wood, Lilienfeld, et al. (2000a, 2000b).
7. Aronow (2001); Exner (1995a, 2001a); Hunsley and Di Giulio (2001); Meyer (2001b); Nezworski and Wood (1995); Widiger (2001); Wood, Nezworski, et al. (2001a, 2001b).
8. Exner (1996); Wood et al. (1996a, 1996b).
9. Lilienfeld et al. (2001b); Weiner (2001c).
10. Lilienfeld et al. (2000).
11. Garb et al. (2002).
12. Lilienfeld et al. (2001a).
13. Wood et al. (2002).
14. Goode (2001).
15. These numbers are based upon information in the tables of T. Shaffer et al. (1999). See also Wood, Nezworski, et al. (2001a).
16. According to T. Shaffer et al. (1999, p. 311), the average $X+\%$ ("XplusPer") is .51, and the average $F+\%$ ("FPlusPer") is .53.
17. Weiner (1999, pp. 336-337).
18. John Exner as quoted by Goode (2001).
19. Rose et al. (2000, p. 167).
20. Wittenborn and Sarason (1949, p. 22).
21. Calden and Cohen (1953); Henry and Rotter (1956).
22. Exner (1993, pp. 64-65).
23. Exner (1993, p. 68).
24. Exner (1993, p. 68).
25. Exner (1993, p. 68).
26. Exner (1993, p. 65).
27. Exner (1993, p. 67).
28. Exner (1993, pp. 72-73).
29. Exner (1993, p. 73).
30. Bornstein (2001); Meyer (1997b, p. 326).
31. As we noted in Chapter Six, vocabulary level as measured by the Rorschach provides a rather good estimate of intelligence. However, modern approaches to the test do not use this approach.
32. Grossman, Wasyliw, Benn, and Gyoerkoe (2002).
33. Meyer (1996, p. 572) states: "Clearly, Rorschach scores are not unrestricted MRIs of the psyche."
34. Albert, Fox, and Kahn (1980), McDougall (1996), Mittman (1983; see also description in Exner, 1991, pp. 431-436), Netter and Viglione (1994), Perry and Kinder (1992); but see

I. Bash and Alpert (1980), Seamons et al. (1981). See also reviews by Perry and Kinder (1990) and Schretlen (1997).

35. Regarding faking and depression, see Caine et al. (1995) and Meisner (1988). Regarding faking and PTSD, see Frueh and Kinder (1994) and Popper (1991/1992). See also reviews by Perry and Kinder (1990) and Schretlen (1997).

36. Schretlen (1997).

37. Schretlen (1997, p. 217).

38. Grossman et al. (2002, p. 499).

39. There were three main problems with the Grossman et al. (2002) study. The study did not include a comparison group of normal individuals, but instead made comparisons to the norms of Exner (2001b) and T. Shaffer et al. (1999). The methodological problems of using norms as a comparison group have been discussed by Wood, Lilienfeld, et al. (2001b) and Wood, Nezworski, et al. (2001a). In addition, several substantive conclusions in the article were based on eyeball comparisons of subjects with normative data, without any statistical test. And approximately half of the central variables in the study (*D* Score, Adjusted *D, H,* and Sex) lack well-demonstrated validity. It's difficult to know what significance, if any, can be attributed to the finding that minimizers and nonminimizers received similar scores on unvalidated Rorschach variables.

40. Meloy and Gacono (1995, p. 419, Note 4).

41. McCann (1998).

42. McKinzey and Ziegler (1999).

43. Irving Weiner (2002, p. 3) has said regarding critics of the Comprehensive System that "their limited background has not prevented them from calling for a moratorium on the teaching and use of certain tests and questioning the professional ethics of psychologists who continue to use them."

Epilogue

1. Biederman and Cerbus (1971); Shemberg and Keeley (1970); Thelen, Varble, and Johnson (1968).

— ⁓⁓ — References

Abrams, E. N. (1955). Prediction of intelligence from certain Rorschach factors. *Journal of Clinical Psychology, 11,* 81–83.

Abt, L. E., & Bellak, L. (1950). *Projective psychology.* New York: Knopf.

Acklin, M. W. (1995). Integrative Rorschach interpretation. *Journal of Personality Assessment, 64,* 235–238.

Acklin, M. W. (1999). Behavioral science foundations of the Rorschach Test: Research and clinical applications. *Assessment, 6,* 319–324.

Acklin, M. W., & Oliveira-Berry, J. (1996). Return to the source: Rorschach's *Psychodiagnostics. Journal of Personality Assessment, 67,* 427–433.

Acklin, M. W., McDowell, C. J., Verschell, M. S., & Chan, D. (2000). Interobserver agreement, intraobserver reliability, and the Rorschach Comprehensive System. *Journal of Personality Assessment, 74,* 15–47.

Albee, G. W. (1968). Conceptual models and manpower requirements in psychology. *American Psychologist, 23,* 317–320.

Albee, G. W. (1970). The uncertain future of clinical psychology. *American Psychologist, 25,* 1071–1080.

Albert, S., Fox, H. M., & Kahn, M. (1980). Faking psychosis on the Rorschach: Can expert judges detect malingering? *Journal of Personality Assessment, 44,* 115–119.

Allard, G., Butler, J., Faust, D., & Shea, M. T. (1995). Errors in hand scoring objective personality tests: The case of the Personality Diagnostic Questionnaire-Revised (PDQ-R). *Professional Psychology: Research and Practice, 26,* 304–308.

Allard, G., & Faust, D. (2000). Errors in scoring objective personality tests. *Assessment, 7,* 119–129.

Allen, R. M., Richer, H. M., & Plotnik, R. J. (1964). A study of introversion-extroversion as a personality dimension. *Genetic Psychology Monographs, 69,* 297–322.

Altus, W. D., & Thompson, G. M. (1949). The Rorschach as a measure of intelligence. *Journal of Consulting Psychology, 13,* 341–347.

American Medical Association. (1989). *Current opinions: The Council on Ethical and Judicial Affairs of the American Medical Association.* Chicago: American Medical Association.

American Psychological Association. (1985). *Standards for educational and psychological testing.* Washington, DC: Author.

American Psychological Association. (1992). Ethical principles of psychologists and code of conduct. *American Psychologist, 47,* 1597–1611.

American Psychological Association. (1999). *Standards for educational and psychological testing.* Washington, DC: American Educational Research Association.

Ames, L. B. (1970). Great Man Award: Dr. Marguerite Hertz. *Journal of Projective Techniques and Personality Assessment, 34,* 445–448.

379

Ames, L. B., Learned, J., Metraux, R., and Walker, R. N. (1952). *Child Rorschach responses.* New York: Hoeber-Harper.

Anastasi, A. (1982). *Psychological testing* (5th ed.). New York: Collier Macmillan.

Anastasi, A. (1988). *Psychological testing* (6th ed.). New York: Macmillan.

Anastasi, A., & Urbina, S. (1997). *Psychological testing* (7th ed.). Upper Saddle River, NJ: Prentice Hall.

Anderson, H., & Anderson, G. (Eds.). (1951). *An introduction to projective techniques.* Upper Saddle River, NJ: Prentice Hall.

Archer, R. P. (1999). Some observations on the debate currently surrounding the Rorschach. *Assessment, 6,* 309–311.

Archer, R. P., & Gordon, R. A. (1988). MMPI and Rorschach indices of schizophrenic and depressive diagnoses among adolescent inpatients. *Journal of Personality Assessment, 52,* 276–287.

Archer, R. P., & Krishnamurthy, R. (1997). MMPI-A and Rorschach indices related to depression and conduct disorder: An evaluation of the incremental validity hypothesis. *Journal of Personality Assessment, 69,* 517–533.

Archer, R. P., & Newsom, C. R. (2000). Psychological test usage with adolescent clients: Survey update. *Assessment, 7,* 227–235.

Armitage, S. G., Greenberg, P. D., Pearl, D., Berger, D. G., and Daston, P. G. (1955). Predicting intelligence from the Rorschach. *Journal of Consulting Psychology, 19,* 321–329.

Armitage, S. G., & Pearl, D. (1957). Unsuccessful differential diagnosis from the Rorschach. *Journal of Consulting Psychology, 21,* 479–484.

Armstrong, J., Silberg, J. L., & Parente, F. J. (1986). Patterns of thought disorder on psychological testing: Implications for adolescent psychopathology. *Journal of Nervous and Mental Disease, 174,* 448–456.

Arnett, J. J. (1999). Adolescent storm and stress, reconsidered. *American Psychologist, 54,* 317–326.

Aron, L. (1980). The Rorschach: Stressful life events and locus of control (Doctoral dissertation, St. John's University, 1980). *Dissertation Abstracts International, 41,* 1489B.

Aron, L. (1982). Stressful life events and Rorschach content. *Journal of Personality Assessment, 46,* 582–585.

Aronow, E. (2001). CS norms, psychometrics, and possibilities for the Rorschach technique. *Clinical Psychology: Science and Practice, 8,* 383–385.

Aronow, E., & Koppel, M. (1997). The evolution of Hermann Rorschach's thought. *British Journal of Projective Psychology, 42,* 1–4.

Aronow, E., & Reznikoff, M. (1973). Attitudes toward the Rorschach Test expressed in book reviews: A historical perspective. *Journal of Personality Assessment, 37,* 309–315.

Aronow, E., & Reznikoff, M. (1976). *Rorschach content interpretation.* New York: Grune & Stratton.

Aronow, E., Reznikoff, M., & Moreland, K. L. (1995). The Rorschach: Projective technique or psychometric test? *Journal of Personality Assessment, 64,* 213–228.

Atkinson, L. (1986). The comparative validities of the Rorschach and MMPI: A meta-analysis. *Canadian Psychology, 27,* 238–247.

Baker, D. B., & Benjamin, L. T. (2000). The affirmation of the scientist-practitioner: A look back at Boulder. *American Psychologist, 55,* 241–247.

Baldwin, D. M. (1998). *The inter-subjective effects of Rorschach administration method: A com-*

parison of the Rapaport-Schafer and Exner systems administration. Unpublished doctoral dissertation, Long Island University.

Ball, J. D., Archer, R. P., Gordon, R. A., & French, J. (1991). Rorschach depression indices with children and adolescents: Concurrent validity findings. *Journal of Personality Assessment, 57,* 465–476.

Ball, J. D., Archer, R. P., & Imhof, E. A. (1994). Time requirements of psychological testing: A survey of practitioners. *Journal of Personality Assessment, 63,* 239–249.

Bandura, A. (1954a). The Rorschach White Space response and "oppositional" behavior. *Journal of Consulting Psychology, 18,* 17–21.

Bandura, A. (1954b). The Rorschach White Space response and perceptual reversal. *Journal of Experimental Psychology, 48,* 113–118.

Barzun, J. (1961). *Classic, romantic and modern.* Chicago: University of Chicago Press.

Bash, I. Y., & Alpert, M. (1980). The determination of malingering. *Annals of New York Academy of Sciences, 347,* 86–99.

Bash, K. W. (1955). Einstellungstyupus and Erlebnistypus: C. G. Jung and Hermann Rorschach. *Journal of Projective Techniques, 19,* 236–242.

Bash, K. W. (1982). Masters of shadows. *Journal of Personality Assessment, 46,* 1–6.

Baughman, E. E. (1951). Rorschach scores as a function of examiner differences. *Journal of Projective Techniques, 15,* 243–249.

Baughman, E. E. (1954). A comparative analysis of Rorschach forms with altered stimulus characteristics. *Journal of Projective Techniques, 18,* 151–164.

Baughman, E. E. (1958). The role of the stimulus in Rorschach responses. *Psychological Bulletin, 55,* 121–147.

Baughman, E. E. (1959). An experimental analysis of the relationship between stimulus structure and behavior on the Rorschach. *Journal of Projective Techniques, 23,* 134–183.

Baughman, E. E. (1967). The problem of the stimulus in Rorschach's test. *Journal of Projective Techniques and Personality Assessment, 31*(5), 23–25.

Beck, S. J. (1936). Autism in Rorschach scoring: A feeling comment. *Character and Personality, 5,* 83–85.

Beck, S. J. (1937a). *Introduction to the Rorschach method: A manual of personality study.* American Orthopsychiatric Association Monograph, I.

Beck, S. J. (1937b). Some present Rorschach problems. *Rorschach Research Exchange, 2,* 15–22.

Beck, S. J. (1939). Thoughts on an impending anniversary. *American Journal of Orthopsychiatry, 9,* 806–808.

Beck, S. J. (1944). *Rorschach's test: Vol. 1. Basic processes.* New York: Grune & Stratton.

Beck, S. J. (1945). *Rorschach's test: Vol. 2. A variety of personality pictures.* New York: Grune & Stratton.

Beck, S. J. (1949). *Rorschach's test: Vol. 1. Basic processes* (2nd ed., revised). New York: Grune & Stratton.

Beck, S. J. (1952). *Rorschach's test: Vol. 3. Advances in interpretation.* New York: Grune & Stratton.

Beck, S. J. (1955). Personality research and theories of personality structure: Some convergences. *Journal of Projective Techniques, 19,* 361–371.

Beck, S. J. (1959). Review of the Rorschach Inkblot Test. In O. K. Buros (Ed.), *The fifth mental measurements yearbook* (pp. 273–276). Highland Park, NJ: Gryphon Press.

Beck, S. J. (1960). *The Rorschach experiment: Ventures in blind diagnosis.* New York: Grune & Stratton.

Beck, S. J. (1968). *Reality, Rorschach and perceptual theory.* In A. I. Rabin (Ed.), *Projective techniques in personality assessment* (pp. 115–135). New York: Springer.

Beck, S. J. (1972). How the Rorschach came to America. *Journal of Personality Assessment, 36,* 105–108.

Beck, S. J., Beck, A. G., Levitt, E. E., & Molish, H. B. (1961). *Rorschach's test: Vol. 1. Basic processes* (3rd ed.). New York: Grune & Stratton.

Beck, S. J., & Molish, H. B. (1967). *Rorschach's test: Vol. 2. A variety of personality pictures* (2nd ed.). New York: Grune & Stratton.

Beck, S. J., Rabin, A. I., Thiesen, W. G., Molish, H., & Thetford, W. N. (1950). The normal personality as projected in the Rorschach Test. *Journal of Psychology, 30,* 241–298.

Belter, R. W., & Piotrowski, C. (2001). Current status of doctoral-level training in psychological testing. *Journal of Clinical Psychology, 57,* 717–726.

Benjamin, J. D. (1937). Discussion on "Some recent Rorschach problems." *Rorschach Research Exchange, 2,* 46–48.

Benton, A. L. (1950). The experimental validation of the Rorschach Test. *British Journal of Medical Psychology, 23,* 45–58.

Berger, D. (1954). Examiner influence on the Rorschach. *Journal of Clinical Psychology, 10,* 245–248.

Bergman, A., & Schubert, J. (1974). The Rorschachs of normal and emotionally disturbed children: A review of the literature. *British Journal of Projective Psychology and Personality Study, 19,* 7–13.

Berlin, I. (Ed.). (1956). *The age of enlightenment: The 18th century philosophers.* New York: New American Library.

Berlin, I. (1999). *The roots of romanticism.* Princeton, NJ: Princeton University Press.

Bernstein, L. (1956). The examiner as inhibiting factor in clinical testing. *Journal of Consulting Psychology, 20,* 287–290.

Bialick, I., & Hamlin, R. M. (1954). The clinician as judge: Details of procedure in judging projective material. *Journal of Consulting Psychology, 18,* 239–242.

Biederman, L., & Cerbus, G. (1971). Changes in Rorschach teaching. *Journal of Personality Assessment, 35,* 524–526.

Bilett, J. L., Jones, N. F., & Whitaker, L. C. (1982). Exploring schizophrenic thinking in older adolescents with the WAIS, Rorschach and WIST. *Journal of Clinical Psychology, 38,* 232–243.

Binder, H. (1932). Die helldunkeldeutungen in psychodiagnostischen experiment von Rorschach (Light-dark interpretations in Rorschach's psychodiagnostic experiment). *Schweiz Archives Neurologie und Psychiatrie, 30,* 1–67.

Binder, H. (1937a). Discussion on "Some recent Rorschach problems." *Rorschach Research Exchange, 2,* 43–44.

Binder, H. (1937b). The "light-dark" interpretations in Rorschach's experiment (J. Carlson, Trans.). *Rorschach Research Exchange, 2,* 37–42.

Blais, M. A., Norman, D. K., Quintar, B., & Herzog, D. B. (1995). The effect of administration method: A comparison of the Rapaport and Exner Rorschach systems. *Journal of Clinical Psychology, 51,* 100–107.

Blatt, S. J. (1986). Where have we been and where are we going? Reflections on 50 years of personality assessment. *Journal of Personality Assessment, 50,* 343–346.

Blatt, S. J., & Allison, J. (1963). Methodological considerations in Rorschach research: The *W* response as an expression of abstractive and integrative strivings. *Journal of Projective Techniques and Personality Assessment, 27,* 269–278.

Block, J. (1995). A contrarian view of the Five-Factor approach to personality description. *Psychological Bulletin, 117*, 187–215.

Block, N. J., & Dworkin, G. (1976). *The IQ controversy: Critical readings.* New York: Pantheon Books.

Board of Professional Affairs, American Psychological Association. (1998). Awards for distinguished professional contributions: John Exner. *American Psychologist, 53*, 391–92.

Bochner, R., & Halpern, F. (1942). *The clinical application of the Rorschach Test.* New York: Grune & Stratton.

Bochner, R., & Halpern, F. (1945). *The clinical application of the Rorschach Test* (2nd ed.). New York: Grune & Stratton.

Bohm, E. (1958). *A textbook in Rorschach Test diagnosis.* New York: Grune & Stratton. (Original work published 1951).

Bonifacio, P. P., & Schaefer, C. E. (1969). Creativity and the projection of movement responses. *Journal of Projective Techniques and Personality Assessment, 33*, 380–384.

Booth, G. C. (1937). Discussion on "Some recent Rorschach problems." *Rorschach Research Exchange, 2*, 48–53.

Bornstein, R. F. (1996). Construct validity of the Rorschach Oral Dependency Scale: 1967–1995. *Psychological Assessment, 8*, 200–205.

Bornstein, R. F. (2001). The clinical utility of the Rorschach Inkblot Method: Reframing the debate. *Journal of Personality Assessment, 77*, 39–47.

Borstelman, L. J., & Klopfer, W. G. (1953). The Szondi test: A review and critical evaluation. *Psychological Bulletin, 50*, 112–132.

Borum, R., & Grisso, T. (1995). Psychological test use in criminal forensic evaluations. *Professional Psychology: Research and Practice, 26*, 465–473.

Boswell, D. L. (1989). Rorschach *EB* as a predictor of imaging style. *Perceptual & Motor Skills, 68*, 1001–1002.

Bricklin, B. (2001). Nostalgia, integration, validity issues, and generative power: Some thoughts on Zygmunt A. Piotrowski. *Journal of Personality Assessment, 76*, 194–199.

Bricklin, B., & Bricklin, P. M. (1987). Zygmunt A. Piotrowski (1904–1985). *American Psychologist, 42*, 261–262.

Bricklin, P. M. (2001). Honoring Zygmunt A. Piotrowski: Memories and influence. *Journal of Personality Assessment, 76*, 200–202.

Broad, W., & Wade, N. (1982). *Betrayers of the truth.* New York: Simon & Schuster.

Brockway, A. L., Gleser, G. C., & Ulett, G. A. (1954). Rorschach concepts of normality. *Journal of Consulting Psychology, 18*, 259–265.

Brown, F. (1953). An exploratory study of dynamic factors in the content of the Rorschach protocol. *Journal of Projective Techniques, 17*, 251–279.

Brown, W. R., & McGuire, J. M. (1976). Current psychological assessment practices. *Professional Psychology, 7*, 475–484.

Bruno Klopfer Distinguished Contribution Award (1980). *Journal of Personality Assessment, 44*, 562.

Buros, O. K. (Ed.). (1949). *The third mental measurements yearbook.* New Brunswick, NJ: Rutgers University Press.

Buros, O. K. (Ed.). (1953). *The fourth mental measurements yearbook.* Highland Park, NJ: Gryphon Press.

Buros, O. K. (Ed.). (1959). *The fifth mental measurements yearbook.* Highland Park, NJ: Gryphon Press.

Buros, O. K. (Ed.). (1965). *The sixth mental measurements yearbook.* Highland Park, NJ: Gryphon Press.

Buros, O. K. (Ed.). (1972). *The seventh mental measurements yearbook. Vol. 1.* Highland Park, NJ: Gryphon Press.

Caine, S. L., Frueh, B. C., & Kinder, B. N. (1995). Rorschach susceptibility to malingered depressive disorders in adult females. In J. N. Butcher & C. D. Spielberger (Eds.), *Advances in personality assessment. Vol. 10* (pp. 165–174). Hillsdale, NJ: Erlbaum.

Calden, G., & Cohen, L. B. (1953). The relationship between ego-involvement and test definition to Rorschach Test performance. *Journal of Projective Techniques, 17,* 300–311.

Calkins, D. L. (1981). The Rorschach Egocentricity Index: A study of its relationship to self-esteem (Doctoral dissertation, Brigham Young University, 1980). *Dissertation Abstracts International, 42,* 365B.

Camara, W. J., Nathan, J. S., and Puente, A. E. (2000). Psychological test usage: Implications in professional psychology. *Professional Psychology: Research and practice, 31,* 141–154.

Carlson, R. (1969). Rorschach prediction of success in clinical training: A second look. *Journal of Consulting and Clinical Psychology, 33,* 699–704.

Carlson, S. (1985, December 5). A Double Blind Test of Astrology. *Nature, 318,* 419.

Carter, C. L., & Dacey, C. M. (1996). Validity of the Beck Depression Inventory, MMPI, and Rorschach in assessing adolescent depression. *Journal of Adolescence, 19,* 223–231.

Carter, J. W. (1950). The community services program of the National Institute of Mental Health, U.S. Public Health Service. *Journal of Clinical Psychology, 6,* 112–117.

Cerbus, G., & Nichols, R. C. (1963). Personality variables and response to color. *Psychological Bulletin, 60,* 566–575.

Chambers, G. S., & Hamlin, R. M. (1957). The validity of judgments based on "blind" Rorschach records. *Journal of Consulting Psychology, 21,* 105–109.

Chapman, L. J., & Chapman, J. P. (1967). Genesis of popular but erroneous psychodiagnostic observations. *Journal of Abnormal Psychology, 72,* 193–204.

Chapman, L. J., & Chapman, J. P. (1969). Illusory correlation as an obstacle to the use of valid psychodiagnostic signs. *Journal of Abnormal Psychology, 74,* 271–280.

Charny, I. W. (1959). A normative study of Rorschach "sex populars" for males. *Journal of Projective Techniques, 23,* 12–23.

Churchill, S. D. (2000). Phenomenological psychology. In A. E. Kazdin (Ed.), *Encyclopedia of psychology. Vol. 6* (pp. 163–168). Oxford, England: Oxford University Press.

Churchill, S. D., & Richer, P. (2000). Phenomenology. In A. E. Kazdin (Ed.), *Encyclopedia of psychology. Vol. 6* (pp. 168–173). Oxford, England: Oxford University Press.

Cialdini, R. B. (1993). *Influence: Science and practice* (3rd ed.). New York: HarperCollins.

Cicchetti, D. V. (1994). Guidelines, criteria, and rules of thumb for evaluating normed and standardized assessment instruments in psychology. *Psychological Assessment, 6,* 284–290.

Cicchetti, D. V., & Sparrow, S. S. (1981). Developing criteria for establishing the interrater reliability of specific items in a given inventory. *American Journal of Mental Deficiency, 86,* 127–137.

Cleveland, S. E. (1976). Reflections on the rise and fall of psychodiagnosis. *Professional Psychology, 7,* 309–318.

Cohen, J. (1960). A coefficient of agreement for nominal scales. *Educational and Psychological Measurement, 20,* 37–46.

Commager, H. S. (1977). *The empire of reason.* Garden City, NY: Anchor Press.

Cowles, M. (2001). *Statistics in psychology: An historical perspective* (2nd ed.). Mahwah, NJ: Erlbaum.

Cromer, A. (1994). Uncommon sense: The heretical nature of science. *Science, 265,* 688.

Cronbach, L. J. (1948). A validation design for qualitative studies of personality. *Journal of Consulting Psychology, 12,* 365–374.

Cronbach, L. J. (1949a). *Essentials of psychological testing.* New York: HarperCollins.

Cronbach, L. J. (1949b). "Pattern tabulation": a statistical method for analysis of limited patterns of scores, with particular reference to the Rorschach Test. *Educational and Psychological Measurement, 9,* 149–171.

Cronbach, L. J. (1949c). Statistical methods applied to Rorschach scores: A review. *Psychological Bulletin, 46,* 393–429.

Cronbach, L. J. (1950a). Statistical methods for multi-score tests. *Journal of Clinical Psychology, 6,* 21–25.

Cronbach, L. J. (1950b). Studies of the Group Rorschach in relation to success in the college of the University of Chicago. *Journal of Educational Psychology, 41,* 65–82.

Cronbach, L. J. (1954). Report on a psychometric mission to clinicia. *Psychometrika, 19,* 263–270.

Cronbach, L. J. (1955). Review of the book *Developments in Rorschach technique: Vol. I: Technique and theory. Journal of Educational Psychology, 46,* 121–123.

Cronbach, L. J. (1956). Assessment of individual differences. *Annual Review of Psychology, 7,* 173–196.

Cronbach, L. J. (1960). *Essentials of psychological testing* (2nd ed.). New York: HarperCollins.

Cronbach, L. J. (1984). *Essentials of psychological testing* (4th ed.). New York: HarperCollins.

Cronbach, L. J. (1989). Lee J. Cronbach. In G. Lindzey (Ed.), *A history of psychology in autobiography. Vol. 8* (pp. 62–93). Stanford, CA: Stanford University Press.

Cruz, E. B., Brier, N. M., & Reznikoff, M. (1997). An examination of the relationship between form level ratings on the Rorschach and learning disability status. *Journal of Psychology, 131,* 167–174.

Culross, R. R., & Nelson, S. (1997). Training in personality assessment in specialist-level school psychology programs. *Psychological Reports, 81,* 119–124.

Cummings, N. A. (2001). The professional school movement: Empowerment of the clinician in education and training. In R. Wright & N. Cummings (Eds.), *The practice of psychology: The battle for professionalism* (pp. 70–103). Phoenix, AZ: Zeig, Tucker & Theisen.

Cummings, S. T. (1954). The clinician as judge: Judgments of adjustment from Rorschach single-card performance. *Journal of Consulting Psychology, 18,* 243–247.

Cundick, B. P. (1985). Review of the Holtzman Inkblot Technique. In J. V. Mitchell (Ed.), *Ninth Mental Measurements Yearbook, Vol. 1* (pp. 661–662). Lincoln, NE: Buros Institute of Mental Measurements, University of Nebraska.

Dana, R. H. (1965). Review of the Rorschach Inkblot Test. In O. K. Buros (Ed.), *The sixth mental measurements yearbook* (pp. 492–495). Highland Park, NJ: Gryphon Press.

Dana, R. H. (1968). Six constructs to define Rorschach *M. Journal of Projective Techniques and Personality Assessment, 32,* 138–145.

Dana, R. H., & Cocking, R. R. (1968). Cue parameters, cue probabilities, and clinical judgment. *Journal of Clinical Psychology, 24,* 475–480.

Darcangelo, S. M. (1997). Psychological and personality correlates of the Massachusetts Treatment Center classification system for rapists (Doctoral dissertation, Simon Fraser University, 1996). *Dissertation Abstracts International, 58,* 2115B.

Davis, H. S. (1961). Judgments of intellectual level from various features of the Rorschach including vocabulary. *Journal of Projective Techniques, 25,* 155–157.

Dawes, R. M. (1994). *House of cards: Psychology and psychotherapy built on myth.* New York: Free Press.

Dawes, R. M. (1999). Two methods for studying the incremental validity of a Rorschach variable. *Psychological Assessment, 11,* 297–302.

DeCato, C. M. (1993a). On the Rorschach *M* response and monotheism. *Journal of Personality Assessment, 60,* 362–378.

DeCato, C. M. (1993b). Piotrowski's enduring contribution to the Rorschach [Review of the book *Perceptanalysis*]. *Journal of Personality Assessment, 61,* 584–595.

Deri, S. K. (1949). *Introduction to the Szondi test: Theory and practice.* New York: Grune & Stratton.

Dodge, K. A., & Frame, C. L. (1982). Social cognitive deficits and biases in aggressive boys. *Child Development, 53,* 8–22.

Dodge, K. A., Murphy, R. R., & Buchsbaum, K. (1984). The assessment of intention-cue detection skills in children: Implications for developmental psychopathology. *Child Development, 53,* 8–22.

Durlak, J. (1995). Understanding meta-analysis. In L. G. Grimm and P. R. Yarnold (Eds.), *Reading and understanding multivariate statistics* (pp. 319–352). Washington, DC: American Psychological Association.

Dush, D. M. (1985). Review of the Holtzman Inkblot Technique. In J. V. Mitchell (Ed.), *Ninth Mental Measurements Yearbook, Vol. 1* (pp. 602–603). Lincoln, NE: Buros Institute of Mental Measurements, University of Nebraska.

Dutton, D. L. (1988). The cold reading technique. *Experientia, 44*(4), 326–332.

Eagle, M. N. (2000). Rapaport, David. In A. E. Kazdin (Ed.), *Encyclopedia of psychology. Vol. 6.* Oxford, England: Oxford University Press.

Earle, L. (1995). *The classic reading.* Washington, DC: Binary Star Publications.

Egozi-Profeta, V. L. (1999). A comparison of the Roemer and the Rorschach Tests as tools for distinguishing characteristics of psychopathy (Doctoral dissertation, Miami Institute of Psychology of the Caribbean Center for Advanced Studies, 1998). *Dissertation Abstracts International, 60,* 1345B.

Ellenberger, H. F. (1954). The life and work of Hermann Rorschach (1884–1922). *Bulletin of the Menninger Clinic, 18,* 173–219.

Ellenberger, H. F. (1993). *Beyond the unconscious.* Princeton, NJ: Princeton University Press.

Eron, L. D. (1965). Review of the Rorschach Inkblot Test. In O. K. Buros (Ed.), *The sixth mental measurements yearbook* (pp. 495–501). Highland Park, NJ: Gryphon Press.

Exner, J. E. (1958). *The influence of color in projective testing.* Unpublished doctoral dissertation, Cornell University.

Exner, J. E. (1966). *A workbook in the Rorschach technique emphasizing the Beck and Klopfer systems.* Springfield, Ill.: Thomas.

Exner, J. E. (1969a). Rorschach responses as an index of narcissism. *Journal of Projective Techniques and Personality Assessment, 33,* 324–330.

Exner, J. E. (1969b). *The Rorschach systems.* New York: Grune & Stratton.

Exner, J. E. (1974). *The Rorschach: A Comprehensive System. Vol. 1.* New York: Wiley.

Exner, J. E. (1978). *The Rorschach: A Comprehensive System: Vol. 2. Current research and advanced interpretation.* New York: Wiley.

Exner, J. E. (1980). But it's only an inkblot. *Journal of Personality Assessment, 44,* 563–577.

Exner, J. E. (1981). Obituary: Samuel J. Beck (1896–1980). *American Psychologist, 36,* 986–987.

Exner, J. E. (1985). *A Rorschach workbook for the Comprehensive System* (2nd ed.). Asheville, NC: Rorschach Workshops.

Exner, J. E. (1986). *The Rorschach: A Comprehensive System: Vol. 1. Basic foundations* (2nd ed.). New York: Wiley.

Exner, J. E. (1990). *A Rorschach workbook for the Comprehensive System* (3rd ed.). Asheville, NC: Rorschach Workshops.

Exner, J. E. (1991). *The Rorschach: A Comprehensive System: Vol. 2. Interpretation* (2nd ed.). New York: Wiley.

Exner, J. E. (1992a). Some comments on "A conceptual critique of the *EA:es* comparison in the Comprehensive Rorschach System." *Psychological Assessment, 4,* 297–300.

Exner, J. E. (1992b). *R* in Rorschach research: A ghost revisited. *Journal of Personality Assessment, 58,* 245–251.

Exner, J. E. (1993). *The Rorschach: A Comprehensive System: Vol. 1. Basic foundations* (3rd ed.). New York: Wiley.

Exner, J. E. (1995a). Comment on "Narcissism in the Comprehensive System for the Rorschach." *Clinical Psychology: Science and Practice, 2,* 200–206.

Exner, J. E. (1995b). *A Rorschach workbook for the Comprehensive System* (4th ed.). Asheville, NC: Rorschach Workshops.

Exner, J. E. (1996). A comment on "The Comprehensive System for the Rorschach: A critical examination." *Psychological Science, 7,* 11–13.

Exner, J. E. (1997). The future of Rorschach in personality assessment. *Journal of Personality Assessment, 68,* 37–46.

Exner, J. E. (1999). The Rorschach: Measurement concepts and issues of validity. In S. E. Embretson & S. L. Hershberger (Eds.), *The new rules of measurement: What every psychologist and educator should know* (pp. 159–183). Mahwah, NJ: Erlbaum.

Exner, J. E. (2000). *A primer for Rorschach interpretation.* Asheville, NC: Rorschach Workshops.

Exner, J. E. (2001a). A comment on "The misperception of psychopathology: Problems with the norms of the Comprehensive System for the Rorschach." *Clinical Psychology: Science and Practice, 8,* 386–388.

Exner, J. E. (2001b). *A Rorschach workbook for the Comprehensive System* (5th ed.). Asheville, NC: Rorschach Workshops.

Exner, J. E. (2002a). A new nonpatient sample for the Rorschach Comprehensive System: A progress report. *Journal of Personality Assessment, 78,* 391–404.

Exner, J. E. (2002b). The Rorschach archives and museum. *SPA Exchange, 13*(1), 4.

Exner, J. E., Armbruster, G. L., & Viglione, D. (1978). The temporal stability of some Rorschach features. *Journal of Personality Assessment, 42,* 474–482.

Exner, J. E., & Exner, D. E. (1972). How clinicians use the Rorschach. *Journal of Personality Assessment, 36,* 403–408.

Exner, J. E., & Martin, L. S. (1983). The Rorschach: A history and description of the Comprehensive System. *School Psychology, 12,* 407–413.

Exner, J. E., & Sendin, C. (1997). Some issues in Rorschach research. *European Journal of Psychological Assessment, 13,* 155–163.

Exner, J. E., & Weiner, I. B. (1982). *The Rorschach: A Comprehensive System: Vol. 3. Assessment of children and adolescents.* New York: Wiley.

Exner, J. E., & Weiner, I. B. (1995). *The Rorschach: A Comprehensive System: Vol. 3. Assessment of children and adolescents* (2nd ed.). New York: Wiley.

Exner, J. E., Weiner, I. B., & Schyler, W. (1976). *A Rorschach workbook for the Comprehensive System.* Bayville, NY: Rorschach Workshops.

Eysenck, H. J. (1945). A comparative study of four screening tests for neurotics. *Psychological Bulletin, 42,* 659–662.

Eysenck, H. J. (1959). Review of the Rorschach Inkblot Test. In O. K. Buros (Ed.), *The fifth mental measurements yearbook* (pp. 276–278). Highland Park, NJ: Gryphon Press.

Faust, D. (1984). *The limits of scientific reasoning.* Minneapolis: University of Minnesota Press.

Fielding, B., & Brown, F. (1956). Prediction of intelligence from certain Rorschach factors. *Journal of Clinical Psychology, 12,* 196–197.

Finn, S. E. (2002). How SPA can help promote personality assessment. *SPA Exchange, 13*(1, Winter), 1–2.

Fischoff, B. (1975). Hindsight does not equal foresight: The effect of outcome knowledge on judgment under uncertainty. *Journal of Experimental Psychology: Human Perception and Performance, 1,* 288–299.

Fisher, S. (1967). Projective methodologies. *Annual Review of Psychology, 18,* 165–190.

Fiske, D. W., & Baughman, E. E. (1953). Relationships between Rorschach scoring categories and the total number of responses. *Journal of Abnormal and Social Psychology, 48,* 25–32.

Fleiss, J. L. (1981). *Statistical methods for rates and proportions* (2nd ed.). New York: Wiley.

Fletcher, R. (1991). *Science, ideology, and the media: The Cyril Burt scandal.* New Brunswick, NJ: Transaction.

Fonda, C. P. (1951). The nature and meaning of the Rorschach White Space response. *Journal of Abnormal and Social Psychology, 46,* 367–377.

Fonda, C. P. (1960). The white-space response. In M. A. Rickers-Ovsiankina (Ed.), *Rorschach psychology* (pp. 80–105). New York: Wiley.

Fonda, C. P. (1977). The white-space response. In M. A. Rickers-Ovsiankina (Ed.), *Rorschach psychology* (2nd ed.), (pp. 113–156). Huntington, NY: Krieger.

Ford, M. (1975). *The application of the Rorschach Test to young children.* Westport, CT: Greenwood Press. (Originally published in 1946 by the University of Minnesota).

Forer, B. R. (1949). The fallacy of personal validation: A classroom demonstration of gullibility. *Journal of Abnormal and Social Psychology, 44,* 118–123.

Fowler, R. D. (1992). The American Psychological Association: 1985 to 1992. In R. B. Evans, V. S. Sexton, & T. C. Cadwallader (Eds.), *100 years. The American Psychological Association: A historical perspective* (pp. 263–299). Washington, DC: American Psychological Association.

Foxhall, K. (2000, October). Platform for a long-term push. *Monitor on Psychology, 31*(9), 30–31. This article is also available at http://www.apa.org/monitor/oct00/push.html. Access date: October 22, 2002.

Frank, G. (1976). On the validity of hypotheses derived from the Rorschach: I. The relationship between Color and affect. *Perceptual and Motor Skills, 43,* 411–427.

Frank, G. (1979). On the validity of hypotheses derived from the Rorschach: VI. *M* and the intrapsychic life of individuals. *Perceptual and Motor Skills, 48,* 1267–1277.

Frank, G. (1993a). C' and depression. *Psychological Reports, 72,* 1184–1186.

Frank, G. (1993b). On the meaning of movement responses on the Rorschach. *Psychological Reports, 73,* 1219–1225.

Frank, G. (1993c). On the validity of hypotheses derived from the Rorschach: The relationship between Color and affect; Update 1992. *Psychological Reports, 73,* 12–14.

Frank, G. (1993d). On the validity of Rorschach's hypotheses: The relationship of Space responses to oppositionalism. *Psychological Reports, 72,* 1111–1114.

Frank, L. (1939a). Comments on the proposed standardization of the Rorschach method. *Rorschach Research Exchange, 3,* 101–105.

Frank, L. (1939b). Projective methods for the study of personality. *Journal of Psychology, 8,* 389–413.

Frank, L. (1948). *Projective methods.* Springfield, Ill.: Thomas.

Freud, S. (1965). *New introductory lectures on psychoanalysis.* New York: Norton. (Originally published 1933).

Frueh, B. C., & Kinder, B. N. (1994). The susceptibility of the Rorschach Inkblot Test to malingering of combat-related PTSD. *Journal of Personality Assessment, 62,* 280–298.

Furnham, A., & Schofield, S. (1987). Accepting personality test feedback: A review of the Barnum effect. *Current Psychological Research & Reviews, 6,* 162–178.

Gacono, C. B. (1989). A Rorschach analysis of object relations and defensive structure and their relationship to narcissism and psychopathy in a group of antisocial offenders (Doctoral dissertation, United States International University, 1988). *Dissertation Abstracts International, 49,* 4536B.

Gacono, C. B. (1990). An empirical study of object relations and defensive operations in antisocial personality disorder. *Journal of Personality Assessment, 54,* 589–600.

Gacono, C. B., DeCato, C. M., Brabender, V., & Goertzel, T. G. (1997). Vitamin C or Pure C: The Rorschach of Linus Pauling. In J. R. Meloy, M. W. Acklin, C. B. Gacono, J. F. Murray, & C. A. Person (Eds.), *Contemporary Rorschach interpretation* (pp. 421–451). Mahwah, NJ: Erlbaum.

Gacono, C. B., Loving, J. L., and Bodholdt, R. H. (2001). The Rorschach and psychopathy: Toward a more accurate understanding of the research findings. *Journal of Personality Assessment, 77,* 16–38.

Gacono, C. B., & Meloy, J. R. (1991). A Rorschach investigation of attachment and anxiety in antisocial personality disorder. *Journal of Nervous and Mental Disease, 179,* 546–552.

Gacono, C. B., & Meloy, J. R. (1992). The Rorschach and the DSM-III-R antisocial personality: A tribute to Robert Lindner. *Journal of Clinical Psychology, 48,* 393–406.

Gacono, C. B., & Meloy, J. R. (1994). *The Rorschach assessment of aggressive and psychopathic personalities.* Hillsdale, NJ: Erlbaum.

Gacono, C. B., Meloy, J. R., & Berg, J. L. (1992). Object relations, defensive operations, and affective states in narcissistic, borderline, and antisocial personality disorder. *Journal of Personality Assessment, 59,* 32–49.

Gacono, C. B., Meloy, J. R., & Heaven, T. R. (1990). A Rorschach investigation of narcissism and hysteria in antisocial personality. *Journal of Personality Assessment, 55,* 270–279.

Ganellen, R. J. (1996a). Comparing the diagnostic efficiency of the MMPI, MCMI-II, and Rorschach: A review. *Journal of Personality Assessment, 67,* 219–243.

Ganellen, R. J. (1996b). *Integrating the Rorschach and the MMPI-2 in personality assessment.* Mahwah, NJ: Erlbaum.

Ganellen, R. J. (2001). Weighing evidence for the Rorschach's validity: A response to Wood et al. (1999). *Journal of Personality Assessment, 77,* 1–15.

Garb, H. N. (1984). The incremental validity of information used in personality testing. *Clinical Psychology Review, 4,* 641–655.

Garb, H. N. (1998). *Studying the clinician: Judgment research and psychological assessment.* Washington, DC: American Psychological Association.

Garb, H. N. (1999). Call for a moratorium on the use of the Rorschach Inkblot in clinical and forensic settings. *Assessment, 6,* 313–315.

Garb, H. N., Florio, C. M., & Grove, W. M. (1998). The validity of the Rorschach and the Minnesota Multiphasic Personality Inventory: Results from meta-analyses. *Psychological Science, 9,* 402–404.

Garb, H. N., Florio, C. M., & Grove, W. M. (1999). The Rorschach controversy: Reply to Parker, Hunsley, and Hanson. *Psychological Science, 10,* 293–294.

Garb, H. N., Klein, D. F., & Grove, W. M. (2002). Comparison of medical and psychological tests. *American Psychologist, 57,* 137–138.

Garb, H. N., Wood, J. M., Lilienfeld, S. O., & Nezworski, M. T. (2002). Effective use of projective techniques in clinical practice: Let the data help with selection and interpretation. *Professional Psychology: Research and Practice, 33,* 454–463.

Garb, H. N., Wood, J. M., & Nezworski, M. T. (2000). Projective techniques and the detection of child sexual abuse. *Child Maltreatment, 5,* 161–168.

Garb, H. N., Wood, J. M., Nezworski, M. T., Grove, W. M., & Stejskal, W. J. (2001). Towards a resolution of the Rorschach controversy. *Psychological Assessment, 13,* 433–448.

Garfield, S. L. (2000). The Rorschach Test in clinical diagnosis: A brief commentary. *Journal of Clinical Psychology, 56,* 431–434.

Gibby, R. G. (1952). Examiner influence on the Rorschach inquiry. *Journal of Consulting Psychology, 16,* 449–455.

Gibby, R. G., Miller, D. R., & Walker, E. L. (1953). The examiner's influence on the Rorschach protocol. *Journal of Consulting Psychology, 17,* 425–428.

Gist, R., & Lubin, B. (1999). *Response to disaster: Psychosocial, community, and ecological approaches.* Philadelphia: Brunner/Mazel.

Goddard, H. H. (1908). The Binet and Simon tests of intellectual capacity. *Training School Bulletin, 5*(10), 3–9.

Goddard, H. H. (1910). A measuring scale for intelligence. *Training School Bulletin, 6,* 146–155.

Goddard, H. H. (1912). *The Kallikak family: A study in the heredity of feeble-mindedness.* New York: Macmillan.

Goddard, H. H. (1914). *Feeblemindedness: Its causes and consequences.* New York: Macmillan.

Goggin, J. E., & Goggin, E. B. (2000). *Death of a "Jewish science": Psychoanalysis in the Third Reich.* West Lafayette, IN: Purdue University Press.

Goldberg, L. R. (1991). Human mind versus regression equation: Five contrasts. In D. Cicchetti and W. M. Grove (Eds.), *Thinking clearly about psychology: Vol. 1. Matters of public interest* (pp. 173–184). Minneapolis: University of Minnesota Press.

Goldberg, L. R. (1993). The structure of phenotypic personality traits. *American Psychologist, 48,* 266–275.

Goldfried, M. R., Stricker, G., & Weiner, I. B. (1971). *Rorschach handbook of clinical and research applications.* Upper Saddle River, NJ: Prentice Hall.

Golding, S. L., & Rorer, L. G. (1972). Illusory correlation and subjective judgment. *Journal of Abnormal Psychology, 80,* 249–260.

Goode, E. (2001). What's in an inkblot? Some say, not much. *New York Times,* February 20, D1.

Goodenough, F. L. (1949). *Mental testing: Its history, principles, and applications.* New York: Rinehart.

Gottesman, I. I. (1991). *Schizophrenia genesis.* New York: Freeman.

Gottfredson, G. D., & Dyer, S. E. (1979). Health service providers in psychology. In C. A. Kiesler, N. A. Cummings, & G. R. VandenBos (Eds.), *Psychology and national health insurance: A sourcebook* (pp. 85–110). Washington, DC: American Psychological Association.

Grant, M. Q., Ives, V., & Ranzoni, J. H. (1952). Reliability and validity of judges' ratings of adjustment on the Rorschach [Whole issue]. *Psychological Monographs, 66*(2).

Gray, W. D. (1991). *Thinking critically about New Age ideas.* Belmont, CA: Wadsworth.

Great Man Award: Bruno Klopfer. (1966). *Journal of Projective Techniques and Personality Assessment, 30,* 509–511.

Greaves, A. R. (2000). *A validation of Wagner's Rorschach autism classification system.* Unpublished doctoral dissertation, Forest Institute of Professional Psychology.

Greene, R. L. (2000). *The MMPI-2: An interpretive manual.* Boston: Allyn & Bacon.

Greenwald, D. F. (1990). An external construct validity study of Rorschach personality variables. *Journal of Personality Assessment, 55,* 768–780.

Greenwald, D. F. (1991). Personality dimensions reflected by the Rorschach and the 16PF. *Journal of Clinical Psychology, 47,* 708–715.

Greenwald, D. F. (1999). Relationships between the Rorschach and the NEO-Five Factor Inventory. *Psychological Reports, 85,* 519–527.

Gross, L. R. (1959). Effects of verbal and nonverbal reinforcement on the Rorschach. *Journal of Consulting Psychology, 23,* 66–68.

Grosskurth, P. (1991). *Secret ring: Freud's inner circle and the politics of psychoanalysis.* Reading Mass.: Addison-Wesley.

Grossman, L. S., Wasyliw, O. E., Benn, A. F., & Gyoerkoe, K. L. (2002). Can sex offenders who minimize on the MMPI conceal psychopathology on the Rorschach. *Journal of Personality Assessment, 78,* 484–501.

Groth-Marnat, G. (1990). *Handbook of psychological assessment* (2nd ed.). New York: Wiley.

Groth-Marnat, G. (1997). *Handbook of psychological assessment* (3rd ed.). New York: Wiley.

Grove, W. M., & Barden, R. C. (1999). Protecting the integrity of the legal system: The admissibility of testimony from mental health experts under *Daubert/Kumho* analyses. *Psychology, Public Policy, and Law, 5,* 224–242.

Grove, W. M., Barden, R. C., Garb, H. N., & Lilienfeld, S. O. (2002). Failure of Rorschach Comprehensive System–based testimony to be admissible under *Daubert–Joiner–Kumho* Standard. *Psychology, Public Policy, and the Law, 8,* 216–234.

Grove, W. M., Zald, D. H., Lebow, B. S., Snitz, B. E., & Nelson, C. (2000). Clinical versus mechanical prediction: A meta-analysis. *Psychological Assessment, 12,* 19–30.

Guarnaccia, V., Dill, C. A., Sabatino, S., & Southwick, S. (2001). Scoring accuracy using the Comprehensive System for the Rorschach. *Journal of Personality Assessment, 77,* 464–474.

Guilford, J. P. (1948). Some lessons from aviation psychology. *American Psychologist, 3,* 3–11.

Guirdham, A. (1937). Discussion on "Some recent Rorschach problems." *Rorschach Research Exchange, 2,* 72–73.

Gurvitz, M. S. (1951). A forerunner of Rorschach. *Journal of Consulting Psychology, 15,* 120–121.

Hagen, M. A., & Castagna, N. (2001). The real numbers: Psychological testing in custody evaluations. *Professional Psychology: Research and Practice, 32,* 269–271.

Haines, J. D. (2002). The king of quacks: Albert Abrams, M.D. *Skeptical Inquirer, 26*(3), 45–48.

Haller, N., & Exner, J. E. (1985). The reliability of Rorschach variables for inpatients present-ing symptoms of depression and/or helplessness. *Journal of Personality Assessment, 49,* 516–521.

Hamel, M., Shaffer, T. W., & Erdberg, P. (2000). A study of nonpatient preadolescent Rorschach protocols. *Journal of Personality Assessment, 75,* 280–294.

Handler, L. (1994). Bruno Klopfer, a measure of the man and his work [Review of *Develop-ments in the Rorschach Technique: Volumes I, II, and III*]. *Journal of Personality Assess-ment, 62,* 562–577.

Handler, L. (1996). John Exner and the book that started it all [Review of *The Rorschach Sys-tems*]. *Journal of Personality Assessment, 66,* 650–658.

Hare, R. D. (1991). *Manual for the Revised Psychopathy Checklist.* Toronto: Multi-Health Sys-tems.

Harper, G., & Scott, R. (1990). Learning disabilities: An appraisal of Rorschach response pat-terns. *Psychological Reports, 67,* 691–696.

Harriman, P. L. (1946). Review of *Rorschach's Test. II. A Variety of Personality Pictures. Rorschach Research Exchange, 10,* 37–39.

Harris, D. B. (1963). *Children's drawings as measures of intellectual maturity: A revision and extension of the Goodenough Draw-a-Man Test.* Orlando: Harcourt Brace.

Harris, J. G. (1960). Validity: The search for a constant in a universe of variables. In M. A. Rickers-Ovsiankina (Ed.), *Rorschach psychology* (pp. 380–439). New York: Wiley.

Harrower, M. R. (1950). Group techniques for the Rorschach Test. In L. E. Abt and L. Bellak (Eds.), *Projective psychology* (pp. 146–184). New York: Knopf.

Harrower, M. R. (1954). Clinical aspects of failures in projective techniques. *Journal of Projec-tive Techniques, 18,* 294–302.

Harrower, M. R., & Steiner, M. E. (1951). *Large scale Rorschach techniques: A manual for the Group Rorschach and Multiple Choice tests* (2nd ed.). Springfield, Ill.: Thomas.

Harrower-Erickson, M. R. (1943). A multiple choice test for screening purposes (for use with the Rorschach cards or slides). *Psychosomatic Medicine, 5,* 330–341).

Harrower-Erickson, M. R., & Steiner, M. E. (1945). *Large scale Rorschach techniques: A manual for the Group Rorschach and Multiple Choice Test.* Springfield, Ill.: Thomas.

Hastorf, A. H., & Cantril, H. (1954). They saw a game: A case study. *Journal of Abnormal and Social Psychology, 49,* 129–134.

Hathaway, S. R., & McKinley, J. C. (1951). *MMPI manual.* New York: Psychological Corpora-tion.

Hathaway, S. R., & Meehl, P. E. (1951). *An atlas for the clinical use of the MMPI.* Minneapolis: University of Minnesota Press.

Hauser, R. J. (1963). The validity of the formal and linguistic aspects of the Rorschach in pre-dicting intelligence (Doctoral dissertation, New York University, 1962). *Dissertation Abstracts International, 24,* 833.

Hayes, S. C. (1989). An interview with Lee Sechrest: The courage to say "We do not know how." *APS Observer, 2*(4), 8–10.

Heilbrun, K. (1992). The role of psychological testing in forensic assessment. *Law and Human Behavior, 16,* 257–272.

Henry, E., & Rotter, J. B. (1956). Situational influence on Rorschach responses. *Journal of Con-sulting Psychology, 20,* 457–462.

Hersen, M., & Greaves, S. T. (1971). Rorschach productivity as related to verbal reinforcement. *Journal of Personality Assessment, 35,* 436–441.

Hertz, M. R. (1935). The Rorschach Ink-Blot Test: Historical summary. *Psychological Bulletin, 32,* 33–66.

Hertz, M. R. (1937). Discussion on "Some recent Rorschach problems." *Rorschach Research Exchange, 2,* 53–65.

Hertz, M. R. (1940). The Shading response in the Rorschach Inkblot Test: A review of its scoring and interpretation. *Journal of General Psychology, 23,* 123–167.

Hertz, M. R. (1942). Rorschach: Twenty years after. *Psychological Bulletin, 39,* 529–572.

Hertz, M. R. (1951). Current problems in Rorschach theory and technique. *Journal of Projective Techniques, 15,* 307–338.

Hertz, M. R. (1959). The use and misuse of the Rorschach method. I. Variations in the Rorschach procedure. *Journal of Projective Techniques, 23,* 33–48.

Hertz, M. R. (1970a). Bruno Klopfer: An appreciation. In B. Klopfer, M. Meyer, F. Brawer, & W. Klopfer (Eds.), *Development in the Rorschach technique: Vol. 3. Aspects of personality structure* (pp. ix-xiv). Orlando: Harcourt Brace.

Hertz, M. R. (1970b). Projective techniques in crisis. *Journal of Projective Techniques and Personality Assessment, 34,* 449–467.

Hertz, M. R. (1977). The organization activity. In M. A. Rickers-Ovsiankina (Ed.), *Rorschach psychology* (2nd ed.), (pp. 29–82). Huntington, NY: Krieger.

Hertz, M. R. (1986). Rorschachbound: A 50-year memoir. *Journal of Personality Assessment, 50,* 396–416.

Hess, A. K., & Weiner, I. B. (1999). *The handbook of forensic psychology* (2nd ed.). New York: Wiley.

Higgins, E. T., & Bargh, J. A. (1987). Social cognition and social perception. *Annual Review of Psychology, 38,* 369–425.

Hilgard, E. R. (1987). *Psychology in America: A historical survey.* Orlando: Harcourt Brace.

Hill, E. F. (1972). *The Holtzman inkblot technique.* San Francisco: Jossey-Bass.

Hiller, J. B., Rosenthal, R., Bornstein, R. F., Berry, D.T.R., Brunell-Neuleib, S. (1999). A comparative meta-analysis of Rorschach and MMPI validity. *Psychological Assessment, 11,* 278–296.

Hilsenroth, M. J., Fowler, J. C., Padawer, J. R., & Handler, L. (1997). Narcissism in the Rorschach revisited: Some reflections on empirical data. *Psychological Assessment, 9,* 113–121.

Hilsenroth, M. J., & Handler, L. (1995). A survey of graduate students' experiences, interests, and attitudes about learning the Rorschach. *Journal of Personality Assessment, 64,* 243–257.

Himelstein, P. D. (1984). Construct validity of two measures of narcissism (Doctoral dissertation, Florida Institute of Technology, 1983). *Dissertation Abstracts International, 44,* 3528B.

Hines, T. (1988). *Pseudoscience and paranormal: A critical examination of the evidence.* Buffalo, NY: Prometheus Books.

Hobbs, N. (1963). Statement on mental illness and mental retardation. *American Psychologist, 18,* 295–299.

Hoffer, E. (1963). *The true believer.* New York: Time Reading Program. (Originally published 1951).

Holbrook, S. H. (1959). *The golden age of quackery.* New York: Macmillan.

Holt, R. R. (1967a). David Rapaport: A memoir. In R. R. Holt (Ed.), *Motives and thought: Psychoanalytic essays in honor of David Rapaport* (pp. 7–17). New York: International Universities Press.

Holt, R. R. (1967b). Diagnostic testing: Present status and future prospects. *Journal of Nervous and Mental Disease, 144,* 444–465.

Holtzman, W. H. (1950). Validation studies of the Rorschach Test: Shyness and gregariousness in the normal superior adult. *Journal of Clinical Psychology, 6,* 343–347.

Holtzman, W. H. (1988). Beyond the Rorschach. *Journal of Personality Assessment, 52,* 578–609.

Holtzman, W. H. (2000). Application of the Holtzman inkblot technique in different cultures. In R. H. Dana (Ed.), *Handbook of cross-cultural and multicultural personality assessment* (pp. 393–417). Mahwah, NJ: Erlbaum.

Holtzman, W. H., Díaz-Guerrero, R., & Swartz, J. D. (1975). *Personality development in two cultures.* Austin: University of Texas Press.

Holtzman, W. H., & Sells, S. B. (1954). Prediction of flying success by clinical analysis of test protocols. *Journal of Abnormal and Social Psychology, 49,* 485–490.

Holtzman, W. H., & Swartz, J. D. (1990). Use of the Holtzman Inkblot Technique (HIT) with children. In C. R. Reynolds & R. W. Kamphaus (Eds.), *Handbook of psychological and educational assessment of children* (pp. 187–203). New York: Guilford Press.

Holtzman, W. H., Thorpe, J. S., Swartz, J. D., & Herron, E. W. (1961). *Inkblot perception and personality.* Austin: University of Texas Press.

Hooker, E. (1960). The fable. *Journal of Projective Techniques, 24,* 240–245.

Hornstein, G. A. (1992). The return of the repressed: Psychology's problematic relations with psychoanalysis, 1909–1960. *American Psychologist, 47,* 254–263.

Houck, R. L., & Dawson, J. G. (1978). Comparative study of persisters and leavers in seminary training. *Psychological Reports, 42,* 1131–1137.

Hunsley, J., & Bailey, J. M. (1999). The clinical utility of the Rorschach: Unfulfilled promises and an uncertain future. *Psychological Assessment, 11,* 266–277.

Hunsley, J., & Bailey, J. M. (2001). Whither the Rorschach? An analysis of the evidence. *Psychological Assessment, 13,* 472–485.

Hunsley, J., & Di Giulio, G. (2001). Norms, norming, and clinical assessment. *Clinical Psychology: Science and Practice, 8,* 378–382.

Hunt, M. (1999). *How science takes stock: The story of meta-analysis.* New York: Russell Sage Foundation.

Hunter, J. E., & Schmidt, F. L. (1990). *Methods of meta-analysis: Correcting error and bias in research findings.* Thousand Oaks, CA: Sage.

Hyman, R. (1981). Cold reading: How to convince strangers that you know all about them. In K. Frazier (Ed.), *Paranormal borderlands of science* (pp. 79–96). Buffalo, NY: Prometheus.

Ilonen, T., Taiminen, T., Karlsson, H., Lauerma, H., Leinonen, K.-M., Wallenius, E., Tuimala, P., & Salokangas, R. (1999). Diagnostic efficiency of the Rorschach schizophrenia and depression indices in identifying first-episode schizophrenia and severe depression. *Psychiatry Research, 87,* 183–192.

Jackson, C. W., & Wohl, J. (1966). A survey of Rorschach teaching in the university. *Journal of Projective Techniques, 30*(2), 115–134.

Jacques, M. F. (1991). The Rorschach Egocentricity Index: A validation study (Doctoral dissertation, California School of Professional Psychology, San Diego, 1990). *Dissertation Abstracts International, 52,* 1064B.

Jansak, D. M. (1997). The Rorschach Comprehensive System Depression Index, depression heterogeneity, and the role of self-schema (Doctoral dissertation, California School of

Professional Psychology, San Diego, 1996). *Dissertation Abstracts International, 57,* 6576B.

Jensen, A. R. (1958). Personality. *Annual Review of Psychology, 9,* 295–322.

Jensen, A. R. (1959). The reliability of projective techniques: Review of the literature. *Acta Psychologica, 16,* 108–136.

Jensen, A. R. (1965). Review of the Rorschach Inkblot Test. In O. K. Buros (Ed.), *The sixth mental measurements yearbook* (pp. 501–509). Highland Park, NJ: Gryphon Press.

Jensen, A. R. (1995). IQ and science: The mysterious Burt affair. In N. J. Mackintosh (Ed.), *Cyril Burt: Fraud or framed* (pp. 1–12). Oxford, England: Oxford University Press.

Jensen, A. R. (1998). *The g factor: The science of mental ability.* Westport, CT: Praeger.

Jensen, M. B., & Rotter, J. B. (1945). The validity of the Multiple Choice Rorschach Test in officer candidate selection. *Psychological Bulletin, 42,* 182–185.

Johnston, M. H., & Holzman, P. S. (1979). *Assessing schizophrenic thinking.* San Francisco: Jossey-Bass.

Jorgensen, K., Andersen, T. J., & Dam, H. (2000). The diagnostic efficiency of the Rorschach depression index and the schizophrenia index: A review. *Assessment, 7,* 259–280.

Joynson, R. B. (1989). *The Burt affair.* London: Routledge.

Kaplan, R. (2001). *Science says: A collection of quotations on the history, meaning, and practice of science.* New York: Freeman.

Kaplan, R. M., & Saccuzzo, D. P. (1982). *Psychological testing: Principles, applications, and issues.* Monterey, CA: Brooks/Cole.

Kaufman, A. S., & Lichtenberger, E. O. (1999). *Essentials of WAIS-III assessment.* New York: Wiley.

Kaufman, A. S., & Lichtenberger, E. O. (2000). *Essentials of WISC-III and WPPSI-R assessment.* New York: Wiley.

Keehn, J. D. (1953a). Rorschach validation: III. An examination of the role of Colour as a determinant in the Rorschach Test. *Journal of Mental Science, 99,* 410–438.

Keehn, J. D. (1953b). Rorschach validation: II. The validity of Colour Shock in the diagnosis of neuroticism. *Journal of Mental Science, 99,* 224–234.

Kelly, E. L., & Fiske, D. W. (1950). The prediction of success in the VA training program in clinical psychology. *American Psychologist, 5,* 395–406.

Kelly, E. L., & Fiske, D. W. (1951). *The prediction of performance in clinical psychology.* Ann Arbor: University of Michigan Press.

Kelly, E. L., & Goldberg, L. R. (1959). Correlates of later performance and specialization in psychology: A follow-up study of the trainees assessed in the VA Selection Research Project [Whole issue]. *Psychological Monographs, 73* (482).

Kelly, R. J., & Ben-Meir, S. (1993). Emotional effects. In J. Waterman, R. J. Kelly, M. K. Oliveri, and J. McCord (Eds.), *Behind the playground walls: Sexual abuse in preschools* (pp. 106–119). New York: Guilford Press.

Kennedy, M. L., Faust, D., Willis, W. G., & Piotrowski, C. (1994). Social-emotional assessment practices in school psychology. *Journal of Psychoeducational Assessment, 12,* 228–240.

Kerman, E. F. (1959). Cypress knees and the blind: Response of blind subjects to the Kerman Cypress Knee Projective Technic (KCK). *Journal of Projective Techniques, 23,* 49–56.

Kessler, J. W. (1994). Marguerite R. Hertz (1899–1992). *American Psychologist, 49,* 1084.

Kleiger, J. H. (1992a). A conceptual critique of the EA:es comparison in the Comprehensive Rorschach System. *Psychological Assessment, 4,* 288–296.

Kleiger, J. H. (1992b). A responses to Exner's comments on "A conceptual critique of the EA:es comparison in the Comprehensive Rorschach System." *Psychological Assessment, 4,* 301–302.

Kleiger, J. H. (1993). The enduring Rorschach contributions of David Rapaport. *Journal of Personality Assessment, 61,* 198–205.

Kleiger, J. H. (1999). *Disordered thinking and the Rorschach.* Hillsdale, NJ: Analytic Press.

Klopfer, B. (1937a). Discussion on "Some recent Rorschach problems." *Rorschach Research Exchange, 2,* 66–68.

Klopfer, B. (1937b). The present status of the theoretical development of the Rorschach method. *Rorschach Research Exchange, 1,* 142–147.

Klopfer, B. (1937c). The technique of the Rorschach performance. *Rorschach Research Exchange, 2,* 1–14.

Klopfer, B. (1939). Shall the Rorschach method be standardized? *Rorschach Research Exchange, 3,* 45–54.

Klopfer, B. (1940). Personality aspects revealed by the Rorschach method. *Rorschach Research Exchange, 4,* 26–29.

Klopfer, B. (Ed.). (1956). *Developments in the Rorschach technique: Vol. 2. Fields of application.* Yonkers-on-Hudson, NY: World Book.

Klopfer, B. (1957). Psychological variables in human cancer. *Journal of Projective Techniques, 21,* 331–340.

Klopfer, B. (1961). C. G. Jung—1875–1961. *Journal of Projective Techniques, 25,* 250–251.

Klopfer, B., Ainsworth, M. D., Klopfer, W. G., & Holt, R. R. (Eds.). (1954). *Developments in the Rorschach technique: Vol. 1. Technique and theory.* Yonkers-on-Hudson, NY: World Book Company.

Klopfer, B., & Davidson, H. H. (1937). Record blank for the Rorschach method. *Rorschach Research Exchange, 2*(1), Appendix.

Klopfer, B., & Davidson, H. H. (1944). Form level rating: A preliminary proposal for appraising mode and level of thinking as expressed in Rorschach records. *Rorschach Research Exchange, 8,* 164–167.

Klopfer, B., & Davidson, H. H. (1962). *The Rorschach technique: An introductory manual.* Orlando: Harcourt Brace.

Klopfer, B., & Kelley, D. M. (1942). *The Rorschach technique.* Yonkers-on-Hudson, NY: World Book.

Klopfer, B., & Kelley, D. M. (1946). *The Rorschach technique* (2nd ed.). Yonkers-on-Hudson, NY: World Book.

Klopfer, B., Kirkner, F., Wisham, W., & Baker, G. (1951). Rorschach Prognostic Rating Scale. *Journal of Projective Techniques and Personality Assessment, 15,* 425–428.

Klopfer, B., Meyer, M., Brawer, F., & Klopfer, W. (Eds.). (1970). *Developments in the Rorschach technique. Vol. 3. Aspects of personality structure.* Orlando: Harcourt Brace.

Klopfer, B., & Sender, S. (1936). A system of refined scoring symbols. *Rorschach Research Exchange, 1,* 19–22.

Klopfer, W. G. (1968). Current status of the Rorschach Test. In P. McReynolds (Ed.), *Advances in psychological assessment. Vol. 1* (pp. 131–149). Palo Alto, CA: Science and Behavior Books.

Klopfer, W. G. (1971). In memory of Bruno Klopfer. *Journal of Personality Assessment, 35,* 501.

Klopfer, W. G., & Taulbee, E. S. (1976). Projective tests. *Annual Review of Psychology, 27,* 543–567.

Kohn, A. (1986). *False prophets.* Oxford, England: Basil Blackwell.

Korchin, S. J. (1960). Form perception and ego functioning. In M. A. Rickers-Ovsiankina (Ed.), *Rorschach psychology* (pp. 109–129). New York: Wiley.

Korchin, S. J., & Larson, D. G. (1977). Form perception and ego functioning. In M. A. Rickers-Ovsiankina (Ed.), *Rorschach psychology* (2nd ed.), (pp. 159–187). Huntington, NY: Krieger.

Krasner, L. (1958). Studies of the conditioning of verbal behavior. *Psychological Bulletin, 55,* 148–170.

Krugman, M. (1940). Out of the ink well: The Rorschach method. *Rorschach Research Exchange, 4,* 91–101.

Krugman, M. (1949). Review of the Rorschach Inkblot Test. In O. K. Buros (Ed.), *The third mental measurements yearbook* (pp. 132–133). New Brunswick, NJ: Rutgers University Press.

Kubiszyn, T. W., Meyer, G. J., Finn, S. E., Eyde, L. D., Kay, G. G., Moreland, K. L., Dies, R. R., & Eisman, E. J. (2000). Empirical support for psychological assessment in clinical health care settings. *Professional Psychology: Research and Practice, 31,* 119–130.

Kunce, J. T., & Tamkin, A. S. (1981). Rorschach Movement and Color responses and MMPI social extraversion and thinking introversion personality types. *Journal of Personality Assessment, 45,* 5–10.

Landis, J. R., & Koch, G. G. (1977). The measurement of observer agreement for categorical data. *Biometrics, 33,* 159–174.

Lazarus, R. S. (1949). The influence of Color on the protocol of the Rorschach Test. *Journal of Abnormal and Social Psychology, 44,* 508–516.

Lerner, H., & Lerner, P. (1987). Review of the Rorschach Inkblot Test. In D. J. Keyser & R. C. Sweetland (Eds.), *Test critiques compendium* (pp. 372–401). Kansas City, MO: Test Corporation of America.

Lerner, P. (2000). A nonreviewer's comment: On the Rorschach and baseball. *Journal of Clinical Psychology, 56,* 439.

Lesser, E. (1961). Popularity of Rorschach training in the United States. *Journal of Projective Techniques, 25,* 179–183.

Levine, M., Spivack, G., & Wight, B. (1959). The inhibition process: Rorschach Human Movement responses and intelligence: Some further data. *Journal of Consulting Psychology, 23,* 306–312.

Levy, D. A. (1997). *Tools of critical thinking: Metathoughts for psychology.* Boston: Allyn & Bacon.

Levy, L. H. (1962). The skew in clinical psychology. *American Psychologist, 17,* 244–249.

Light, R. J. (1971). Measures of response agreement for qualitative data: Some generalizations and alternatives. *Psychological Bulletin, 76,* 365–377.

Lilienfeld, S. O. (1999a). Projective measures of personality and psychopathology: How well do they work? *Skeptical Inquirer, 23 (May),* 32–39.

Lilienfeld, S. O. (1999b). Pseudoscience in contemporary clinical psychology: What it is and what we can do about it. *Clinical Psychologist, 51,* 3–9.

Lilienfeld, S. O. (2002a). A funny thing happened on the way to my American Psychologist publication. *American Psychologist, 57,* 225–227.

Lilienfeld, S. O. (2002b). When worlds collide: Social science, politics, and the Rind et al. (1998) Child sexual abuse meta-analysis. *American Psychologist, 57,* 176–188.

Lilienfeld, S. O., Wood, J. M., & Garb, H. N. (2000). The scientific status of projective techniques. *Psychological Science in the Public Interest, 1,* 27–66. (Copies of this article are available without charge at http://www.psychologicalscience.org/newsresearch/publications/journals/pspi1_2.html. Access date: October 22, 2002.)

Lilienfeld, S. O., Wood, J. M., & Garb, H. N. (2001a, May). What's wrong with this picture? *Scientific American, 284*(5), 80–87.

Lilienfeld, S. O., Wood, J. M., & Garb, H. N. (2001b, December). The Rorschach Test is scientifically questionable. *The Harvard Mental Health Letter,* pp. 5–6.

Lindner, R. M. (1946). Content analysis in Rorschach work. *Rorschach Research Exchange, 10,* 121–129.

Lindner, R. M. (1950). The content analysis of the Rorschach protocol. In L. E. Abt and L. Bellak (Eds.), *Projective psychology* (pp. 75–90). New York: Knopf.

Lipovsky, J. A., Finch, A. J., & Belter, R. W. (1989). Assessment of depression in adolescents: Objective and projective measures. *Journal of Personality Assessment, 53,* 449–458.

Lipsey, M. W., & Wilson, D. B. (2001). *Practical meta-analysis.* Thousand Oaks, CA: Sage.

Lisansky, E. S. (1956). The inter-examiner reliability of the Rorschach Test. *Journal of Projective Techniques, 20,* 310–317.

Little, K. B., & Shneidman, E. S. (1959). Congruencies among interpretations of psychological test and anamnestic data [Whole issue 476]. *Psychological Monographs, 73*(6).

Loevinger, J. (1998). *Technical foundations for measuring ego development: The Washington University Sentence Completion Test.* Mahwah, NJ: Erlbaum.

Loftus, E. F. (1993). The reality of repressed memories. *American Psychologist, 48,* 518–537.

Lohr, J. M., Fowler, K. A., & Lilienfeld, S. O. (2002). The dissemination and promotion of pseudoscience in clinical psychology: The challenge to legitimate clinical science. *Clinical Psychologist, 55*(3), 4–10. (This article is also available online at http://www.apa.org/divisions/div12/tcp_journals/Tcp_55_3.pdf. Access date: October 22, 2002.)

Lohrenz, L. J., & Gardner, R. W. (1967). The Mayman form-level scoring method: Scorer reliability and correlates of form level. *Journal of Projective Techniques and Personality Assessment, 31*(4), 39–43.

Loosli-Usteri, M. (1937). Discussion on "Some recent Rorschach problems." *Rorschach Research Exchange, 2,* 73–74.

Loosli-Usteri, M. (1938). *Le diagnostic individuel chez l'enfant de moyen du Test de Rorschach* (2nd ed). Paris: Hermann.

Lord, E. (1950). Experimentally induced variation in Rorschach performance [Whole issue 316]. *Psychological Monographs, 64*(10).

Lotsof, E. J. (1953). Intelligence, verbal fluency, and the Rorschach Test. *Journal of Consulting Psychology, 17,* 1953.

Lotsof, E. J., Comrey, A., Bogartz, W., & Arnsfield, P. (1958). A factor analysis of the WISC and Rorschach. *Journal of Projective Techniques, 22,* 297–301.

Loving, J. L. (1998). Selected Rorschach variables of psychopathic male juvenile offenders (Doctoral dissertation, Widener University 1998). *Dissertation Abstracts International, 59,* 0878B.

Loving, J. L., & Russell, W. F. (2000). Selected Rorschach variables of psychopathic juvenile offenders. *Journal of Personality Assessment, 75,* 126–142.

Lubin, B., Larsen, R. M., & Matarazzo, J. D. (1984). Patterns of psychological test usage in the United States: 1935–1982. *American Psychologist, 38,* 451–454.

Lubin, B., Wallis, R. R., & Paine, C. (1971). Patterns of psychological test usage in the United States: 1935–1969. *Professional Psychology, 2,* 70–74.

Lueger, R. J., & Petzel, T. P. (1979). Illusory correlation in clinical judgment: Effects of amount of information to be processed. *Journal of Consulting and Clinical Psychology, 47,* 1120–1121.

Luft, J. (1953). Interaction and projection. *Journal of Projective Techniques, 17,* 489–492.

Machover, K. (1949). *Personality projection in the drawing of the human figure.* Springfield, Ill.: Thomas.

Mackintosh, N. J. (1995a). Declining educational standards. In N. J. Mackintosh (Ed.), *Cyril Burt: Fraud or framed* (pp. 95–110). Oxford, England: Oxford University Press.

Mackintosh, N. J. (1995b). Does it matter? The scientific and political impact of Burt's work. In N. J. Mackintosh (Ed.), *Cyril Burt: Fraud or framed* (pp. 130–151). Oxford, England: Oxford University Press.

Mackintosh, N. J. (1995c). Twins and other kinship studies. In N. J. Mackintosh (Ed.), *Cyril Burt: Fraud or framed* (pp. 45–69). Oxford, England: Oxford University Press.

Mann, L. (1956). The relation of Rorschach indices of extratension and introversion to a measure of responsiveness to the immediate environment. *Journal of Consulting Psychology, 20,* 114–118.

Manners, J., & Durkin, K. (2001). A critical review of the validity of ego development theory and its measurement. *Journal of Personality Assessment, 77,* 541–567.

Masling, J. (1992). The influence of situational and interpersonal variables in projective testing. *Journal of Personality Assessment, 59,* 616–640. (Original published in *Psychological Bulletin* in 1960).

Masling, J., Rabie, L., & Blondheim, S. H. (1967). Obesity, level of aspiration, and Rorschach and TAT measures of oral dependence. *Journal of Consulting Psychology, 31,* 233–239.

Mayman, M. (1970). Reality contact, defense effectiveness, and psychopathology in Rorschach form-level scores. In B. Klopfer, M. M. Meyer, & F. B. Brawer (Eds.), *Developments in the Rorschach technique: Vol. 3. Aspects of personality structure* (pp. 11–46). Orlando: Harcourt Brace.

Mayou, R. A., Ehlers, A., & Hobbs, M. (2000). Psychological debriefing for road traffic accident victims: Three-year follow-up of a randomized controlled trial. *British Journal of Psychiatry, 176,* 589–593.

McCall, R. J. (1959). Review of the Rorschach Inkblot Test. In O. K. Buros (Ed.), *The fifth mental measurements yearbook* (pp. 278–289). Highland Park, NJ: Gryphon Press.

McCann, J. T. (1998). Defending the Rorschach in court: An analysis of admissibility using legal and professional standards. *Journal of Personality Assessment, 70,* 125–144.

McCoy, B. (2000). *Quack! Tales of medical fraud from the Museum of Questionable Medical Devices.* Santa Monica, CA: Santa Monica Press.

McDougall, A. L. (1996). Rorschach indicators of simulated schizophrenia (Doctoral dissertation, California School of Professional Psychology, 1996). *Dissertation Abstracts International, 57,* 2159B.

McDowell, C., & Acklin, M. W. (1996). Standardizing procedures for calculating Rorschach interrater reliability: Conceptual and empirical foundations. *Journal of Personality Assessment, 66,* 308–320.

McFall, R. M. (2000). Elaborate reflections on a simple manifesto. *Applied and Preventive Psychology, 9,* 5–21.

McHugh, P. R. (1994). Psychotherapy awry. *American Scholar, 63,* 17–30.

McKinzey, R. K., & Ziegler, T. (1999). Challenging a flexible neuropsychological battery under Kelly/Frye: A case study. *Behavioral Sciences and the Law, 17,* 543–551.

McNally, R. J. (1996). Cognitive bias in the anxiety disorders. *Nebraska Symposium on Motivation, 43,* 211–250.

Meehl, P. E. (1954). *Clinical vs. statistical prediction.* Minneapolis: University of Minnesota Press.

Meehl, P. E. (1956). Wanted—a good cookbook. *American Psychologist, 11,* 262–272.

Meehl, P. E. (1989). Paul E. Meehl. In G. Lindzey (Ed.), *A history of psychology in autobiography. Vol. 8* (pp. 336–389). Stanford, CA: Stanford University Press.

Meehl, P. E. (1997). Credentialed persons, credentialed knowledge. *Clinical Psychology: Science and Practice, 4,* 91–98.

Megargee, E. I., & Spielberger, C. D. (1992a). Personality assessment in America: An introduction. In E. I. Megargee and C. D. Spielberger (Eds.), *Personality assessment in America* (pp. 1–14). Hillsdale, NJ: Erlbaum.

Megargee, E. I., & Spielberger, C. D. (1992b). Reflections on fifty years of personality assessment and future directions for the field. In E. I. Megargee and C. D. Spielberger (Eds.), *Personality assessment in America* (pp. 170–190). Hillsdale, NJ: Erlbaum.

Meili-Dworetzki, G. (1956). The development of perception in the Rorschach. In B. Klopfer (Ed.), *Developments in the Rorschach technique: Vol. 2. Fields of application* (pp. 104–176). Yonkers-on-Hudson, NY: World Book.

Meisner, S. (1988). Susceptibility of Rorschach distress correlates to malingering. *Journal of Personality Assessment, 52,* 564–571.

Meloy, J. R., & Gacono, C. B. (1995). Assessing the psychopathic personality. In J. N. Butcher (Ed.), *Clinical personality assessment: Practical approaches* (pp. 410–422). New York: Oxford University Press.

Meloy, J. R., & Gacono, C. B. (1998). The internal world of the psychopath. In T. Millon, E. Simonsen, M. Birket-Smith, & R. D. Davis (Eds.), *Psychopathy: Antisocial, criminal, and violent behavior* (pp. 95–109). New York: Guilford Press.

Meloy, J. R., Hansen, T. L., & Weiner, I. B. (1997). Authority of the Rorschach: Legal citations during the past 50 years. *Journal of Personality Assessment, 69,* 53–62.

Meyer, G. J. (1991). An empirical search for fundamental personality and mood dimensions within the Rorschach Test (Doctoral dissertation, Loyola University of Chicago, 1989). *Dissertation Abstracts International, 52,* 1071B-1072B.

Meyer, G. J. (1992a). Response frequency problems in the Rorschach: Clinical and research implications with suggestions for the future. *Journal of Personality Assessment, 58,* 231–244.

Meyer, G. J. (1992b). The Rorschach's factor structure: A contemporary investigation and historical review. *Journal of Personality Assessment, 59,* 117–136.

Meyer, G. J. (1993). The impact of response frequency on the Rorschach constellation indices and on their validity with diagnostic and MMPI-2 criteria. *Journal of Personality Assessment, 60,* 153–180.

Meyer, G. J. (1996). The Rorschach and MMPI: Toward a more scientifically differentiated understanding of cross-method assessment. *Journal of Personality Assessment, 67,* 558–578.

Meyer, G. J. (1997a). Assessing reliability: Critical corrections for a critical examination of the Rorschach Comprehensive System. *Psychological Assessment, 9,* 480–489.

Meyer, G. J. (1997b). On the integration of personality assessment methods: The Rorschach and MMPI. *Journal of Personality Assessment, 68,* 297–330.

Meyer, G. J. (1997c). Thinking clearly about reliability: More critical corrections regarding the Rorschach Comprehensive System. *Psychological Assessment, 9,* 495–498.

Meyer, G. J. (2000). On the science of Rorschach research. *Journal of Personality Assessment, 75,* 46–81.

Meyer, G. J. (2001a). Correction to "On the science of Rorschach research." *Journal of Personality Assessment, 77,* 580.

Meyer, G. J. (2001b). Evidence to correct misperceptions about Rorschach norms. *Clinical Psychology: Science and Practice, 8,* 389–396.

Meyer, G. J. (2002). Exploring possible ethnic differences and bias in the Rorschach Comprehensive System. *Journal of Personality Assessment, 78,* 104–129.

Meyer, G. J., & Archer, R. P. (2001). The hard science of Rorschach research: What do we know and where do we go? *Psychological Assessment, 13,* 486–502.

Meyer, G. J., Finn, S. E., Eyde, L. D., Kay, G. G., Dies, R. R., Eisman, E. J., Kubiszyn, T. W., & Reed, G. M. (2002). Amplifying issues related to psychological testing and assessment. *American Psychologist, 57,* 140–141.

Meyer, G. J., Finn, S. E., Eyde, L. D., Kay, G. G., Kubiszyn, T. W., Moreland, K. L., Eisman, E. J., & Dies, R. R. (1998). *Benefits and costs of psychological assessment in healthcare delivery: Report of the board of professional affairs psychological assessment work group, Part I.* Washington, DC: American Psychological Association. (Copies available from the Practice Directorate, American Psychological Association.)

Meyer, G. J., Finn, S. E., Eyde, L. D., Kay, G. G., Moreland, K. L., Dies, R. R., Eisman, E. J., Kubiszyn, T. W., & Reed, G. M. (2001). Psychological testing and psychological assessment: A review of evidence and issues. *American Psychologist, 56,* 128–165.

Meyer, G. J., & Handler, L. (1997). The ability of the Rorschach to predict subsequent outcome: A meta-analysis of the Rorschach Prognostic Rating Scale. *Journal of Personality Assessment, 69,* 1–38.

Meyer, G. J., Hilsenroth, M. J., Baxter, D., Exner, J. E., Fowler, J. C., Piers, C. C., & Resnick (2002). An examination of interrater reliability for scoring the Rorschach Comprehensive System in eight data sets. *Journal of Personality Assessment, 78,* 219–274.

Meyer, G. J., & Richardson, C. (2001, March). *An examination of changes in Form Quality codes in the Rorschach Comprehensive System from 1974 to 1995.* Paper presented at the Midwinter Meeting of the Society for Personality Assessment, Philadelphia.

Miale, F. R., & Selzer, M. (1975). *The Nuremberg mind.* New York: Quadrangle/New York Times Book Co.

Miller, D., Sanders, R., & Cleveland, S. E. (1950). The relationship between examiner personality and obtained Rorschach protocols: An application of interpersonal relations theory. *American Psychologist, 5,* 322–323. (Abstract).

Miller, J. G. (1946). Clinical psychology in the Veterans Administration. *American Psychologist, 1,* 181–189.

Mills, D. H., Wellner, A. M., & VandenBos, G. R. (1979). The national register survey: The first comprehensive study of all licensed/certified psychologists. In C. A. Kiesler, N. A. Cummings, & G. R. VandenBos (Eds.), *Psychology and national health insurance: A sourcebook* (pp. 111–128). Washington, DC: American Psychological Association.

Mischel, W. (1968). *Personality and assessment.* New York: Wiley.

Mittman, B. L. (1983). Judges' ability to diagnose schizophrenia on the Rorschach: The effect of malingering (Doctoral dissertation, Long Island University, 1983). *Dissertation Abstracts International, 44,* 1248B.

Molish, H. B. (1958). Can a science emerge from Rorschach's test? *Contemporary Psychology, 3,* 189–192.

Moreland, K. L., Reznikoff, M., & Aronow, E. (1995). Integrating Rorschach interpretation by carefully placing more of your eggs in the content basket. *Journal of Personality Assessment, 64,* 239–242.

Morganthaler, W. (1954). Der kampf um das erscheinen der Psychodiagnostik (The struggle for the publication of *Psychodiagnostics*). *Zeitschrift eur diagnostische psychologie und perseonlichkeitsforschung, 2,* 255–271. [An English translation is available upon request from James M. Wood, jawood@utep.edu.]

Munroe, R. L. (1942). An experiment in large scale testing by a modification of the Rorschach method. *Journal of Psychology, 13,* 229–263.

Munroe, R. L. (1944). The inspection technique: A method of rapid evaluation of the Rorschach protocol. *Rorschach Research Exchange, 8,* 46–70.

Munroe, R. L. (1945). Prediction of the adjustment and academic performance of college students. *Applied Psychology Monographs, 7,* 1–104.

Munroe, R. L. (1946). Rorschach findings on college students showing different constellations of subscores on the ACE. *Journal of Consulting Psychology, 10,* 301–316.

Munroe, R. L. (1950). The inspection technique for the Rorschach protocol. In L. E. Abt and L. Bellak (Eds.), *Projective psychology* (pp. 91–145). New York: Knopf.

Muntz, A. (1999). Object relations and defense mechanisms of psychopathic and nonpsychopathic female offenders: A descriptive study (Doctoral dissertation, California School of Professional Psychology, 1998). *Dissertation Abstracts International, 60,* 2954B.

Murphy-Peaslee, D. M. (1995). An investigation of incarcerated females: Rorschach indices and Psychopathy Checklist scores (Doctoral dissertation, California School of Professional Psychology, 1993). *Dissertation Abstracts International, 56,* 0531B.

Murstein, B. I. (1963). *Theory and research in projective techniques.* New York: Wiley.

Murstein, B. I. (1965). *Handbook of projective techniques.* New York: Basic Books.

Myers, D. (2001). *Psychology* (6th ed.). New York: Worth.

Nakata, L. M. (1999). Interrater reliability and the Comprehensive System for the Rorschach: Clinical and non-clinical protocols (Doctoral dissertation, Pacific Graduate School of Psychology, 1999). *Dissertation Abstracts International, 60,* 4296B.

Neisser, U., Boodoo, G., Bouchard, T. J., Boykin, A. W., Brody, N., Ceci, S. J., Halpern, D. F., Loehlin, J. C., Perloff, R., Sternberg, R. J., & Urbina, S. (1996). Intelligence: Knowns and unknowns. *American Psychologist, 51,* 77–101.

Netter, B.E.C., & Viglione, D. J. (1994). An empirical study of malingering schizophrenia on the Rorschach. *Journal of Personality Assessment, 62,* 45–57.

Neuringer, C. (1968). A variety of thematic methods. In A. I. Rabin (Ed.), *Projective techniques in personality assessment* (pp. 222–261). New York: Springer.

Newton, K. R. (1959). Review of the Blacky Pictures. In O. K. Buros (Ed.), *The fifth mental measurements yearbook* (pp. 214–216). Highland Park, NJ: Gryphon Press.

Newton, R. L. (1954). The clinician as judge: Total Rorschachs and clinical case material. *Journal of Consulting Psychology, 18,* 248–250.

Nezworski, M. T., & Wood, J. M. (1995). Narcissism in the Comprehensive System for the Rorschach. *Clinical Psychology: Science and Practice, 2,* 179–199.

Nisbett, R. E., & Ross, L. (1980). *Human inference: Strategies and shortcomings of social judgment.* Upper Saddle River, NJ: Prentice Hall.

Nisbett, R. E., & Wilson, T. D. (1977a). The halo effect: Evidence for unconscious alteration of judgments. *Journal of Personality and Social Psychology, 35,* 250–256.

Nisbett, R. E., & Wilson, T. D. (1977b). Telling more than we can know: Verbal reports on mental processes. *Psychological Review, 84,* 231–259.

Norman, R. D., & Scott, W. A. (1952). Color and affect: A review and semantic evaluation. *Journal of General Psychology, 46,* 185–223.

Nunnally, J. C., & Bernstein, I. C. (1994). *Psychometric theory* (3rd ed.). New York: McGraw-Hill.

O'Donohue, W., & Bradley, A. R. (1999). Conceptual and empirical issues in child custody evaluations. *Clinical Psychology: Science and Practice, 6,* 310–322.

Offer, D. (1969). *The psychological world of the teenager: A study of normal adolescent boys.* New York: Basic Books.

Palmer, J. O. (1956). Attitudinal correlates of Rorschach's Experience Balance. *Journal of Projective Techniques, 20,* 207–211.

Parker, K.C.H., Hanson, R. K., & Hunsley, J. (1988). MMPI, Rorschach, and WAIS: A meta-analytic comparison of reliability, stability, and validity. *Psychological Bulletin, 103,* 367–373.

Parker, K.H.C., Hunsley, J., & Hanson, R. K. (1999). Old wine from old skins sometimes tastes like vinegar: A response to Garb, Florio, and Grove. *Psychological Science, 10,* 291–292.

Pascal, G. R., Ruesch, H. A., Devine, C. A., & Suttell, B. J. (1950). A study of genital symbols on the Rorschach Test: Presentation of a method and results. *Journal of Abnormal and Social Psychology, 45,* 286–295.

Patterson, T. W., & Davis, R. W. (1985). Walter G. Klopfer: Remembrances. *Journal of Personality Assessment, 49,* 338–345.

Perry, G. G., & Kinder, B. N. (1990). The susceptibility of the Rorschach to malingering: A critical review. *Journal of Personality Assessment, 54,* 47–57.

Perry, G. G., & Kinder, B. N. (1992). Susceptibility of the Rorschach to malingering: A schizophrenia analogue. In C. D. Spielberger & J. N. Butcher (Eds.), *Advances in personality assessment.* (Vol. 9, pp. 127–140). Hillsdale, NJ: Erlbaum.

Phelps, R., Eisman, E. J., & Kohout, J. (1998). Psychological practice and managed care: Results of the CAPP practitioner survey. *Professional Psychology: Research and Practice, 29,* 31–36.

Phillips, L., & Smith, J. G. (1953). *Rorschach Interpretation: Advanced Technique.* New York: Grune & Stratton.

Piatelli-Palmarini, M. (1994). *Inevitable illusions: How mistakes of reason rule our minds.* New York: Wiley.

Pichot, P. (1984). Centenary of the birth of Hermann Rorschach. *Journal of Personality Assessment, 48,* pp. 591–596.

Pickren, W. (2000). Piotrowski, Zygmunt A. In A. E. Kazdin (Ed.), *Encyclopedia of psychology. Vol. 6* (pp. 200–201). Oxford, England: Oxford University Press.

Pinkerman, J. E., Haynes, J. P., & Keiser, T. (1993). Characteristics of psychological practice in juvenile court clinics. *American Journal of Forensic Psychology, 11,* 3–12.

Pion, G. M. (1992). Psychologists wanted: Employment trends over the past decade. In R. R. Kilburg (Ed.), *How to manage your career in psychology.* Washington, DC: American Psychological Association.

Piotrowski, C. (1999). Assessment practices in the era of managed care: Current status and future directions. *Journal of Clinical Psychology, 55,* 787–798.

Piotrowski, C., & Belter, R. W. (1999). Internship training in psychological assessment: Has managed care had an impact? *Assessment, 6,* 381–385.

Piotrowski, C., Belter, R. W., & Keller, J. W. (1998). The impact of "Managed Care" on the practice of psychological testing: Preliminary findings. *Journal of Personality Assessment, 70,* 441–447.

Piotrowski, C., & Keller, J. W. (1989). Use of assessment in mental health clinics and services. *Psychological Reports, 64,* 1298.

Piotrowski, C., Sherry, D., & Keller, J. W. (1985). Psychodiagnostic test usage: A survey of the Society for Personality Assessment. *Journal of Personality Assessment, 49,* 115–119.

Piotrowski, H. (2001). A life fully lived, told in brief by his partner. *Journal of Personality Assessment, 76,* 203–208.

Piotrowski, Z. A. (1937a). The M, FM, and m responses as indicators of changes in personality. *Rorschach Research Exchange, 1,* 148–156.

Piotrowski, Z. A. (1937b). The Rorschach inkblot method in organic disturbances of the central nervous system. *Journal of Nervous and Mental Disease, 86,* 525–537.

Piotrowski, Z. A. (1943a). Tentative Rorschach formulae for educational and vocational guidance in adolescence. *Rorschach Research Exchange, 7,* 16–27.

Piotrowski, Z. A. (1943b). Use of the Rorschach in vocational selection. *Journal of Consulting Psychology, 7,* 97–102.

Piotrowski, Z. A. (1957). *Perceptanalysis: A fundamentally reworked, expanded and systematized Rorschach method.* New York: Macmillan.

Piotrowski, Z. A. (1960). The movement score. In M. A. Rickers-Ovsiankina (Ed.), *Rorschach psychology* (pp. 130–153). New York: Wiley.

Piotrowski, Z. A. (1964). Consistently successful and failing top business executives: An inkblot test study. In G. Fisk (Ed.), *The frontiers of management psychology* (pp. 18–28). New York: HarperCollins.

Piotrowski, Z. A. (1977). The movement responses. In M. A. Rickers-Ovsiankina (Ed.), *Rorschach psychology* (2nd ed.), (pp. 189–227). Huntington, NY: Krieger.

Piotrowski, Z. A. (1980). CPR: The psychological x-ray in mental disorders. In J. B. Sidowski, J. H. Johnson, & T. A. Williams (Eds.), *Technology in mental health care delivery systems* (pp. 85–108). Norwood, NJ: Ablex.

Piotrowski, Z. A. (1984). The making of a personologist. In D. P. Rogers (Ed.), *Foundations of psychology: Some personal views.* New York: Praeger.

Piotrowski, Z. A., & Biele, A. M. (1986). *Dreams: A key to self-knowledge.* Hillsdale, NJ: Erlbaum.

Piotrowski, Z. A., & Rock, M. (1963). *The Perceptanalytic Executive Scale: A tool for the selection of top managers.* New York: Grune & Stratton.

Ponder, J. I. (1999). An investigation of psychopathy in a sample of violent juvenile offenders (Doctoral dissertation, University of Texas at Austin, 1998). *Dissertation Abstracts International, 59,* 5105B.

Pope, B., & Jensen, A. R. (1957). The Rorschach as an index of pathological thinking. *Journal of Projective Techniques, 21,* 59–62.

Popper, M. D. (1992). The Rorschach on trial: Attempts to simulate disability (Doctoral dissertation, California School of Professional Psychology, 1991). *Dissertation Abstracts International, 53,* 1073B.

Potkay, C. R. (1971). *The Rorschach clinician.* New York: Grune & Stratton.

Poundstone, W. (1983). *Big secrets: The uncensored truth about all sorts of stuff you are never supposed to know.* New York: Quill.

Presley, G., Smith, C., Hilsenroth, M., & Exner, J. (2001). Clinical utility of the Rorschach with African Americans. *Journal of Personality Assessment, 77,* 491–507.

Psychological Corporation. (1997). *Wechsler Adult Intelligence Scale, Third edition. Wechsler Memory Scale, Third edition. Technical manual.* San Antonio, TX: Author.

Rabin, A. I. (1963). Do we need another projective technique? *Merrill-Palmer Quarterly, 9,* 73–77.

Rabin, A. I. (Ed.). (1968). *Projective techniques in personality assessment: A modern introduction.* New York: Springer.

Rabin, A. I. (1972). Review of the Rorschach Inkblot Test. In O. K. Buros (Ed.), *The seventh mental measurements yearbook. Vol. 1* (pp. 443–446). Highland Park, NJ: Gryphon Press.

Rabin, A. I. (1980). The Rorschach: A new lease on life. *Contemporary Psychology, 25,* 52–53.

Rabin, A. I. (Ed.). (1981). *Assessment with projective techniques: A concise introduction.* New York: Springer.

Rabin, A. I. (2001). Projective techniques at midcentury: A retrospective review of *An introduction to projective techniques* by Harold H. Anderson and Gladys L. Anderson. *Journal of Personality Assessment, 76,* 353–367.

Rabin, A. I., & Haworth, M. R. (Eds.). (1960). *Projective techniques with children.* New York: Grune & Stratton.

Rapaport, D. (1941). The Szondi test. *Bulletin of the Menninger Clinic, 5,* 33–39.

Rapaport, D., Gill, M., & Schafer, R. (1946a). *Diagnostic psychological testing. Vol. 1.* Chicago: Year Book.

Rapaport, D., Gill, M., & Schafer, R. (1946b). *Diagnostic psychological testing. Vol. 2.* Chicago: Year Book.

Rapaport, D., Gill, M., & Schafer, R. (1968). (Ed. by R. R. Holt). *Diagnostic psychological testing* (rev. ed.). New York: International Universities Press.

Reisman, J. M. (1976). *A history of clinical psychology.* New York: Irvington.

Reynolds, W. M., & Sundberg, N. D. (1976). Recent research trends in testing. *Journal of Personality Assessment, 40,* 228–233.

Reznikoff, M. (1972). Review of the Rorschach Inkblot Test. In O. K. Buros (Ed.), *The seventh mental measurements yearbook. Vol. 1* (pp. 446–449). Highland Park, NJ: Gryphon Press.

Reznikoff, M., Aronow, E., & Rauchway, A. (1982). The reliability of inkblot content scales. In C. D. Spielberger & J. N. Butcher (Eds.), *Advances in personality assessment.* (Vol. 1, pp. 83–113). Hillsdale, NJ: Erlbaum.

Riccuiti, H. (1962). Development and application of projective techniques of personality. *Review of Educational Research, 32,* 64–77.

Richards, W. S., & Merrens, M. R. (1971). Student evaluation of generalized personality interpretations as a function of method of assessment. *Journal of Clinical Psychology, 27,* 457–459.

Ritsher, J. B., Slivko-Kolchik, E. B., & Oleichik, I. V. (2001). Assessing depression in Russian psychiatric patients: Validity of MMPI and Rorschach. *Assessment, 8,* 373–389.

Ritzler, B. (1995). Putting your eggs in the content analysis basket: A response to Aronow, Reznikoff, and Moreland. *Journal of Personality Assessment, 64,* 229–234.

Ritzler, B., & Alter, B. (1986). Rorschach teaching in APA-approved clinical graduate programs: Ten years later. *Journal of Personality Assessment, 50,* 44–49.

Ritzler, B., Erard, R., & Pettigrew, G. (2002a). A final reply to Grove and Barden: The relevance of the Rorschach Comprehensive System for expert testimony. *Psychology, Public Policy, and the Law, 8,* 235–246.

Ritzler, B., Erard, R., & Pettigrew, G. (2002b). Protecting the integrity of Rorschach expert witnesses: A reply to Grove and Barden (1999) Re: The admissibility of testimony under *Daubert/Kumho* analyses. *Psychology, Public Policy, and the Law, 8,* 210–215.

Roemer, G. A. (1967). The Rorschach and Roemer Symbol Test series. *Journal of Nervous and Mental Disease, 144,* 185–197.

Rorschach, H. (1964). *Psychodiagnostics.* New York: Grune & Stratton. (Original work published in German in 1921 and in English in 1942).

Rorschach, H., & Oberholzer, E. (1924). The application of the interpretation of form to psychoanalysis. *Journal of Nervous and Mental Diseases, 60,* 225–248, 359–379.

Rose, T., Kaser-Boyd, N., & Maloney, M. P. (2000). *Essentials of Rorschach assessment.* New York: Wiley.

Rosen, M. (1973). Alice in Rorschachland. *Journal of Personality Assessment, 37,* 115–121.

Rosenthal, R., Hiller, J. B., Bornstein, R. F., Berry, D.T.R., & Brunell-Neuleib, S. (2001). Meta-analytic methods, the Rorschach, and the MMPI. *Psychological Assessment, 13,* 449–451.

Roustang, F. (1982). *Dire mastery: Discipleship from Freud to Lacan.* Baltimore: Johns Hopkins University Press.

Routh, D. K. (1994). *Clinical psychology since 1917: Science, practice, and organization.* New York: Plenum.

Russell, E. W. (1967). Rorschach stimulus modification. *Journal of Projective Techniques and Personality Assessment, 31*(5), 20–22.

Sacks, J. M., & Lewin, H. S. (1950). Limitations of the Rorschach as sole diagnostic instrument. *Journal of Consulting Psychology, 14,* 479–481.

Sagan, C. (1995). *The demon-haunted world: Science as a candle in the dark.* New York: Random House.

Salyer, K. M., Holmstrom, R. W., & Noshpitz, J. D. (1991). Learning disabilities as a childhood manifestation of severe psychopathology. *American Journal of Orthopsychiatry, 61,* 230–240.

Samuel Jacob Beck—Citation. (1965). *Journal of Projective Techniques and Personality Assessment, 29,* 414-417.

Samuels, S. (1952). The validity of personality-trait ratings based on projective techniques [Whole issue 337]. *Psychological Monographs, 66*(5).

Sanders, R., & Cleveland, S. E. (1953). The relationship between certain examiner personality variables and subjects' Rorschach scores. *Journal of Projective Techniques, 17,* 34–50.

Sappenfeld, B. R. (1965). Review of the Blacky Pictures. In O. K. Buros (Ed.), *The sixth mental measurements yearbook* (pp. 417–423). Highland Park, NJ: Gryphon Press.

Sarason, S. B. (1954). *The clinical interaction with special reference to the Rorschach.* New York: HarperCollins.

Saville, T. K., & Dewey, H. (date unknown). *Red hot cold reading.* Place and publisher unknown; available in stores catering to stage magicians.

Schachtel, E., & Hartoch, A. (1937). Discussion on "Some recent Rorschach problems." *Rorschach Research Exchange, 2,* 70–72.

Schafer, R. (1954). *Psychoanalytic interpretation in Rorschach Testing.* New York: Grune & Stratton.

Schofield, W. (1950). Research in clinical psychology: 1949. *Journal of Clinical Psychology, 6,* 234–237.

Schretlen, D. J. (1997). Dissimulation on the Rorschach and other projective measures. In R. Rogers (Ed.), *Clinical assessment of malingering and deception* (2nd ed.), (pp. 208–222). New York: Guilford Press.

Seamons, D. T., Howell, R. J., Carlisle, A. L., & Roe, A. V. (1981). Rorschach simulation of mental illness and normality by psychotic and nonpsychotic legal offenders. *Journal of Personality Assessment, 45,* 130–135.

Sechrest, L. (1963). Incremental validity: A recommendation. *Educational and Psychological Measurement, 23,* 153–158.

Sechrest, L. (1992). The past future of clinical psychology: A reflection on Woodworth (1937). *Journal of Consulting and Clinical Psychology, 60,* 18–23.

Sell, J. M., & Torres-Henry, R. (1979). Testing practices in university and college counseling centers in the United States. *Professional Psychology, 10,* 774–779.

Sells, J. E. (1991). A validity study of the DEPI index: The Rorschach Comprehensive System (Doctoral dissertation, University of Utah, 1990). *Dissertation Abstracts International, 51,* 5590B.

Shaffer, L. F (1959). Review of the Rorschach Inkblot Test. In O. K. Buros (Ed.), *The fifth mental measurements yearbook* (pp. 285–289). Highland Park, NJ: Gryphon Press.

Shaffer, T. W., Erdberg, P., & Haroian, J. (1999). Current nonpatient data for the Rorschach, WAIS-R, and MMPI-2. *Journal of Personality Assessment, 73,* 305–316.

Shakow, D. (1965). Seventeen years later: Clinical psychology in the light of the 1947 Committee on Training in Clinical Psychology Report. *American Psychologist, 20,* 353–362.

Shakow, D. (1969). *Clinical psychology as science and profession: A forty-year odyssey.* Hawthorne, NY: Aldine de Gruyter.

Shakow, D., & Rapaport, D. (1964). *The influence of Freud on American psychology.* Cleveland: World Book.

Shapiro, D. (1960). A perceptual understanding of Color response. In M. A. Rickers-Ovsiankina (Ed.), *Rorschach psychology* (pp. 154–201). New York: Wiley.

Shaw, B. (1948). "Sex populars" in the Rorschach Test. *Journal of Abnormal and Social Psychology, 43,* 466–470.

Sheehan, J. G., & Tanaka, J. S. (1983). Prognostic validity of the Rorschach. *Journal of Personality Assessment, 47,* 462–465.

Shemberg, K., & Keeley, S. (1970). Psychodiagnostic training in the academic setting. *Journal of Consulting and Clinical Psychology, 34,* 205–211.

Shermer, M. (1997). *Why people believe weird things: Pseudoscience, superstition, and other confusions of our time.* New York: Freeman.

Shontz, F. C., & Green, P. (1992). Trends in research on the Rorschach: Review and recommendation. *Applied and Preventive Psychology, 1,* 149–156.

Siemsen, R. A. (1999). Relationships of Rorschach and MMPI-2 variables to the Hare Psychopathy Checklist-Revised among mentally ill incarcerated felons (Doctoral dissertation, California School of Professional Psychology at Alameda, 1999). *Dissertation Abstracts International, 60,* 2367B.

Silberg, J. L., & Armstrong, J. G. (1992). The Rorschach Test for predicting suicide among depressed adolescent inpatients. *Journal of Personality Assessment, 59,* 290–303.

Silver, R. J. (2001). Practicing professional psychology. *American Psychologist, 56,* 1008–1014.

Silverman, L. H. (1959). A q-sort study of the validity of evaluations made from projective techniques. *Psychological Monographs: General and Applied, 73,* Whole No. 477.

Simkins, L. (1960). Examiner reinforcement and situational variables in a projective testing situation. *Journal of Consulting Psychology, 24,* 541–547.

Sines, L. K. (1959). The relative contribution of four kinds of data to accuracy in personality assessment. *Journal of Consulting Psychology, 23,* 483–492.

Singer, H. K., & Brabender, V. (1993). The use of the Rorschach to differentiate unipolar and bipolar disorders. *Journal of Personality Assessment, 60,* 333–345.

Singer, J. L. (1960). Some Experience Type: Some behavioral correlates and theoretical implications. In M. A. Rickers-Ovsiankina (Ed.), *Rorschach psychology* (pp. 223–259). New York: Wiley.

Singer, J. L., & Brown, S.-L. (1977). The Experience Type: Some behavioral correlates and theoretical implications. In M. A. Rickers-Ovsiankina (Ed.), *Rorschach psychology* (2nd ed.), (pp. 325–372). Huntington, NY: Krieger.

Singer, J. L., & Herman, J. (1954). Motor and fantasy correlates of Rorschach Human Movement responses. *Journal of Consulting Psychology, 18,* 325–331.

Singer, J. L., & Spohn, H. (1954). Some behavioral correlates of Rorschach's Experience-Type. *Journal of Consulting Psychology, 18,* 1–9.

Singer, J. L., Wilensky, H., & McCraven, V. (1956). Delaying capacity, fantasy, and planning ability: A factorial study of some basic ego functions. *Journal of Consulting Psychology, 20,* 375–383.

Skadeland, D. R. (1986). Bruno Klopfer: A Rorschach pioneer. *Journal of Personality Assessment, 50,* 358–361.

Smith, A. M. (1995). Juvenile psychopathy: Rorschach assessment of narcissistic traits in conduct disordered adolescents (Doctoral dissertation, California School of Professional Psychology, 1994). *Dissertation Abstracts International, 55,* 5088B.

Smith, A. M., Gacono, C. B., & Kaufman, L. (1998). Erratum: A Rorschach comparison of psychopathic and nonpsychopathic conduct disordered adolescents. *Journal of Clinical Psychology, 54,* 1151.

Smith, S. R., Baity, M. R., Knowles, E. S., & Hilsenroth, M. J. (2001). Assessment of disordered thinking in children and adolescents: A Rorschach perceptual-thinking index. *Journal of Personality Assessment, 77,* 447–463.

Snowden, R. F. (1956). Top management and the Rorschach technique. In B. Klopfer (Ed.), *Developments in the Rorschach technique: Vol. 2. Fields of application* (pp. 582–592). Yonkers-on-Hudson, NY: World Book.

Snyder, C. R. (1974). Why horoscopes are true: The effects of specificity on acceptance of astrological interpretations. *Journal of Clinical Psychology, 30,* 577–580.

Snyder, C. R., & Shenkel, R. J. (1975, March). Astrologers, handwriting analysts, and sometimes psychologists use the P. T. Barnum effect. *Psychology Today, 8,* 52–54.

Snyder, C. R., Shenkel, R. J., & Lowery, C. R. (1977). Acceptance of personality interpretations: The "Barnum effect" and beyond. *Journal of Consulting and Clinical Psychology, 45,* 104–114.

Society for Personality Assessment. (2000). Minutes of the meeting of the board of trustees. Washington, DC, September 18–19, 1999. *Journal of Personality Assessment, 75,* 178–182.

Society for Personality Assessment. (2001a). Minutes of the meeting of the board of trustees. Albuquerque, New Mexico. March 23, 2000. *Journal of Personality Assessment, 76,* 583–586.

Society for Personality Assessment. (2001b). Minutes of the meeting of the board of trustees. Washington, DC, September 14–17, 2000. *Journal of Personality Assessment, 77,* 391–396.

Society for Personality Assessment Distinguished Contribution Award. (1971). *Journal of Personality Assessment, 35,* 503–504.

Solovay, M. R., Shenton, M. E., Gasperetti, C., Coleman, M., Kestnbaum, E., Carpenter, J. T., &

Holzman, P. S. (1986). Scoring manual for the Thought Disorder Index. *Schizophrenia Bulletin, 12,* 483–496.

Soskin, W. F. (1954a). Bias in postdiction from projective tests. *Journal of Abnormal and Social Psychology, 49,* 69–74.

Soskin, W. F. (1954b). Frames of reference in personality assessment. *Journal of Clinical Psychology, 10,* 107–114.

Soskin, W. F. (1959). Influence of four types of data on diagnostic conceptualization in psychological testing. *Journal of Abnormal and Social Psychology, 58,* 69–78.

Stanovich, K. E. (1998). *How to think straight about psychology* (5th ed.). New York: Longman.

Stevens, D. T., Edwards, K. J., Hunter, W. F., & Bridgman, L. (1993). An investigation of the color-affect hypothesis in Exner's comprehensive system. *Perceptual and Motor Skills, 77,* 1347–1360.

Stricker, G., & Gold, J. R. (1999). The Rorschach: Toward a nomothetically based, idiographically applicable configurational model. *Psychological Assessment, 11,* 240–250.

Sundberg, N. D. (1961). The practice of psychological testing in clinical services in the United States. *American Psychologist, 16,* 79–83.

Sundberg, N. D. (1977). *Assessment of persons.* Upper Saddle River, NJ: Prentice Hall.

Super, D. E., & Crites, J. O. (1962). *Appraising vocational fitness by means of psychological tests* (Rev. ed.). New York: HarperCollins.

Sutherland, S. (1992). *Irrationality: Why we don't think straight!* New Brunswick, NJ: Rutgers University Press.

Swartz, J. D., Reinehr, R. C., & Holtzman, W. H. (1999). *Holtzman inkblot test: Research guide and bibliography.* Austin, TX: Hogg Foundation for Mental Health.

Symonds, P. M. (1955). A contribution to our knowledge of the validity of the Rorschach. *Journal of Projective Techniques, 19,* 152–162.

Taulbee, E. S. (1955). The use of the Rorschach Test in evaluating the intellectual levels of functioning in schizophrenics. *Journal of Projective Techniques, 19,* 163–169.

The Society for Personality Assessment. (1980). *Journal of Personality Assessment, 44,* 661–662.

Thelen, M. H., Varble, D. L., & Johnson, J. (1968). Attitudes of academic clinical psychologists toward projective techniques. *American Psychologist, 23,* 517–521.

Thorndike, E. L., & Lorge, I. (1944). *The teacher's word book of 30,000 words.* New York: Teachers College, Columbia University.

Thornton, G. R., & Guilford, J. P. (1936). The reliability and meaning of Erlebnistypus scores in the Rorschach Test. *Journal of Abnormal and Social Psychology, 31,* 324–330.

Thurstone, L. L. (1948). The Rorschach in psychological science. *Journal of Abnormal and Social Psychology, 43,* 471–475.

Toomey, L. C., & Rickers-Ovsiankina, M. A. (1960). Tabular comparison of Rorschach scoring systems. In M. A. Rickers-Ovsiankina (Ed.), *Rorschach psychology* (pp. 441–465). New York: Wiley.

Trier, T. R. (1958). Vocabulary as a basis for estimating intelligence from the Rorschach. *Journal of Consulting Psychology, 22,* 289–291.

Trull, T. J., & Phares, E. J. (2001). *Clinical psychology* (6th ed.). Belmont, CA: Wadsworth.

Tucker, W. H. (1997). Re-reconsidering Burt: Beyond a reasonable doubt. *Journal of the History of the Behavioral Sciences, 33,* 145–162.

Turner, D. R. (1966). Predictive efficiency as a function of amount of information and level of professional experience. *Journal of Projective Techniques and Personality Assessment, 30,* 4–11.

Tversky, A., & Kahneman, D. (1973). Availability: A heuristic for judging frequency and probability. *Cognitive Psychology, 5,* 207–232.

Ulrich, R. E., Stachnik, T. J., & Stainton, N. R. (1963). Student acceptance of generalized personality interpretations. *Psychological Reports, 13,* 831–834.

Urist, J. (1977). The Rorschach Test and the assessment of object relations. *Journal of Personality Assessment, 41,* 3–9.

Van Hutton, V. (1994). *House-Tree-Person and Draw-a-Person as measures of abuse in children: A quantitative scoring system.* Odessa, FL: Psychological Assessment Resources.

Viglione, D. J. (1985). Review of the Rosenzweig Picture-Frustration Study. *Ninth mental measurements yearbook, 2,* 1295–1297.

Viglione, D. J. (1999). A review of recent research addressing the utility of the Rorschach. *Psychological Assessment, 11,* 251–265.

Viglione, D. J., Brager, R. C., & Haller, N. (1988). Usefulness of structural Rorschach data in identifying inpatients with depressive symptoms: A preliminary study. *Journal of Personality Assessment, 52,* 524–529.

Viglione, D. J., & Hilsenroth, M. J. (2001). The Rorschach: Facts, fictions, and future. *Psychological Assessment, 13,* 452–471.

Vorhaus, P. G. (1960). Bruno Klopfer: A biographical sketch. *Journal of Projective Techniques, 24,* 232–237.

Wade, T. C., & Baker, T. B. (1977). Opinions and use of psychological tests: A survey of clinical psychologists. *American Psychologist, 32,* 874–882.

Wade, T. C., Baker, T. B., Morton, T. L., & Baker, L. J. (1978). The status of psychological testing in clinical psychology: Relationships between test use and professional activities and orientations. *Journal of Personality Assessment, 42,* 3–10.

Wagner, E. E. (1965). Exhibitionistic Human Movement responses of strippers: An attempt to validate the Rorschach *M. Journal of Projective Techniques and Personality Assessment, 29,* 522–524.

Wagner, E. E. (1985). Review of the Rosenzweig Picture-Frustration Study. *Ninth mental measurements yearbook, 2,* 1297–1298.

Wagner, E. E. (2001). *The logical Rorschach.* Los Angeles: Western Psychological Services.

Wagner, E. E., & Hoover, T. O. (1971). Exhibitionistic *M* in drama majors: A validation. *Perceptual and Motor Skills, 32,* 125–126.

Wagner, E. E., & Hoover, T. O. (1972). Behavioral implications of Rorschach's Human Movement response: Further validation based on exhibitionistic *Ms. Perceptual and Motor Skills, 35,* 27–30.

Waldman, I. D. (1996). Aggressive boys' hostile perceptual and response biases: The role of attention and impulsivity. *Child Development, 67,* 1015–1033.

Waller, R. W., & Keeley, S. M. (1978). Effects of explanation and information feedback on the illusory correlation phenomenon. *Journal of Consulting and Clinical Psychology, 46,* 342–343.

Watkins, C. E., Campbell, V. L., Nieberding, R., & Hallmark, R. (1995). Contemporary practice of psychological assessment by clinical psychologists. *Professional Psychology: Research and Practice, 26,* 54–60.

Watkins, J., & Stauffacher, J. (1952). An index of pathological thinking. *Journal of Projective Techniques, 16,* 276–286.

Weiner, I. B. (1972). Does psychodiagnosis have a future? *Journal of Personality Assessment, 36,* 534–546.

Weiner, I. B. (1983). The future of psychodiagnosis revisited. *Journal of Personality Assessment, 47,* 451–461.

Weiner, I. B. (1985). Editorial policies and procedures: A note from the incoming editor. *Journal of Personality Assessment, 49,* 451–453.

Weiner, I. B. (1995). Variable selection in Rorschach research. In J. E. Exner (Ed.), *Issues and methods in Rorschach research* (pp. 73–98). Mahwah, NJ: Erlbaum.

Weiner, I. B. (1996). Some observations on the validity of the Rorschach inkblot method. *Psychological Assessment, 8,* 206–213.

Weiner, I. B. (1997). Current status of the Rorschach inkblot method. *Journal of Personality Assessment, 68,* 5–19.

Weiner, I. B. (1998). *Principles of Rorschach interpretation.* Mahwah, NJ: Erlbaum.

Weiner, I. B. (1999). What the Rorschach can do for you: Incremental validity in clinical applications. *Assessment, 6,* 327–338.

Weiner, I. B. (2000). Using the Rorschach properly in practice and research. *Journal of Clinical Psychology, 56,* 435–438.

Weiner, I. B. (2001a). Advancing the science of psychological assessment: The Rorschach inkblot method as exemplar. *Psychological Assessment, 13,* 423–432.

Weiner, I. B. (2001b). Considerations in collecting Rorschach reference data. *Journal of Personality Assessment, 77,* 122–127.

Weiner, I. B. (2001c, December). The value of Rorschach assessment. *Harvard Mental Health Letter,* 4–5.

Weiner, I. B. (2002). Advocating for assessment: Coordinators report. *SPA Exchange, 13*(1), 3.

Weiner, I. B., Exner, J. E., & Sciara, A. (1996). Is the Rorschach welcome in the courtroom? *Journal of Personality Assessment, 67,* 422–424.

Weiner, I. B., & Hess, A. K. (1987). *The handbook of forensic psychology.* New York: Wiley.

Weller, A. C. (2001). *Editorial peer review: Its strengths and weaknesses.* Medford, NJ: Information Today.

Welsh, R. K. (1999). Psychopathy and psychological risk markers of violent recidivism (Doctoral dissertation, Rosemead School of Psychology, Biola University, 1999). *Dissertation Abstracts International, 60,* 2968B.

Whitehead, W. C. (1985). *Clinical decision making on the basis of Rorschach, MMPI, and automated MMPI report data.* Unpublished doctoral dissertation, University of Texas Health Science Center at Dallas.

Wickes, T. H. (1956). Examiner influence in a testing situation. *Journal of Consulting Psychology, 20,* 23–26.

Widiger, T. A. (2001). The best and the worst of us? *Clinical Psychology: Science and Practice, 8,* 374–377.

Williams, G., & Kellman, S. (1956). The Rorschach technique in industrial psychology. In B. Klopfer (Ed.), *Developments in the Rorschach technique: Vol. 2. Fields of application* (pp. 545–581). Yonkers-on-Hudson, NY: World Book.

Williams, H. L., & Lawrence, J. F. (1953). Further investigation of Rorschach determinants subjected to factor analysis. *Journal of Consulting Psychology, 17,* 261–264.

Wilson, M. S., & Reschly, D. J. (1996). Assessment in school psychology training and practice. *School Psychology Review, 25,* 9–23.

Wilson, T. D., & Nisbett, R. E. (1978). The accuracy of verbal reports about the effects of stimuli on evaluations and behavior. *Social Psychology, 41,* 118–131.

Wittenborn, J. R. (1949). Review of the Rorschach Inkblot Test. In O. K. Buros (Ed.), *The third mental measurements yearbook* (pp. 133–134). New Brunswick, NJ: Rutgers University Press.

Wittenborn, J. R., & Sarason, S. B. (1949). Exceptions to certain Rorschach criteria of pathology. *Journal of Consulting Psychology, 13,* 21–27.

Wolpert, L. (1992). *The unnatural nature of science: Why science does not make (common) sense.* Cambridge, MA: Harvard University Press.

Wood, J. M., Garb, H. N., Lilienfeld, S. O., & Nezworski, M. T. (2002). Clinical assessment. *Annual Review of Psychology, 53,* 519–543.

Wood, J. M., & Lilienfeld, S. O. (1999). The Rorschach Inkblot Test: A case of overstatement? *Assessment, 6,* 341–349.

Wood, J. M., Lilienfeld, S. O., Garb, H. N., & Nezworski, M. T. (2000a). Limitations of the Rorschach as a diagnostic tool: A reply to Garfield (2000), Lerner (2000), and Weiner (2000). *Journal of Clinical Psychology, 56,* 441–448.

Wood, J. M., Lilienfeld, S. O., Garb, H. N., & Nezworski, M. T. (2000b). The Rorschach Test in clinical diagnosis: A critical review, with a backward look at Garfield (1947). *Journal of Clinical Psychology, 56,* 395–430.

Wood, J. M., Lilienfeld, S. O., Nezworski, M. T., and Garb, H. N. (2001). Coming to grips with negative evidence for the Comprehensive System for the Rorschach: A comment on Gacono, Loving, and Bodholdt; Ganellen; and Bornstein. *Journal of Personality Assessment, 77,* 48–70.

Wood, J. M., Nezworski, M. T., Garb, H. N., & Lilienfeld, S. O. (2001a). The misperception of psychopathology: Problems with the norms of the Comprehensive System for the Rorschach. *Clinical Psychology: Science and Practice, 8,* 350–373.

Wood, J. M., Nezworski, M. T., Garb, H. N., & Lilienfeld, S. O. (2001b). Problems with the norms of the Comprehensive System for the Rorschach: Methodological and conceptual considerations. *Clinical Psychology: Science and Practice, 8,* 397–402.

Wood, J. M., Nezworski, M. T., & Stejskal, W. J. (1996a). The Comprehensive System for the Rorschach: A critical examination. *Psychological Science, 7,* 3–10.

Wood, J. M., Nezworski, M. T., & Stejskal, W. J. (1996b). Thinking critically about the Comprehensive System for the Rorschach. A reply to Exner. *Psychological Science, 7,* 14–17.

Wood, J. M., Nezworski, M. T., & Stejskal, W. J. (1997). The reliability of the Comprehensive System for the Rorschach: A comment on Meyer (1997). *Psychological Assessment, 9,* 490–494.

Wood, J. M., Nezworski, M. T., Stejskal, W. J., & Garven, S. (2001). Advancing scientific discourse in the controversy surrounding the Comprehensive System for the Rorschach. A rejoinder to Meyer (2000). *Journal of Personality Assessment, 76,* 369–378.

Wooten, A. J. (1984). Effectiveness of the *K* correction in the detection of psychopathology and its impact on profile height and configuration among young adult men. *Journal of Consulting and Clinical Psychology, 52,* 468–473.

Wright, R., & Cummings, N. (Eds.). (2001). *The practice of psychology: The battle for professionalism.* Phoenix, AZ: Zeig, Tucker & Theisen.

Wysocki, B. A. (1956). Differentiation between introvert-extravert types by Rorschach method as compared with other methods. *Journal of Psychology, 43,* 41–46.

Wysocki, B. A. (1957). Assessment of intelligence level by the Rorschach Test as compared with objective tests. *Journal of Educational Psychology, 48,* 113–117.

Young, G. R., & Wagner, E. E. (1993). Behavioral specificity in the Rorschach Human Movement response: A comparison of strippers and models. *Journal of Clinical Psychology, 49,* 407–412.

Young, J. H. (1961). *The toadstool millionaires: A social history of patent medicines in America before federal regulation.* Princeton, NJ: Princeton University Press.

Young, J. H. (1967). *The medical messiahs: A social history of health quackery in twentieth-century America.* Princeton, NJ: Princeton University Press. (This book can be read without charge on the World Wide Web at http://www.quackwatch.com/. Access date: October 22, 2002.)

Young, M. H., Justice, J. V., Erdberg, P. S., & Gacono, C. B. (2000). The incarcerated psychopath in psychiatric treatment: Management or treatment. In C. B. Gacono (Ed.), *The clinical and forensic assessment of psychopathy: A practitioner's guide* (pp. 313–331). Mahwah, NJ: Erlbaum.

Zax, M., Stricker, G., & Weiss, J. H. (1960). Some effects of non-personality factors on Rorschach performance. *Journal of Projective Techniques, 24,* 83–93.

Zenderland, L. (1998). *Measuring minds: Henry Herbert Goddard and the origins of American intelligence testing.* Cambridge, England: Cambridge University Press.

Zillmer, E. A., Harrower, M., Ritzler, B. A., & Archer, R. P. (1995). *Quest for the Nazi personality.* Hillsdale, NJ: Erlbaum.

Zubin, J. (1941a). A psychometric approach to the evaluation of the Rorschach Test. *Psychiatry, 4,* 547–566.

Zubin, J. (1941b). A quantitative approach to measuring regularity of succession in the Rorschach experiment. *Character and Personality, 10,* 67–78.

Zubin, J. (1954). Failures of the Rorschach technique. *Journal of Projective Techniques, 18,* 303–315.

Zubin, J., Eron, L. D., & Schumer, F. (1965). *An experimental approach to projective techniques.* New York: Wiley.

～～～ About the Authors

James M. Wood is an associate professor of psychology at the University of Texas at El Paso. He received a master's degree in divinity from the Yale Divinity School in 1979 and a Ph.D. in clinical psychology from the University of Arizona in 1990. Since that time he has worked in university settings doing research and teaching. His research has focused on issues in psychology and law, particularly the suggestibility of adult and child witnesses, and the decision-making strategies of professionals in child abuse cases. Although he received training in the Rorschach in graduate school, he didn't become deeply interested in the test until he encountered it in the context of a case of alleged child abuse. He can be reached by e-mail at jawood@utep.edu.

M. Teresa Nezworski is an associate professor in the School of Behavioral and Brain Sciences at the University of Texas at Dallas and director of psychological services at the Callier Center. She has a joint appointment as clinical professor in the Graduate School of Biomedical Sciences at UT Southwestern Medical Center. She received a dual Ph.D. in clinical psychology and experimental child psychology from the University of Minnesota in 1983. She has worked in university settings doing research, teaching, and providing clinical services. Teresa has been fascinated with individual differences in coping and resiliency and her early work focused on sequelae to individual differences in infant attachment patterns. She is currently working in the area of behavioral medicine with projects that include examination of successful coping in cochlear implant patients and personality adjustment following closed head injury.

Teresa taught graduate courses in personality assessment using the Comprehensive System for the Rorschach in APA-approved doctoral psychology programs for many years. Originally trained in the Klopfer approach, she greatly appreciated the improved scoring rules introduced by the Comprehensive System. She has used the Rorschach as a tool for generating hypotheses in particularly difficult diagnostic cases. As a "dustbowl empiricist" she was surprised to learn that some psychologists use information from the Rorschach as the primary support for diagnoses and life changing decisions such as competency to stand trial or parent. Teresa began closely reviewing the empirical basis of the Comprehensive System after encountering startling examples of misdiagnosis.

Scott O. Lilienfeld is an associate professor of psychology at Emory University in Atlanta. He received his Ph.D. in clinical psychology from the University of Minnesota in 1990, and has worked in universities as a researcher and teacher. Scott's primary research focuses on psychopathy, a condition characterized by such personality traits as lack of guilt, dishonesty, callousness, poor impulse control, and superficial charm. In addition, he's interested in pseudoscientific and unvalidated practices in clinical psychology, and is founder and editor of *The Scientific Review of Mental Health Practice,* a new journal that aims to distinguish scientifically supported from unsupported assessment and therapeutic techniques. Scott learned the Comprehensive System for the Rorschach in graduate school and administered the test on numerous occasions during his early clinical work as a graduate student. Nevertheless, he began to harbor increasing doubts concerning this measure after being exposed to the research literature on its validity.

Howard N. Garb is coordinator of the Anxiety and Adjustment Disorders Clinic at the Pittsburgh Veterans Administration Healthcare System and clinical associate professor of psychiatry in the School of Medicine at the University of Pittsburgh. He received a double-major Ph.D. in clinical psychology and "psychological measurement and research methodology" from the University of Illinois at Chicago in 1984. A full-time clinician, he also conducts research, teaches at the university, and testifies in court as an expert witness. Howard is best known for his work on the strengths and weaknesses of decision making by mental health professionals. His book *Studying the Clinician: Judgment Research and Psychological Assessment* is a bestseller of the American Psychological Association. While in graduate school Howard learned the Beck System for the Rorschach. Subsequently, he routinely used the test while working on a schizophrenia research unit. However, he no longer uses the Rorschach in his clinical work, due to its limited validity and utility.

⁓ Name Index

A

Abrams, A., 77–78, 158
Acklin, M., 229–230, 232, 233, 234
Albee, G. W., 193
Ames, L., 259
Anastasi, A., 106, 212–213, 215
Archer, R., 20
Armitage, S., 141
Aron, L., 222–223
Aronow, E., 191–192, 217, 279, 287

B

Bacon, F., 160
Bailey, J. M., 1, 217, 226
Bandura, A., 174, 260
Barden, C., 317
Barnum, P. T., 166
Baughman, E. E., 150–151, 154, 224
Beck, S., 50, 98–99, 107, 123, 148, 259;
  administration procedures of,
  197–198; background on, 49; blind
  interpretation and, 101; Bohm and,
  127, 129; on Color responses, 153,
  154; death of, 212; disregard of, for
  scientific evidence, 156, 180, 182,
  186, 260, 263; empiricist position of,
  94; Exner and, 194, 195, 203, 213;
  Hertz and, 74–76, 94, 178, 181, 182;
  Klopfer conflict with, 54–55, 68–76,
  94, 129–130, 195, 264; later years of,
  128, 129–132; manual and textbooks of, 70, 72, 74, 86, 129; new
  scoring categories of, 130–132; popularity of, 196; psychoanalytic/con-
  tent approach and, 89, 117;
  psychometric approach and, 54–55,

130; Rabin and, 211; on Rorschach's
  infallibility, 99
Bell, D., 9–16
Ben-Meir, S., 237
Benjamin, J. D., 70–71
Berra, Y., 286
Bhagavan Das, 120
Binder, H., 72, 127, 128
Binet, A., 23, 26, 45, 55, 56, 59, 60, 61,
  81, 146
Binggeli, J., 26
Blatt, S., 126
Bleuler, E., 24, 25, 28, 43–44, 81–82
Boas, F., 50
Bochner, R., 85, 91, 111–112, 113, 121
Bohm, E., 99, 123, 126–128, 153,
  188–189; Beck and, 127, 129; book
  published by, 127–128
Bohr, N., 293
Bornstein, R., 250, 259
Botticelli, 23
Bradley, A., 297
Brockway, A. L., 148
Brown, F., 112
Bryan, W. J., 60
Buck, C., 57
Buros, O. K., 182
Burt, C., 221

C

Campagna, V., 310
Chambers, G., 141
Chapman, J., 161–163
Chapman, L., 161–163
Cialdini, R., 288, 295
Cochran, J., 316

━◆━ Subject Index

A

Accuracy. *See* Prediction accuracy; Rorschach Inkblot Test accuracy

Ad antiquitem fallacy, 289

Ad populum fallacy, 289

Adelphi University, 94, 208, 226

Adjusted D, 205, 206–207, 235

Adjustment ratings, research studies of Rorschach for, 140–141, 148

Administration procedures: Beck's, 197–198; in Exner's Comprehensive System, 197–199, 311–313; H. Rorschach's, 197; violations of, in legal cases, 302–303, 311–313

Administrators: friendly *versus* unfriendly, 152; influence of, on Rorschach Inkblot Test responses, 151–153, 158, 310–313; Klopfer's category of, 80. *See also* Artists/experts/wizards, Rorschach

Advocates. *See* Promoters and supporters

"Advocating for Assessment: Coordinators Report" (Weiner), 322

Affect: Barnum statements regarding, 172–173; Color responses and, 31–33, 36–37. *See also* Emotional inhibition or suppression

Affective Ratio, 235

African American policeman, racial discrimination case, 301, 306, 308

Age, Color responses and, 37

Aggressive or hostile responses, 121, 222

Agreement, percentage of, 227–229

Alice in Rorschachland, 149

Alternate-form reliability: concept of, 65–66; of Exner's Comprehensive System, 201–202; solutions to, 188

Alternative tests, lack of, 296

Amazon.com, 21

Ambiequal individuals, 33

Ambiguous phrasing, in Rorschach interpretations, 163

American Biodyne, 208–209

American Medical Association, 210

American Psychological Association (APA), 285, 290; Board of Professional Affairs, 209, 215–216, 257, 261, 266, 269–271; clinical psychologists and, 53; Comprehensive System and support of, 193, 215–216, 267, 268, 269–271, 275, 323; Ethical Principles of Psychologists of, 264, 265, 318, 319–321; Ethics Office of, filing complaints with, 321; growth of, 207; post–WWII graduate programs and, 91–92; practitioner control of, 93–94, 209–210, 270–271; Psychological Assessment Work Group (PAWG) of, 266, 269–271, 275; romantic-empiricist division in, 93–94; *Standards for Educational and Psychological Testing,* 20, 221; tolerance of, for unscientific practices, 209–210, 267

American Psychological Society, 93, 209

American Psychologist, 137–139, 215–216, 270

Amsterdam Rorschach conference, 235–236, 239, 242

Analytic ability: accuracy of predicting, 8; responses indicative of, 3, 8